READERS LOVE
WALT DISNEY WORLD FOR COUPLES!

For Just the Two of You

"This book is a wonderful tool for two people to plan a celebration of their love together in a most magical place." —*Jim and Lauri*

"A warm, charming, and insightful exploration of all the romance and magic of a Walt Disney World vacation. If you're a couple planning a trip to the Happiest Place on Earth, this guidebook is your E-Ticket to a vacation filled with love and life-long memories."
—*Jeff and Ann Marie*

"After I bought this book, I couldn't put it down—in fact, I read it in one night. I found great ideas for romance as well as for budgeting a WDW vacation." —*Heather*

For Planning a Honeymoon

"This book was all we needed to plan our honeymoon."
—*Brendan and Appen*

"My fiancée and I are planning a wedding and honeymoon at Walt Disney World. We've read about ten books on Disney, and by far this is the most detailed and best written book on the market."
—*David and Debbie*

Great for All Couples—
Even Couples with Kids

"The Perlmutters' exuberance and excitement as they describe their Disney experiences raise this guide to a higher level. Whether it is your first trip or fifteenth, *Walt Disney World for Couples* can help make your dream come true." —*Sherry*

"Incredibly helpful, informative, and entertaining!" —*Laura*

"This guidebook has changed the way we approach Walt Disney World. Now we slowly savor the parks, the restaurants, the resorts, and all the rest of the World! Descriptions are accurate and beautifully written." —*Connie*

"As someone in the travel industry, I want to express my appreciation for this book. The detail about hotel rooms is exactly what I have been looking for, and the restaurant info and comments are great. Even though I am an avid WDW visitor, I learned a lot from this book!"

—*Amy*

"The one and only complete guide to Walt Disney World."

—*Chrissi*

"Your book has helped make my visits to WDW the best they could possibly be. Thank you for our fantastic memories!"   —*Jennifer*

Don't forget to write!

Do you have tips you'd like to share? Have we missed or misstated something? How did you like our book? All your experiences—both positive and negative—matter to us. Do drop us a line in care of editors@fodors.com or at 1745 Broadway, New York, New York 10019.

WALT DISNEY
WORLD®
for Couples

RICK & GAYLE PERLMUTTER

Fodor's

Published by Fodor's Travel Publications, a unit of Fodors LLC
Fodor's is a registered trademark of Random House, Inc.
www.fodors.com

The prices herein reflect 2003–2004 figures. Rates for resorts, prices for meals, and ticket costs are all subject to change.

Every effort has been made to make this book complete and accurate as of the date of publication. In a time of rapid change, however, it is difficult to ensure that all information is entirely up-to-date. Although the publisher and authors cannot be liable for any inaccuracies or omissions in this book, they are always grateful for corrections and suggestions for improvement.

All products mentioned in this book are trademarks of their respective companies. This book is not affiliated with, sponsored by, or licensed by Walt Disney World.

Maps by Rick Perlmutter

Previously published by Prima Publishing.

Fifth Edition

ISBN 0-7615-3022-3
ISSN 1091-5850

Printed in the United States of America
10 9 8 7 6 5 4 3 2 1

To our mothers,
who taught us how to enjoy life.
And to our children,
who we hope learned it from us.

Contents

Acknowledgments

We'd like to thank the following people for their help in making our book what it is: Michelle Baumann at Disney Media Relations, Camille Dudley at Universal Orlando, Korri McFann and the team at Disney Fairy Tale Weddings, Mariska Elia at the Disney Vacation Club, Rebecca Michaels at Wolfgang's, Connie Casipit at the Grand Floridian, Kelly Burnett at the Wyndham Palace, Amy MacGuire, Christie Erwin at the Disney Cruise Line, Treva Marshall at TJM Communications, Arthur Levine, and our grandkids Ben and Guin Leggett, for letting us take them to the theme parks.

Introduction:
Why You Should Use
a Disney Guide Book

It never ceases to amaze us how many people visit Walt Disney World without doing a little research beforehand. Often, we see these bewildered travelers wandering around the parks wondering what they want to see and not even sure what there is to do. These are usually the very same folks who can't get a table at that character breakfast or dinner show they'd had their hearts set on, or who discover too late that they should have stayed in a different resort. The truth about Walt Disney World is that not only is it BIG, but also it changes from year to year. Even if you've been before, it's wise to learn what's changed since your last Walt Disney World visit.

During the 1990s, Walt Disney World expanded at a furious pace. Its 42 square miles literally exploded with new attractions and rides, new resorts and restaurants, and even a new theme park. These things are, in fact, just the tip of the Disney iceberg. There has been much more: Downtown Disney, the Wide World of Sports, the Disney Speedway, and Blizzard Beach are just a few. Walt Disney World has simply become so large and so diverse that the days when you could see it all in a single visit are ancient history.

What does this mean for you? Simply, it means that if you wish to make good use of your limited (and expensive) vacation time, you'll need to have some idea before you arrive about what you most want to see and do at Disney. With four theme parks, more than twenty resorts, two water parks, and a dozen other attractions, the more you know beforehand, the better prepared you'll be to get what you want out of your Disney vacation and the less likely you'll be to go home with a long list of things you should have done differently. What to bring, how to book your room, what types of admission passes you really need, the best places to eat, and how to get around Disney are just a few of the many things we can tell you.

We want to make your Disney vacation all it should be. We want to show you how to avoid getting so tired at Disney that you'll return home needing a week's rest. We want to show you that hidden inside the Walt Disney World of thrill rides, musical shows, and parades is a world of lavish resorts, dazzling nightlife, world-class wining and dining, and unforgettable romance.

Who Is This Book For, Anyway?

To begin with, we've written this book for adult sensibilities. If you're a couple coming to Walt Disney World for a romantic time, this is the book for you. We'll tell you how to have a wonderful, relaxing, and romantic vacation at Disney and how to find those special and intimate moments that make vacations the stuff of dreams.

If you're visiting with your children, we want to remind you of something you might have forgotten. You're still a couple! Sure, you're coming to Disney with the kids and are planning to have some real family fun, but you should know that you can also have some grown-up fun of your own. Our aim is to get you and your family to Disney, to help you have some terrific times together, and to show how the two of you can get off together for some of Disney's own special brand of romance.

We Want to Make Your Vacation a Better One

We've created this book to help you plan your vacation from top to bottom. Since where you stay will be an important decision, we've put together the most complete and detailed guide of the Disney resorts anywhere, and we've done it by staying everywhere at least twice and most places, many times. We'll cover vacation packages, your first and last days, how to get the most for your money, and lots more. What makes us the experts? Simple: We spend a lot of time at Walt Disney World. In fact, we spend months every year checking out resorts, restaurants, rides, recreation, and especially what's new at Disney.

We'll tell you about what attractions are suitable for your young ones and which have an especially adult appeal, and we'll paint an accurate picture of every attraction, one that will provide more than enough information for you to decide which you most want to see and those you can skip.

After you've arrived, our book will help you avoid those pitfalls most common to theme-park vacations. We'll give you tips on how to find a pace that will keep you from getting exhausted, and we'll give you all the latest information on avoiding lengthy waits, huge crowds, and long lines.

So, get ready for some real insider information, the kind of stuff you can only get by spending a lot of time carefully searching for it, which is exactly what we've done. From African safaris to mariachi music, from high tea to high-wire acts, from nightclubbing to unique honeymoon suites, we promise to reveal all our discoveries and to make your vacation a better one.

Walt Disney World: It's Not Just for Kids!

There's a lot more to Walt Disney World than just the world's greatest theme parks. Much more. World-class wining and dining, themed luxury resorts, golf, tennis, boating, and a dazzling world of nightlife are just some of the things that make the Walt Disney World Resort unique among vacation destinations. Sure there are great rides, but if you thought that was all, you'd be missing out on a whole other side of Disney excitement: theaters, nightclubs, dancing, luxurious spas, and the wonderful Florida sunshine are just a few of the faces of this "other side" of Disney. If you still think that Walt Disney World is just for kids, let this be your wake-up call.

The Romantic Side of Walt Disney World

We're frequently asked what we think is most romantic about Walt Disney World. After a decade of Disney, our answer is now swift and certain: It's the Disney Resorts. Sure, there are moonlight strolls, quiet beaches at sunset, luxurious spas, and intimate dining, but what really creates the backdrop for all these things and sets the mood for any great vacation is where we are staying.

Not merely places to sleep, the magical Disney resorts have been created to make your Disney vacation something that isn't put on hold when you leave the theme parks. Each resort tells a story, and a stay in one will enfold you in that fantasy. From the Victorian splendor of the Grand Floridian to the safari adventure of the Animal Kingdom Lodge, these resorts are guaranteed to immerse you in the romance and the magic of Disney.

But, of course there's more romance to Walt Disney World than just the resorts. For us, a romantic Disney vacation means a slow stroll around Epcot's World Showcase, the enchantment of an early-morning safari, and the excitement of a musical show. It means live jazz followed by an intimate nightcap. It means dining, hot tubs, fine wine, and slow dancing. Team Disney continues to find new and better ways to create magic for couples. For incurable romantics such as us, the possibilities become endless.

Finding Romance at Walt Disney World

It was a special day, even by Disney standards. We awoke in our Turret Honeymoon suite at the Grand Floridian to our unforgettable view of Cinderella Castle and the Magic Kingdom. This is Disney's most magical room, and we will forever call it "our ivory tower."

Our day's adventures began with an early safari at the Animal Kingdom. Next, we strolled the shady trails of Pangani Forest and later, sat awhile in the aviary in Asia's Maharaja Jungle Trek. It was a beautiful morning, and we spent it slowly and carefully, enjoying the sights, sounds, and smells of Disney's most exotic lands.

For afternoon fun, we shifted gears and took on the challenge of Disney's highest thrill ride. Not the Tower of Terror, but parasailing 400 feet above Bay Lake. It was peaceful and beautiful, not to mention quietly thrilling. The view of Disney, and indeed of central Florida, was unforgettable. We followed our airborne adventure with waterskiing and tubing, and finished just in time to make it to our next destination: the Grand Floridian Spa.

An hour together in the spa's couples room for aromatherapy massages got us in the perfect mood to make an unexpected return to our room. Later, as we were enjoying a romantic, in-room, candlelit dinner, the lights dimmed over the Magic Kingdom. We opened our windows, knowing what was about to take place. There in our magical room, with an unimaginably special view, and a wonderful meal in front of us, we watched spellbound as the glittering fireworks and memorable music wove their spell. For us, it was a special moment and an unforgettable day. It was the kind of experience that we take vacations hoping to find, and it left us with a wonderful feeling of togetherness.

While romance is a personal thing (and we don't pretend to know what will make everyone experience it), we do feel that there are ingredients conducive to romance, as well as elements that are incompatible with it. This kind of intimacy can occur when you are alone on a beach at sunset, or it can happen in a crowded theater. It is a special feeling of closeness that transports you together to a place far away from the everyday. It is something special and out of the ordinary that seems to occur for just the two of you.

As you read through this guidebook, look for heart symbols (♥) that suggest this special feeling. The more ♥'s you see, the more likely we think you will be able to ignite this chemistry. We have tried to savor a place for its ability to enhance our own feelings of togetherness, for its potential to elevate us above the everyday, and to let us know that this special thing is happening just for us. Not surprisingly, Disney has a knack for creating these moments. Sometimes romance just happens, and sometimes we can help it along.

♥	A hint of romance
♥♥	An air of romance
♥♥♥	Intimate and enchanting
♥♥♥♥	Unforgettable, sublimely romantic

Also look for the 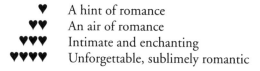 symbol. These mark those things at Disney that are new to this book or restaurants that have totally new menus. The **$** symbol will be your guide for budget tips.

Key to Icons

Throughout the book we'll give you hints and tips to save money and time and add an extra touch of romance to your vacation. Look for the following icons:

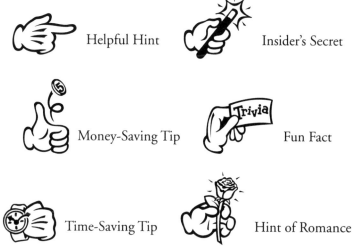

Helpful Hint

Insider's Secret

Money-Saving Tip

Fun Fact

Time-Saving Tip

Hint of Romance

List of Maps

List of Quick Guides

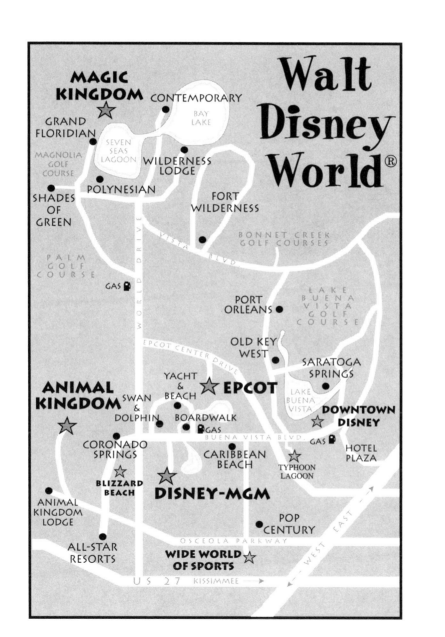

PART 1
What to Do Before You Leave Home

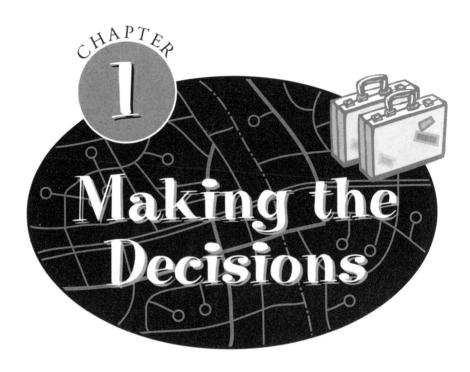

CHAPTER

1

Making the Decisions

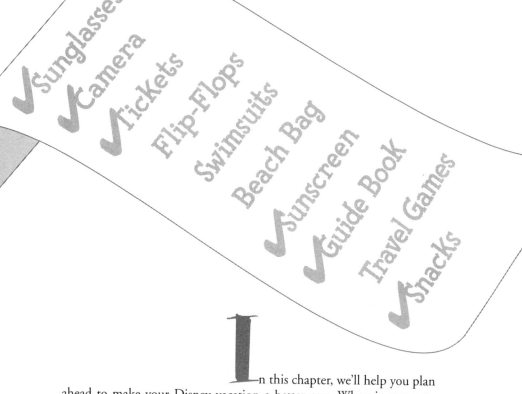

n this chapter, we'll help you plan ahead to make your Disney vacation a better one. When it comes to Walt Disney World, the more you plan, the more smoothly your vacation will go. We'll help you make the big decisions: when to visit, where to stay, and how to fit it all into your budget. You'll also want to have an idea about what you most want to see and do at Disney. If you're interested in a particular restaurant or show, make reservations ahead of time so there is one less thing to do during your holiday. We believe that the more you know about Walt Disney World and the more you can do before you arrive, the better time you'll have when you get there.

What's New at Disney

Even for us, keeping up with Disney isn't easy. Things change continually. It's wise to expect that a few of the details in this book will become out of date: a menu change, an increased ticket price, or even an attraction suddenly being retired. These things can and do happen unannounced and unforeseen. Such is the way of things when you're writing a guidebook about a destination as fluid and as changing as Walt Disney World. However, there are several ways to get up-to-speed on the latest changes, and we'll tell you about them on page 191.

This said, we can tell you what we know will be new at Disney in 2003. The big event of 2003 is no doubt be the opening of the new Epcot pavilion, *Mission: Space*. Presented by Compaq Computers in association with NASA engineers, this new attraction launches guests on a simulated space adventure. Also new in 2003 is the Fantasyland 3-D show, *Mickey's PhilharMagic,* and the live *Character RoundUp* in Liberty Square. *Motion* is already making waves as the hot new club at Pleasure Island and 2003 might actually see the long-delayed opening of Disney's newest value lodgings, the Pop Century Resort. In 2004, Team Disney will unveil its newest home-away-from-home resort creation, Disney's Saratoga Springs Resort & Spa.

Of course, along with the new comes "out with the old." Here's what you will no longer find at Walt Disney World: the Villas at the Disney Institute, River Country water park, the Disney Club, and free valet parking for resort guests at the Disney resorts. Gone from the theme parks are *Doug Live!* and the *Hunchback of Notre Dame* show at MGM, and the *Diamond Horseshoe Revue* and the *Legend of the Lion King* at the Magic Kingdom.

When to Go

Choosing what time of year to visit Walt Disney World may be more important than you think. The "Disney Seasons" have everything to do with how busy Walt Disney World is and almost nothing to do with the regular yearly seasons. Visit at a good time and you'll enjoy fewer people everywhere and even discounted resorts. You'll get to see and do more, and it should cost you less. Pick the wrong time and you'll spend your expensive Disney vacation battling crowds, standing in long lines, and feeling frustrated that you are not getting your money's worth. Like much of life, a Disney vacation is a matter of good timing.

The Seasons of Walt Disney World

Forget about summer, fall, winter, and spring. We'll talk about them later. The Disney seasons go like this:

Holiday Season means the ten days around Christmas. This is the most expensive time of year and the most crowded (except for Fourth of July and Thanksgiving week). Resort rates during the holiday season are more than 30 percent higher than during the value season, which ends a mere week before Christmas.

Peak Season means the traditional Florida winter tourist season and spring break, which runs from mid-February to mid-April. During peak season, the parks are very crowded. Some discounts are available, but they're few and hard to get. Peak season means that the Disney resort rates are higher than at any other time of year except holiday season and 21 to 27 percent higher than during the value season.

Regular Season for the moderate and value resorts runs from mid-April to the last week of August and for the month of October. For Ft. Wilderness, regular season runs from mid-April through the first week of August, and for the Disney deluxe and home-away-from-home resorts, regular season is from late April to the Fourth of July and for the month of October.

During the summer, kids are out of school and the parks are mobbed and running at full-throttle. Discounts are rare, lines are long, and Florida is hot, HOT, HOT. October, which used to be value season, is not as crowded as summer and the weather is nicer. It is one of the regular season's nicest months.

$ *Value Season* is the bargain season at Walt Disney World. It used to be longer than it is now, and the reason for this is simple. More and more people visit Disney every year and more and more have discovered Disney's off-season. Hence, less need for discounts. So while the "off-season" isn't as slow as it once was, it is still the time when crowds are relatively easy to avoid, when resort rates are at their lowest, and discounts and specials are available. Value season includes all of January to mid-February, the end of August to the end of September, and all of November and the first three weeks of December. Value season for most of Disney's deluxe and home-away-from-home resorts also includes after the Fourth of July weekend to the end of September. It is well worth mentioning that value season for the deluxe and home-away-from-home resorts is 180 days long, nearly half the year.

Insider's Secret

Tuesday through Friday are the least busy days of the Disney week. Plan your vacation accordingly.

Your Visit and the Central Florida Weather

Summer, fall, winter, and spring will play a role in your Disney vacation because whatever the weather, you'll find yourselves out in it much of the time. It's wise to get a good idea of what to expect so you can pack accordingly.

Pluses and Minuses

Holiday, Peak, and Regular Seasons

+ Theme parks stay open later

+ Numerous special events, such as fireworks,
parades, and parties

− From more crowded to too crowded

− More expensive: few, if any, discounts and higher resort rates

Value Season

+ Fewer people; every place is less crowded

+ Fewer lines and shorter waits.
(You'll get to see more and do more.)

+ Lower resort rates and numerous specials

− Parks close earlier

− Fewer special events, such as fireworks and parades

While Central Florida enjoys a progression of seasons, the weather does not vary as much as in a region like New England or the Midwest. Winters at Disney usually mean warm days and cool nights. As cold fronts pass through the state, nights become a bit cooler and days a little less warm. Extremely cold weather is rare in Central Florida, but it does happen. If you manage to avoid holidays, the winter months are a wonderful time to visit Disney.

Summers at Disney range from hot to HOT, with temperatures usually in the mid-90s and humidity about the same. It's even hot and sticky in the evening hours. Afternoon thundershowers can be relied on.

Spring and fall are a mix of warm and cool weather, a sort of left-overs time. Hot days are typical in September and become rarer in October as the weather moderates. The heat of summer begins to sneak back in during May. Pick and choose your times and these months can be quite nice when it comes to weather.

Here's a month-by-month look at how weather and crowds work at Disney:

January

Weather: Average high: 72°. Average low: 49°. Occasional cold spells common.

Park Conditions: **$** Value season all month, minimal crowds, especially after first week. A great time to visit.

February

Weather: Average high: 73°. Average low: 50°. Cool nights, warm days, and brief, wintry cold snaps. A nice month.

Park Conditions: **$** Value season until mid-month, then peak season. Attendance is lowest in first week. Avoid the crowded President's Week.

March

Weather: Average high: 78°. Average low: 55°. Peak season all month. One of the wetter winter months. Rarely very cold.

Park Conditions: Attendance up. Avoid the spring break season and Easter.

April

Weather: Average high: 84°. Average low: 60°. A nice month. Breezy, warm days and balmy nights.

Park Conditions: Avoid Easter week. Busy season until mid-April, then regular season.

May

Weather: Average high: 88°. Average low: 66°. Nice weather. Spring in central Florida.

Park Conditions: Regular season all month, but less-than-average crowds. Avoid Memorial Day weekend.

June

Weather: Average high: 91°. Average low: 71°. Hot days; evenings still fairly pleasant.

Park Conditions: Regular season all month. The first week okay, but after schools get out, the hoards arrive.

July

Weather: Average high: 92°. Average low: 73°. HOT with afternoon thundershowers.

Park Conditions: Regular season all month for most resorts (see above). Very crowded, worst around the Fourth of July. A month to avoid.

August

Weather: Average high: 92°. Average low: 73°. Hot days, hot nights, afternoon thundershowers.

Park Conditions: Regular season for most resorts (see above). Busy for first three weeks, then slow.

September

Weather: Average high: 90°. Average low: 73°. Still summer in Florida. Hot days and hot nights.

Park Conditions: $ Value season all month. Not too crowded. Week after Labor Day is the slowest of the year.

October

Weather: Average high: 84°. Average low: 65°. Warm, but rarely hot. Balmy nights. A good month.

Park Conditions: Regular season after the first of the month, with attendance up, but not terrible.

November

Weather: Average high: 78°. Average low: 57°. Nice! Days are warm and evenings are cool.

Park Conditions: $ Value season all month. A great month except Thanksgiving week (stay home!).

December

Weather: Average high: 73°. Average low: 57°. Usually nice, but occasionally cold.

Park Conditions: $ Value season until last ten days, then holiday season. Attendance okay for first three weeks, then too crowded.

Some Special Times to Visit

During the course of the year, Disney features many special and seasonal events. Whether it's the Fourth of July, Christmas, or Halloween, the folks at Disney love to throw a party. In addition to the usual "big name" holidays, you will find celebrations of the Walt Disney World Marathon (January), Mardi Gras (February), St. Patrick's Day (March), Mother's Day (May), and ABC Supersoap Weekend, and the Festival of the Masters (November). In fact, there's always something going on at Walt Disney World.

Recommendations by Season

Our Winter Recommendations

• Expect any kind of weather except very hot; be prepared clothing-wise: try layering clothes.

• Don't forget your bathing suits. Pools and water attractions are all heated, and there are always the hot tubs.

• Avoid holidays (especially Christmas) or school break periods.

Our Summer Recommendations

• Prepare for heat and high humidity: bring lots of light, loose clothing, hats, bathing suits, and sunscreen.

• Make full use of Disney pools and water attractions during the hottest part of the day.

• Be prepared for brief afternoon thundershowers. Umbrellas and "Mickey ponchos" will come in handy.

Our Spring and Fall Recommendations

• Pack for almost any weather except very cold or very hot (except for September: it's still fairly hot).

• Avoid holidays such as Labor Day weekend or Thanksgiving week.

One of the best times to visit is during January. The weather is usually good, it's value season, and the parks are not crowded. Another of our favorite times is during the three weeks after Thanksgiving. It's a great time to enjoy the holiday festivities without battling the awful crowds of the Christmas holidays. We also love visiting during the Epcot Spring Flower & Garden Festival (late April to early June) and especially during the Epcot International Food & Wine Festival (late October and November). For

Helpful Hint

If you are visiting Disney in the weeks prior to Christmas, ask your Disney resort's guest relations for the schedule of the special Christmas entertainment featured nightly in the lobbies of many Disney resorts.

more details about this, one of our favorite Disney events, see chapter 6. The truth is that we much prefer these small and special celebrations to the overcrowded big-name holidays. For exact dates and more information about Disney's special events, call Disney Information at (407) 824-4321.

A Few Words About When *Not* to Go

If we could give you only one bit of advice about your Disney vacation (and we're glad that isn't so), it would be to avoid a visit on or near any major holiday. Avoid it like the plague. Sure, these times of year feature special celebrations, but the big holidays at Disney are so crowded that you'll find yourselves suffocating in a sea of humanity. You'll be standing in line not only for rides and attractions, but also for an ice cream bar, a T-shirt, and even for going to the bathroom. Attendance records are shattered every year on the Fourth of July, around Easter, during Thanksgiving week, and during the last week of December. These are tough times to visit if you are expecting to see much of Walt Disney World. If you must come during a holiday period, get to the theme parks early and make the best possible use of *FASTPASS* to avoid long lines.

Money-Saving Tip

If possible, go during value season, taking advantage of numerous resort discounts, smaller crowds, and discount vacation packages.

Then leave when it gets too busy. Another good way to deal with the crowds is to simply spend more of your time outside of the theme parks. Take in a game or match out at Disney's Wide World of Sports, visit one of Disney's lavish spas, see Cirque du Soleil, or spend your afternoons enjoying some of Disney's recreation. Play golf or tennis, ride a horse, rent a boat, or simply enjoy the pool at your resort. Know, too, that Disney resort rates are significantly higher during the two weeks around Christmas.

Helpful Hint

Avoid visiting Walt Disney World on or around any major holiday. At some Disney resorts, Christmas holiday season resort rates are about 30 percent higher than value season.

Where to Stay at a Glance

- **On-Site.** Stay on-property! It will make for a more relaxing vacation. You'll see more and without the frustration of traffic jams, long lines at park entrances, and too much time spent coming and going. We are convinced that staying at a Disney resort will make a more memorable vacation. If you've already done it, you know what we are talking about.
- **Off-Site.** If you feel you simply must stay off-property, do your homework. Find out exactly how much it will cost and precisely what you will get for your money. Extra persons, miscellaneous charges, and transportation costs can raise the price of your bargain room to as much or more than what you'd spend staying at Disney. If you're going to be relying on a shuttle service, find out how often it runs.

To make your Disney resort stay more affordable and to get just the room you want, make an extra effort to plan as far in advance as possible. There are many ways to get discounted Disney rooms and we'll tell you all about them.

Where to Stay

Yes, this is an important decision and making it will have more effect on your Walt Disney World vacation than you may know. Your accommodations will set the backdrop and mood for your entire visit. Convenience, luxury, and even romantic atmosphere are all about where you stay.

You have two basic choices of accommodations for your Walt Disney World vacation. You can stay at Walt Disney World or you can stay near Walt Disney World. Staying at Disney, known to cast members (the Disney folks) as "on-property," means staying in one of the Disney resorts. Staying near Walt Disney World, or "off-property," means staying in one of the many hotels or motels in surrounding areas such as Kissimmee, Lake Buena Vista, and Orlando.

There are some 100,000 hotel rooms in the Orlando area and without doubt, many provide wonderful accommodations. What's more, many may seem less expensive than staying in a Disney resort. But, be careful! Even though an off-property motel may claim that it is "five minutes from Disney," this doesn't mean that it will take only five minutes to make the trip. It may actually be a five-minute drive to Disney's front gate, but by the time you add traffic, parking, getting in from the parking lots, and a host of other impediments, we would be surprised if you would be able to leave your off-property room during the busy morning rush hour and get into a Disney theme park in less than an hour.

If you stay off-property, you'll quickly discover that all of this going back and forth wastes precious vacation time. And what's worse, staying this far away usually means that it's impractical to return to your hotel room for an hour's rest, an afternoon together, or even to change clothes for an evening out. If you're driving, the traffic jams in the mornings and at closing times mean frustration and more lost vacation time. And if you're relying on a hotel shuttle, then you'll find yourself on somebody else's schedule and not your own. Getting places will take on a whole new level of considerations.

Now consider what it would be like to stay at Disney. Every room on-property is located in a "themed resort." Each Disney resort has its own fantasy atmosphere and lodgings that have been carefully created to enfold you in Disney's unique brand of magic. Everything at Disney's award-winning Animal Kingdom Lodge, for example, reflects the exotic flavor of Africa, from the live creatures that inhabit its grounds to the lodge's African restaurants. Not just the look of the resort but the costumes of its cast members and even room decor—everything down to the smallest and most entertaining detail, enhances the African theme. Once you've left the theme parks and returned to your resort, you won't feel as though you've left the magic behind. You will have entered your very own special part of Walt Disney World.

And this is really just the beginning. Staying in a Disney Resort will make your vacation easier and more fun. You'll be right next door to all the magic and you'll enjoy all the benefits of Disney transportation. Whether by boat, bus, or monorail, you'll be able to make much better use of your vacation time. And, as Disney resort guests, you'll enjoy special benefits such as early admission to the theme parks and the Ultimate Park Hopper Pass (see page 14 for details).

If you are thinking that it costs a fortune to stay at a Disney resort, think again. There are now Disney resorts for most every budget, with prices beginning around $86 per night. In chapter 2, we'll tell you all about them and about how to find the one that suits your tastes and your budget. Later in this chapter, we'll tell you how to find resort discounts that will make a stay in one of the Disney resorts even more attractive.

Admission Options

Whether you opt to buy your admission passes before you get to Walt Disney World or not, you'll certainly want to know what's available. If you are a couple with children, you'll want to know that children under 3 years of age do not require admission passes to any of the Disney attractions. There is a children's pass for ages 3 to 9 years, and for all visitors 10 years of age and over, general admission is required.

Following is the assortment of Disney tickets and passes. Remember that admission prices often go up several times a year and sometimes, even the assortment of passes might change. Note that the following prices already include 6½ percent Florida sales tax.

One-Day/One-Park Ticket

This ticket is the simplest one of all: buy one and get admission to one of the four Disney theme parks for one day only (Epcot, the Magic Kingdom, Disney-MGM, or the Animal Kingdom).

- General admission price: $53.25 ($42.60 for ages 3 to 9)

- Tips: Good for short visit or to fill in days not covered by other passes. Most expensive per-day cost

- Does NOT include park hopping (going to more than one park in one day)

Four- or Five-Day Park Hopper Pass

These passes provide either four or five days of admission to the Magic Kingdom, Disney-MGM Studios, Epcot, and the Animal Kingdom. Visit one or all of these parks on any of the days (called "park-hopping"). Passes need not be used on consecutive days, and unused days never expire.

- Four-Day Park Hopper Pass: $211.95 ($169.35 for ages 3 to 9)

- Five-Day Park Hopper Pass: $243.90 ($195.97 for ages 3 to 9)

Insider's Secret
Park Hopper Pass is a good choice for your first visit to WDW.

Park Hopper Plus Pass

This pass provides unlimited park-hopping to all four theme parks. The "plus" means a specified number of visits to either of the Disney water parks or to Pleasure Island. With the five-day pass, you get two "plus visits," with the six-day pass, three, and with the seven-day pass, four additional visits. How you use these passes will affect how many days you get out of them. Unused days never expire.

- Five-Day Park Hopper Plus (includes two plus visits): $275.85 ($221.53 for ages 3 to 9)

- Six-Day Park Hopper Plus (includes three plus visits): $307.80 ($247.09 for ages 3 to 9)

- Seven-Day Park Hopper Plus (includes four plus visits): $339.74 ($272.65 for ages 3 to 9)

Money-Saving Tip

Stretch a five-day Hopper pass to seven days by using each "plus visit" for a one-day admission to one of the water parks.

Ultimate Park Hopper Pass

Available only to Disney resort guests, this pass provides unlimited admission to all Disney attractions for the duration of your Disney visit, no matter the length. This includes all four theme parks as well as Blizzard Beach, Typhoon Lagoon, Pleasure Island, the Wide World of Sports (valid only on event days), and DisneyQuest. The longer your stay, the less the average cost per day. Ultimate Park Hopper Passes are available for any length of stay. Here's the breakdown for general passes:

- One-night/two-day Ultimate Park Hopper Pass: $126.75 ($102.24 for ages 3 to 9)

- Two-night/three-day Ultimate Park Hopper Pass: $171.47 ($137.39 for ages 3 to 9)

- Three-night/four-day Ultimate Park Hopper Pass: $232.17 ($186.38 for ages 3 to 9)

- Four-night/five-day Ultimate Park Hopper Pass: $277.97 ($225.59 for ages 3 to 9)

- Five-night/six-day Ultimate Park Hopper Pass: $312.05 ($250.28 for ages 3 to 9)

- Six-night/seven-day Ultimate Park Hopper Pass: $346.13 ($276.90 for ages 3 to 9)

Insider's Secret

The Ultimate Park Hopper Pass is the only Hopper Pass that includes DisneyQuest.

Money-Saving Tip

If you arrive late on your first day or depart early on your last day, you can shorten your Ultimate Hopper Pass to avoid paying theme park admission for the partial day. This can only be done if you purchase your tickets at your Disney resort during check-in. Be sure to request it at that time. For tips about what to do for such a "partial" day at Disney, see page 28.

Disney Water Parks: Typhoon Lagoon or Blizzard Beach

- One-day, one-park pass: $33 ($27 for ages 3 to 9)

- Admission to Blizzard Beach and Winter Summerland Miniature Golf: $38.50 ($30.80 for ages 3 to 9)

- Annual pass to both water parks: $106 ($86 for ages 3 to 9)

- Annual pass to both water parks and to DisneyQuest: $137 ($105 for ages 3 to 9)

Pleasure Island

- One evening pass: about $21

- Annual pass: $59

- Add five consecutive nights to one-night Pleasure Island admission ticket: $5

Disney's Wide World of Sports

- One-day, general admission: $9.75 ($7.50 for ages 3 to 9). Charged only on days when events are scheduled; some events require special admission.

DisneyQuest (at Downtown Disney)

- ℮ Single-day DisneyQuest admission: $33.00 ($26.63 for ages 3 to 9)

- ℮ DisneyQuest Annual Pass: $84.13 ($67.10 for ages 3 to 9)

- ℮ DisneyQuest/Waterparks Annual Pass $137 ($105 for ages 3 to 9)

Cirque du Soleil (at Downtown Disney)

Provides admission to one show. See page 291 for more information about this amazing show.

- ℮ Category One seating $87.33 ($52.19 for ages 3 to 9)

- ℮ Category Two seating $76.68 ($46.86 for ages 3 to 9)

Disney Annual Passes

Disney also offers a selection of passes for an entire year of admission. Of course, you need to visit often enough to make one worth the investment. However, with resort discounts for annual pass holders sometimes as high as 40 percent, an annual pass can pay for itself in a single visit. For more details, see the section on the Disney World of discounts on page 22.

Theme Park Annual Pass

This pass provides unlimited admission to all four theme parks for one year from date of first use.

- ℮ Pass price: $393 ($334 for ages 3 to 9)

- ℮ $ Tip: If you are going to be spending more than seven days in a given year at Walt Disney World, the Theme Park Annual Pass saves money.

Premium Annual Pass

Providing unlimited admission for one year from date of voucher redemption, to all four theme parks: Blizzard Beach, Typhoon Lagoon, Pleasure Island, the Wide World of Sports, and DisneyQuest.

- ℮ Pass price: $521 ($443 for ages 3 to 9)

- ℮ $ Tip: Not counting resort discounts, you'll have to spend ten days at Disney within one year for the Premium Annual Pass to earn its keep. However, with resort discounts, this pass can pay for itself in a single visit. Making your next year's visit within the life of the pass will save even more. For details on both annual pass holder resort discounts, see page 23.

Tips for Disney Attraction Admissions

- AAA Club in Florida is a good source of discounted WDW admission tickets and passes.

- A good source for ticket discounts, especially the Ultimate Hopper Pass, is www.Disneyworld.com.

- Admission price increases are yearly events at Disney. To get the exact figures for your visit, call (407) W-DISNEY (934-7639), or check online at www.disneyworld.com.

- $ To fill in days not covered by your passes, consider spending a day at Downtown Disney. Other options that would save the cost of a theme park ticket would be one of the Disney water parks, DisneyQuest, or the Wide World of Sports.

- $ Florida residents get discounts on annual passes and a special resident's seasonal pass. See page 26 for details.

Where to Purchase Your Disney Admission Passes

- When you check in to your Disney resort

- Tickets by phone or online (multiday tickets only; allow three weeks for delivery and add $3 service charge; Ultimate Hopper Pass no service charge to order ahead.)

- Tickets by phone: (407) 824-4321

- Tickets online: www.disneyworld.com

- Disney Store: select passes only

- At the theme park ticket booths (most time consuming)

- Florida AAA offices: Any AAA member can buy discounted tickets at any Florida AAA office

Vacation Packages

These days nearly everyone in the travel industry offers a Walt Disney World vacation package. Some are independent travel companies or tour services, while others are discount travel wholesalers. Many provide off-property lodgings, theme park admission, and often little else. This is the type of package deal that you're likely to see in your local newspaper. If you are considering one of them, we warn you to be extremely careful. Off-property accommodations are often not what they sound like in ads or look like in photos. And once you get to Walt Disney World, you may be surprised by the condition of your lodgings and at what these "all-inclusive" offers don't include.

Vacation plans created by the Walt Disney Travel Company will be our focus. With these, you will be able to enjoy the convenience and benefits of staying right on Disney property (or nearby, if that is your wish). We suggest you begin your odyssey by visiting a local travel agent and picking up the fifty-page catalog of packages. Once armed with package basics and Disney's list prices, you'll be ready to shop around for the best deal.

Disney Vacation Package Basics

Disney vacation plans are calculated on a per-person, per-night cost. Youngsters fall into one of two cost levels: juniors (ages 10 to 17) or children (ages 3 to 9). Children under 3 years of age are free. Different packages and prices are available for the entire spectrum of Disney resorts. If you opt for a vacation package, you should know that after your initial deposit, the complete balance of your package cost is due no later than thirty days before the first day of your vacation.

All Walt Disney Travel Company vacation packages will provide each member of your party with an Ultimate Hopper Pass, good for your entire length of stay. This pass will admit you to all four Disney theme parks plus DisneyQuest, Blizzard Beach, Typhoon Lagoon, Pleasure Island, and Disney's Wide World of Sports (does not include special sports events), each as many times and on any days you wish.

Sources of Disney Vacation Packages

- WDW Central Reservations Office (CRO): (407) 934-7639

- American Automobile Association's (AAA) Vacations: Call your local AAA

- Delta Dream Vacations: (800) 872-7786

- Your local travel agent

- Wholesale clubs like Sam's Club, Price Club, Costco, and BJ's

Types of Disney Vacation Packages for 2003

Disney's basic vacation package is called the Dream Maker Plan. This package vacation includes three nights or more of accommodations, Ultimate Hopper Passes, two free Disney pins and lanyards, and the choice of either miniature golf, a Disney character storytelling, or two images at Epcot's Leave a Legacy (see page 220 for details). Prices begin at $349 per person ($222 junior/$177 child) for three nights at a Disney value resort during value season. Staying in a more expensive resort or staying during a more expensive season will add dollars to these figures.

You can upgrade your Dream Maker Plan by purchasing "add-ons." There are four basic add-on plans: the Silver, the Gold, the Platinum, and the Romance. Everyone in your party must be on the same package add-on. Here's a brief rundown on what you get with each:

Dream Maker Silver Plan

To the basic Dream Maker plan, add $67 adults or juniors ($54 child) per person, per night to get the addition of two "Magical Wishes" per person, per night. Magical Wishes include:

- Dining: one breakfast, lunch, or dinner in 125 select Disney restaurants (includes character meals and dinner shows); also includes gratuities

- Dining in "signature restaurants" (counts as two wishes)

- Recreation: Eighteen holes of off-season golf (peak season golf requires two wishes), length-of-stay health club access, thirty minutes of watercraft rental, thirty-minute private golf lesson, golf club rental, or nine holes of par-3 golf. Parasailing requires two wishes.

- Souvenir animated scene photo

- Up to six hours of children's activities with dinner in select Disney resort (see page 36 for details)

- A choice of a select Disney tour

- Variety of specially created Disney merchandise, such as trading pin kit, sculpted figurine, or enameled box

- Souvenir T-shirt

- Admission to Cirque du Soleil (counts as two wishes)

- Select spa treatment (preferred treatment for two wishes)

Dream Maker Gold Plan

To the basic Dream Maker plan, add $139 for adult or junior ($94 child) per person, per night. In addition to basic Dream Maker plan, features include all of the following:

- Breakfast, lunch, and dinner per night at 125 participating Disney restaurants (includes character meals and "signature" restaurants)

- Unlimited recreation includes golf, tennis, fishing, water sports and crafts, and health club access

- Admission to Cirque du Soleil

- Unlimited use of Disney children's activities centers

- Unlimited access to most WDW tours

Dream Maker Platinum Plan

To the basic Dream Maker plan, add $199 for adult or junior ($119 child) per person, per night. The Platinum Plan is good only for staying at a deluxe or a home-away-from-home resort. Features in addition to basic Dream Maker include:

- Personalized pre-arrival itinerary planning

- Three meals daily at any WDW restaurant (includes dinner shows and counter service), plus one snack daily; includes room service and Victoria & Albert's

- Unlimited use of select Disney recreation, including golf and waterskiing

- Admission to Cirque du Soleil

- One luxurous spa treatment

- One exclusive keepsake per room

- Fireworks cruise

- Reserved seating at Fantasmic! (see page 251)

- Unlimited access to Disney Tours plus Epcot's DiveQuest and Dolphins In-Depth

- Unlimited use of Disney children's activities centers

- Private in-room child care

- Nightly turn-down service

Money-Saving Tip

The all-inclusive packages are best for repeat WDW visitors who venture out of the theme parks to make use of the special features of these packages.

Romance Plan Add-On

To the basic Dream Maker plan, add $149 per person. Benefits include a thirty-minute carriage ride with champagne and choice of two Romance Plan features per person for the length of your package. Features include:

- Dinner at a select signature restaurant (excludes alcohol and includes gratuities)

- Admission to Cirque du Soleil

- Select spa treatment or professional photography session (each counts as two features)

$ Are Packages a Bargain?

Yes, packages will save you money. When you look at Walt Disney Travel Company package pricing, remember that these rates already include both a 5 percent Florida resort tax and the 6½ percent Florida sales tax. Add it all up and you save. Given that further discounts are available through travel agents and AAA, these packages look pretty attractive. Besides saving money, another real advantage is that you'll have a much clearer picture about how much your Disney vacation will cost.

If you are thinking that you can do better yourselves, this might also be true. An Annual Pass might be used to create your own bargain package, but you'll have to be lucky enough to get good resort rates, and be ready to vacation only when they are available.

As for the Gold, Silver, Platinum, and Romance add-ons, these will save you money *only* if you make the best possible use of all their features. We think these offerings are particularly good deals if you have been to Disney often enough that you'll spend time using the sports, recreation, and dining features of these packages. The real advantage of these all-inclusive packages is that you will be more focused on seeing Cirque du Soleil, waterskiing or golfing, and enjoying the finest of Disney dining than you will be on how much it all costs. This amounts to a *major* difference in attitude. All in all, we think that if you're going to make use of the extra features, a Walt Disney Travel Company package vacation is worth a good, long look.

To give you an idea of prices, here's a quick look at a small variety of Walt Disney Travel Company Packages for 2003. Remember, the following prices are calculated for value season, standard view rooms and include tax:

Package	Length	Resort	Two Adults	Junior 10–17	Child 3–9
Dream Maker	3 nights	Disney's Caribbean Beach	$886	$222	$177
Dream Maker	5 nights	Disney's Caribbean Beach	$1,334	$298	$239
Dream Maker Silver	5 nights	Disney's Caribbean Beach	$2,004	$633	$509
Dream Maker Gold	5 nights	Disney's Caribbean Beach	$2,724	$993	$709
Dream Maker Silver	5 nights	Disney's Yacht & Beach	$2,870	$633	$509
Dream Maker Platinum	3 nights	Disney's Yacht & Beach	$2,600	$819	$534

$ The Disney World of Discounts

No doubt about it, a Disney vacation is expensive. The good news is that there are a variety of discounts for resorts, package vacations, meals, admission tickets, and more. The bad news is that discounts aren't what they used to be. With the demise of the Disney Club at the end of 2003, one of the most dependable sources of Disney discounts vanishes. It's not all bad news, though. ✸ A new Disney Visa credit card now offers users reward points applicable toward Disney vacations and merchandise.

Discounts do exist, but almost entirely during value season. Although these savings may not be as hefty as they once were, they will save you plenty of money. The longer you stay, the more money you'll save. Here's what we know about discounts at Walt Disney World:

✸ $ Disney Visa Credit Card

This Visa credit sounds like a darn good deal. The card is usable anywhere Visa is accepted, and like air miles, use of this card will accrue points that will be redeemable toward purchasing Walt Disney World vacations and Disney merchandise. It will also provide special, money-saving offers, and a 0 percent interest rate on Disney vacation packages. These include the Disney Cruise Line, Walt Disney World, and Disneyland. Sounds simple. To acquire one of these cards, call 888-688-4868 and mention code card 7BXJ.

✸ Online Discounts at www.Disneyworld.com

Discounts of all kinds can be had by visiting Disney World's online site: package vacations, resort reservations, even admission tickets.

Timing is everything. Although you might be able to get something better elsewhere, this Web site is certainly worth a look, especially for admission passes and the Ultimate Hopper Pass.

$ Walt Disney World Annual Passes

The Theme Park Annual Pass features some of the best discounts both for the Disney resorts and for dining at Walt Disney World. In addition, only one person in your party needs the pass to get the room discount. If you visit Disney for more than two or three days and take the time to get the good resort rates, an annual pass can pay for itself in a single yearly visit. If you return again within that year, you'll be that much more ahead. You won't even need your pass before you reserve your room. However, expect to present your pass or its voucher at check-in.

The annual pass is available to anyone willing to purchase it. Cost is $393 ($335 for ages 3 to 9). A Premium Annual Pass will add unlimited admission to both Disney water parks, Pleasure Island, Disney's Wide World of Sports, and DisneyQuest. Cost is $521 ($443 for ages 3 to 9). All prices include Florida sales tax.

Discounts and Privileges for Annual Passholders

- Bearer gets unlimited admission to the four theme parks for one full year. (With Premium Pass, add the Disney water parks, Pleasure Island, Disney's Wide World of Sports, and DisneyQuest.)

- Free parking at Disney theme parks (currently $7)

- Seasonal "Mickey Monitor" newsletter with special offers and advance notice of special events

- Seasonal discounts at WDW resort hotels and select Disney Vacation Club properties may be offered. In the past, some resort discounts have been as much as 40 percent.

- Discounted renewal prices for pass

- Special passholder events

- 15 percent off regular boat rentals at Walt Disney World (excludes specialty cruises)

- 10 percent off lunch at select Downtown Disney, Disney resort restaurants, and Epcot World Showcase restaurants for passholder and up to three guests

- 10 percent off dinner at Portobello Yacht Club, Fulton's, and Planet Hollywood for pass holder and up to three guests

- 10 percent off meals at All Star Cafe for passholder and up to three guests

- 10 percent discounts on merchandise at select shops in Downtown Disney

- 15 percent discounts on most Walt Disney World tours (see page 361)

- 10 percent off regular price of any single treatment per visit at Grand Floridian Spa

- 30 percent off golf at select times of year (good for passholder and three guests)

- 10 percent discount at Sammy Duvall's Watersports on parasailing, waterskiing, wakeboarding

- Discounts of $4 (adult), $3 (ages 3 to 9) on admission for friends and family for DisneyQuest, Pleasure Island, and Disney water parks

- 10 percent discount on Richard Petty Driving Experience

- 50 percent off one admission to Fantasia or Winter Summerland miniature golf and 15 percent off for up to three guests

- Complimentary admission to O-Ray games at Wide World of Sports

- 20 percent discount at Alamo and National Car Rentals

Please note that annual pass dining discounts do not include alcoholic beverages.

$ American Automobile Association (AAA)

With the end of the Disney Club, AAA has become one of only a few dependable sources for discount packages, resort discounts, and discount admission passes. If you factor in the automotive advantages of membership along with the Disney discounts, AAA makes good sense. AAA members of any state can purchase discounted Disney passes at any Florida AAA office. However, Florida resident passes may only be purchased by Florida residents.

Discounts and Privileges for AAA Members

- Special benefits when booking AAA Vacations: 10 to 20 percent discount on room portion of package (depends on season and room availability)

- At Florida and some other AAA offices: 10 to 20 percent discount on Disney resort rooms (depends on season and room availability)

@ At Florida AAA Clubs, as well as some other states: discounted Disney admission to all attractions, including Pleasure Island and DisneyQuest

$ *AAA Vacations*

AAA Vacations is one of several travel services provided by AAA. The privileges and discounts that follow apply only to packages purchased through AAA Vacations. You do not have to be a AAA member to get these packages.

@ AAA Vacations Diamond Card for discounted tours, dining, merchandise, recreation, dinner shows, and more at Walt Disney World

Money-Saving Tip

AAA members get discounts on AAA Vacation packages.

@ Use of the Magic Kingdom AAA VIP Lounge (comfortable and free beverages, too)

@ Preferred viewing areas for Magic Kingdom and Epcot fireworks

@ Preferred parking at select Disney theme parks

@ Discounts on select rentals on Disney Cruise Line's Castaway Cay

$ Disney Central Reservations Office: (407) W-DISNEY (934-7639)

Central Reservations (or CRO) takes reservations for all things Disney. The few discounts that are available through CRO are usually package deals, including airfare, resort room, and admission tickets. However, it's worth a few calls to see what might be available for the time you're planning to visit. Special discounts are known to happen.

$ Random Mailings to Previous Disney Guests

If you've already been to Walt Disney World or have visited the Disney Web site, you might already be on a list for resort discount offerings. These promotions go to past guests, theme park visitors who are surveyed as they exit, and those who take the surveys that sometimes appear on the Walt Disney World Web site (see page 22 for details). In our experience, these are some of the best discounts we've seen—up to 34 percent off regular resort rates. Unfortunately, if you qualify for a random mailing, the only thing you can do is wait for one to arrive.

$ Your Local Travel Agent

Disney offers discount vacation packages to travel agents, which enables your local agents to be competitive in the Disney travel market, especially during value season. Call your agent to learn what kind of deals you can get.

$ Wholesale Clubs

Organizations such as Sam's Club, BJ's, and Costco offer discount travel services. These usually include a variety of Walt Disney Travel Company packages and even offerings of the Disney Cruise Line. If you are a member of one of these wholesale club, check to see what is available.

Non-Disney Online Discount Sources

$ Unofficial Disney sites can provide useful information about what special discounts are available. See page 464 for a list of other useful Disney Internet sites.

  ℯ *Mousesaver.com*   This site has more information on Disney discounts than we've ever seen in one place. Mary, who runs it, seems to keep things pretty current. Check it out at www.mousesaver .com.

$ Florida Resident Discounts

When it comes to Disney discounts, being a Florida resident really pays off. Usually offered during value season, discounts include resort rates, packages, and admission tickets. If you are Florida residents planning a visit, you will certainly want to take advantage of these offers. Simply call Disney Central Reservations at (407) W-DISNEY (934-7639) and ask what Florida residents' specials are being offered and when. $ Disney also offers to Florida residents discounted Theme Park Annual Passes and Premium Annual Passes.

The $ **Florida Resident Seasonal Pass** is a great deal for Floridians. With it, you get unlimited admission to all four theme parks for an entire year, excluding mid-June to late August, the Christmas holiday season, and around Easter. The pass is good for nearly 270 days of the year, and the price (including tax) is a mere $201 ($171 for ages 3 to 9). It also entitles the bearer to the same resort discounts available to Annual Pass holders. However, it does not provide free theme park parking. Still, it's a great deal.

The **After 4 P.M. Epcot Pass** is another ticket for Florida residents. For $111 ($94 for ages 3 to 9), including tax, owners of this pass can visit Epcot on any evening for a full year.

The **$ Disney Dining Experience** is a one of the best perks for Florida residents. The $75 annual membership provides a 20 percent discount in a large selection of Disney restaurants. This includes both food and alcoholic beverages and is good for a party of up to six. It also entitles the bearer to buy tickets to a variety of Disney Dining Experience special functions throughout the year, half-price admission to Pleasure Island, and free admission to BoardWalk's Atlantic Dance Hall. If you are a Florida resident and enjoy food, wine, and Disney, this card can pay for itself in a few meals. Call (407) 566-5858 for information.

Money-Saving Tips

Florida residents who are members of AAA can get a discount on the seasonal and annual passes.

Money-Saving Tips

- Be comparative shoppers. Check out every possible source. Be persistent.
- Don't pass up a good deal while waiting for the perfect one. Make your reservation and cancel it later when a better deal arrives.
- When talking with a CRO reservationist, be sure to ask questions. Carefully explain what you are looking for. These people know a lot, but they also seem trained to not offer the cheapest alternative unless you ask for it.
- For best-room availability, try calling Central Reservations in the morning, before 11 A.M. , eastern time. This really works.
- Book early and visit during value season.

Figuring Out What It Will All Cost

It's important to know beforehand what your Walt Disney World vacation is going to cost. You won't want to spend your time at Disney worrying about how much money you're spending. If you're traveling on one of Disney's all-inclusive package plans, you'll already be enjoying its greatest advantage: you'll know what you'll be spending for just about everything except souvenirs. Most of us, however, make our own plans and work within our own self-imposed budgets.

Fortunately, figuring out how much it will all cost is not terribly difficult. The basic expenses of a Disney vacation are travel to Orlando (we'll leave this one for you to figure out), resort accommodations, admission passes, food, and such miscellaneous expenses as souvenirs.

Determining the Cost of Accommodations

Figuring out what your resort or hotel will cost should be easy. Take a look at our guide to the Disney resorts in chapter 2 and see which resort meets your expectations. Modest price increases are yearly events at Disney, so you might want to check with Central Reservations to make sure that you have the most current rates. Our prices already include a combined Florida state sales and county resort tax of 11½ percent.

Calculating Admission Expenses

There's a variety of Disney admission passes, but cost per day doesn't seem to vary greatly. Expect to spend around $53 per day per adult ($42 for children ages 3 to 9) for admission to the Disney theme parks. For more precise amounts and the variety of Disney passes, see page 12.

Money-Saving Tip

If your first or last day at Disney is just half a day, avoid using a full-day theme park pass (about $53). Instead, play at Disney-Quest ($33), shop at Downtown Disney (no admission), or visit the Wide World of Sports ($10) if there is an event scheduled.

How Much Will It Cost to Eat at Disney?

Figuring your food expenses is a bit more complicated. Whatever your tastes, you should know that eating three meals a day at Disney World will constitute a significant part of your vacation budget. Just how big a part will depend on where and how you eat.

As a general rule, if you're willing to eat only at counter-service restaurants (and we don't suggest that you do this), it would be possible for two adults to eat three meals a day at Walt Disney World on $80 a day (add $25 for each child). For a more realistic figure, we'd suggest a daily food budget for two of $140 per day (and $40 for each child). This would mean fast food for one meal a day and table service meals for the other two. Of course, the larger your budget, the more lavish your dining. For three table-service meals a day in Disney's better (but not premium) restaurants, expect to spend $160 per day for two adults ($60 for each child). A dinner for two at one of Disney's premium restaurants can easily top $100. These prices include a daily snack and drink, taxes, and tips where applicable. If you are one of those people who always orders the most expensive thing on the menu (one of our kids could be relied on for this), expect our figures to come in a little on the low side.

It should be easy to eat within the ranges we provide but we should warn you that our figures don't include alcoholic beverages. For this, figure about $10 a glass for wine, about $5 for a beer, and $8 or $9 for a cocktail.

Putting It All Together: What Will It Cost?

Now that you have some idea of what the major costs will be, all that remains is to add them up and to see what you get. To give you a good idea of the scope of possibilities, we have constructed two sample budgets, with stays at the Animal Kingdom Lodge. Don't forget to add your transportation expenses to and from Walt Disney World and any other anticipated expenses such as alcoholic beverages or child care.

Know too that these figures do not include souvenirs, which can be expensive. Given that a logo T-shirt can cost over $25 (and we've seen some for twice that amount) and even the smallest of souvenirs is at least $5, we suggest that you set a budget for vacation mementos and do your best to stick to it. Prices below include all taxes.

Four-Night/Five-Day Stay for Two at Animal Kingdom Lodge (Regular Season)

Savannah view room	$1,405
Resort gratuities	20
Meals and gratuities	700
Ultimate Hopper Passes	528
TOTAL	$2,653

Four-Night/Five-Day Stay for Two at Animal Kingdom Lodge (Value Season), with Annual Pass Discount

Savannah view room with 35% Pass Holder discount	$930
Resort gratuities	20
Meals and gratuities with annual pass discounts	675
Premium Annual Pass for one	521
Ultimate Hopper Pass for one	264
TOTAL (saves $243)	$2,410

Tips for Doing It on a Budget

$ Take advantage of every discount you can get. Plan ahead.

$ Book ahead for a value season special to get the best resort rate.

$ Avoid the two weeks around Christmas.

$ Explore a variety of resorts and admission ticket combinations before making your final decision.

$ Try a Disney vacation package.

$ Make a budget and stick to it.

Making Your Resort Reservations

There are more than a thousand cast members at the Disney Central Reservations Office (CRO) taking an incredible seven million reservations a year. The discounted and least-expensive rooms are the first to go, so we suggest that you reserve your rooms as far in advance as you are able. Have alternatives in the event that your choice is not available. Here are the numbers to call (Monday–Friday 7 A.M.–10 P.M., Saturday–Sunday 8 A.M.–8 P.M.):

Disney Central Reservations Office (CRO)
(407) W-DISNEY (934-7639)

Before you make your call, here are some things to think about:

@ Views: A variety of views are available in all of the Disney resorts. Selecting one of these will be part of making your reservations. Expect to pay more for rooms with views of water, castles, and theme parks.

@ Types of beds: Most resort rooms come with two queen beds or two doubles, but there are a number of king-size beds available at most of the Disney resorts. This is the time to reserve one of these if that is your choice. Making a king-size bed reservation usually means that the view cannot be guaranteed. In some resorts, a king bed can no longer be guaranteed, but it can be requested. Be forewarned, rooms with king beds (regardless of view) at the moderate resorts cost the same as water view rooms.

@ Room location: In our guide to the Disney resorts in chapter 2, we describe the various choices of room locations for each resort. If you have a preference for a certain location, you should make this request when you reserve your resort room. Although no guarantee can be made, a mention of this will be attached to your reservation.

@ Smoking or non-smoking room: Be sure to mention your preference when making your call.

@ Connecting rooms: If you are bringing your children along, consider a room that connects to your own. Disney reservations can guarantee connecting rooms when children are a part of your reservation.

@ **$** Discounts or specials: Always ask about specials or promotions when you make your reservations.

@ Certain restaurants are so popular that if you are planning a meal there, you should make priority seating arrangements when you make your room reservations. These include Cinderella's Royal Table (especially the character breakfast), Victoria and Albert's, the Coral Reef (dinner only), and the California Grill. See chapter 6 for tips on making priority seating arrangements.

@ Dinner show reservations: If you're planning on a dinner show, such as the Hoop-Dee-Doo Musical Revue, you need to make reservations when you reserve your room.

@ From October to April, if you are interested in playing golf, reserve your tee times when you book your room.

@ Children under 17 years of age stay for free in your Disney resort room.

@ Disney resorts charge extra for more than two adults per room. The charge is $10 per night at the value resorts, $15 per night at the moderates, $25 per night at the deluxe resorts and the Swan or Dolphin, and $5 for the Wilderness Cabins. There are no extra charges at the Disney Vacation Club properties.

@ Special comments: If this is your honeymoon, anniversary, or birthday, be sure to tell your reservationist. Mention it again when you check in. Often, your Disney resort will do something for you—usually a card or a special pin. If your occasion is a big one, such as a twenty-fifth anniversary, be sure to tell them.

Making Reservations

You will probably want to begin your reservation odyssey by gathering the most current information. Once you get a Disney reservationist on the telephone, you will discover that the system is designed to make reservations, not to dispense information. The very first thing they'll want to know is the date of your visit. If you are simply shopping for prices and haven't picked a date, make up one. Use any date during value season to get those prices, any date during regular season to compare prices, and so forth. (See page 4 for the dates of the Disney seasons.) To hold your Disney resort reservation, a deposit in the amount of your first night's stay will be required and you can either do this with a credit card when you make your reservation or by check, no later than fourteen days prior to your arrival.

Money-Saving Tips

To get the best room deal:

- Be persistent. Keep trying, calling every day if need be.
- Call early, before 11 A.M.

Reservation Tips

- Make your reservations in the morning, before 11 A.M. For some reason, resort availability seems best at this time.

- Keep trying if at first you are unable to get what you really want. There are plenty of cancellations that produce more available rooms.

- **$** Reservations that begin at a value season rate maintain that low rate for your entire visit, even if you stay into a more expensive season. Since some value season discounts can be as much as 30 percent, simply arriving a day earlier for the last day of value season can pay for several nights of a holiday season visit.

The Romantic Family Trip

If having children meant the end to romance for married couples, we'd all come from very small families. We hope that if you have children, romance is alive and well in your lives. If it isn't, let this be your wake-up call. With a bit of planning, you should be able to visit Walt Disney World as a family and still have your romantic moments.

Making a family trip to Disney World is a large undertaking, one that will take even more planning than a visit for two. It will be more expensive, and there will be a greater number of logistical concerns, especially if you are traveling with very young children or an infant. Consider, though, that it's a free ride for kids under 3 years of age at Disney World. No admission tickets are necessary, they are not an extra expense at Disney resorts, and they eat for free at buffet meals. Walt Disney World has been "Imagineered" with families in mind. When it comes to meeting the needs of a family, the facilities are impressive.

Making Plans: When to Go

For most of us, when we vacation is determined by when we can get time off. If you have some choice in the matter, know that the best time to visit Walt Disney World is during the off-season. Yes, this means taking your kids out of school.

September and the first three weeks of both November and January are all good times for a Walt Disney World vacation. Off-season is also the value season. Resort rates, packages, and admission tickets are all available at discounted rates. People are still at the parks, but are significantly fewer in number. You will see much more, do much more, have a more relaxed time of it, and spend less money. Any more questions?

Accommodations: An Even Bigger Decision for a Family

For us, staying off-property with children is even less appealing than doing it by ourselves. There's a lot of travel, a host of logistics, and lots of lost time. It's much easier to get the kids back to a Disney resort for an afternoon of rest than it is to get them back to a motel on Highway 192.

Along with the choice of staying off-property or on, you will be faced with the decision of how to accommodate all of you. There are more options than you think.

One Family, One Room

Sharing a room with your family will not make having a romantic time impossible; it simply makes things more of a challenge. Getting a room in a Disney resort is expensive enough. Getting two may be a fatal blow to an already stretched budget. While we cannot speak for accommodations outside of Disney World, we can tell you that children younger than 17 stay for free at all Disney resorts. Standard resort rooms feature two large beds, and cribs are available at every Disney resort at no extra cost.

Most Disney resorts permit a maximum of four people in each room. In addition to standard rooms with two queens, both the Wilderness and Animal Kingdom Lodges have rooms with one queen bed and a set of bunk beds, a more interesting option for a family of four. Many of the deluxe resorts accommodate five. This is managed with two queen beds and a daybed/sofa. Port Orleans Riverside features trundle beds in many rooms for a fifth person, and many of the hotels at Downtown Disney's Hotel Plaza can also sleep five, some even more.

If you have a family larger than five, you'll have to do something besides share a standard resort room.

One Family, Two Rooms

All Disney resorts offer connecting rooms, and some feature a room with two beds connected to a room with one king-size bed. This seems perfect for a small family. If you're considering sharing a room at one of the premium resorts, for about the same expense, you should be able to get two adjoining rooms at one of the value or moderate resorts.

A Suite for a Family

Suites offer yet another route to accommodate a family. Virtually all of the premium resorts offer a selection of suites, some with as many connecting rooms as you care to add. While these can be the perfect place for a family, they are expensive.

Family-Sized Accommodations

These are Disney's home-away-from-home lodgings, and besides providing enough room for just about any large family, each has some kind of kitchen, giving you an economical alternative to eating every meal in a restaurant. **$** For a little more than the cost of a single room at the Yacht or the Beach Clubs, you can get a luxurious one-bedroom villa at either Old Key West, the Villas at the Wilderness Lodge, the BoardWalk Villas, or the new Beach Club Villas. Any of these accommodations provides a complete kitchen, washer and dryer, a living room with fold-out queen bed, and your own king-size bedroom. Add to this a balcony and a Jacuzzi tub, and your romance family vacation starts looking pretty good. These places are beautiful and spacious and perfect for a family Disney vacation. Most home-away-from-home accommodations also feature two bedroom villas.

On the budget end of the spectrum are the **$** Fort Wilderness Cabins, which can sleep six, or the **$** DoubleTree Guest Suites at Downtown Disney, which can accommodate two adults and two children with ease. Both are available off-season at very reasonable rates. For more information about these accommodations, see chapter 2.

Family Necessities

$ If you have an infant, bring all the baby supplies that are practical to carry. You can buy them at Disney, but choices are limited and prices are high. Extra pacifiers are also a good idea and so are snacks and drinks for the kids. If you can, bring your own folding stroller. While both single and double strollers can be rented at the theme parks, you will find yourselves standing in line to get one (and to return it). Your own stroller will also come in handy at your resort and at Downtown Disney. Be sure to mark it with your name and your resort.

If you wish to buy snacks and drinks or baby supplies, your best bet for variety is Gooding's Market, but prices here are still steep. See page 46 for directions.

Kids and Food

Disney knows what picky eaters kids can be, and Disney restaurants specialize in all the favorites. Milk and chocolate milk are available virtually everywhere, and they're usually cheaper than soft drinks. Buffets provide a good way for children to find something they want to eat and to try new things. And of course, there are reasonably priced children's menus, even at the fine dining places. These offerings include just the kind of stuff most kids like: burgers, hot dogs, chicken strips, macaroni and cheese, pizza, and other finger foods.

You'll surely wish to enjoy a Disney character meal. Whether for breakfast, lunch, or dinner, these buffets feature Disney characters who go from table to table for fun visits and unsurpassed photo opportunities. For more information, see page 306.

Preparing the Kids

When our kids were young, we took them to Walt Disney World as a surprise. "Let's go out for donuts," we told them as we woke them at 6 A.M. All the way to the front gate (it was two hours), we pretended that we had no intention of actually going in. We just wanted to look at it, we told them. Meanwhile, the kids whined and cried. By the time we'd gotten our tickets, they were beginning to smell a rat. Or at least, a Mouse.

While this makes a great story, none of us were prepared for our visit, and pandemonium reigned supreme. We suggest that you do a few simple things to prepare your children for the kind of Disney vacation you wish to have. Get them set to enjoy spending some leisure time at your resort, and, if you plan to take advantage of the many and varied children's activities, you might prime them for these. We're sure that you know just how to do it.

A few days before you leave for Disney, you might also ask Central Reservations what attractions will be closed ("in rehab," as insiders say) during your visit. Better to head off expectations now than deal with disappointment later.

Setting Your Pace

Let your family know that this visit will not mean spending every waking moment trying to see every attraction. Sure, you'll spend plenty of time in the theme parks, but you'll also be taking time to relax around the pool and to explore other areas of Walt Disney World. Take them for a boat ride or explore Downtown Disney. Try to keep to your child's regular schedule. If naps are the rule at home, then they should be at Disney, too. Try to eat and snack at the normal times. Remember how much energy this kind of stimulation will demand from your children and do your best to keep them rested and happy. This goes for yourselves, too.

If you are out late, try relaxing around the pool in the morning and then spending the afternoon in one of the waterparks, shopping at Downtown Disney, or taking a leisurely stroll around the World Showcase Lagoon. Avoid staying out late and getting an early start every day. Slow down and pace yourselves.

Logistical Concerns

Disney World is built to accommodate families and you will find resources for every imaginable situation. Each of the theme parks has a baby care center where you will find facilities for heating formula, rocking chairs for bottle- and breast-feeding, and an assortment of expensive baby supplies and formulas. There's even a video game room to keep the rest of your family occupied. Diaper-changing stations are available in both men's and women's rest rooms throughout Walt Disney World.

Traveling with Teenagers

Taking a teenager (or several) to Disney World brings with it a whole new level of concerns. If your teenagers are planning to get away on their own, we suggest that you rent pagers. They are available at all Disney resorts. This will give you the resources to contact them whenever you wish. Know also that at check-in you will have the option to make your resort card, and not theirs, work as a charge card.

Getting Time Alone Together

Being here in "The Happiest Place on Earth" will be a joy for you and your family. There are lots of things to do here together, and there should be no shortage of time to enjoy each other's company. We have always found that being at Disney with our kids made us feel more together. Having this kind of family fun is something that none of you will ever forget. A Disney vacation will bring you nearer to your children and it will make you, as a couple, feel closer. If this isn't romance, we don't know what is.

Still, having time alone together is both natural and healthy for a couple in love. You may wish to spend an evening together, have a romantic dinner, and go out for some grown-up entertainment. No problem.

If you are traveling with an infant or very young children, Kids Night Out, Disney's in-room sitting service, will be your best choice.

With older children, the options also include Disney activity centers and Disney "educational" programs.

Kids Night Out

This in-room baby-sitting service is the only option for children under 4 years of age. We tried this once with our grandkids, Ben and Guin. The sitter showed up with a bag of toys and the kids felt comfortably "at home." By the time we returned, they were having such a good time that they asked if the sitter could spend the night.

Reservations must be made in advance. Cost is $13.50 per hour for one child, $15.50 for two, $17.00 for three, and $19.00 for four. There is a four-hour minimum and an $8.00 transportation charge per reservation.

For meals, caregivers can either order from room service or go to a restaurant in your

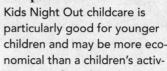

Helpful Hint

Kids Night Out childcare is particularly good for younger children and may be more economical than a children's activity center if you have two or more children.

resort (with your permission, of course). With advance notice, sitters may take one or two children 4 years of age or older, to a theme park. You will have to provide admission for the sitter (and of course, your children).

For information and reservations, call Kids Night Out at (407) 827-5444, or visit www.kidsniteout.com.

Disney Children's Activities Centers

If your child is at least 4 years old and potty-trained (and younger than 12), then one of these marvelous "clubs" will be the perfect choice. Any one will provide a memorable evening of entertainment and your child's very own Disney experience. There are five such centers for the children of Disney resort guests. We have heard many wonderful things about them and can tell you, firsthand, that children love them—ours did, during our visit to the Polynesian years ago. Hours for all centers open from 4:00 to 4:30 P.M. and stay open to midnight. Cost is $10 per hour, per child. Dinners include all the foods kids love: chicken strips, pizza, peanut butter and jelly sandwiches, and hot dogs. Snacks and beverages are also included.

Reservations for these centers are an absolute must and we recommend you do it when you make your room reservations. For more information or to make reservations, call (407) WDW-DINE (939-3463).

Neverland Club   The Neverland Club at the Polynesian features a Peter Pan–themed adventure that begins with a trip through the "window" of Wendy's bedroom and into Neverland. Activities include video and board games, a Disney feature film, and a picture with Goofy.

Cub's Den   The Cub's Den is located at the Wilderness Lodge. Its western-themed adventure is great for boys and girls, and features board games, western arts and crafts, and a nightly Disney feature film.

Sandcastle Club   This children's center is located at the Beach Club and is available to guests at the Yacht and the Beach Clubs. The Sandcastle Club has plenty for kids to do: computers, video games, a large library, and arts and crafts are just a few of the offerings here.

Harbor Club   Located at the BoardWalk, this children's activities center features board and video games, Disney movies, supervised arts and crafts, and snack time.

Simba's Cubhouse   This activity center is at the Animal Kingdom Lodge and features African costumes and storytelling, puppet making, Disney movies, and a unique variety of arts and crafts.

Other Childcare Options

For childcare, there are several other options around Walt Disney World.

Mouseketeer Clubhouses   Though these childcare centers do not offer the theming of the previous five, they do provide a supervised evening of entertainment for your children. There are two Mouseketeer Clubhouses: one at the Contemporary and the other at the Grand Floridian. While the clubhouse at the Contemporary is open to all Disney resort guests, the one at the Grand Floridian is available only to its guests. Cost at either is $10 per hour per child. Reservations are strongly suggested and may be arranged through the Mouseketeer Clubhouses at the Contemporary after 4:30 P.M. by calling (407) 824-3038 or at the Grand Floridian at (407) 824-2985. If you bring your children before 6:45 P.M., dinner will be included.

Camp Dolphin   The Swan and Dolphin offer a program for children, which includes arts and crafts, movies, music and books, and other supervised activities. Afternoon camp is from 1:30 P.M. to 4:30 P.M. and dinner camp, from 6:00 P.M. to 11:00 P.M. Cost is $10 per hour per child.

Childcare at Downtown Disney Hotel Plaza   There are a variety of childcare options available at the seven Downtown Disney hotels along Hotel Plaza Boulevard. If you are staying at any of these resorts, we suggest that you consult their guest services desk or reservationists for complete details.

Romancing with Kids: Our Recommendations

- ℮ $ Take your vacation during the off-season. It will be less expensive and more relaxing.

- ℮ Thoroughly explore the possibilities of getting your own room or your own bedroom. It will make a big difference.

- ℮ Keep your pace a relaxed one. Don't wear yourselves out. Spend time at your resort. The kids will play happily in the pool and not get cranky and overtired. Same for you.

- ℮ It is important that both of you share the chores involved in taking care of your children. It's no fun for one person to be stuck with all of the work while everyone else is vacationing.

- ℮ Rent your teen a beeper, so you can keep in touch (available at all Disney resorts).

- ℮ Be sure to make your reservations for the children's activity centers when you book your room, especially for the Neverland Club.

> ### Helpful Hint
>
> Kids love petting live creatures. There are three opportunities for this at Walt Disney World: The Living Seas at Epcot, Fort Wilderness Campground, and Rafiki's Planet Watch at the Animal Kingdom.

- ℮ If you haven't made childcare reservations or if you have more than one child or an infant, Kids Night Out is a good choice.

- ℮ Try a family activity such as bike riding or boating. Do something special together.

Taking Your Pet to Disney

If you are traveling with a member of the family who wears a little fur coat, you'll need to know a few important things. First, none of the Disney resorts will allow you to keep your pet with you in your room. The closest you'll be able to get is a pet-designated campsite in Fort Wilderness (for more details, see page 88). If you're not camping, your options are one of the five Disney kennels or something outside of Walt Disney World.

There is one Disney kennel at the Ticket and Transportation Center near the Magic Kingdom, another at Fort Wilderness, and one each at Epcot, Disney-MGM Studios, and the Animal Kingdom. Together, the kennels of Disney have a total of 700 animal spaces. The rules are the same for each kennel: $9 per pet for overnight ($11 for non-Disney resort guests), and $6 per pet for day boarding. You must bring your pet's current shot record and you will be expected to walk your pet twice a day (three times for puppies). No animals younger than 8 weeks will be accepted, and small animals other than cats or dogs must be kept in their own cages. Friskies dry food is available at no charge, but it is suggested that you bring the food your pet is used to, and for overnighters, pet beds and toys are also suggested. No farm animals are accepted but the folks here at Disney have had some strange boarders: fish, iguanas, and even a basket of hermit crabs. For details and reservations, call (407) 824-2735.

What to Bring

- Don't forget a liberal amount of sunscreen with a minimum SPF 15. The Florida sun will burn you, especially on an overcast day. We recommend that you not only bring sunscreen but that you use it, too.

- If you are staying in one of the deluxe resorts, be sure you have a handful of dollar bills for tipping.

- **$** Bring your own snacks and beverages (even alcoholic, if you wish). We strongly suggest bringing some bottled water.

What's Available at the Disney Resorts

Housekeeping will be happy to provide you with an assortment of items. Available at every resort, for no charge, will be extra pillows, blankets, iron and ironing board, and hairdryers (now standard in many rooms).

If you need a refrigerator in your room, whether for pleasure or medical reasons, you should know that most resorts charge $10 per day for them. A limited number of microwave ovens are available at the Grand Floridian. Coffeemakers are standard at the Caribbean Beach and Coronado Springs, the Swan and Dolphin, and most concierge-level rooms. A coffeemaker is available upon request at all resorts except the All-Stars, Pop Century, Yacht and Beach, and Grand Floridian.

Some deluxe resort rooms have "mini-butlers." These small refrigerators are stocked with wines, liquors, soft drinks, candy, and snacks. The selection is impressive. So are the prices.

Each Disney resort has a "sundries" section in one of its shops. Here you'll find sunscreen, magazines and newspapers, film, insect repellent, Band-Aids, and items to ward off everything from a headache to the munchies.

Your First Day at WDW

Whether you are arriving early or late, it's sensible to give some thought to your first day at Disney. If you are arriving by automobile, you'll be delighted to know that the roadways are very well marked. Once on property, you'll find that Walt Disney World has its own system of road signs. They are brightly colored and easy to read.

If you are staying in a Disney resort, you'll need to know which resort area your resort belongs to. Simply follow the Florida highway signs to the exit for that area and then follow the red and purple Disney signs to your resort's guest check-in area.

Hint of Romance

Town car service is wonderfully personal, even a bit romantic.

If you are flying into Orlando, you may be surprised to learn that Disney World isn't there. It's 20 miles south, in Lake Buena Vista. Fear not. An entire industry has evolved to transport guests from the airport to Disney. There are a variety of cabs, limousines, and van services that will take you directly to your resort (or not so directly, if you wish to stop for snacks or groceries). Several transportation options are available.

There are two dependable town car services that will meet you at the baggage claim area of the airport and bring you directly to your Disney resort. We suggest using Florida Town Cars. The round-trip fare for five persons or less is $85 ($95 for Magic Kingdom resort

Helpful Hint

Expect to add a 15 percent gratuity for town car, limousine, and taxi drivers.

area). You are promised the same driver on both ends of your vacation. We have heard glowing reports of this company. Arrangements and inquiries from out of Florida should be directed to Florida Town Cars at (800) 525-7246 (www.floridatowncar.com).

Tiffany Town Cars provides a similar service, charging $80 (or $90) for the round-trip. Tiffany also features a round-trip van service for $95 that can handle more than five people. To make arrangements, call (888) 838-2161 (www.tiffanytowncars.com).

Mears is the other company providing similar services. Shuttle service (round-trip) is $24 ($14 one-way) for each adult and $17 ($10 one-way) for each child under 11 years of age (children under 3 ride free). Mears Town Car service is $122 round-trip. Arrangements should be made in advance with Mears at (800) 759-5219. A Mears booth can be found at the Orlando International Airport on the second level. You can make arrangements upon arrival at this kiosk but be forewarned, lines here can get very long. Don't forget that a 15 percent gratuity is expected by the drivers of all these services.

Time-Saving Tips

• Avoid shuttle services as they often make many stops and can take several hours to get you to your resort from the airport.

• Be sure to arrange your airport transportation before you leave home.

Cab fare from either the Orlando train station or airport to a Disney resort is about $50 (plus tip) each way, making the round-trip fare no bargain.

Rental Cars: Getting Your Own Wheels

Is having a car while you're at Walt Disney World a good idea? We think a car would come in especially handy at Disney's less "well-located" resorts, such as Fort Wilderness, Old Key West, Hotel Plaza, any of the value or moderate resorts, the Wilderness Lodge, Saratoga Springs, and the Animal Kingdom Lodge. A rental car will also save you money in airport transportation. If you are planning a trip to Universal Orlando or somewhere else off-property (or if you are staying off-property), a rental car will certainly be a good idea. For traveling to other Disney resorts (to dine, for example) and to Downtown Disney, a

Time-Saving Tip

If you're flying into Orlando and are planning on renting a car, only National, Budget, Avis, L and M, and Dollar are located right at the airport. All others require a shuttle ride for pick-up and after drop-off.

car would save time if you can find your way around. Maps of Walt Disney World are available at guest services in all Disney resorts, and the Disney roads are well marked.

Helpful Hint

Your Disney resort parking permit will allow you to park for free at the theme parks and at other Disney resorts.

Arriving at Your Disney Resort

Check-in time at the Disney Resorts is 3 P.M. (4 P.M. at Vacation Club properties). If you arrive earlier than this, you'll be able to register, have your luggage put in storage, and begin your Disney vacation. You'll be able to get your resort ID cards (see chapter 2) and admission passes and return later to move into your room. On occasion (and subject to availability), we've even managed to get into our room early in the day. Be sure to ask.

If you are arriving by car, know that the deluxe Disney resorts charge $6 per day for valet parking (plus gratuities). Self parking, however, is free. You have the option of unloading your luggage, declining valet parking, parking your car yourself, then checking in. If you can easily manage your own luggage (we travel with two rolling bags), you can also decline bell service to your room. Although this will save you some money, let us warn you that at many Disney deluxe resorts, it can be a hike to your room.

It is important to note that Disney resorts now require at least one person in your party to have a photo ID.

Time-Saving Tip

Before you rush off to the parks on your first day, take the time to familiarize yourself with your resort and look over your theme park guidemaps to get an idea of what there is to see and do.

Special Requests, Last-Minute Changes, and Upgrades

If you were unable to get the room that you had originally desired, you may be able to remedy this when you check in. While there is no guarantee, cancellations and last-minute changes may pay off. Also, if you are checking in to a standard-view room, ask if you can get one with a view of something pleasant, such as a garden or courtyard. It also may be to your advantage to ask what upgrades are available.

Money-Saving Tips

- Avoid taxis at the airport. They are too expensive.
- Arriving late? Avoid paying for a full day's park admission and go to Downtown Disney (no charge, except to Pleasure Island, which is only $21 after 7 P.M.)

Your Last Day at WDW

Your last day at Disney, like your first, demands some thought. Checkout at Disney resorts is 11 A.M. If you plan to leave Disney World before that time, no problem. Simply get packed up and depart. If you're flying out of Orlando, plan on leaving your Disney resort two hours prior to your flight time.

Money-Saving Tip

If you're only going to be at Disney for part of the day, avoid paying for a whole day's park admission and visit Downtown Disney, spend a few hours at the pool, or take a tour of the Disney resorts.

If you are departing later in the day, morning checkout will mean that you will have to vacate your room no later than 11 A.M. You will be able to place your luggage in storage until you actually leave. Your resort ID cards and Unlimited Magic passes will be good until midnight of your last day, so you will be able to carry on with your Disney adventures.

Late Checkout

Disney resorts are usually able to grant a 1 P.M. checkout each day for a limited number of rooms. Depending on your schedule, these two extra hours can make a big difference. If you want late checkout, call the front desk at your resort on your last night to see what that resort's policy is. Know that late check-out is difficult to get during busier seasons and that there is no late check-out at any of the Vacation Club properties.

Some Things You Might Need to Know

A Few Tips on Gratuities

Tipping situations often make both tipper and tippee uncomfortable. However, knowing when to tip and what amount is appropriate should alleviate the awkwardness. Here are our recommendations:

- Cab, limo, town car drivers: 15%

- Valet parking: $2, when you take the car out only

- Bell persons: $1 per bag

- Housekeeping, maid service: $2 per day per person

- Room service: 15% is included in bill, add more as desired

- Housekeeping, delivery: $2

- Table-service restaurants: 15 to 20%

- Buffet restaurants: 10%

- Cocktail service: 15 to 20%

- Spa treatments: 15 to 20%

> **Helpful Hint**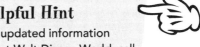
>
> For updated information about Walt Disney World, call (407) 824-4321.

Banking Around Walt Disney World

If you find yourselves needing a little cash while you're at Disney, no problem. Banking facilities and automated tellers are everywhere. There are ATMs in the lobbies of each resort except the BoardWalk, where you'll find it on the promenade near Wyland Gallery. At the theme parks, you'll find one near each park entrance. Both Epcot and the Magic Kingdom have several others as well, and there are four ATMs at Downtown Disney, two on the West Side and one in each of the other areas. Check your guidemaps for specific locations.

- For full service: SunTrust Bank on Buena Vista Boulevard, directly opposite the Downtown Disney Marketplace.

- Foreign currency can be exchanged at the guest services of all four theme parks, at the SunTrust Bank, and at all Disney resort guest services.

- Disney resort front desks will cash personal checks for resort guests.

Food Shopping

If you are staying in one of the many Disney home-away-from-home lodgings that has a kitchen, or even if you are simply looking for a place to buy beverages and snacks, you'll probably need a supermarket. While the Gourmet Pantry at the Downtown Disney Marketplace is certainly handy for limited groceries, lots of baked goods, and a good selection of wines, it's expensive. An alternative is not far away. Gooding's Market is a large and modern supermarket located at the Crossroads Shopping Plaza at the end of Hotel Plaza Boulevard. Directly across from the Downtown Disney Marketplace is Hotel Plaza Boulevard. Turn onto it and continue through the intersection at Route 535 and into the shopping plaza.

The Care and Feeding of Your Car

Located in the Magic Kingdom Auto Plaza is the AAA Car Care Center. It offers full mechanical services and free towing on-property. It's open Monday through Saturday. The center's phone number is (407) 824-0976.

There are three places to fill up at Walt Disney World: the Magic Kingdom Auto Plaza, a station across the street from the BoardWalk, and another across the street from Pleasure Island. Prices are high, so it's best to fill up just before you get on Disney property.

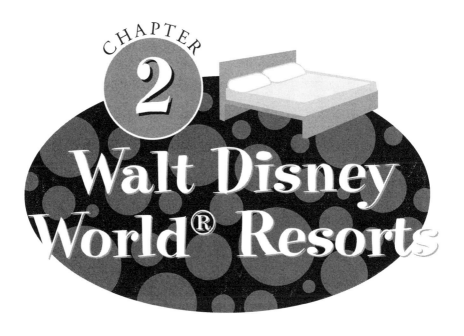

CHAPTER 2

Walt Disney World® Resorts

and the
Disney Cruise Line

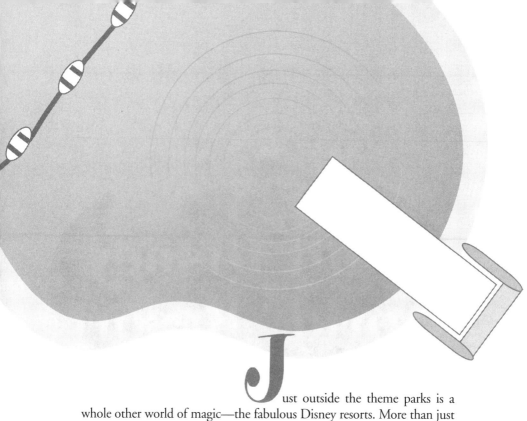

J ust outside the theme parks is a whole other world of magic—the fabulous Disney resorts. More than just places to sleep, these resorts will enfold you in their storytelling magic. If you stay in a Disney resort, you'll find that your adventure won't end the minute you walk out of the theme parks, but will continue throughout your vacation. Your resort room will be your own little piece of the Disney magic. We honestly believe that staying in a Disney resort will make for a better, more relaxing, and "more Disney" vacation. If you are skeptical about what we say, we can only tell you to give it a try. After a stay in one of Walt Disney World's fabulous resorts, we're sure you'll be a convert.

With more than twenty resorts and hotels at Walt Disney World, you'll want to learn about them all before you decide which one is right for your Disney holiday. A name and a theme are just the beginning of what you'll need to know. What the cost will be, how convenient each resort is to the attractions that you'll be visiting, the atmosphere of its guest rooms, where in the resort you should book your room, and what kind of accommodations are available are just a few of the many things that will help you make this important decision.

This chapter is an inside look at the wonderful assortment of resorts and hotels at Walt Disney World. During the last decade, we've stayed everywhere at Disney, and most places numerous times. We have firsthand experience with standard guest rooms, suites, villas, and virtually every kind of lodging available. We have not relied upon surveys, press releases, or the judgments of others. We've simply been there ourselves, looking things over carefully. Our dogged determination to get right even the smallest detail is, we think, what sets our guidebook apart from the others.

Services Available to Disney Resort Guests

As a Disney resort guest, you'll enjoy many unique services. Some are simply not available elsewhere. Note that although they're on Disney property, the Dolphin, the Swan, Shades of Green, and the seven hotels along Hotel Plaza at Downtown Disney are neither owned nor operated by Walt Disney World. Therefore, the following discussion of available services will not apply to these establishments, although they may well offer some. See the descriptions of each of these resorts for its list of available services, later in this chapter. Here are the services and perks available to Disney Resort Guests:

Guaranteed Admission to Disney Theme Parks

On the busiest days of the year, the theme parks are sometimes filled to capacity. However, Disney resort guests are always guaranteed admission.

The Ultimate Hopper Pass

This pass is available only to Disney resort guests and provides unlimited admission to all four Disney theme parks for your entire length of stay. Admission to DisneyQuest, the Disney water parks, Wide World of Sports, and Pleasure Island is also included. The Ultimate Hopper Pass is the least costly pass that will provide daily admission to all Disney attractions for just the days of your vacation. For the pluses and minuses of this pass and a few tips about using it, see page 14.

Resort ID Cards: Your Keys to the World

Everyone in your party will receive one of these cards at check-in, and you'll soon cherish them. These plastic cards will be both your room keys and if guaranteed with a credit card, they can be your Disney charge cards as well, allowing you to put all your expenses right on your room account. Souvenirs, fast food, fine dining: this card's everywhere you're going to be. You'll marvel at how easy they'll make your vacation. And if you purchase Ultimate Hopper Passes (see above), these will also be added to your ID cards, making them just about the only thing you'll need to carry.

Helpful Hint

Your Disney Resort ID can be your all-in-one ticket to Disney fun: admission to the theme parks, charging all expenses, and your resort room key.

On the morning of your departure, or at any time during your visit, a fully detailed bill can be prepared to give you a complete picture of what you've spent. These cards are valid from check-in or pre-registration to midnight on the day of your departure.

The Extra Magic Hour

This is a powerful perk that will admit you to a different, select theme park each day, one hour before the general public. It will give your day a real head start. For more details, see page 199.

E-Ride Nights

This neat program is available only to Disney resort guests with an Ultimate Hopper Pass, a Park Hopper Pass, an annual pass, or a Florida resident seasonal pass. For about $13 ($11 for kids), this ticket will admit you to the Magic Kingdom after regular hours to ride the park's most popular attractions. For more information, see page 204.

Guest Services

This essential service, located at or near the registration desk of each resort, will help you plan your stay at Walt Disney World. Use guest services to buy tickets or to make your reservations for dinner, tennis, golf, or for such entertainment as Cirque du Soleil. Guest services will also be your source of Disney information. Brochures, menus, and schedules for virtually everything Disney are available here. Whether you want to know the time for a parade or ignition time for a fireworks show, your guest services should have it all.

The Resort Newspaper

Each resort has its own themed information "newspaper" that you should receive at check-in. The BoardWalk's paper is the BoardWalk Bugle and the one at Port Orleans is called The Sassagoula Times. Each paper will give you lots of information about your resort, its restaurants and shops, and its services. We suggest that you read the one for your resort so that you'll be familiar with what's available and where and when you'll find it.

$ The Refillable Resort Cup

Each of the Disney resorts offers its own logo thermal cup. It's a quality and useful souvenir, and you'll get free drink refills at your resort's fast-food outlet for as long as you're staying. These cups cost around $11; with prices for soft drinks, coffee, and tea near $2, it won't take long for them to pay for themselves.

First Aid

Emergency service and in-room health care are available on a twenty-four-hour basis. Guests are responsible for any charges.

Wake-Up Service

If you need to be up early, simply press the appropriate button on your room telephone to arrange a wake-up call. You might be surprised who will call to wake you.

Wheelchairs

Each Disney resort has a limited number of wheelchairs for its guests. There's no charge, but a credit card deposit is required. The chair may be used everywhere throughout Walt Disney World and can be kept for the length of your visit.

Additional Services and Amenities at All Disney Resorts

- Valet parking $6 per day at deluxe resorts (gratuity not included, see page 45)

- Free self parking

- Free parking at Disney theme parks with resort ID

- Hairdryers and ironing boards

- Refrigerators $10 per day (limited number; reserve when you book room)

- Data ports on all Disney resort room telephones

- Guest messaging system, free on all resort telephones

- Pager rental

- Walt Disney World Foreign Language Center

- Same-day theme park dining reservations by telephone (dial 55 on your room phone)

- Four full-service barber and beauty shops

- Luggage assistance or bell service

- Overnight use of Walt Disney World kennels; for information, call (407) 824-2735

@ Package delivery to your resort room from any shop at Walt Disney World

@ Children's activities centers and in-room baby-sitting (see page 36)

@ Coin-operated laundry and laundry service

@ Quality two-hour film developing

@ Walt Disney World Florist is available to deliver a variety of floral arrangements, food baskets, and wine or champagne to any Disney resort room, including your own; call (407) 827-3505. Send someone you love a rose.

Types of Disney Resorts

Like Mickey and his friends, the Disney resorts come in a variety of shapes and sizes. However, there are four basic levels, based on price and services available: value, moderate, deluxe, and home-away-from-home.

Basically, the deluxe resorts are all hotels. This means that you'll enter a lobby and then reach your room via a hallway. Most guest rooms in deluxe resorts feature balconies or patios with views of everything from castles to giraffes. The moderate and value resorts are laid out like motels, where you'll reach your room along exterior walkways. Rooms in the moderate and value resorts have neither balconies nor patios.

The big difference here (and we think it is a big difference) is that at the deluxe resorts, you'll be able to relax in your room (on the balcony or with curtains open) and enjoy the sun, the stars, and the view. Not so at the moderate or value resorts, where your only windows open on to trafficked walkways.

The home-away-from-home resorts all feature some sort of kitchen, either a wet bar with small refrigerator and microwave or everything from range to dishwasher. You'll find these unique accommodations in a variety of resorts around Walt Disney World, including Fort Wilderness Resort & Campground. Many of these accommodations offer enough room for a large family.

Disney's Value Resorts

Prices range from $86 to $121 per night (prices include taxes)

Disney's All-Star Music Resort
Disney's All-Star Sports Resort
Disney's All-Star Movies Resort
NEW Disney's Pop Century Resort

These colorful places are styled like motels. Themed yes, but not to the richness of the moderate resorts. Rooms are small (266 square feet) but still comfortable, and offer a choice of two double beds or one king. Maximum occupancy is four adults. Value resorts have only food courts. While recreation means only themed pool areas, all value resort guests are free to use recreation at any other Disney resorts. Transportation to all Disney attractions is by bus. These accommodations are well-suited to visitors who plan to spend most of their time at the Disney attractions.

Disney's Moderate Resorts

Prices range from $148 to $232 per night (prices include taxes)

Disney's Port Orleans Resort Riverside and French Quarter
Disney's Caribbean Beach Resort
Disney's Coronado Springs Resort

The moderate resorts are enchantingly themed and beautifully landscaped. Rooms are well appointed, relatively spacious (314 square feet) and feature either two double beds or a single king. Accommodations are limited to four adults but certain rooms at Port Orleans Riverside can accommodate five (see page 154).

Each of the moderate resorts has a large food court and a single, table-service restaurant. Resort theming is very much a presence everywhere from check-in to guest rooms and from gardens to pools. All of the moderates feature a variety of recreational offerings, from bike to boat rentals. Transportation to Disney attractions from the moderate resorts is by bus.

Disney's Deluxe Resorts

Prices begin at $221 per night for the Wilderness Lodge (price includes taxes)

Disney's Animal Kingdom Lodge
Disney's BoardWalk Inn
Disney's Contemporary Resort
Disney's Grand Floridian Resort and Spa
Disney's Polynesian Resort
The Walt Disney World Swan and Dolphin
Disney's Wilderness Lodge Resort
Disney's Yacht Club and Beach Club Resorts

As you would expect, the Disney deluxe resorts offer an impressive level of luxury and theming. From meticulously landscaped grounds to lavish lobbies, these are first-rate hotels with beautiful and spacious accommodations (around 390 square feet for many rooms, 366 square feet for the Wilderness Lodge). Some feature nightly turndown service (by request), while others provide sumptuous bathrobes. Amenities typically include bell service, valet service, and in-room dining. Two queen beds or a single king are usual and many deluxe resort rooms even include a daybed for a fifth person.

Dining choices are numerous and include at least several restaurants at each resort (there are seven at the Grand Floridian!). Pool areas are large and elaborately themed, and recreation usually includes boat and bike rentals. Transportation to Disney attractions may be by monorail, by boat, by foot, or by bus, depending upon resort location and your destination.

We'll tell you again that value season at the Disney deluxe resorts runs for nearly half the year.

Disney's Home-Away-from-Home Resorts

Prices begin at $255 per night for a Wilderness Cabin (price includes taxes)

Disney's Old Key West Resort
The Villas at the Disney Wilderness Lodge
Disney's Fort Wilderness Resort
Disney's BoardWalk Villas
Disney's Beach Club Villas
Disney's Saratoga Springs Resort & Spa (coming 2004)

Besides providing room enough for a family, the big advantage of this type of lodging is that you can prepare at least some meals in your room. Preparing breakfast alone would save money. By doing some off-property shopping and dining out only occasionally, you'll enjoy significant savings. If you're traveling with kids, another advantage would be accommodations large enough to provide your own bedroom. Some of these are not as expensive as you may think. See page 32 for more information on taking kids to Disney.

Many home-away-from-home properties are part of the Disney Vacation Club and when not booked by members, are available to resort guests. One of our favorite places to stay at Disney is the one-bedroom villa at either the BoardWalk or Beach Club Villas.

Concierge Service

This service is known by seasoned travelers as "the hotel within a hotel," and let us tell you, it will spoil you. Basically, concierge service means a room on a private, concierge floor that features a comfortable lounge for concierge guests, with offerings throughout the day of snacks, beverages, hors d'oeuvres, and wines. Guest rooms typically offer such upgraded amenities as bathrobes, fancy toiletries, and guests enjoy a private desk staff dedicated to making everything go as smoothly as possible. Weeks before you arrive, the concierge staff will contact you so that they may begin creating your own personal vacation itinerary. They'll want to make your dinner and entertainment reservations, and do virtually anything you wish. This might mean setting up your room for an anniversary or other special occasion or arranging a special event. Whatever your wish, they'll be prepared for your visit.

Money-Saving Tip

If you're traveling with children, you can save money on breakfasts with the concierge continental breakfast offerings, which always include milk, juice, and cold cereals.

Once, while staying at the Royal Palm Club concierge at the Grand Floridian, we requested priority-seating arrangements for a 7 P.M. dinner at Narcoossee's. Although the computer said "no," the concierge called the restaurant and our arrangements were made.

Concierge service will add about $125 to $150 to the cost of a day's stay. Is it worth it? Well, this certainly is not something for those traveling on a tight budget. But if you're looking for something truly special, we'd recommend this wonderful upgrade without a moment's hesitation.

Insider's Secret

If you decide at check-in that you want a concierge room, ask if an upgrade is available.

The Resorts by Area

There are five resort areas at Walt Disney World. Each occupies its own little piece of Disney turf, and each has a unique offering of resorts.

The Magic Kingdom Resorts

Disney's Polynesian Resort
Disney's Contemporary Resort
Disney's Grand Floridian Resort and Spa
Disney's Wilderness Lodge Resort
Villas at Disney's Wilderness Lodge

Disney's Fort Wilderness Resort & Campground
Shades of Green

The Epcot Resorts

Disney's Yacht Club and Beach Club Resorts
NEW Disney's Beach Club Villas
Disney's BoardWalk Inn and BoardWalk Villas
The Walt Disney World Swan and Dolphin
Disney's Caribbean Beach Resort

The Animal Kingdom Resorts

Disney's Animal Kingdom Lodge
Disney's Coronado Springs Resort
Disney's All-Star Sports Resort
Disney's All-Star Music Resort
Disney's All-Star Movies Resort

The Disney Wide World of Sports Complex Resort Area

NEW Disney's Pop Century Resort
   (Opening in 2003 or 2004)

The Downtown Disney Resorts

Disney's Port Orleans French Quarter and Riverside
Disney's Old Key West Resort
NEW Disney's Saratoga Springs Resort and Spa
   (coming 2004)
Wyndham Palace Resort & Spa
Courtyard by Marriott
DoubleTree Guest Suites Resort
Grosvenor Resort
The Hilton
Hotel Royal Plaza
Best Western Lake Buena Vista Resort

The Magic Kingdom Resorts

The resorts in this group are all good choices if you're traveling with children and wish to be near the Magic Kingdom. The Contemporary, the Polynesian, and the Grand Floridian are all right on the monorail loop that encircles the Seven Seas Lagoon. All three provide unsurpassed convenience to the Magic Kingdom. Both the Wilderness Lodge and Fort Wilderness Resort and Campground are located along the shores of nearby Bay Lake while Shades of Green overlooks the golf courses near the Polynesian.

Disney's Polynesian Resort

The Polynesian is a fanciful re-creation of the South Seas and it is one of the most popular of the Disney resorts. The Polynesian was Walt Disney World's first resort (it opened two weeks before the Contemporary), and it was also our first experience staying on-property (in 1974!). In the past few years, it has been re-created to better represent the real cultures of the South Pacific rather than an imaginary Disney version. The resort and grounds have been decorated with colorful Polynesian paintings and sculpture, and the rooms now feature the authentic designs and colors of South Seas fabrics. We're not exaggerating to say that the Polynesian has improved with age.

Located on a pristine white-sand beach directly across the lagoon from Cinderella Castle, the "Poly" enjoys one of the most spectacular views in all of Walt Disney World. Over the years, its lush grounds have grown dense with tropical foliage. Candlenut trees, gardenias, banana trees, hibiscus, and orchids are but a few of the more than seventy-five species of exotic plants that make this resort a veritable garden. Its many meandering footpaths invite an evening stroll, and we can tell you it's a magical one. The flickering torches, balmy lagoon breezes, and South Seas music from Luau Cove all combine to create a potent piece of Polynesia. Kick off your shoes and walk along the lagoon to discover the quiet beach areas at either end of the resort. Here you'll find hammocks and bench swings where you can relish a few quiet moments alone late in the evening. The Polynesian is exciting and romantic.

The Great Ceremonial House is the center of life in Disney's South Seas. It is surrounded by a profusion of exotic plants and fish ponds. Native statues stand sentry at its entrance. Inside, the mingling of Hawaiian music and the sounds of rushing water set the stage for your Polynesian adventure. Mammoth hewn beams, stone floors, and woven bamboo are the makings of this place, all trimmed carefully with hanging baskets of brightly colored orchids and birds of paradise.

The centerpiece of the Great Ceremonial House is its towering garden of palms, volcanic rock, and splashing water. It reaches to the domed ceiling three stories above. The gurgling waterfalls, brilliant blossoms, and verdant foliage produce a sensation that is both cool and soothing.

The Great Ceremonial House is home for this resort's front desk, guest services, shops, and restaurants. "Aloha" is the usual greeting here at the Polynesian, where there's a Hawaiian word for nearly every occasion. The Polynesian's guest rooms are located in colorful "longhouses" that surround the Great Ceremonial House. With names such as Tonga, Fiji, Tuvalu, and Rapa Nui, they offer not only a variety of locations, but also an assortment of accommodations. Some of the buildings are near the Great Ceremonial House, others surround the pools, and still

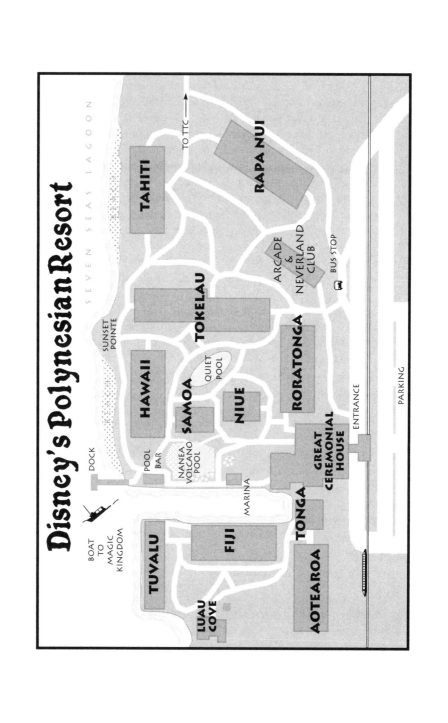

Disney's Polynesian Resort

SEVEN SEAS LAGOON

BOAT TO MAGIC KINGDOM

DOCK

SUNSET POINTE

TAHITI

TO TTC →

RAPA NUI

ARCADE & NEVERLAND CLUB

BUS STOP

TOKELAU

HAWAII

QUIET POOL

SAMOA

RORATONGA

NIUE

POOL BAR

NANEA VOLCANO POOL

MARINA

TONGA

GREAT CEREMONIAL HOUSE

ENTRANCE

TUVALU

FIJI

LUAU COVE

AOTEAROA

PARKING

others can be found along the sparkling sand beach of the lagoon. The Tonga houses the Polynesian's suites, while Hawaii is home to the Royal Polynesian concierge service. Given the lay of the land and the size of this resort, certain longhouses are closer to some things and farther away from others. But nothing is very far, and walking around the Polynesian is one of its greatest pleasures.

The Nanea Volcano pool is a recent addition at the Polynesian. This towering volcanic peak features waterfalls, a shady sitting area, and a water slide. But if you're looking for something a bit quieter, you'll find it nearby at the Polynesian's quiet pool or perhaps out on the sparkling sand beach along the lagoon, comfortably snoozing in the shade of a cabana or catching some sun in one of the hammocks. One of the themes of this charming resort can best be expressed by "ho 'onanea," which means the passing of time in ease, pleasure, and peace.

Rooms at the Polynesian

Polynesian guest rooms are large (409 square feet) and splendidly themed. Fabrics feature traditional Polynesian designs of browns and greens and furniture is wicker and bamboo. A room at the Poly provides more than a mere hint of tropical paradise. It immerses you in the magic of the South Seas.

Guest rooms each have two queen-size beds and a daybed. None of the standard rooms feature king beds. Each room also has a small table and several handsome wicker chairs. A large tropical armoire hides the television and, along with the closet, provides room enough even for travelers like ourselves, who can never seem to travel light. Beautiful marble baths feature counters of green and black with a spacious vanity and shower-tub combination. Coffeemakers are available upon request.

There are nine three-story longhouses. Tokelau, Tahiti, and Rapa Nui all have rooms that enjoy either patios or balconies. Except for Niue and Tonga, the remainder of the longhouses have ground-floor patios and balconies on the third floors only. Second-floor rooms have sliding glass

Room Rates as of 2004 for Disney's Polynesian Resort (prices include taxes)

Accommodation	Value Season	Regular Season	Peak Season	Holiday Season
Garden View	$333	$384	$450	$523
Lagoon View	$429	$479	$563	$624
Concierge Garden	$435	$491	$574	$641
Concierge Lagoon	$524	$585	$675	$753

doors that open onto wooden railings. Niue has only two floors, with ground-floor rooms featuring a patio. Selections can be requested when you make your reservations, and we advise asking again at check-in.

Polynesian rooms feature garden or lagoon views. Naturally, the most expensive overlook the lagoon, its white sandy beach, and Cinderella Castle. If you can afford the difference, you will find the view memorable and romantic. Garden rooms are beautiful as well; at night, the torch-lit footpaths and dense greenery will transport you.

Royal Polynesian Concierge Service

The Hawaii longhouse is located right on the lagoon and is home to the Polynesian's concierge service. Lagoon-view rooms boast extraordinary views. Determined to get a firsthand experience of everything, we have happily stayed here in the tropical lap of Polynesian luxury. Royal Polynesian concierge service provides additional room amenities such as bathrobes, and a full array of toiletries.

As concierge guests, we relished the use of Hawaii's lounge. Amid the plush Polynesian furnishings, we savored a day-long offering of foods with a tropical touch, snacks, beverages, and desserts. Each evening found us sipping cordials, nibbling desserts, and watching the fireworks over the lagoon. Like passengers on a small cruise ship, we were able to chat with other guests, some of whom we had seen at breakfast.

A knowledgeable and dedicated staff was ready to spring into action for reservations, transportation, and any of our other concerns. We found the Polynesian's concierge service to be romantic and unforgettable—the perfect choice for any couple in love.

Suites at the Polynesian

The Tonga longhouse, located next door to the Great Ceremonial House, accommodates the Polynesian's suites. Tonga is much smaller and more intimate than the other longhouses. It has only two stories and a dozen or so suites.

While all of the suites and rooms at Tonga include concierge service, the concierge lounge is far enough away to make it inconvenient. To accommodate guests of the suites, a small continental breakfast is served in the Tonga lobby. The concierge staff is available, and use of Hawaii's concierge lounge is encouraged.

The smallest and least expensive suite here isn't really a suite at all; it's a single oversized room. While considerably larger than the regular resort room, this luxurious accommodation is grand enough to accommodate a comfortable sitting area, a small desk and chair, and a dining table. The bathroom is large and offers a shower-tub and bidet. With either a single king bed or twin queens, this room comes as a garden-view room only. Marina-view versions are available on the lagoon side of the building, but they offer only dual queen-size beds. Garden kings or queens cost around $758 per night. These rooms are exceptionally nice and are on our small list of favorite Disney accommodations. The King Kamehameha suite is one of the most lavish in Walt Disney World. This two-level set of rooms commands a panoramic view of the marina area and lagoon. This suite is the stuff that dreams are made of. It has a large living room downstairs with a wet bar and enough space for a small wedding reception or party. The upstairs king bedroom is luxurious and perfectly themed. The bathroom features an oversized Jacuzzi tub. With its adjoining bedroom, this suite can easily accommodate a large family. The King Kamehameha costs more than $2,000 nightly.

Transportation and Convenience

The Polynesian is right on the main monorail loop that runs around the lagoon. The monorail station is located on the second floor of the Great Ceremonial House and is a relatively short walk from most of the long-houses, giving this resort a real convenience to the Magic Kingdom and the other resorts around the lagoon. A boat runs from the Magic Kingdom to the Grand Floridian and then to the Polynesian and back to the Magic Kingdom. From the longhouses along the lagoon, getting to the Magic Kingdom by boat is especially convenient and pleasant.

If you are staying at either Rapa Nui or Tahiti, you might find that walking to the Ticket and Transportation Center (TTC) or to the ferry-boat landing might provide more convenient transportation to either Epcot or the Magic Kingdom. Other Disney destinations can be reached by bus from a bus stop near the arcade and the Neverland Club.

- To the Magic Kingdom: monorail, boat from dock, or by foot to ferry from TTC
- To Epcot: monorail or by foot to TTC, then transfer to Epcot monorail
- To Disney-MGM Studios, the Animal Kingdom, Blizzard Beach: direct bus
- To Downtown Disney and Typhoon Lagoon: direct bus
- To BoardWalk: bus to Downtown Disney or any open park and take BoardWalk bus

Dining at the Polynesian

With three restaurants at the Polynesian and many others at nearby resorts, your dining options are considerable. 'Ohana offers both a character breakfast and a Disney-style South Seas dinner feast. The Kona Cafe is one of our favorites for breakfast, lunch, or dinner. Adjacent to it is the Kona Cafe coffee bar, serving specialty coffees and a variety of tempting pastries (open 6:30 A.M. to 11:00 A.M.). No resort would be complete without some sort of fast-food offering, and at the Polynesian it's Captain Cook's Snack Isle, which is open twenty-four hours a day (grill closes at 11 P.M.) with the usual selection of Disney fast foods. Polynesian in-room dining is available from 6:30 A.M. to midnight.

There's a lovely dinner show here at the Polynesian and if you're thinking about an evening of food and entertainment, you'll want to make reservations for the Polynesian Luau. For more information, see page 308. The Polynesian also offers an in-room romance dining experience. Available from room service, it includes a lavish meal, desserts, wine, and two keepsake glasses.

For reviews and more information about the restaurants at the Polynesian Resort, see chapter 6.

Lounges at the Polynesian

There are two tropical lounges at the Polynesian: the Tambu and the Barefoot Bar. Both offer a tantalizing selection of specialty drinks. The Tambu, which adjoins 'Ohana, features live entertainment during busy months. Appetizers are from the firepit of 'Ohana. The Barefoot Bar is poolside and features snacks as well as a selection of refreshing tropical concoctions.

Shops at the Polynesian

Trader Jack's is located on the second floor of the Great Ceremonial House. It offers character merchandise, toys, gifts, films, postcards, Polynesian logo items, and an assortment of beers, wines, liquors, sundries, and snacks. There's an excellent selection of clothing shops on the ground floor of the central building. Whether you are looking for something special for yourselves or for a gift to bring home, these places definitely have nice stuff.

Recreation at Disney's Polynesian

- Nanea Volcano feature pool, with slide
- Quiet pool
- Watercraft rentals
- Evening fireworks cruises
- Moana Mickey's Video Arcade
- The Neverland Club children's activity center and dinner club
- Scheduled children's activities: hula dancing, pool games
- 1½-mile jogging and walking path (map available at guest services)

Our Impressions of the Polynesian

- This is a beautifully themed resort. Its guest rooms are large and some of the finest at Disney. We think that the Polynesian is both memorable and romantic. It's a first-class place to stay, and its motto says it all: "Aita Peatea" (there will be another day tomorrow just like today).

- Convenience to the Magic Kingdom is good to very good; convenience to other Disney destinations is only average.

- The new pool and surrounding areas have brought some great new theming to this resort. It's a beautiful and fun place. However, there is still no hot tub here at the Polynesian.

- Many families with small children stay at the Polynesian, and we found that the resort's beaches and pools remain busy throughout the day.

Recommendations for Disney's Polynesian Resort

- Spring for a lagoon view. You'll be happy you did.

- Smoking rooms are located in the Samoa and Tuvalu longhouses.

Romance at the Polynesian

- The rooms at the Polynesian ♥♥♥

- Royal Polynesian concierge service or garden king room at Tonga ♥♥♥♥

- Breakfast in bed ♥♥♥♥

- In-room romance dining experience ♥♥♥

- Breakfast on your balcony or patio ♥♥♥

- Strolling around the grounds after dark, especially the two quiet beaches at either end of the resort ♥♥♥

- In the evening, taking the walkway around the lagoon to the Grand Floridian, having dinner, enjoying a cocktail in one of the lounges there, or simply seeing the sights ♥♥♥

- The Polynesian Luau ♥♥

- Viewing the Electric Water Pageant or fireworks from Sunset Pointe, a small grassy area along the beach near the Hawaii or Tahiti longhouses, or one of the two quiet beaches ♥♥♥

- Fireworks cruise for two, available at the marina ♥♥♥

- Renting a boat and taking a cruise ♥♥

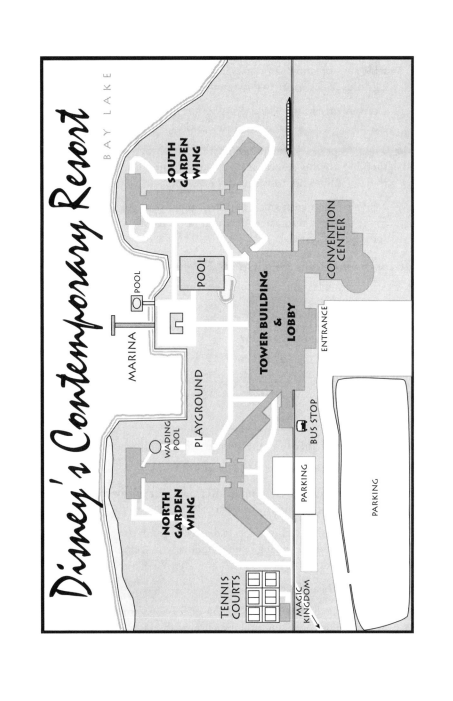

Disney's Contemporary Resort

BAY LAKE

SOUTH GARDEN WING

NORTH GARDEN WING

MARINA

POOL

POOL

WADING POOL

PLAYGROUND

TENNIS COURTS

TOWER BUILDING & LOBBY

CONVENTION CENTER

ENTRANCE

BUS STOP

PARKING

PARKING

MAGIC KINGDOM

Disney's Contemporary Resort

In the early 1970s, when the Contemporary first opened, it was at the forefront of architectural innovation: modular construction, a cavernous atrium lobby, and a monorail that ran right through it all. It was an impressive display of the vision and imagination of Walt Disney. During the past quarter-century, while the rest of the architectural world has been playing catch-up, the Contemporary has remained an impressive site on the Disney horizon. It is a marvel of glass, steel, and concrete, and it is itself a Disney icon.

This may be one of Disney's oldest resorts, but it's no dowager. Constant improvements and refurbishing have kept it seeming as new as the day it opened. During the past three decades, the Contemporary has maintained a firm grip on its first-rate status. It offers a variety of spacious rooms and suites as well as a complete package of resort amenities. These, and its unequaled proximity to the Magic Kingdom, are what this exciting place is all about. The ambience here at the Contemporary is definitely modern. It is fast-paced, fun, and high-energy.

The resort's main building is called the Tower. Adjacent to it are two newer additions called the Garden Wings, which lie along the north and south sides of the Tower building and are connected to it by short, covered walkways. The Tower building is an enormous fifteen-story, A-frame structure. Its atrium-style lobby is the Grand Canyon Concourse. Tiers of guest rooms hang suspended from its sides. The ends of the building are large, open expanses of glass. Within them is an entire world of restaurants, shops, and lounges. A dazzling mosaic leaps hundreds of feet from floor to ceiling.

Rooms at the Contemporary

Room decor is a modern art theme, complete with brightly colored cubist bedspreads and geometric shapes of purples and oranges. Sconce lights resemble artist's palettes and baths feature black and white marble with a large vanity and shower-tub combination. The net effect is colorful, fun, and entertaining. These rooms, at 422 square feet, are some of the largest standard rooms at Disney (compare them to the All-Star's 260 square feet).

All of the rooms in the Tower have balconies; none of the standard rooms in the Garden Wings do. Rooms in the Tower building face either the Magic Kingdom or Bay Lake with views that range from very good to astounding. Furnished with several chairs and a small table, balconies in the Tower are large and comfortable. Our room was located on the twelfth floor overlooking the Magic Kingdom. After dark, the view was spectacular. Tower rooms with panoramas of the Magic Kingdom are the most requested at the Contemporary. So, if this is your wish, reserve early.

Rooms of the Garden Wings overlook the parking area or landscaped gardens and Bay Lake. With only three floors here, views are pleasant but not panoramic. The larger Junior Suites feature a small foyer and spacious bath with either a single king bed or one queen with foldout sleeper/sofa. Views from these rooms are particularly pleasant. Not as convenient to the services of the Tower building, these rooms do offer a certain tranquility and sense of seclusion not found in the Grand Canyon Concourse.

Most rooms at the Contemporary offer the usual two queen beds and a daybed/sofa. There are only thirty-three rooms with king beds, counting both the Tower and Garden Wings, and many of these are suites. The standard rooms at the Contemporary do not have mini-butlers. Coffeemakers are available upon request.

Concierge Service and Suites at the Contemporary

The Contemporary's private fourteenth floor is reserved for concierge guests. The luxurious lounge on this floor features a stunning panoramic view, continental breakfast, midday snacks, afternoon hors d'oeuvres and champagne, as well as evening cordials and desserts. Guests also get their own concierge staff with private check-in and check-out. The two presidential suites each offer spacious king beds and Jacuzzi tubs (the only rooms with whirlpool tubs at this resort). With wet bar, dining area, large parlor room with sofa and chairs, two oversized balconies, and an extra bedroom, either of the suites will provide over-the-top luxury and privacy. More than once, an Arab prince and entourage have occupied this entire floor.

There are a limited number of regular guest rooms on the fourteenth floor, two king rooms and three rooms with double queens. All enjoy the full amenities of this exceptional concierge level. Prices begin around $535 per night.

Room Rates as of 2004 for Disney's Contemporary Resort (prices include taxes)

Accommodation	Value Season	Regular Season	Peak Season	Holiday Season
Garden Wing, standard	$266	$294	$345	$384
Garden Wing, garden	$307	$340	$396	$457
Jr. Suites	$335	$379	$435	$479
Tower room	$374	$413	$485	$530
Tower Club	$440	$485	$563	$608
Concierge, 14th floor	$535	$602	$680	$753

The twelfth floor of the Contemporary is the Tower Club and it features a limited concierge service. A small lounge has been set up near the elevators, and here guests of this floor can enjoy a continental breakfast and some light snacks and beverages in the afternoon. There is a concierge staff here from 7 A.M. to 4 P.M. Rooms on this floor also feature refrigerators.

There are suites in the Garden Wings too, but they do not include concierge service. With 1,313 square feet, you'll certainly not feel cramped in one of these luxurious accommodations. Each provides a large bedroom with adjoining parlor and pull-down "sico" bed and, depending on view and season, cost from $869 to $1,244 nightly. This is plenty of room for a family, but at these prices, you'd be better off with two Tower rooms.

Transportation and Convenience

With the Contemporary right on the monorail loop, travel to and from the Magic Kingdom is both easy and exciting. Arrivals and departures are from the monorail station on the Tower's fourth floor. Be advised that during peak hours, the trip to the Magic Kingdom can take upward of fifteen minutes. There's also a pleasant walking path to the Magic Kingdom. The walk is especially convenient from the north Garden Wing.

Except for the pleasant monorail ride to Epcot, travel to other Disney destinations, while not quite so much fun, is relatively easy.

@ To the Magic Kingdom: monorail or a pleasant walk

@ To Epcot: monorail, then transfer at TTC to Epcot monorail

@ To Disney-MGM Studios, Animal Kingdom, Blizzard Beach: direct bus

@ To Downtown Disney and Typhoon Lagoon: direct bus

@ To BoardWalk: bus to Downtown Disney or any open park and take BoardWalk bus

Helpful Hint

The Contemporary is just a short walk from the Magic Kingdom.

Dining at the Contemporary

Dining at the Contemporary is outstanding. Along with its three full-service restaurants, room service, and fast-food eatery, you will find many fine choices at the other resorts around the Lagoon. Atop the Contemporary is the California Grill, one of Walt Disney World's finest and most exciting dining destinations. The Concourse Steakhouse is another good choice, with a variety of well-prepared breakfasts and lunches. Evenings feature fine dining with seafood and cuts of beef. Chef Mickey's Buffet is the Contemporary's place for Disney character meals with both breakfast and dinner buffets. For more information and our reviews of these table-service restaurants, see chapter 6.

On the first floor, located near the front desk, is the Contemporary's espresso bar, Contemporary Grounds, offering fresh-brewed coffee concoctions and a small selection of pastries. The Food 'n Fun Center is nearby, adjacent to the video arcade. A bit noisy, the Food 'n Fun Center offers a typical selection of Disney fast foods and is open twenty-four hours (grill is only open from 11 A.M. to 10 P.M.).

Lounges at the Contemporary

The California Grill Lounge is located right inside the restaurant and shares its top-of-the-world view. Besides an extensive wine list and a full complement of liquors, it offers a menu of appetizers, sushi, taster plates, and pizzas from the Grill.

The Outer Rim Cocktail Lounge is on the fourth floor of the Tower building, overlooking Bay Lake and Discovery Island. Open from noon to midnight, this lounge offers an assortment of cocktails and appetizers. Smoking is permitted, and it is often crowded with guests waiting to get into Chef Mickey's Buffet. The Sand Bar is located in the marina complex near the pool, on the lakeside of the resort. This lounge operates seasonally.

Shops at the Contemporary

All of the Contemporary's shops can be found on the fourth floor in the Grand Canyon Concourse. Concourse Sundries and Spirits should take care of any loose ends. Whether you're in search of souvenirs, snacks, newspapers or magazines, film or tobacco products, or nonprescription medicines, here's where you will go. Concourse Sundries has a large offering of beers, wines, and liquors. Bay View Gifts is the perfect place to stop for that little something special. Men's and women's resort wear and unique gifts are the specialty here. Fantasia offers character merchandise and children's apparel.

Recreational Activities at the Contemporary

- Two heated swimming pools
- Two hot tubs
- Kiddie pool and play fountain
- The Olympiad Health Club and Tanning Salon

- Marina Pavilion with watercraft rentals
- Waterskiing, parasailing, and fishing excursions
- Six lighted tennis courts, backboards, ball machine
- Volleyball and shuffleboard
- Lakefront beach area
- Children's playground and spray fountain
- Fourth Floor Skywalk Observation Deck for Magic Kingdom fireworks
- Food 'n Fun Center video arcade
- Fireworks cruises

Our Impressions of the Contemporary

- As bright and as colorful as a work of modern art, the Contemporary is a fun and exciting place to stay. We like it.
- This resort is exceptionally convenient to the Magic Kingdom.
- Lakeside water recreation here is as good as it gets: check out Sammy Duvall's Watersports (see chapter 7).

Recommendations for Disney's Contemporary Resort

- Tower rooms offer the best views and are the most convenient to transportation and dining.
- Neither Garden Wing is convenient to the Tower building or the monorail. The north wing is, however, convenient to the tennis courts and the footpath to the Magic Kingdom.
- Both Garden Wings offer pleasant and quiet surroundings.

Romance at the Contemporary

- Resort theming ♥
- Breakfast in bed ♥♥♥♥
- Breakfast on your balcony overlooking Disney World or Bay Lake ♥♥♥
- Fourteenth Floor Concierge King Bed ♥♥♥♥
- Having a drink or dinner at the California Grill during the evening fireworks show ♥♥♥
- Garden wing deluxe room with a King bed ♥♥
- A stroll on the beach behind either Garden Wing, then watching the Electric Water Pageant from the beach ♥♥♥♥

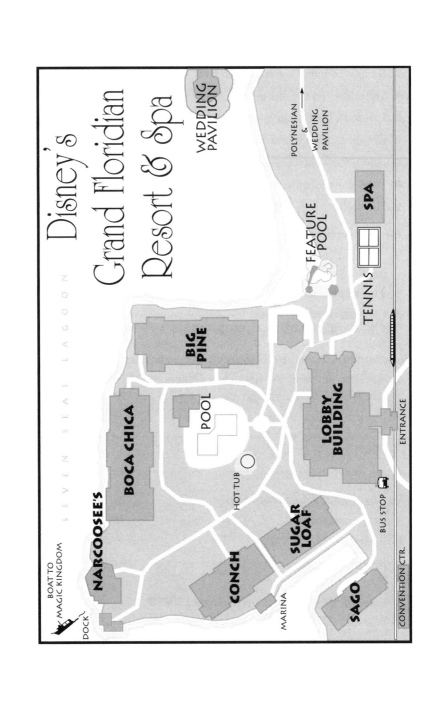

Disney's Grand Floridian Resort and Spa

Even from a distance, there is something sublimely romantic about this place. Its red-shingled roofs, ornate turrets, and intricate latticework all seem to belong to a time long past. We confess gladly to a little thrill each time we are near it. In our hearts, this lovely resort represents an unhurried age when the quality of life was held dear and when time was something to be savored. Here amid the stately palms and gas lamps, and among the verandas and the rose gardens, old-world crafts-manship has been brought to life.

This is the Grand Floridian, and it is the jewel in the Disney crown. A stay here will immerse you in a richness and elegance that will be the stuff of your romantic dreams. Details are everything at the Grand. From flawless service to sumptuous bathrobes, the luxurious and the lavish come standard. Arriving at the Grand Floridian is definitely excit-ing, and it is likely something that you will never forget. The tree-lined drive leads through manicured gardens and up to an entrance where a dozen costumed valets and bell persons scurry about. Knickers, knee socks, and pastel jackets are the uniforms of the day. Once inside the huge lobby, you begin to understand why this place is called Grand. Level upon level of formal balconies surround this great hall and lead the eye upward toward the domed ceiling high above. Rows of turned white posts are capped with rails of gleaming mahogany. Light filters through stained-glass skylights onto sparkling chandeliers.

Fabrics, decor, and design are all in perfect harmony. Details attract your eye: A topiary Cinderella Castle occupies one space, while above it an old-fashioned cage elevator ascends slowly. This striking Grand lobby is an awesome and even a dizzying sight. Everything about the Grand Floridian appears to be first-class, and everything most certainly is first-class. A stay here will be a celebration of everything that is special and memorable.

Set perfectly along a combed, white-sand beach on the Seven Seas Lagoon, the Grand Floridian is but a stone's throw from Cinderella's front door. The monorail slips quietly from the station and whisks guests away to Disney adventures.

The Grand's five lodge buildings are along the shores of Bay Lake. Connected by garden walkways, these buildings reflect the Victorian charm of the lavish lobby and house the resort's luxurious guest rooms. Each lodge is named for a Florida key: Sago, Boca Chica, Conch, Big Pine, and Sugar Loaf.

Insider's Secret

On Mondays and Fridays at 8 A.M. at the Grand Floridian, the housekeepers do their Parasol Parade.

Rooms at the Grand Floridian

Grand Floridian guest rooms are decorated much as they might have been a century ago. Every room includes a delicate lace curtain behind its formal drapes, conveying a tangible sense of the Victorian era. Honey-maple furnishings with carved bedsteads are a charming remembrance of an age gone by. Each lodge features one of four themes: Swan, Cameo, Floral, or Alice in Wonderland, and each theme features the introduction of "hidden Mickeys" and other Disney characters. While colors vary slightly from theme to theme, all rooms feature colorful spreads and wallpapers of pastel floral patterns and room accents of pale yellows, blues, roses, and greens.

Grand Floridian guest rooms are cozy, warm, and elegant. Each features a large television armoire, a ceiling fan, and a delightful carved wooden Mickey lamp (available in one of the lobby shops, if you must have one). Large glass doors open onto spacious balconies that look onto the lovely garden grounds. Costumed housekeepers arrive each day with wicker baskets of fresh linens.

Rooms are large (391 square feet) and comfortable. They are the flawless marriage of the elegance of yesterday and of the creature comforts of today. Most rooms at the Grand feature two queen beds, although there are about eight king bedrooms in the lodge buildings. However, the rooms with king beds are difficult to reserve because of their limited number.

Every guest room features several chairs and a small table. A sofa bed makes the perfect place to lounge or for a fifth person to sleep. Every guest room also features twin marble vanities in a spacious and well-lit area adjacent to the bathroom.

Because of the unusual shapes of the lodge buildings, standard room sizes and shapes vary slightly within each building. Top-floor "attic

Room Rates as of 2004 for Disney's
Grand Floridian Resort and Spa (prices include taxes)

Accommodation	Value Season	Regular Season	Peak Season	Holiday Season
Garden View	$378	$428	$495	$573
Lagoon View	$446	$507	$597	$663
Lodge Tower	$463	$530	$624	$753
Lodge Concierge	$502	$580	$669	$736
Concierge	$652	$736	$825	$920
Concierge Deluxe	$663	$747	$842	$937
Honeymoon	$663	$747	$842	$936

rooms," while a bit smaller, feature quaint dormer balconies and vaulted ceilings (our lovely attic room, number 7515, had a king bed). Lodge tower rooms are a bit more expensive and are a little larger than the standard rooms; a comfortable sitting area substitutes for the balcony or patio.

Rooms at the Grand enjoy two different views, of either the garden or lagoon. Each has its charm. Many of the rooms overlooking the lagoon feature an impressive panorama of Cinderella Castle. The sparkling water, fireworks, and the Electric Water Pageant all make evenings here magically romantic. Whatever your choice, the Grand Floridian is a luxurious place to celebrate your honeymoon, anniversary, or romantic Disney vacation.

Concierge Service and Suites at the Grand Floridian

The luxurious concierge rooms at the Grand are located on the private, upper floors of the main lobby building. All 90 rooms include plush bathrobes, slippers, VCRs, and complimentary movies. This is the life! The beautiful and comfortable concierge lounge is located on the fourth floor, and here you will enjoy a sumptuous offering of treats served throughout the day: continental breakfast, midday refreshments, afternoon tea, and hors d'oeuvres and wine before dinner. Drop by in the evening, sip cordials, and share a dessert while you listen to the music of the Grand's orchestra waft up from the landing below. Once you have been a guest here, you will understand why so many who have visited before will never consider a stay elsewhere.

There are a variety of rooms in concierge that range from a standard resort room to the extravagant, two-bedroom Walt Disney suite. There's a concierge deluxe room, too, and it's larger than the standard. One of the most popular lodgings is the newly created Victorian Suite. This charming one-bedroom suite perfectly evokes the Victorian era in splendid and lavish luxury. Its picture-perfect charm features restful pastel walls with elegant floral spreads and drapes. A spacious living room with dining area is enhanced with such marvelous details as a working Victrola (complete with a playable 78 rpm recording) and wall nooks, displaying antique dishes. The master bedroom is magnificently appointed with honey maple king bed, dresser, and desk, and the master bath with a shower and whirlpool tub. Prices for this unforgettable accommodation begin around $1,300 per night.

The Grand Floridian also features two types of exceptionally romantic concierge rooms, and our favorite is the Turret honeymoon suite. Six of these octagonal rooms are located in the two towers of the main building. Each features a large bathroom, walk-in closet, and a bedroom with a spectacular panorama. Several command views of Cinderella Castle right from the four-poster king bed. From our own experience, we can tell you that for sheer magic, these suites have no equal

here at Walt Disney World. The other honeymoon rooms are on the secluded Clarendon concierge level. Room amenities here include a
Jacuzzi tub and love seat. These are enchanting and romantic. Know
that the Turret rooms do not have balconies.

Lodge concierge means a stay in the Sugarloaf Lodge where the
ground-floor lobby is a comfortable lounge, serving continental breakfast and a day-long offering of snacks and beverages. The desk staff will
happily help fill all your needs, from admission passes to priority seating. With the exception of after-dinner desserts and cordials, lodge
concierge service is the same as that in the main building.

Transportation and Convenience

Guests at the Grand Floridian enjoy the same monorail and bus transportation as the Contemporary and the Polynesian. In addition, there is
a boat that travels from a dock near Narcoossee's to the Magic Kingdom.

- To the Magic Kingdom: monorail or water taxi

- To Epcot: monorail with transfer at the Ticket and Transportation
  Center (TTC) to Epcot monorail

- To Disney-MGM Studios, the Animal Kingdom, Blizzard Beach:
  direct bus

- To Downtown Disney and Typhoon Lagoon: direct bus

- To BoardWalk: bus to Downtown Disney or any open park and
  take BoardWalk bus

 Time-Saving Tip

From the Grand Floridian, it's quickest to take the monorail to
the Magic Kingdom, and *return* by boat.

Dining at the Grand Floridian

Several of Walt Disney World's finest restaurants are located here. Victoria and Albert's ♥♥♥♥, a romantic dining experience, is Orlando's
only Five-Diamond restaurant. The award-winning Cítricos is another
wonderful choice, and one we highly recommend. Lakeside is Narcoossee's, which specializes in fresh seafood and fine cuts of meat, all elegantly prepared. And adjacent to the lobby is the Grand Floridian
Cafe. Its interesting menus make it perfect for breakfast or lunch.

As if these weren't enough, 1900 Park Fare is a delightful breakfast
and dinner buffet-style restaurant. It features Mary Poppins and friends

for breakfast and Cinderella and her storybook friends at dinner, as well as some of Walt Disney World's best buffet food. For snacks and fast food twenty-four hours a day, visit the Gasparilla Grill, which serves up a small variety of better-than-average Disney fast foods. To complete the largest selection of restaurant offerings in any Disney resort, the Grand also offers the Garden View Lounge and its elegant afternoon tea ♥♥♥. The Grand also has round-the-clock room service. For more details regarding these and other Disney dining spots, see chapter 6.

The private Romance Dinner is yet another dining option available only to guests of the Grand Floridian. This unforgettably romantic service provides a private dining experience delivered to the Grand Floridian location of your choice. Enjoy it in your room, on your balcony, on the third floor lobby veranda, or on the resort's luxurious yacht, The Grand One. Just about any location is possible. The meal is served white-gloved, with crisp linens and candlelit table setting. For information, call room service.

Lounges at the Grand Floridian

Mizner's Lounge is located on the second floor of the main building and is one of only a few smoking lounges at Disney. Specialties include ales, ports, and select brandies. Each evening, the Grand Floridian Society Orchestra plays on the landing next to this handsome and comfortable lounge. Cítricos bar is a particularly pleasant place to enjoy something from its huge selection of fine wines. Other offerings of this full-service bar include ports, cognacs, champagnes, and aperitifs. Lakeside, Narcoossee's also has a small, full-service bar. There are also two poolside snack bars with beer, wine, specialty drinks, and a small assortment of food.

Shops at the Grand Floridian

There's an interesting selection of shops here at the Grand Floridian, all of which are located in the lobby building. On the ground floor, Summerlace features a selection of women's resort wear. Sandy Cove is this resort's gift and sundries shop. It's where to go for film, sunscreen, and this resort's carved Mickey Lamp ($250) and "teacup" pillows. Upstairs is M. Mouse Mercantile, truly a "Grand" Disney merchandise store. Nearby, you'll find the Ivy Trellis hair salon, men's and women's resort apparel, and the exceptional leather goods of Bally's.

Grand Floridian Spa ♥♥♥♥ and Health Club

Get yourselves in the perfect mood for romance with pampering treatments at this luxurious spa. From an exceptional variety of soothing massages to relaxing mineral soaks, facials, wraps, and aromatherapies, this is certainly a place you'll want to experience. For more details, see page 350.

Helpful Hint
If you're leaving late on your last day, join the health club (around $12) and use its lockers and showers after spending your last hours at the pool.

Recreational Activities at the Grand Floridian

Located along the sparkling sands of Hemingway Cove, the Grand's themed pool features perfectly landscaped Victorian surroundings, a waterfall, slide, kiddie fountain, and children's play area. It is a place of excitement and fun for the younger set and, with shady lounges and poolside snack bar, a place of lakeside relaxation for parents. It is the perfect complement to this lavish resort. In the resort courtyard is the Grand's other larger and quieter swimming pool.

For boating fun, the Grand offers a complete array of watercraft rentals, including the Grand One, the resort's 48-foot luxurious power yacht, available for dining, proposals, and small parties. Arrangements can be made in advance by calling (407) 824-2439. For complete details on watercraft rentals, see page 357.

- One large, heated swimming pool, open twenty-four hours a day

- One heated and themed swimming pool with slide

- One large hot tub

- White sand beach on Seven Seas Lagoon

- Marina complex with watercraft rentals

- In-room massage, by appointment

- Jogging and walking path

- Wingfield tennis courts (see chapter 7)

- Children's activity center

- Video arcade

- Fireworks cruises

Special Children's Activities

No other resort seems to offer anything like the memorable and special activities designed for young visitors. Offered here is the Wonderland Tea Party, Disney's Pirate Adventure, the Perfectly Princess Tea, and Grand Kid Adventures in Cooking. See chapter 7 or inquire at guest services for details. Other children's activities include poolside games and arts and crafts, storytelling on Monday evenings, and crafts on Wednesday evenings at M. Mouse Mercantile.

Our Impressions of the Grand Floridian

@ The Grand Floridian is an enchanting and romantic resort. The rooms are luxurious, and a stay here will have you feeling special and pampered.

@ This resort is almost the dining capital of Disney World.

@ Service here at the Grand is exceptional. Nightly turndown to all rooms is part of the "usual" service.

@ The downside is that the Grand is expensive. Specials and discounted rooms are occasionally available, but rates are rarely outstanding. Holiday season rates have become particularly expensive.

Recommendations for Disney's Grand Floridian Resort & Spa

@ The best views of Cinderella Castle are from the Boca Chica lodge building. The next best view is from Conch, with rooms ending in 25 to 31. After that, Big Pine rooms ending in 41 to 47 have great views.

@ Both Boca Chica and Conch are no-smoking buildings.

@ Make your reservation for Victoria & Albert's when you reserve your room.

@ The Turret suites with the views of the castle are 4021, 4221, and 4321 (we still call this one "our room").

@ Call for bathrobes if there are none in your room.

@ If you wish nightly turndown, be sure that the "privacy please" sign is not on your door.

@ Don't miss housekeeping's Parasol Parade at 8 A.M. on Mondays and Fridays.

Romance at the Grand Floridian

- Unsurpassed service, accommodations, and ambience ♥♥♥♥

- Restaurant selection (the best in the World) ♥♥♥♥

- The Victorian Suite ♥♥♥♥

- A Honeymoon or Turret room ♥♥♥♥

- A lagoon-view room ♥♥♥♥

- Breakfast in bed ♥♥♥♥

- Afternoon tea at the Garden View Lounge in time to hear the orchestra and pianist (music starts at 3 P.M.) ♥♥♥

- Dining at Cítricos ♥♥♥

- An intimate dinner at Victoria & Albert's ♥♥♥♥

- The Romance Dinner ♥♥♥♥

- Watching the fireworks from one of the swings on the beach ♥♥♥♥

- A late-night swim in the pool or hot tub ♥

- A fireworks cruise ♥♥♥

Disney's Wilderness Lodge and The Villas at Disney's Wilderness Lodge

Located in the woods near the Magic Kingdom is one of Disney's most majestic resort creations, the Wilderness Lodge. It is a magnificent tribute, both architecturally and thematically, to the great lodge houses built by the U.S. Park Service around the turn of this century. We have visited many of the lodges after which the Wilderness Lodge was styled, such places as the Ahwahnee at Yosemite, the Lake McDonald Lodge at Glacier National Park, and Yellowstone's Old Faithful Inn. We can tell you that the Wilderness Lodge has been created with great care and that the mood it achieves is impressive. When it comes to magic and theming, the Wilderness Lodge is one of our favorites.

Near the resort's front entrance, a whimsical topiary buffalo and calf graze. The Lodge's bell staff wear the costumes of Park Service Rangers, from knotted kerchiefs to hiking boots. Once inside the great doors, you will know that you have made the right selection. The cavernous lobby soars eight stories above you and surrounds you with balconies of log railings. Two colossal totems face off across the huge expanse, and a shaft of sunlight enters through windows high among the timbers. There is a faint and delicious scent of campfire in the air.

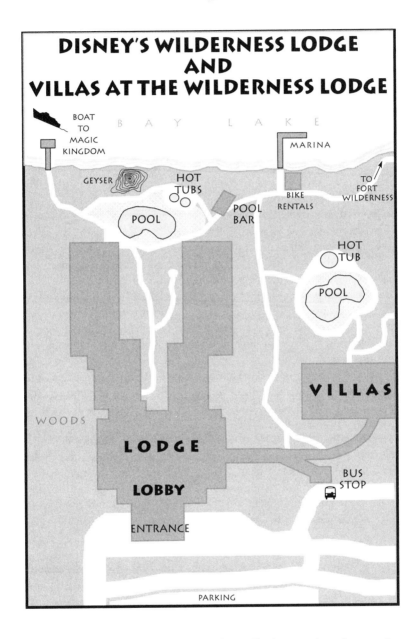

The lobby of the Wilderness Lodge will take your breath away. Its grandeur and detailing are stunning. The decor is American Indian, and the lobby is a showcase of native craftwork. Behind the front desk is an exhibit of authentic Indian cradleboards, while around the lobby are glass showcases of feathered headpieces, the intricate handiwork of

Native American artisans. In a far corner is a fireplace that befits the grand scale of the Lodge. The stonework of its massive chimney rises over 80 feet to the beamed ceiling above. A multitude of hued layers simulate the bedrock of the Grand Canyon. The forged iron hearth is artwork, and its hinges are carefully tooled to resemble quivers, each one full of iron arrows.

As grand as it may be, the Lodge is a place for people, too. Comfortable sitting areas, cozy corners, and fireplaces invite you to linger a while. This is a place of creature comforts, with sofas, ottomans, and hearthside rockers. It's a place for holding hands and for sitting quietly together by the fire. Spectacular and huge, the Lodge also manages to be intimate and inviting. It may take you days or it may take you only a few moments, but you will discover that the charm and the rustic ambience of the Wilderness Lodge are unrivaled at Walt Disney World.

From a distance, the Lodge resembles a frontier fort. The hewn log walls and green roofs of its great central building turn gracefully into two long wings. The swimming pool is formed by a manmade hot spring that bubbles up in the lobby and flows out into the Lodge's rocky courtyard. As the stream builds to a torrent, it becomes a waterfall, splashing noisily over huge artificial granite boulders and tumbling into the swimming pool.

The resort overlooks Bay Lake and each evening, the Electric Water Pageant passes by with its music and lights. It's the perfect end to each magical day. The Disney Imagineers have even provided a steaming geyser that erupts hourly.

The pool at the Lodge is themed and beautiful. During the summer months, there is one hot tub and one cold tub. During the cooler seasons, the cold tub is heated. The lakefront forms a small, sandy swimming beach, and its marina rents a variety of boats and bicycles. Walking, jogging, and cycling paths will take you around the lake to Fort Wilderness. It's a trip you should make time for.

Rooms at the Wilderness Lodge

The standard rooms at the Lodge have a high-timber, western sensibility. Though a bit smaller than those of the other deluxe resorts (about 366 square feet), the rooms are comfortable and well-appointed. Each is woodsy and charming. The furniture is simple and natural, and includes two queen beds and a colorful "quilted" spread. There is a large pine armoire with ample drawer space and a large television set. A small table and several chairs provide the ideal place for in-room dining. The bathroom is fairly standard, with a twin vanity and the usual tub-shower.

All rooms at the Wilderness Lodge have balconies with a variety of views. Standard-view rooms overlook small parking areas, while woods-view rooms open onto the dense forest surrounding the resort. Our woods-view room was on the side of the resort that faces the Magic Kingdom. At night, we were able to see the fireworks above the treetops.

Courtyard rooms provide views of the courtyard and pool, while lake-view rooms enjoy magnificent vistas of Bay Lake. Most of the standard rooms come with the usual dual queen-size beds, and two other offerings are available in limited numbers. There are about forty rooms with single king beds. These have been designed for the physically challenged, and they are handsome rooms. Some rooms also offer a single queen bed and a bunk bed. These seem to capture the western feeling of the Lodge and are ideal for families with one or two children. Coffeemakers are available upon request.

Concierge Service and Suites at the Wilderness Lodge

Concierge service here at the Lodge is on the exclusive seventh floor, where the private concierge lounge is located on the balcony overlooking the lobby. Here you'll enjoy several comfortable seating areas and day-long offerings of continental breakfast, snacks, beverages, late-afternoon hors d'oeuvres, and in the evening, desserts and cordials. And of course, Wilderness Lodge concierge includes pre-arrival planning and a private desk staff eager to please.

A small assortment of suites is available at the Lodge and all feature concierge service. We particularly like the four charming Honeymoon "suites." While not really suites, each has a king-size bed and a large bathroom with whirlpool tub. These reasonably priced rooms are special, intimate, and private. They are the only rooms on the seventh floor overlooking the lobby.

Also on the private seventh floor are the Yellowstone and Yosemite suites, which are the presidential and vice-presidential suites, respectively. These suites are two of our favorites at Walt Disney World. Prices begin at $909 and $803 per night. The Yellowstone features an elegant, western motif. From the suite's double doors and large foyer with elk horn chandelier to the lavish, marble bath, this place is first-class all the way. The suite's four-poster king bed is a unique sculpture of wood, and the spacious suite of rooms is furnished with a large, wooden dining table, stuffed leather chair, and antique books. The Yosemite is nearly as large and enjoys much more of a cowboy sensibility. Rawhide curtains, branding-iron towel racks, and saloon doors on the kitchen/wet bar are just a few of the memorable and whimsical

Room Rates as of 2004 for Disney's Wilderness Lodge Resort and Villas (prices include taxes)

Accommodation	Value Season	Regular Season	Peak Season	Holiday Season
Standard View	$222	$266	$322	$361
Woods View	$244	$283	$333	$378
Courtyard View	$279	$323	$379	$429
Lodge Concierge	$390	$429	$485	$530
Concierge Honeymoon Suite	$401	$446	$507	$546
Villa Studio	$311	$350	$423	$484
One-bedroom Villa	$424	$474	$574	$624
Two-bedroom Villa	$597	$769	$931	$1098

details. Either suite comes with a large whirlpool tub (the Yellowstone's is bigger). We've promised ourselves a stay in one of these suites.

The Lodge Deluxe Room costs about $413 per night during value season. This room has a standard bedroom with two queen beds or one king and a small sitting room with pull-out sofa and wet bar. A standard adjoining room may be added to this suite.

Villas at Disney's Wilderness Lodge

Another stunning Disney creation, the Villas evoke the turn-of-the-century hotels built by railroad workers in the Old West national parks. Though on a much smaller scale, we found the lobby here as magnificent as the Lodge's, and this is really saying something. For us, the stunning log rotunda, a massive stone fireplace, hewn-log animal sculptures, and comfortable sitting rooms recall the unforgettable Ahwahnee Lodge at Yosemite National Park.

These beautiful and rustic villas are part of Disney's Vacation Club and are located in the woods on the south side of the Lodge. Their 181 accommodations are all deluxe home-away-from-home rooms and are either one-bedroom studios with two queen beds, wet bar, microwave, and small refrigerator, or spacious one-bedroom villas. Our villa was a little apartment, with completely equipped kitchen, living room with entertainment center and pull-out queen sleeper-sofa, king bedroom, and bath with whirlpool tub and large vanity. A villa and studio can be interconnected to create a spacious two-bedroom villa, large enough to comfortably accommodate eight.

Theming in our one-bedroom villa was woodsy and western. Dark woodwork, paintings from the great parks of the west, and room accents of pine cones, acorns, and leaves lent it a pleasant sense of rugged adventure. We made good use of our kitchen, enjoying fresh coffee and breakfast in the comfort of our own little "home." At the end of a long day of Disney exploration, our evenings centered around the whirlpool tub. During our visit, we even made use of the washer and dryer.

The Villas at the Wilderness Lodge has its own quiet pool with hot tub and a full-service fitness center (with sauna). Connected to the nearby Wilderness Lodge by a short covered walkway, this wonderful place enjoys all the comforts of home yet still manages all the excitement and theming of one of Disney's most majestic resort creations. It's a premier offering.

Transportation and Convenience

Convenience is not, we're sorry to tell you, one of the strong suits here at the Wilderness Lodge. Still, it is acceptable.

- @ To the Magic Kingdom: by boat, arrivals and departures from the lakeside dock

- @ To Epcot, Disney-MGM Studios, the Animal Kingdom, Blizzard Beach: direct bus

- @ To Typhoon Lagoon and Downtown Disney: direct bus

- @ To BoardWalk: bus to Downtown Disney or any open park and take BoardWalk bus

Dining at the Wilderness Lodge

The Lodge has three western-themed restaurants; two with table service, and one with fast food. The Artist Point ♥♥ is the Wilderness Lodge's premier eating place. Dinner specialties are the freshest of meats, seafood, game, and wines from the Pacific Northwest.

The "all-purpose" restaurant is the Whispering Canyon Cafe. It's a fun place to eat and the food is acceptable. Each of the day's hearty meals is served family-style, all you care to eat, or à la carte. Reservations for either of these restaurants is strongly suggested (dial 55 on your room telephone). For our reviews of these restaurants, see chapter 6.

The Lodge has a themed counter-service eatery called the Roaring Fork. Open 6 A.M. to midnight, this self-serve restaurant offers a selection of breakfasts, burgers, sandwiches, fried foods, salads, and desserts (grill closes at 11 P.M.). The Lodge also has 7 A.M. to midnight room service with a menu that includes barbecued ribs, pizza, grilled fish, and prime rib. Foods come from either the Artist Point or Whispering Canyon. Wines, beers, and mixed drinks are also available.

Lounges at the Wilderness Lodge

The picturesque Territory Lounge is located adjacent to the Artist Point and serves a selection of microbrewery beers, specialty drinks, and wines. If the Artist Point is too crowded or if you simply prefer it, you may order from the Artist Point or Whispering Canyon menus.

The Trout Pass Pool Bar enjoys a nice view of the Lodge and of the lake and beach and offers an interesting selection of specialty drinks and a small variety of snacks and sandwiches.

Shops at the Wilderness Lodge

The Lodge Mercantile is this resort's shop and just outside its door sits an amusing totem pole of Disney characters. It's a great photo opportunity. Inside, you'll find handsome Lodge logo merchandise and the usual assortment of sundries such as film, sunscreen, and snacks. With the new home-away-from-home Villas, the Mercantile now features a modest assortment of basic foodstuffs, including frozen foods and milk.

Sturdy Branches Fitness Center

Located in the Villas, this full-service fitness center features a large variety of Cybex equipment, a sauna, and a staff of trainers. It even has two beautiful massage rooms. Lodge or Villa guests may use this center for $15 per day or $25 for length of stay.

Recreational Activities at the Wilderness Lodge

- Heated swimming pool with small water slide at the Lodge
- Heated swimming pool with bubbling springs at the Villas
- One hot and one cold spa at the Lodge, one hot tub at the Villas
- Lodge children's activities: fireside storytelling, duck races, penny toss
- White sand beach and marina with assorted boat rentals
- Bicycle and surrey quadri-cycle rentals
- Video arcade
- Fishing excursion
- The Cub's Den children's activity center

The Wilderness Lodge Tours

- On various days, the Lodge conducts a free tour that begins in the lobby at 9:30 A.M. Even if you aren't staying here, we'd recommend one.

Our Impressions of the Wilderness Lodge and Villas

@ A beautifully themed resort. The fantasy element here is so powerful that a visit will be a real adventure. As elusive as romance is, we'd have to say that the Lodge has it.

@ One of the most "transporting" Disney resorts

@ $ The Lodge is a good value. It falls in cost somewhere between the deluxe resorts and the moderates, yet offers extraordinary theming, well-decorated rooms, and the services found at more expensive resorts.

@ The ambience, comforts, and conveniences of the Villas are hard to beat. We love the Vacation Club accommodations. The pool is a bit small for a hotel with nearly 800 rooms. Even during the winter months, the Lodge's two hot tubs are simply not enough.

@ A car would come in handy here, especially for dining at other Disney resorts. Transportation can be slow.

@ This is definitely one of our favorite resorts. Even if you aren't staying here, we suggest you drop by just to see its award-winning lobby.

Recommendations for Disney's Wilderness Lodge and Villas

@ A lodge room that is on one of the lobby's balconies is considered a woods-view room. Ask for one when you make your reservations, if this is your wish. Occasionally, noise from the lobby can be heard in these rooms.

@ $ The Honeymoon suite is a great choice for a romantic visit.

@ The Wilderness Lodge concierge is the least expensive concierge at WDW.

@ Courtyard-view rooms are picturesque but noisy; woods-view rooms are quiet.

@ Some of the lower-level lake-view rooms have stunning balconies of "granite."

@ At the Villas, ask for lodgings on the lakeside of the building.

Romance at the Wilderness Lodge and Villas

@ Resort theming ♥♥♥

@ A Honeymoon "suite" ♥♥♥

- A room in concierge ♥♥

- A one-bedroom villa: luxury, a Jacuzzi, and your own private bedroom—perfect ♥♥♥

- Morning cup of coffee in front of the fireplace on the third-floor landing above the main door ♥♥

- The Artist Point restaurant ♥♥

- The Territory Lounge ♥

- Taking a stroll or a bike ride over to Fort Wilderness ♥

- Searching for the sixteen hidden Mickeys at the Lodge ♥

Disney's Fort Wilderness Resort and Campground

If you've never been to Fort Wilderness, you'll find that there's a lot more going on out here than just a campground. More than any other Walt Disney resort area, Fort Wilderness is a world unto itself. With 750 beautifully wooded acres, Fort Wilderness would have little trouble drawing guests even without the nearby Disney attractions. This amazing place offers a sandy beach, two swimming pools, a host of watercraft, sports activities, a petting farm, two popular dinner shows, a restaurant, and some shopping. And besides offering a real variety of quality campsites and motor home hookups, Fort Wilderness has its very own lodgings, the Wilderness Cabins. To say that Fort Wilderness is a campground would be like calling the Magic Kingdom an amusement park.

Fort Wilderness has a distinctly western flavor. Weathered log buildings, rough-hewn timbers, split-rail fences, and meadows filled with wildflowers are set amid a shady forest of slash pine, cypress, and live oak. It really doesn't feel much like Florida at all. In fact, it reminds us of the many national parks we've visited in the West.

Accommodation Rates as of 2004 for Disney's Fort Wilderness Resort and Campground (prices include taxes)

Accommodation	Value Season	Regular Season	Peak Season	Holiday Season
Wilderness Cabin	$255	$300	$33	$367
Preferred Campsite	$55	$75	$85	$96
Campsite, full hookup	$46	$69	$79	$90
Campsite, partial hookup	$40	$58	$67	$77

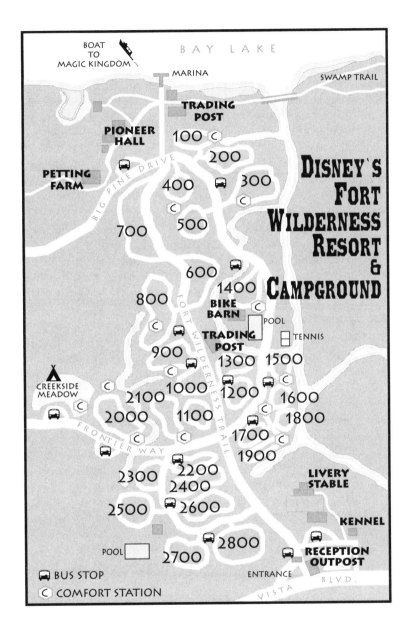

There are two basic types of accommodations at Fort Wilderness: the campsites and the Wilderness Cabins. Each offers something quite different. The Wilderness Cabins are Disney resort lodgings. The campsites, of course, furnish a place to either pitch your tent or hook up your motor home or trailer.

Fort Wilderness Campsites

Fort Wilderness is Disney, and that means everything is something special. The campsites, whether for tents, motor homes, or travel trailers, are all large and relatively private. Each comes with either a full or partial hookup. Full hookups include water, sewer, electric, and cable television. Partials supply only electric and water. All offer ample space, a small barbecue grill, and a picnic table, and all provide 110- and 220-volt electricity.

Wherever your campsite, you won't be far from an air-conditioned (or heated) Comfort Station. Each of these features private showers and restrooms, an ice machine, and a coin-operated laundry. They are all clean and well maintained.

There are also a number of campsites where guests are allowed to have pets. Availability is limited and costs an additional $5 per night. If you want to bring your pet on a Disney adventure, be sure to reserve one of the pet-designated loop sites (300 for preferred site; other sites, loops 1600–1900). Proof of vaccinations is required for dogs and cats.

Wilderness Cabins

The Wilderness Cabins are why this area is called a "resort." Each of these small, air-conditioned 12-by-50-foot cabins features a full kitchen, including utensils, pots and pans, microwave oven, and dishwasher. The living room has a pull-down double bed, and the bedroom has both a double bed and bunk beds. Every cabin has a raised, outside deck, a picnic table, and an outdoor grill. All are relatively new and feature log siding and a rough-hewn beam interior. Theming here is at its best and so are creature comforts.

Money-Saving Tip

At various times throughout the year, there are good discounts on the Wilderness Cabins.

While not equal to the luxury found at Old Key West, the Wilderness Cabins have real charm. Furnishings are comfortable, quaint, and homey. Chairs and table are woodsy and rustic. The overall feeling is surprisingly pleasant and each is large enough to accommodate a large family or six adults. This is truly one Disney accommodation that's a real bargain.

If you are visiting Disney with your children, a Wilderness Cabin will provide the privacy for your romantic Disney holiday. Being able to prepare many of your own meals will save you some serious money as well. Maid service is included and this means dishwashing, too. So cook up a storm and leave the dishes for Disney.

Location, Location, Location

As the old adage goes, there are three important elements to real estate. The same is true for Fort Wilderness. The central area is around Pioneer Hall, where you will find the resort's restaurants, guest services, the Settlement Depot, the beach, River Country, and most of the recreational activities. We suggest that you locate yourselves as close to it as possible in one of the preferred campsites.

Fort Wilderness is large. The roads here wind lazily through the resort's 750 forested acres. The campsites and homes are all located on small "loop" roads that connect to the larger streets. There are nearly thirty such loops. Some are closer to things than others. Some offer a bit more seclusion. Others offer convenience to the pools or to the beach or bus stops. Each loop is numbered, with the series beginning at Loop 100 and ending with Loop 2800.

Loops 100 through 500 are the Preferred Campsites, and you will pay about $8 more per night to stay in one. They are all full hookups. It's well worth the small expense, and we suggest that you request one when you make your reservation. We also suggest that you make your reservation as far in advance as possible. These puppies go fast.

If you are planning a stay in one of the Wilderness Cabins, you'll be a bit farther away. These occupy loops 2100 through 2800. The partial hookup campsites are also a little farther out, occupying loops 1500 to 2000.

Occupancy rates are based on two adults per accommodation; children under 17 years of age are no extra charge. A maximum of six persons is allowed in each cabin, with ten persons maximum at any one campsite. Extra adults at the cabins are $5 each per night and $2 each per night at the campsites.

Transportation and Conveniencee

- ℮ To all Fort Wilderness areas: by internal buses

- ℮ To Magic Kingdom: bus or walk to Settlement Depot, then take boat launch from Bay Lake dock

- ℮ To all other Disney destinations: bus or walk to Outpost Depot, then bus to your final destination

- ℮ Epcot (alternate route): bus to TTC, then take monorail to Epcot

Since Disney asks that you not drive your car at Fort Wilderness except to arrive and depart, you'll want to give some thought to getting around this large resort. Rental electric carts are available either for your length of stay or by the day. At $46 per day or $40 for a twenty-four-hour period, these carts are expensive, but if you are in one of the more distant areas, one will come in handy. You can reserve one up to a year before your arrival date. There are also rental bicycles, available either by the hour or for $21 per day. With miles of peaceful, wooded paths, a couple of bikes would be nice. During our time at Fort Wilderness, we noticed many people riding around on their own bicycles.

Restaurants and Eating at Fort Wilderness

Most guests staying at Fort Wilderness fix their own meals. Whether you are visiting in your motor home or staying in a Wilderness Cabin, one economical advantage of Fort Wilderness is being able to feed yourselves.

We suggest that on your way through one of the surrounding communities, you stop for groceries. There are two Trading Posts here at Fort Wilderness, and while they offer a decent selection of basic foodstuffs, they do so at Disney prices. If you are looking for a real supermarket, Gooding's at the Crossroads Plaza near the Downtown Disney Marketplace is convenient, though still expensive. See page 46 for directions.

There are several restaurants at Fort Wilderness, and two of them are dinner shows: the Hoop-Dee-Doo Musical Revue and Mickey's Backyard Barbecue (see page 308 for details). $ Trail's End Restaurant is located next door to Pioneer Hall and features bargain buffet meals for breakfast and lunch, and a reasonably priced buffet dinner. There's plenty of good food: fried chicken, ribs, pizza, sandwiches, and much more. Dinners even include hand-carved roast beef.

Crockett's Tavern is Fort Wilderness's picturesque lounge. It's a nice place for specialty drinks and even offers pizza and appetizers. Hours are 4 P.M. to 10 P.M.

Recreational Activities at Fort Wilderness

- Two heated swimming pools and white-sand beach
- Marina with rental craft
- Bike and surrey quadri-cycle rentals
- Private, evening horse-drawn carriage rides (see chapter 7 for details)
- Tri-Circle D Ranch
- Horseback riding
- Two lighted tennis courts
- Jogging and walking paths
- Two video arcades
- Swamp Trail nature walk
- Petting farm

- Supervised children's activities
- Nightly wagon ride
- Evening movies and snacks and campfire sing along
- Volleyball, tetherball, basketball, horseshoes, and "yolf"
- Fishing excursions, waterskiing, and parasailing

Our Impressions of Fort Wilderness

- No doubt, this is a super campground. The facilities are first-rate—sparkling and clean. There's so much to do here that you hardly have to go anywhere to have fun.
- $ We love the Wilderness Cabins and think that they are great family lodging.
- Although transportation at Fort Wilderness has improved over the past few years, a car will come in handy.

Recommendations for Fort Wilderness

- To get either a preferred campsite or one that permits pets, make your reservations as far ahead of time as possible.
- Reserve your electric cart when you make your reservations

Romance at Fort Wilderness

- Taking an evening stroll around the resort ♥♥
- Having a nightcap on the porch at Crockett's Tavern ♥
- Taking a late-afternoon dip in the lake on a hot summer day ♥
- The evening carriage ride ♥♥
- Having your privacy when you bring your family to a Wilderness Cabin ♥
- Watching the Electric Water Pageant from the beach ♥

Shades of Green Resort

This resort, once known as the Disney Inn, is now reserved for use by active and retired military personnel, employees of the Department of Defense, and members of the National Guard and military reserves. Owned by the U.S. government, Shades of Green provides an affordable Disney vacation for the men and women of the U.S. armed services and their families. As we write this, Shades has been closed for more than a year in order to more than double the number of rooms and to

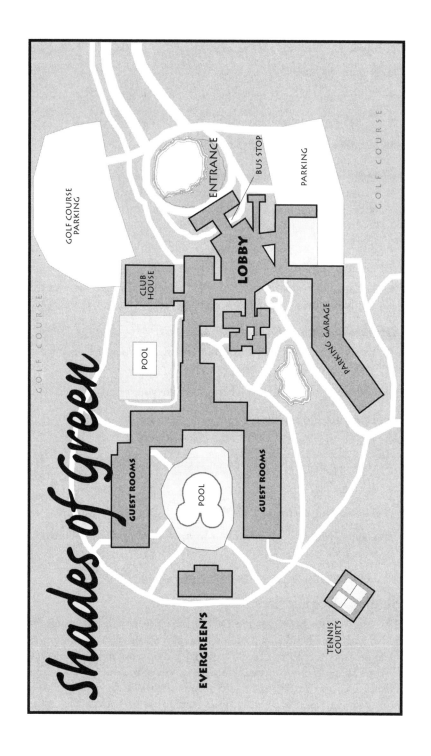

make significant upgrades to the entire resort. It will reopen in December of 2003.

Shades of Green is nestled between two of Disney's championship golf courses, the Magnolia and the Palm, and features a peaceful, woodsy ambience. The porte cochere at the resort entrance is reached via a circular drive that surrounds a quiet pond fed by a series of rocky waterfalls. Palms, azaleas, and philodendrons create a tranquil picture of Central Florida elegance.

Rates at Shades are based on rank and range from very reasonable to downright deserving. Discount passes to Disney (10% off) and other attractions are available and Shades of Green restaurants offer meals at reduced prices. Although guests at Shades of Green do enjoy the Extra Magic Hour, they do not get Disney Resort ID cards. Every effort at Shades is made to make the Disney experience an affordable one for our people in uniform.

Special arrangements can be made for small weddings at the resort's own garden gazebo. Everything from family reunions and modest parties to large conventions can be handled by the resort's professional staff. These events can be as grand or as modest as you can afford, and the many rules and regulations regarding such happenings at Disney resorts are not a consideration here. Staff members make a real effort to get to know their guests, and we suspect that repeat customers are the rule rather than the exception.

It is worth noting that no taxpayer funds are used to support this resort. Shades of Green and all other Armed Forces Recreation Centers are completely self-supporting.

Rooms at Shades of Green

All accommodations are located in the resort's three three-story guest wings. Guest rooms face the landscaped central courtyard, the pool, or the golf course. There's no such thing as a bad view here, and the rooms, at 450 square feet, are the largest standard rooms at Disney World. Of the resort's 586 rooms, all but its eleven suites feature two queen beds. Each room has a sofa bed, small table and chairs, and balcony or patio. Other amenities include a large, remote-controlled color television, coffeemaker, hairdryer, iron, and ironing board.

The eleven suites at Shades of Green each feature a living room, master bedroom with large bath, and a second bedroom, with two queen beds and bath. Each can accommodate up to eight people.

Because all rooms at Shades are either undergoing redecorating or are under construction, we are unable to tell you any other details. We are confident, however, that all resort accommodations will be comfortable and well appointed.

2004 Room Rates for Shades of Green (prices include tax)

Military/Civilian Grade	Standard Room	Poolside Room
E1–E5:	$78	$89
E6–E9, O1–O3, WO1–CW3, GS1–GS10, NF1–NF3, widows, and disabled veterans:	$106	$117
O4–O6, CW4–CW5, GS11–GS15, NF4–NF5:	$113	$124
O7–O10, retired DOD civilians, NF6:	$118	$129

About the only downside to this resort is that in the past, the number of guests has far exceeded room availability. In short, this is one very popular place. "Overflow" guests have been put up at just about every Disney resort and at several of the hotels along Hotel Plaza Blvd. at Downtown Disney. We are told that this policy will continue as long as demand exceeds supply.

Valid military ID or current LES and Department of Defense (DOD) pay grade verification is required at check-in. Room rates at Shades of Green are based on rank and civil service rate and double occupancy.

Special "Gold Leaf" package vacations are offered and include accommodations, meals, and admission to the Disney theme parks. Reservations for rooms and packages can be made by calling Shades of Green reservationists at (888) 593-2242.

Transportation at Shades of Green

Transportation to all Disney destinations is by Shades of Green buses. These are not Walt Disney World buses. They run on a schedule that is available at the front desk. Service is on par with that of Disney, and having a printed schedule will take the guesswork out of travel.

Restaurants and Lounges at Shades of Green

The "new" Shades of Green will feature a variety of restaurants, from fine dining to a quick bite. Mangino's will be this resort's premier dining destination, a Northern Italian themed trattoria. Shades will also feature a large eatery with four themed buffet dining rooms, all connected by bridges.

Poolside will still be Evergreen's. This sports bar and restaurant will continue to offer its selection of salads and sandwiches. And right near the bus stop entrance of the resort will be a fast-food counter, offering coffee, beverages, and baked goods. It's the perfect morning stop on the way to the theme parks.

Shops at Shades of Green

Although plans are yet to be finalized, Shades will feature a variety of retail outlets, including an Army–Air Force Exchange and a Disney merchandise outlet as well as several other shops.

Services Available at Shades of Green

- Room service
- Coin-operated laundry facilities
- Small refrigerators
- Travel services

Recreational Activities at Shades of Green

- Discounted golf on Disney courses for after-10 A.M. tee times
- Two large standard swimming pools and one hot tub
- Two tennis courts
- One kiddie pool
- A children's playground
- Fitness room
- Video arcade

Our Impressions of Shades of Green

- This is a very nice resort and provides an affordable way for military personnel to visit Walt Disney World and to stay on-property.

Romance at Shades of Green

- Resort theming ♥
- A suite ♥♥♥
- Ask about special room amenities, such as flowers ♥

The Epcot Resorts

This is our favorite resort area not simply because it's home to our favorite resort, but because it's so well located. The Yacht and Beach Clubs, the BoardWalk, and the Swan and Dolphin all surround Crescent Lake. All are deluxe resorts and all are within walking distance of both Epcot and Disney-MGM Studios. Dining and entertainment choices here are virtually unlimited and for us, this is the "adult" corner of Disney and *the* place to be. We relish a stay in any of these beauties.

The Caribbean Beach is a bit farther away and while it may lack the convenience of the other Epcot resorts, it's a beautifully themed and moderately priced resort.

Disney's Yacht Club and Beach Club Resorts

Maybe we love these resorts so much because we're New Englanders, or maybe it's just because the resorts are such beautiful period pieces. Whatever the reasons, we think that the Yacht and the Beach Clubs and the Beach Club Villas are among Disney's most enchanting creations. All are lovely visions of nineteenth-century luxury where you will be immersed in a setting that is perfectly exciting, lavishly relaxing, and splendidly romantic. The gray and blue clapboard buildings of the Yacht Club and Beach Club and Villas evoke a bygone era of grace and hospitality. These picturesque resorts share a quaint, turn-of-the-century New England seaside theme. The Yacht Club reflects a more formal nautical charm, while the Beach Club and Beach Club Villas are reminiscent of the casual ambience of the shore.

Lakeside, a rope-slung boardwalk, a beached shipwreck, a lighthouse, and the white-sand beach complete the seaside fantasy. The Disney magic is everywhere, from the antique "woody" station wagon at the front door of the Beach Club to the intricate ship models in the Yacht Club's elegant lobby. These places are classy and unforgettable and are first-rate resorts from top to bottom. Their intimate, relaxed atmospheres will embrace you, enhancing the chemistry for your romantic escape. And their location puts you right next door to much of the adult excitement of Walt Disney World.

The feature pool is Stormalong Bay—an extraordinary and magical place. More like a river than a pool, it meanders from the Yacht Club to the Beach Club. Along the way are bubbling springs, whirlpool eddies, waterfalls, and two hot tubs nestled along its rocky "shore." There's even a sand beach for children. At the Beach Club end of the sand-bottom Stormalong Bay is a wild and winding slide that begins in the crow's nest of the shipwreck and ends in the pool with a sudden splash. After a morning of theme park activity, you'll be anxious to spend a blissful afternoon here, swimming and sunning.

Along with Stormalong Bay, each resort also has its own quiet pool and hot tub, and all share a common area that includes Periwig's Salon and Barber, a video arcade, and the Ship Shape Health Club with its old-fashioned, tiled indoor spa. Along the waterfront, the Yacht Club features a marina of rental watercraft, while the Beach Club enjoys a

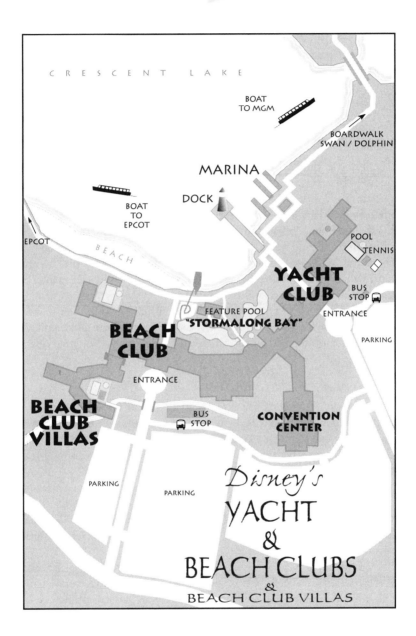

lazy stretch of white sand. These areas are separated by a long wooden pier at the end of which is a charming lighthouse, one of the signature sights of these idyllic resorts.

The landscaping at the Yacht and Beach Clubs is a showcase of Disney's penchant for details. Colorful gardens and manicured shrubbery will be an inspiration to home gardeners. Long stretches of trimmed lawns lead gracefully to the lake. On one of the lawns is the lovely gazebo used by Disney Fairy Tale Weddings. Amid beguiling gardens of roses and the carved, wooden cupids, happy couples tie the knot, Disney-style.

Disney's Yacht Club Resort

The lobby of the Yacht Club showcases its nautical theme. A large antique globe sits amid the elegant splendor. We wonder where Disney gets things like this. There are intricate ship models in glass cases that invite more than just a casual glance. Ornate brass chandeliers, polished hardwood floors, and decorative ropework recall the finery of New England's old yachting establishments. Tufted leather sofas and chairs will tempt you with the promise of luxurious comfort. Muted reds, whites, and blues herald the colors of the grand old yacht clubs of Cape Cod, Marblehead, and Bar Harbor.

This lobby area is more formal but is no less inviting than that of the casual Beach Club. There is a certain classiness to this place and, as one of our mothers said when we arrived, "Now, *this* is the style I'm accustomed to!"

Rooms at the Yacht Club

The recently refurbished guest rooms at the Yacht Club feel light and airy and enjoy a bit of a formal charm. Ship's-wheel bedsteads are made of white wood and the wall lamps, of polished brass. Bedspreads of classic yachts on a field of sky blue enhance the nautical decor and feature hidden Mickey knots.

Rooms at the Yacht Club have either two queen beds or a single king and each room has a spacious vanity area with twin sinks. New to the decor is an interesting desk that features a pull-out table on wheels. High-speed Internet access is on the agenda for the near future.

Most rooms have a daybed, providing space for a fifth guest, and every room at the Yacht Club has a large balcony with several chairs and a small table where you'll want to enjoy an early morning breakfast, read a good book, or simply watch Disney World awaken. We know from our blissful time here that the Yacht Club will embrace you with the luxurious comforts found only at first-class hotels: large soft towels, Disney toiletries, and a stocked mini-butler.

At the Yacht, the assortment of views includes waterfront (pool or lagoon) and garden.

Concierge Service at the Yacht Club

This is the way to see Disney. Before you arrive, you'll be phoned by the concierge staff, who will be anxious to help plan your Disney vacation: dinner reservations, tickets to Cirque du Soleil, or whatever you wish. After your arrival and private check-in, you'll begin to understand the meaning of personalized service. You'll have a desk staff dedicated to making your Disney vacation go as smoothly as possible.

The Yacht Club's private fifth floor is home to a hotel within the hotel. Guest rooms feature upgraded amenities, such as bathrobes and signature toiletries. The cozy concierge lounge serves a variety of food and drink throughout the day. Each morning's continental breakfast features pastries, croissants, fruits, cereals, and muffins, while midday snacks include tea, chips and salsa, fruit, and cookies and milk. Late afternoons mean wine and cheese, a vegetable tray, and a marvelous selection of hors d'oeuvres. In the evening, cordials and desserts are offered.

Suites at the Yacht Club

Our favorite Yacht Club suite is the large and lavishly furnished, two-bedroom Commodore. It's charming and romantic—the perfect place for a honeymoon, an anniversary, or a romantic getaway. With a comfortable sitting room, a large bedroom with a king-size sleigh bed, and concierge service, a stay here will make your time dreamy and idyllic.

The Commodore's bathroom is large and luxurious. Complete with television, dual vanity areas, a walk-in shower, and Jacuzzi tub, it's absolutely world-class. If you can afford the $1,300 per night price tag (value season!), we are sure that it will not disappoint you.

The Turret suites occupy the first three floors of the resort's beautiful tower-like structure. Each includes an octagonal sitting room in the turret, two large bedrooms, and a spacious living room. Each Turret room is sunny and bright, offering a thrilling panorama of Stormalong Bay and Crescent Lake. If you're looking for something really spectacular, there is the Presidential, which is the fourth floor of the Turret suites. It includes a large dining area, Jacuzzi tub, and two balconies. The suite costs more than $1,700 per night. Disney CEO Michael Eisner is frequently a guest here during his Disney visits.

The Yacht's premier suite is the Admiral. It is one of only a handful on Disney property that offer such luxury. Furniture is dark and varnished, and there is enough room for a large family or even a small wedding reception. The dining room table will easily seat a dozen, and the wet bar is designed to be a serving area for a large room-service event.

The dark wood theme is carried throughout, with a large armoire and four-poster king bed in the master bedroom. The bath has an over-sized shower and tub. This suite of rooms also has a 40-foot-wide patio, which opens onto its own secluded garden and pond.

Disney's Beach Club Resort

The relaxed and romantic atmosphere of the Beach Club has lured us back time and again. We like to think of this place as our home-away-from-home. We confess that staying elsewhere has been done with some reluctance. The casual atmosphere here is elegant yet informal. For us, the Beach Club is simply inviting.

The Beach's lobby is a canvas of pastels, pink marble, and fine woodwork. Large windows facing the lake make the lobby airy and bright. Comfortable wicker furnishings are everywhere on plush car-pets of floral designs, and wooden birdcages and large potted palms add just the right touches of warmth.

Around the resort are porches with rockers, beaches with cabanas, and lovely gardens with benches. Enjoying the Disney attractions for a few hours at a time will not be hard. After a morning in the parks, you'll be ready to return.

Rooms at the Beach Club

The "seaside" rooms are sunny and bright. Ensconced amid the luxuri-ous furnishings, you will not for a minute forget that you are enjoying a romantic vacation at the beach. The verdigris-finished bedsteads and seahorse lamps seem weathered by their "years" at the seashore. The sand-colored bedspread with vignettes of classic Disney characters at the Beach adds a real touch of whimsy, and the framed prints of beach scenes complete the image. This is a place of creature comforts, your own intimate and private retreat. You've landed in the lap of luxury and, if you're like us, you won't be anxious to depart.

Beach Club rooms are indeed inviting. Like her "sister ship," the Beach Club offers either a single king or double queen beds with a large vanity area and twin sinks. Many rooms include a daybed/sofa providing space for a fifth guest. Balconies are either full-size, with patio furniture, or standing room only. Beach Club rooms feature the same desk with pull-out table as her sister resort. Expect to see high-speed Internet access here in 2003.

There is the usual Disney complement of views. Standard-view rooms look out onto well-landscaped gardens, beyond which are the re-sort's parking lots. Ground-floor, standard-view rooms have charming little patios that open onto beautiful gardens. Water-view rooms at the

Beach overlook Stormalong Bay or the quiet pool area. Other rooms command views of the various gardens on the lakeside of the building, and some rooms provide views of Epcot and IllumiNations, the nightly fireworks show.

Concierge Service at the Beach Club

The Beach Club's concierge area offers all the privileges enjoyed at her sister ship next door. An exclusive floor and private lounge, as well as private check-in and a desk staff, are dedicated to making your Disney vacation as much as it can be. The Beach Club concierge lounge features a small children's entertainment area. For more details, see "Concierge Service at the Yacht Club."

Suites at the Beach Club

From the luxurious to the lavish, the Beach Club offers a variety of suites. The Newport is this resort's two-bedroom presidential suite. It features a king bedroom with a large vanity, bath, and large Jacuzzi tub. The formal living room is arranged around a fireplace and includes a spacious dining area, wet bar, and room enough for a small party. Located on a corner of the fifth floor, the Newport has a narrow balcony that runs the entire width of the living room and bedroom. The view of Stormalong Bay and the lagoon is commanding. So is the price: $1,739 nightly for value season.

The Nantucket is the Beach's vice-presidential suite. With a beautiful king bedroom, comfortable second bedroom, and a smaller and less formal living room, it seems better suited for a honeymoon or family holiday. Located on the second floor, the Nantucket overlooks a pleasant garden area. It is charming and is conveniently located near the lobby. Expect to pay about $850 during value season. The Beach also offers deluxe rooms. At about $507 nightly, there are two varieties, each with a large king bedroom: Deluxe A features a sitting area that is part of the bedroom, and Deluxe B offers a separate sitting area with French doors and a daybed. Deluxe B is a nice choice for a family with one child.

Disney's Beach Club Villas

We were very excited when we first arrived at the Beach Club Villas. These accommodations combine two of our favorite things about Disney resorts: the Beach Club and the home-away-from-home properties of the Disney Vacation Club. The Beach Club Villas were designed by the Yacht & Beach's original architect, Robert A. M. Stern. The clapboard exterior and porches, turrets, and Victorian gingerbread marry this resort perfectly to both the Yacht and Beach Clubs.

After our check-in at the Beach Club, we headed next door to the adjacent villas. On our way, we passed through the Solarium, the Villas' sun-filled sitting room. Modeled after a Victorian-era sun porch, the Solarium connects the Villas to the Beach Club and offers a comfortable and relaxing sitting area with a pleasant view of the main garden and resort entrance.

Later, we discovered the Drawing Room, another common room, which is adjacent to the Villas' lobby. Here, we found seaside watercolor paintings, a Victorian dollhouse, vintage posters that advertise the Atlantic coast's seaside attractions, and a large-screen television showing Disney movies.

The Beach Club Villas features the "usual" Vacation Club variety of rooms: one-room studios, spacious one-bedroom villas, and two-bedroom villas. The one-room studio accommodation offers one queen bed and a queen sleeper/sofa, a small refrigerator, coffeemaker, toaster, and microwave oven. A spacious one-bedroom villa means a full kitchen, a cozy living room with pull-out queen sleeper, side chair, sea chest coffee table, and a spacious king bedroom. The two-bedroom villa adds a second bedroom (sometimes a connecting studio) to this already luxurious arrangement. Both the one- and two-bedroom villas feature a washer-dryer.

Rooms here also feature large-screen televisions and DVD players, with loaner movies for Vacation Club members.

Whatever your choice, you'll find each beautifully and comfortably furnished. Lodgings feature a restful backdrop of peach and pale aqua with floral drapes. A lighthouse lamp, colorful prints of coastal scenes, and an eclectic collection of furnishings enhance the home-away-from-home cottage theme. Bedsteads are white iron. Bedpreads are beige with blue morning glories climbing a white trellis and feature subtle, Classic Disney characters. Studio bedspreads are a muted turquoise and also feature Classic Disney characters.

Even by home standards, the open villa kitchen is both attractive and practical. Each features a range, microwave, toaster, coffeemaker, and full-size refrigerator. Granite countertops, seahorse tilework, and all the necessary equipment to prepare whatever meal you desire will give you the option of eating in or dining out (and at Disney restaurant prices, a villa could actually save you money). There's both a breakfast bar and a small table for dining.

We really appreciate the villas' split bathroom. One area features a shower, vanity, and private toilet while the other provides a spacious vanity and whirlpool tub with French doors that open onto the king bedroom. The Beach Club Villas may seem a bit smaller than other Vacation Club villas, but we found our accommodation to be casually plush and invitingly cozy. We never wanted for space.

Room Rates as of 2004 for Disney's Yacht and Beach Club Resorts (prices include taxes)

Accommodation	Value Season	Regular Season	Peak Season	Holiday Season
Standard View	$322	$367	$439	$500
Water or Pool View	$385	$440	$507	$569
Concierge Garden View	$474	$535	$613	$680
Concierge Lagoon View	$524	$591	$663	$736

The Beach Club Villas has its own quiet pool and spa, the Dunes Cove Pool. This charming area feels as though it is tucked in among the sea-grass–covered dunes of Cape Cod or the North Shore.

We can't stress enough just how perfect the Vacation Club one-bedroom villas are when it comes to a Disney vacation. Having a kitchen, a laundry, a whirlpool tub, and so much space makes a stay at Disney something very, very special, especially if you are traveling with children. We must warn you though, the Beach Club Villas are *very* popular. If you aren't a Vacation Club member, you'll have to do some advanced planning to manage reservations here. Becoming a member makes more sense to us every year. For Beach Club Villa rates, see BoardWalk Villas, page 112.

Transportation and Convenience

The Yacht and Beach Clubs and Beach Club Villas are only minutes from almost any Disney destination. Whether by boat, foot, or bus, transportation to anywhere is about as easy as it gets.

Reaching Disney-MGM Studios or Epcot from either resort is by Friendship motor vessel. Arrivals and departures are from the lighthouse dock on the beach side of the resorts. The trip to Epcot takes only a few minutes by boat and even less time by foot. All other Disney destinations are by direct buses, and each resort has a bus stop near its front entrance.

- To Disney-MGM Studios: short boat trip from resort dock or longer walk along footpath

- To Epcot: short walk or boat ride to International Gateway

- To Magic Kingdom, the Animal Kingdom, Typhoon Lagoon, Downtown Disney, Blizzard Beach: direct bus

- To the BoardWalk (or Swan and Dolphin): a short stroll around the lake

Dining at the Yacht and Beach Clubs and Beach Club Villas

One of the many advantages here is the outstanding dining. Each resort boasts its own array of themed restaurants and lounges, and all are within easy walking distance of either resort. You'll also find many other fine restaurants at the BoardWalk, the Swan and Dolphin, and Epcot's World Showcase.

At the Beach Club is the Cape May Cafe and its delightful seaside decor. Mornings here feature Goofy's Beach Club character breakfast buffet, and in the evenings, a New England–style clambake and all-American buffet. At the Yacht are the Yacht Club Galley and the superb Yachtsman Steakhouse. The Galley serves a large and varied menu for breakfast and lunch, including a breakfast buffet. The Yachtsman is open only for dinner, with its specialty of fine cuts of aged, prime beef.

Money-Saving Tip

Each Disney Resort features a souvenir mug with free refills for your entire length of stay. See page 50 for details.

In and around the pool area are two other restaurants: Beaches and Cream Soda Shop and Hurricane Hanna's. Beaches is a delightful fifties-style soda fountain, and its mean double-chocolate ice cream soda is always a part of our visits. Hamburgers, some good sandwiches, and Disney's best hot dogs are also on the menu. Hanna's is the Y & B's poolside bar and eatery, serving an assortment of drinks, coffees, beer and wine, and good sandwiches. Either of these places is ideal for a light meal while relaxing around Stormalong Bay.

The Yacht Club Galley is the source of in-room dining at both resorts. We have made good use of it on our numerous visits and have always found both the food and the service outstanding. For more details and our reviews of the table-service restaurants, see chapter 6.

Lounges at the Yacht and the Beach

Martha's Vineyard Lounge is the Beach's lounge, and it is a charming and cozy hideaway. Its soft lighting, wicker furnishings, and rose hues create a pleasant atmosphere. Drop by Martha's some evening and enjoy a wine flight.

The Crew's Cup Lounge at the Yacht Club is next door to the Yachtsman Steakhouse and offers a complete selection of beers, wines, and mixed drinks with a cozy clubhouse ambience. Comfortable booths, sofas, and plenty of varnished wood and polished brass make it charming and inviting. With a varied offering of appetizers, finger foods, and sandwiches from the Yacht Club Galley, you might want to consider it for lunch or for a light evening meal.

Both resorts feature comfortable and themed lobby lounges. Both the Ale & Compass at the Yacht and the Rip Tide at the Beach feature full-service bars and specialty drinks. Each also serves a continental breakfast from 6:00 A.M. to 7:30 A.M.

Shops at the Yacht and the Beach

Each resort features its own shop. The Atlantic Wear and Wardrobe Emporium can be found at the Beach Club, and Fairings and Fittings is over at the Yacht. Both shops offer a large selection of sundries, character merchandise, and gifts. Each also features its own line of logo resort wear

Recreational Activities at the Yacht and the Beach

- Stormalong Bay pool complex ♥♥ with rental floats and tubes
- Six hot tubs/spas ♥♥♥
- Three quiet pools ♥
- Sand beach on the lake (no swimming) with lounge chairs
- Lafferty Place video arcade
- Fireworks cruises ♥♥♥
- Complimentary tennis court (at the Yacht Club)
- Jogging and walking paths (map available at the front desk)
- Ship Shape Health Club, state-of-the-art fitness center with sauna, massage room, and whirlpool tub
- Bayside Marina with a variety of rental boats
- Volleyball (ball at health club)

Our Impressions of the Yacht and Beach Clubs and Beach Club Villas

- These are lovely, charming, and romantic resorts—our favorites here at Disney.
- With such proximity to the BoardWalk, Epcot, and Disney-MGM, a stay here will have you in the middle of all the fun and excitement. This is the best corner of Walt Disney World.
- Dining is outstanding. To these choices add the convenience of the restaurants at Epcot, the Swan and Dolphin, and the BoardWalk,

and you'll have to narrow your choices from nearly thirty restaurants, all within walking distance.

@ Our penchant for hot tubs is most certainly satisfied here. There are two lovely hot tubs near Stormalong Bay, one more at each of the quiet pools, and one in the health club.

Recommendations for Disney's Yacht & Beach Clubs and Beach Club Villas

@ If you have reserved a standard room, ask at check-in for one that overlooks a garden area.

@ If you want real convenience to Epcot and the BoardWalk, ask for a room near the Beach's quiet pool.

@ If you wish to be in one of the Beach Club's upper-floor rooms facing Epcot, ask for one when you reserve and again when you check in.

@ Consider a Vacation Club one-bedroom villa (this is the way to visit Disney!)

@ Real versus tiny balconies at the Beach Club are hit or miss. On your reservation and at check-in, be sure to request a room with a real balcony.

@ Some of the rooms can be a trek from the main elevators. If this is not to your liking, mention it at check-in.

@ Don't forget to request nightly turndown (call housekeeping). Not available at the Villas.

Romance at the Yacht and Beach Clubs

@ Overall resort theming ♥♥♥♥

@ Room ambience ♥♥♥

@ A concierge stay ♥♥♥♥

@ A family vacation in a one-bedroom villa ♥♥♥♥

@ The Commodore suite, with concierge service ♥♥♥♥

@ Stormalong Bay pool area ♥♥

@ Breakfast in bed ♥♥♥♥

@ Hot tubs at day's end or late night ♥♥♥

@ A wine flight at Martha's Vineyard Lounge ♥♥

@ A stroll to the World Showcase for IllumiNations ♥♥

@ A swim in Stormalong, and then a double-chocolate ice cream soda from Beaches and Cream ♥

@ The Breathless IllumiNations Cruise for Two (see chapter 7) ♥♥♥♥

@ Watching IllumiNations from the beach ♥♥♥

@ $ A "Breathless Glide" (see chapter 7) ♥♥

Disney's BoardWalk Inn and BoardWalk Villas

This resort is a charming remembrance of America's bygone era of seaside holidays. It is the golden years of such places as Coney Island, Atlantic City, Cape May, Nantasket, and Revere Beach brought marvelously to life. If in your youth you were lucky enough to enjoy a vacation at one of these shoreside gems, you'll find the BoardWalk to be a powerful piece of nostalgia. If you never did, you'll discover here a magical re-creation of a time you may have only imagined.

The BoardWalk is both a resort and an entertainment district, and it brings together more than just a few of our favorite elements. It's a delightful and exciting period piece and after dark it comes alive with romantic magic: dining, dancing, and entertainment. You'll find it all here as you stroll the BoardWalk Promenade. Located directly across Crescent Lake from the Yacht and the Beach Clubs, the BoardWalk is the perfect creation to cohabit in this, our favorite corner of Walt Disney World.

The BoardWalk features two very different resorts joined by a bustling, barrel-vaulted, Victorian lobby. The elegant entrance reminisces an era of American culture. This is the 1930s Atlantic seaside, and here you'll be transported to that age when Americans vacationed on the shore amid the splendor of sprawling resorts and the excitement of oceanside promenades. The lobby's centerpiece is a miniature carousel, seventy years old and perfect in every minute detail. Overhead, the unique "Hoppocampus Electrolier" chandelier weaves its magical spell of wonder and delight. Overstuffed sofas, large potted palms, fan-back wicker chairs, and the old photographs and curious relics of this period's long-vanished amusement parks create a powerful sense of nostalgia. Disney's knack for this kind of re-creation remains unmatched.

The Inn and The Villas are the BoardWalk's two resorts. The Inn is Disney's smallest and most intimate. With only 378 rooms, this romantic, Victorian-style resort features well-appointed rooms, awning-covered balconies, private courtyards, and a host of unforgettable "seaside" and garden views. Explore the Inn's hallways to discover cozy sitting areas and fascinating artifacts from the amusement parks of this era. Everything has a tale, and we urge you to spend the time learning

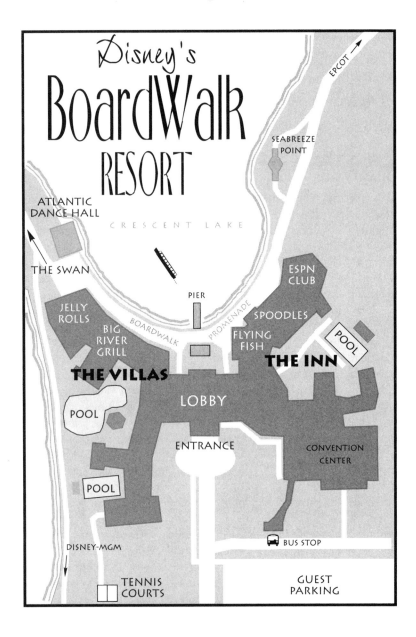

the story behind this place. The Inn has one quiet pool and an accompanying hot tub/spa, both set in a lovely and peaceful garden area.

The 532 rooms of the BoardWalk Villas fall into Disney's home-away-from-home category. Accommodations range from the single-bedroom studios to the luxurious Grand Villas. Part of the Disney

Vacation Club, these accommodations are also available to Disney resort guests. All of the Villa's lodgings feature some sort of cooking facility; most offer full kitchens and laundries. A stay here will allow you to eat "at home" and dine out only as often as you wish. The Villas have two pool areas: one is a quiet pool with a community clubhouse and another more resembles an amusement park. Luna Park is an exciting place, featuring a roller coaster–like water slide, a carousel lounge and eatery, and a carnival-like children's play area.

More than a resort, the BoardWalk's charm is that of a seaside village of the mid-Atlantic coast. Its grounds are beautiful, hospitable, and relaxing. Mowed lawns, picket fences, beguiling gardens, and manicured shrubbery carefully accentuate its varieties of architecture. The effect enhances the sensation that this place evolved over time, that it truly is a small shoreside town.

Once settled into your room, the excitement begins. The magic of the BoardWalk comes alive after dark. You'll find shops, restaurants, nightclubs, sidewalk vendors and entertainers, and boats arriving and departing from the Promenade Pier. And there's more: magicians, games of skill, fire-eaters, and portrait artists. Everywhere is the magic that you have been expecting, and it is all just outside your door. Stroll the Promenade, then enjoy a quick snack or some fine dining. Rent a bicycle "surrey," or walk to Epcot. You can dance the night away at Atlantic Dance or simply sit and enjoy the nightlife. This is one of the neatest places at Disney. For more about the BoardWalk, see chapter 4.

Rooms at the BoardWalk Inn

This is a deluxe resort and a stay here means that you'll be immersed in both the luxury and magic of Disney. The Inn is a showpiece of Victorian charm, featuring an eclectic blend of elegant furnishings styled to create the ambience of a bed and breakfast. Iron and brass bedsteads, antique photographs of old seaside resorts, vintage furniture, and papered wainscoting all evoke an enchanting sense of the past. Accommodations feature either twin queen beds or a single king. Standard rooms are large (390 square feet), and most include child-size daybeds. Marble baths are roomy, and spacious vanities feature large mirrors and dual sinks. Draperies use the images of actual postcards of this period. The Inn's rooms feature the colors of blue and white, with bedspreads of botanical specimens accented with floral greens and pastels.

All rooms at the Inn have balconies. Water-view rooms look right out onto the Promenade and enjoy all the charm and romance of the BoardWalk. Lodgings here are surprisingly quiet with balcony doors closed. Standard rooms overlook either the front of the resort or the lovely Rose Courtyard. Here, among flower-covered trellises and in the

Room Rates as of 2004 for Disney's BoardWalk Inn (prices include taxes)

Accommodation	Value Season	Regular Season	Peak Season	Holiday Season
Standard View	$322	$367	$439	$501
Water View	$401	$452	$524	$591
Concierge	$474	$535	$613	$680
Concierge Deluxe	$563	$619	$680	$753
Garden Suites	$608	$669	$747	$870

shadow of Epcot's Eiffel Tower, your Disney romance will come to life. The Rose Courtyard only seems a world away from the excitement of the nearby Promenade.

Concierge Service and Suites at the BoardWalk Inn

Known as the Innkeeper's Club, the Inn's concierge service is small and sublime. From our own blissful experience here, we know you'll relish the plush bathrobes, the luxurious lounge, and the highly personal service. A continental breakfast with coffees, teas, and a variety of pastries, bagels, fruit, and cereals will be the perfect beginning to each morning. Available throughout the day are a variety of beverages and snacks. After 3 P.M., enjoy tea, sandwiches, and pastries. Late-afternoon snacks include wine, cheese, and a hot dish from one of the BoardWalk's fine restaurants. The friendly and helpful concierge staff will be most pleased to make all your arrangements. After dinner, you'll want to return to the lounge's balcony to sip cordials, nibble desserts, and enjoy IllumiNations. This is romantic Disney at its finest.

The Innkeeper's Club offers only three king beds among its standard rooms. The remainder have two queen beds. Concierge deluxe rooms feature two queen beds and a large sitting area with a pull-out queen. Junior suites each have a king master bedroom and Jacuzzi tub with adjacent parlor room featuring a plush sitting area, pull-out queen, and second bath.

The Inn's presidential suite is called the Steeplechase, and it is the most elaborate and grandest on the property. Extravagant furnishings, a Promenade view, and its incredible size combine to make this suite of rooms (at more than $2,100 per night) something unique even among presidential suites. Canopied king bed, giant Jacuzzi tub, and a full patio with potted palms are but a few of its many memorable features.

The Inn's garden suites are some of the most unique accommodations at Disney. Perfect for any honeymoon or romantic getaway, each features a private entrance through the gate of its own unique rose garden. Complete with birdhouse, mailbox, arbor, and picket fence, each suite is the quintessential love nest. Just a bit secluded, all fourteen garden suites offer downstairs sitting areas and upstairs king bedrooms with couple-sized Jacuzzi baths. Furnishings are typically luxurious and follow color schemes similar to standard rooms.

Except for several of the concierge deluxe rooms on the third floor and the garden suites, which are in the Rose Courtyard, all suites and concierge rooms are located in the fourth floor's exclusive Club area. All garden suites and concierge deluxe rooms, regardless of location, include concierge access.

Rooms at the BoardWalk Villas

The sunny seaside accommodations of the Villas come in a variety of shapes and sizes, each with a roomy balcony. These bright and colorful lodgings all offer a simple decor of casual comfort. Floral prints, brass fixtures, and gleaming white woodwork are reminiscent of the family vacation cottage at the beach. Ceiling fans, large tiled baths, and cozy creature comforts will have you feeling right at home.

The studio features a single king bed and a queen sleeper/sofa. A small wet bar provides refrigerator, microwave oven, and coffeemaker. Request a toaster from housekeeping, if you like. Some studios also offer a child-size daybed, providing enough sleeping space for four adults and one child.

The spacious one-bedroom vacation home is one of our favorite accommodations at Disney. It is the perfect place for a small family, a romantic escape, or both. These villas each feature a complete kitchen with dishwasher, toaster, blender, range, refrigerator, and enough equipment to cook just about any meal you might desire. The living area features an entertainment center with VCR and TV as well as several chairs and a pull-out queen sleeper. Let's not leave out the breakfast bar, dining area, washer and dryer, or the rest of this splendid place. The master bedroom's king bed adjoins the tiled bath and its Jacuzzi tub. This villa's comfortable 720 square feet and its location at the BoardWalk make it one of the World's most attractive accommodations.

By adding a connecting studio to a one-bedroom vacation home, you'll get a two-bedroom. The Grand Villa is a luxurious, three-bedroom apartment. It includes two baths, a living area with sleeper/sofa, dining room, complete kitchen, master bedroom with a four-poster king, and a large Jacuzzi tub.

Room Rates as of 2004 for the BoardWalk Villas (prices include taxes)

Accommodation	Value Season	Regular Season	Peak Season	Holiday Season
Studio	$322	$367	$439	$500
One-bedroom Villa	$435	$485	$538	$636
Two-bedroom Villa	$608	$786	$992	$1,126
Three-bedroom Grand Villa	$1,472	$1,684	$1,890	$2,135

Transportation and Convenience

Located in our favorite corner of Walt Disney World, the BoardWalk shares the same transportation system as the Yacht and the Beach Clubs and the Swan and Dolphin. Whether by foot, bus, or boat, you'll feel right next door to every Disney destination.

- @ To Disney-MGM Studios: short boat trip from the Promenade Pier or pleasant footpath
- @ To Epcot: short walk or boat from Promenade Pier
- @ To Magic Kingdom, the Animal Kingdom, Downtown Disney, Typhoon Lagoon, Blizzard Beach: direct bus

Dining at the BoardWalk

Dining choices here at the BoardWalk are so good that you might not care to venture elsewhere for a meal. But if you do, be ready to make a decision, because there are more than two dozen good restaurants within walking distance.

At the BoardWalk, try the fine dining and imaginative cuisine of the Flying Fish Cafe. This is one of the World's hottest places for a great meal and one not to miss. Spoodles and its "cuisine of the sun" is another outstanding BoardWalk eatery. Featured here is an excellent breakfast menu. Dinner at Spoodles means a wonderful Mediterranean cuisine, a tasty selection of tapas, and wood-fired pizzas. There's more along the BoardWalk: Try the super sandwiches, pastas, and salads at ESPN Club or the Big River Grille & Brewing Works' pleasing selection of grilled entrées, ribs, salads, gourmet burgers, and five hand-crafted beers. For more detailed information and reviews of these and other Disney eateries, see chapter 6.

The BoardWalk also offers twenty-four-hour room service, delivering food from its variety of restaurants. If what you feel like eating isn't on the menu, ask for it. Room service also features a sumptuous assortment of themed "amenities baskets" such as might be left in your room while you are out. Just a few of these treats include a chef's special chocolate turndown, elaborate welcome baskets, and cookies and milk.

The BoardWalk Promenade also features an interesting and often amusing selection of treats more suited to a nibble, a quick lunch, or snack. The BoardWalk Bakery will tempt you with muffins, bagels, croissants, and a luscious offering of pastries. The Bakery also manages a selection of juices, coffee, milk, espresso, and cappuccino: the perfect continental breakfast. Seashore Sweets is the Promenade's old-fashioned sweet shop. Saltwater taffy, ice cream, and a selection of beverages and coffees make this a place to check out. Spoodles sidewalk cafe even has an "express" pizza window, open from noon to midnight.

In the evening, along the Promenade are a host of vendors and carts offering an entertaining variety of treats: popcorn, hot dogs, chicken fingers, fried onion rings, shaved ice cones, crêpes-on-a-stick, and fresh fruits and juices. There's even BoardWalk Joe's coffee wagon with a variety of outstanding specialty coffees and pastries (hours vary seasonally).

Lounges at the BoardWalk

The BelleVue Room is the Inn's 1930s-style sitting room. Drop in here for a flight of single-malt scotch, small-batch bourbons, or Grand Marnier. Cozy, comfortable, and quiet, this full-service bar is open from 11 A.M. to midnight, with the nostalgic music and radio shows of the 1930s. Leaping Horse Libations is the pool lounge at the Villas. Looking more like a carousel, the Leaping Horse offers an assortment of sandwiches and alcoholic or nonalcoholic specialty drinks.

Down on the boardwalk, there's dancing every night at Atlantic Dance, and next door, you'll find the zany antics of dueling pianists at Jellyroll's. For more on these clubs and after-dark activities at the BoardWalk Promenade, see page 295.

Shops at the BoardWalk

Adjacent to the lobby is Dundy's Sundries, the place for BoardWalk logo merchandise and the usual variety of film, souvenirs, and gifts. The Promenade's Screen Door General Store is just the place for packaged drinks, snacks, and a modest selection of groceries. Thimbles and Threads is the BoardWalk's source for swimwear and resort apparel, while character merchandise can be found at the Character Carnival.

For the serious collector and interested browser alike, Wyland Gallery displays and sells a truly amazing collection of stunning artwork. Both sculptures and murals here are not to be missed.

Recreational Activities at the BoardWalk

- Luna Park swimming area with the 250-foot-long Keister Koaster waterslide and large pool

- Two quiet pools

- Three hot tub spas, one at each pool area

- Muscles and Bustles Health and Fitness Center

- Children's playground at Luna Park

- Harbor Club (children's activity center)

- Bicycle rentals at the Villas Community Hall

- Surrey rentals on the BoardWalk Promenade (four-wheeled pedal cars for two, four, or six persons)

- Two lighted tennis courts (equipment and lessons available)

- Rentals at Villas Community Hall: video movies, bikes, pool floats

- Fantasia Gardens miniature golf (see page 354 for details)

- BoardWalk fireworks cruise (see page 356)

- Sideshow Games video arcade

Our Impressions of the BoardWalk

- The Inn is luxurious and romantic—a first-class establishment in every way.

- The Villas offer unique and comfortably homelike accommodations. The one-bedroom villa is a real gem.

- Overall, this resort is really something special: beautifully themed, romantic, and exciting. There is so much to do here that you could keep busy without ever visiting a single theme park. One of Disney's premier destinations.

Recommendations for Disney's Boardwalk

- For couples with children, try a one-bedroom villa.

- Try a one-bedroom villa or studio to save money on meals. Look for off-season specials.

- If you want a room with a Jacuzzi, go for a one-bedroom villa, junior suite, garden suite, Steeplechase, or Sonora.

- Be sure to call housekeeping and request nightly turndown service.

Romance at the BoardWalk

- @ Overall theming ♥♥♥♥
- @ King bed at the Inn ♥♥♥
- @ A stay at the Innkeeper's Club ♥♥♥♥
- @ A garden suite ♥♥♥♥
- @ Dinner at the Flying Fish ♥♥♥
- @ Rent a surrey for two and ride around the lake ♥♥♥
- @ Dancing at Atlantic Dance ♥
- @ A nightcap and radio show at the BelleVue Room ♥♥♥
- @ A late-night swim at the quiet pool or hot tub ♥♥♥
- @ A drink and appetizer on the outside patio of Atlantic Dance ♥♥
- @ Breakfast in bed ♥♥♥♥
- @ IllumiNations from the second-floor outside balcony of Atlantic Dance ♥♥

The Walt Disney World Swan and Dolphin

These fantastic resorts are the product of Michael Eisner's unwillingness to settle for less. When he came aboard as Disney CEO, Eisner insisted on something other than the structures planned for this site. "Come meet my architect," he told the planners. And of course, he was talking about the world-renowned Michael Graves. What ensued was an architectural competition, and the result was these unique resorts.

The Swan and the Dolphin are perfectly aligned, set together like sisters and neatly nestled between Epcot and the Disney-MGM Studios. Separate, yet part of a greater whole, they share something special. The corals and aquas of their exteriors, their giant murals, and the perfect convergence of shapes tell us that there is a juncture happening here. These fantastic structures were designed from the ground up to occupy each other's space, to be seen together and from each other.

The theme of these resorts is fantasy and fun. Everything from the 47-foot swans perched atop one resort to the nine-story cascading waterfall at the other serves to evoke a feeling of whimsy and delight. The Swan and Dolphin seems to be a fantasy that is bigger and bolder than life. A visit after dark will work a magic spell.

Resort landscaping is beautiful, elaborate, and integral to the confluence of the two structures. Date palms, magnolias, and flower gardens

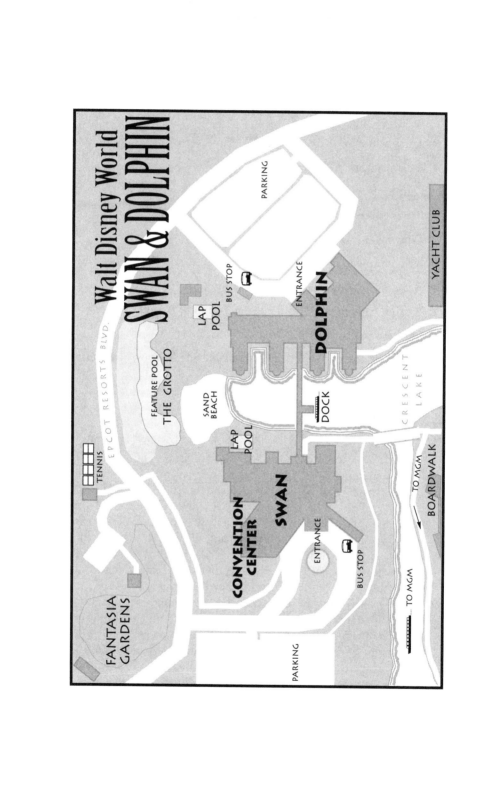

abound. Driveways, walkways, and footpaths are all essential elements in a big and beautiful picture.

Each resort has its own Olympic lap pool with hot tub, and together they share The Grotto. This 3-acre water playground features a large meandering pool, rocky waterfalls, secluded hot tubs, a water volleyball court, a restaurant and bar, a sand beach, and paddleboat rentals. Feature pools don't get much better than this.

The Swan and the Dolphin are owned by the same company, and though neither is a Disney resort, you'll hardly notice. Like the Disney Resorts, both the Swan and the Dolphin offer the Extra Magic Hour as well as the Ultimate Hopper Pass. About the only difference is that the Swan and Dolphin resort card can only be used for charging at these resorts. Otherwise, you'll enjoy virtually all the benefits of staying at a Disney resort: preferred tee times, same-day dinner reservations, and guaranteed park admission, to mention only a few. They feature first-class, deluxe accommodations and services typical of the world's finest hotels. And what's more, they are right in the middle of all the Disney magic.

The Swan was the first resort at Disney that we visited after our kids had grown up and left home. We hadn't been to Disney in more than ten years. We'd never even seen Epcot, and Disney-MGM Studios had just opened. We had no idea what to expect and were ready for just about anything. What we got was a few days of intimate and relaxing fun. We had a wonderful time exploring the theme parks, and we had an even more memorable time at this classy resort. We enjoyed hot tubs, swimming, and fine dining, all accented with occasional touches of Disney magic. We were hooked. And while we didn't know it at the time, this was the beginning of a Disney adventure that would result in the first edition of this book.

On that first trip, we slowed our car as we approached the resorts. We marveled at the ornate cast-iron street lamps and the rows of magnolias and palms. Above and around us loomed two buildings, the likes of which we'd never seen before. The Dolphin features a towering pyramid right in its middle, while the Swan has a unique arched roof upon which sit huge twin swans.

So intriguing are these places that when you arrive, you may feel more like exploring than registering. The tropical theme of the grounds and buildings are carried gracefully into their interiors. In the Swan's lobby, a fountain of swans and a flock of parrot chandeliers are but a few of the many amusing details. The Dolphin's rotunda-style lobby lies under a towering, ten-story fabric tent. Hallways, windows, and porticos in both resorts are all in perfect symmetry. This confluence, we were to discover, is one of the essentials of Michael Graves' design.

Rooms at the Swan and Dolphin

A dozen years and nearly a dozen visits after our first stay, we returned to a Swan that now enjoys completely redecorated rooms. (We have been told that during 2003 rooms at the Dolphin will enjoy an identical upgrade.)

Our guest room was a habitable work of art, every element of which had been completely redesigned by the hotel's original architect. Entering our room, we were struck by its lightness and airiness. The view onto Epcot was dazzling, and the casual maple furnishings were beautiful, yet inviting. Dresser handles, chairs, and stylized metallic lamps were all in perfect harmony. These elements and the room's pale tropical pastels of coral and aqua gave it a refreshing and restful sense of simplicity.

The fluffy white comforter and piles of feather pillows made us feel as though we'd arrived on a cloud. And after one blissful night's sleep, we knew we had. Few hotels anywhere can boast mattresses as comfortable as the Heavenly Beds of these resorts. One night here and you will be forever spoiled.

Swan and Dolphin guest rooms are not only beautiful, restful, and sublimely comfortable, but they are functional as well. Two vanity areas, mini-butler, a coffeemaker (with coffee), a useful desk, and ample drawer space make a stay here effortless. Two-line telephones with data ports are standard, as are iron and ironing board.

Rooms at the Swan are available with either a single king-size bed or double queens, and rooms at the Dolphin have either one king bed or two double beds. The king room at both resorts features a pull-out sleeper sofa, while the double room features a lounge chair and ottoman. Roll-out beds are available only at the Swan.

Although only some rooms at these resorts have balconies, all have interesting views. Some offer thrilling vistas of Epcot and Illumi-Nations; others overlook Disney/MGM Studios. There are pool views and lake views, but there really aren't any bad views, simply better ones. These sister hotels are meant to be seen from each other, and the variety of views provides an interesting insight into the intriguing architecture of Michael Graves.

Our favorite room at the Dolphin is the Premier King View. Located on the end corners of the hotel's wings, these unique rooms look out in two directions and provide an unmatched view of the lake, the Swan, Epcot, and Disney's BoardWalk. Each has a king-size bed and twin balconies. At $425 during the brief regular season, this room enjoys many specials during the remainder of the year.

It is important to note that value season at the Swan and Dolphin is considerably longer than at Disney resorts. It runs from early to mid-

Room Rates as of 2003 for the Swan and Dolphin Resorts (prices include taxes)

Accommodation	Value Season	Peak Season
Standard View	$378	$407
Lake View	$407	$457
Resort View, no balcony	$440	$485
Resort View, balcony	$474	$545
Club Level (concierge)	$507	$579

January and from May 1 to the end of the third week in December. This includes the entire summer.

Room rates also include a $10-per-night resort service fee, which includes free local calls, a high-speed Internet connection, health club membership, and *USA Today* newspaper, Mondays through Fridays.

Transportation and Convenience

The Swan and the Dolphin enjoy the same wonderful transportation that serves the Yacht and the Beach Clubs and the BoardWalk. Both nearby Epcot and Disney-MGM can be reached by boat from a dock on the walkway between these resorts or by foot, along pleasant walkways. The BoardWalk Promenade is but a few steps away, and all other Disney destinations are via direct buses, leaving from the bus stops at the front entrance of each resort.

Concierge Service and Suites at the Swan and Dolphin

Both resorts feature private concierge areas. The Royal Beach Club is located on the exclusive east end of the twelfth floor at the Swan, while the seventy-seven spacious and lavishly decorated guest suites of the Dolphin Tower Club are located in the Dolphin Tower. Concierge level rooms feature a host of luxurious toiletries, plush bathrobes, hairdryers, special stationery, and coffeemakers.

In both concierge lounges, a continental breakfast is served each morning, and hors d'oeuvres and cocktails begin before dinner, with coffee and desserts later in the evening. Alcoholic beverages are served at an honor bar. All in all, you'll receive a day's worth of delights, and the dedicated concierge staffs will be available to assist with all of your reservations and special needs.

There is a variety of suite designs at the Swan, and each has something unique to offer. The studio suite is the most affordable. Each studio comes with a lavishly furnished bedroom, a king bed, desk, and sofa and chairs. The ample living room and dining area feature a round table and chairs. Cloth robes, private bar, and live plants are a few of the indulgences.

The Swan's two presidential suites each feature more than 1,000 square feet. The multi-room suites have a marble entryway, grand piano, fully stocked bar, king bed, whirlpool tub, and a full kitchen stocked with assorted beverages. Furnishings are lavishly extravagant. Even for us, it's hard to imagine traveling in this kind of style.

The Dolphin boasts that it offers more suites than any other resort at Walt Disney World. This may be true, but many of the suites would be better for business purposes. The two types of suites worth mentioning are the junior and the presidential. The junior suites are in various places throughout the resort. Each consists of a parlor connected to a regular resort room with either a single king bed or two doubles. The parlor offers a sitting area with a pull-out sofa bed and several comfortable chairs. You might not feel the need for an extra room, but it is a good place for the kids if they are with you. During the brief regular season, a junior suite will cost around $700 per night. Most of the year, the same suite is about $625.

There are four presidential suites at the Dolphin. Each has been extravagantly decorated with its own exotic personality. At nearly 3,000 square feet, each suite is larger than many private homes. Named Los Presidentes, the Pharaoh's Suite, the Emperor's Suite, and Caesar's Suite, each is the final word in luxury. Service even includes a round-the-clock butler. These two-bedroom suites offer a large entertainment center, gold-plated bathroom fixtures, ten telephones, four VCRs, and a fully stocked kitchen.

Dining at the Swan and Dolphin

Dining at these resorts is exceptional. Whether you stay at the Swan or Dolphin, you'll be close enough to eat at either. And with memorable eating places at the neighboring BoardWalk and the Yacht and the Beach Clubs as well as those at nearby Epcot, your choices will be nearly limitless. For convenient, varied, and outstanding dining, this is *the* corner of Walt Disney World to visit.

Restaurants at the Swan and Dolphin cover all the bases. The Swan offers two inviting table-service eateries. The Garden Grove serves breakfast and lunch in a pleasant garden gazebo. At dinner, it becomes Gulliver's Grill, with seafood, prime rib, and chicken, as well as a unique, nightly buffet complete with Disney characters. The Swan's other offering is Palio, with its upscale Italian dining and a wonderfully romantic atmosphere. Featuring outstanding food and strolling musicians, Palio is one of our favorite dining spots at Disney. If you enjoy sushi or tempura, you'll want to visit Kimonos, a beautiful and stylishly created retreat that features a cozy Asian ambience.

At the Dolphin, the centerpiece of fine dining is Shula's Steakhouse. We can't offer enough superlatives to cover this, one of the finest dining experiences at Disney (or anywhere).

For eating fun, there's the Dolphin Fountain, a 1950s-style soda shop with a menu of American classics. For more information and our reviews of these restaurants, see chapter 6.

Both resorts also offer fast food. At the Swan, you'll find the Splash Grill and Deli, with a selection of pizza, sandwiches, and snacks. At the Dolphin, there's Tubbi's Buffeteria, which features a selection of convenience foods for all three meals. New at Tubbi's is a variety of complete dinners, such as roast chicken and grilled steak, prepared to order. Tubbi's even has a small convenience store with a variety of snacks, beverages, and sundries.

For continental-style breakfasts, try the comfortable lobby lounge of either resort for coffee, juice, and a selection of pastries and muffins. Both the Swan and Dolphin also feature twenty-four-hour room service, with large menus of snacks, complete meals, and beverages. It's the perfect choice for breakfast in bed or intimate, fine dining in your own room.

Several dining changes are in the works for the Dolphin. A fine-dining seafood restaurant, as yet unnamed, will open during late 2003 or early 2004, and the Coral Café will be replaced by a restaurant that will feature fresh-cooked meals at a variey of food stations.

Lounges at the Swan and Dolphin

The lobby lounges of both resorts offer a selection of wines and spirits as well as espresso and cappuccino. The Copa Banana is the Dolphin's "nightclub," and during busier times, you might find live entertainment here. Dance the night away to the rhythm of the islands and enjoy a fruitful selection of tropical drinks. Shula's Bar at the Dolphin and Kimonos at the Swan are two other lounge offerings. Both feature a large selection of wines, beers, and cocktails.

Shops at the Swan and Dolphin

Disney's Cabanas is the Swan's souvenir and Disney character merchandise store. It also offers a large selection of casual men's and women's sportswear and a small variety of sundries. There are four shops in the lobby of the Dolphin. From character and resort logo merchandise to gourmet chocolates, jewelry and fine apparel, these shops should provide some interesting browsing and even something special to celebrate your visit here.

Services Available at the Swan and Dolphin

- Valet parking, $10 per day
- Full bell service
- Valet and laundry service
- Beauty salon
- Concierge desk and Disney guest services desk
- Nightly turndown service, by request
- Pay-per-view movies
- Refrigerators, upon request, $12 a day

Recreational Activities at the Swan and Dolphin

- Lap pools with spas at each resort
- The Grotto, a three-acre feature pool area
- Kiddie pools
- White-sand beach with swan paddleboat rentals
- Complimentary health clubs
- Jogging and walking path
- Tennis club and basketball court
- Camp Dolphin children's activity centers
- Video game rooms
- Fantasia Gardens miniature golf

Recommendations for the Swan and Dolphin

- Reservations for these resorts are handled by Disney CRO at (407) W-DISNEY (934-7639); by Westin Reservations at (800) 228-3000; by Sheraton reservations at (800) 325-3535; and by the Swan/Dolphin reservation system at (800) 227-1500, and on the Swan/Dolphin Web site and the Sheraton, Westin, and Starwood Web sites (see appendix B).

- $ Become a Starwood Preferred Guest and accrue points toward vacations, enjoy special privileges, and get special offers. It's free to join online at www.spg.com.

- The Swan and Dolphin offer impressive discounts (based on availability) for teachers, nurses, government employees, and active military personnel. You must book directly through the hotel at (407) 227-1500.

@ After check-in, drop by the Disney guest services desk to pick up a "World Update," your admission passes, and the theme park guidemaps.

@ After you arrive, call Guest Requests and ask for bathrobes.

@ Reserve a room with a view of IllumiNations.

Romance at the Swan and Dolphin

@ Resort theming ♥♥♥

@ Room amenities ♥♥♥♥

@ Dining at Shula's Steakhouse or Palio ♥♥♥

@ Breakfast on your balcony ♥♥♥

@ Hot tubs ♥♥♥

@ Evening walks to BoardWalk, Epcot countries, and the Yacht and Beach Clubs ♥♥

@ Watching IllumiNations from your balcony ♥♥♥

@ Premier King View room ♥♥♥

@ Beach hammock, under the stars ♥♥♥

@ Breakfast in bed ♥♥♥♥

Our Impressions of the Swan and Dolphin

@ These are beautiful and fanciful resorts. Both seem a bit more adult-oriented than the Disney Resorts, and we think this is a good thing.

@ The most comfortable beds at Disney, hands down.

@ A beach, beautiful pools, hot tubs: you have it all at these resorts.

@ These resorts are right in the middle of our favorite corner of Walt Disney World, near great dining, entertainment, theme parks, and nightlife.

@ We prefer the Swan but only because of its two queen beds (versus the Dolphin's doubles) and because it's a smaller hotel.

Disney's Caribbean Beach Resort

This lovely resort will lend your Disney vacation the colorful and festive flavors of the tropics. From its white-sand beaches to its lush and

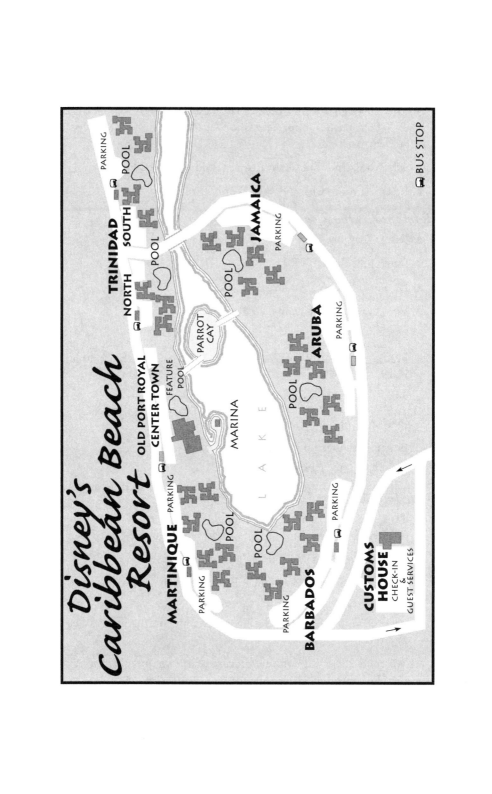

Disney's Caribbean Beach Resort

OLD PORT ROYAL
CENTER TOWN

MARTINIQUE

TRINIDAD
NORTH   SOUTH

PARKING

POOL

POOL

POOL

FEATURE
POOL

PARROT
CAY

MARINA

L A K E

POOL

JAMAICA

PARKING

PARKING

ARUBA

POOL

PARKING

POOL

BARBADOS

PARKING

PARKING

CUSTOMS
HOUSE
CHECK-IN
&
GUEST SERVICES

BUS STOP

verdant foliage, the flowering scents of the islands are in the air: jasmine, mango, and hibiscus. Your Caribbean vacation will be in one of this resort's five "island villages," all of which surround Barefoot Bay, a 50-acre lake. Each of these "tin-roofed" villages enjoys its own unique personality of bright tropical colors and whimsical gingerbread. Their names evoke the exotic ports of the Caribbean: Aruba, Martinique, Jamaica, Barbados, and Trinidad.

You'll begin your Caribbean Beach Resort journey with check-in at the Customs House, Disney's charming re-creation of an old-world island hotel lobby. Ceiling fans, potted palms, and shuttered windows are just a few of its details. Old Port Royale Centertown, Disney's bustling West Indies village, is the resort's central hub and is home for the Caribbean's shops, restaurant, food court, water playground, and marina. Enjoy a soak in the hot tub or a dip in the pool, hop on a bike, rent a boat, or lounge around the Banana Cabana pool bar to the strains of Jimmy Buffet. It's a fun place to be.

In the middle of the lake is Parrot Cay, an island connected by footbridges to the villages on one side of the lake and Old Port Royale Centertown on the other. Winding paths, quiet sitting areas, three lovely gazebos, and a picnic area are all set against its lush backdrop of singing birds, dense bamboo, and stately palms. It's the perfect place for a quiet breakfast or a romantic evening stroll.

The colors, the foliage, and the ambience of this resort will relax you. Take your time to savor this place and your time here. The Caribbean Beach Resort does exactly what the best of resorts anywhere do and what Disney resorts do better than most: It takes you above the everyday and transports you to that unforgettable place called "vacation."

Rooms at the Caribbean Beach

The recently refurbished rooms are bright and colorful. Floral bedspreads and brightly colored drapes lend a tropical air of island excitement, while a colorful and lively wall banner with an undersea theme seems to bring the tropical oceans right into the room. Caribbean accommodations feature either a single king bed or twin doubles. All of the king bedrooms at the Caribbean can connect to rooms with double beds. It's the perfect arrangement if you're visiting with your children or grandchildren.

On our recent Caribbean visit, we enjoyed a king room in the island village of Aruba. It was located on the corner of a building, giving our sitting area two windows, rather than the usual one. With curtains open, our room was exceptionally bright and airy.

Room Rates as of 2004 for Disney's
Caribbean Beach Resort (prices include taxes)

Accommodation	Value Season	Regular Season	Peak Season	Holiday Season
Standard View	$148	$161	$188	$205
Water View	$165	$177	$216	$233
King Bed	$165	$177	$216	$233

Our vanity area featured double sinks and a large mirror and even a privacy curtain. Plenty of room for both of us to get ready for an evening out. The bathroom, a bit on the small side, had the usual shower-tub combination. All rooms at the Caribbean Beach include coffeemakers and complimentary coffee.

Overall, we found our room pleasant and comfortable, and greatly enjoyed our time there. There are a small variety of views here. Water-view rooms overlook either the lake or the pool. Since pool views seem to look onto the walls that surround the pool areas, we suggest that if you are looking for a water view that you opt for one of the lake; ask at check-in. Standard-view rooms feature views of either the courtyard or the parking lots. We suggest that you ask for (and be prepared to wait for) a courtyard view. Ours was quiet and beautiful, and it greatly enhanced our Caribbean Beach Resort visit.

Transportation and Convenience

❧ To all Disney destinations: by bus

❧ An "internal" bus for riding to Old Port Royale Centertown and the Customs House.

Dining at the Caribbean Beach

Recent changes at the Caribbean have worked well to correct what was once this resort's only weak point: food. With the opening of Shutters, this resort now has a real restaurant, one that features very good food at a moderate price. Shutters is open for dinner from 5 P.M. to 10 P.M. For our take on Shutters, see chapter 6.

The Old Port Royale food court is called Market Street, and it is a rather cute little avenue of food shops. Decorated with palms, colorful kites, and other Caribbean artifacts, these exotic storefronts come complete with balconies and "roofs." The effect is delightful. Counter-service shops have names such as Cinnamon Bay Bakery, Montego's Deli, and Bridgetown Broiler. Fare here includes a variety of breakfast offerings, burgers, deli sandwiches, pizza, roasted chicken, barbecued ribs, and lots more. It has a pleasant outside dining area and is open from 7 A.M. to midnight. Although there's no room service here at Disney's Caribbean Beach, there is a delivery service available for pizza, sandwiches, and beverages.

Shops at the Caribbean Beach

Old Port Royale Centertown has several shops. The Straw Market's selection of Caribbean Beach logo merchandise and tropical apparel is worth a look. Next door at the Calypso Trading Post, you'll find the usual variety of Disney character merchandise, postcards and stamps, books and newspapers, and a variety of snacks, souvenirs, and "sundries" such as sunscreen and nonprescription medications.

Recreational Activities at the Caribbean Beach

Recreational activities are one of the Caribbean's strong suits. In addition to a themed main pool, there are six quiet pools, one at each of the island villages. The central pool at Old Port Royale boasts a spa and a kiddie pool. It looks like an "old" Spanish fort, complete with turrets, cannons, and waterfalls. A short slide runs from the ramparts to the water. The pool is exactly the kind of thing that we love so much about Disney resorts: It seems more like a movie set than a hotel pool. Unfortunately, the hot tub here is rather small. Although the Caribbean offers sparkling white-sand beaches, no lake swimming is allowed. With chaise lounges, cabanas, and some nice hammocks, the beaches are attractive places to catch either sunlight or moonbeams.

- One themed pool with kiddie pool and six quiet pools
- One hot tub
- Rental boats and bikes, including surrey quadri-cycles
- Video and game arcade
- Walking and jogging path
- Beach volleyball

Our Impressions of the Caribbean Beach Resort

- Even by Disney standards, this resort (and its rooms) seems exceptionally clean and well kept. Housekeeping service is better than average.
- Guest services is located far away in the Customs House.
- No table-service restaurant for breakfast; food court only.

❧ A car would be of some advantage here, especially for traveling to other resort areas to dine.

❧ This is a very attractive resort. Grounds are lavishly landscaped and rooms are themed and comfortable.

Recommendations for Disney's Caribbean Beach Resort

❧ Barbados and Trinidad South are a bit far from the central resort area, and Trinidad North and Martinique are closest. We prefer either Jamaica or Aruba. Either is a short walk from the central area, a walk that takes you across Parrot Cay. We found this stroll pleasant and, in the evenings, even a bit romantic.

❧ There are no passenger elevators here, so if you have a problem with climbing stairs to a second-floor room, be sure to request one on the ground floor.

Romance at the Caribbean Beach

❧ Resort theming ♥♥

❧ Courtyard-view room ♥♥

❧ King bed resort room ♥♥

❧ Early picnic breakfast on Parrot Cay ♥♥

❧ Late-night swim at a quiet pool ♥♥

❧ Beach hammock by starlight ♥♥♥♥

❧ Evening stroll around the resort ♥♥

The Animal Kingdom Resorts

This resort area features Disney's Animal Kingdom Lodge. Unlike anything else at Disney (or anywhere else we know of), this exotic resort is surrounded by wild animal habitats and takes Disney resort theming to an entirely new level.

Of course, the resorts of this area are all near the Animal Kingdom, but the All-Stars and Coronado are also particularly close to Disney-MGM Studios, the BoardWalk, Blizzard Beach, and Fantasia miniature golf courses. Transportation to all Disney attractions from these resorts is by bus.

Disney's Animal Kingdom Lodge

Half a dozen years ago, a team of Disney Imagineers ventured into darkest Africa. Their journey of discovery took them to some of the

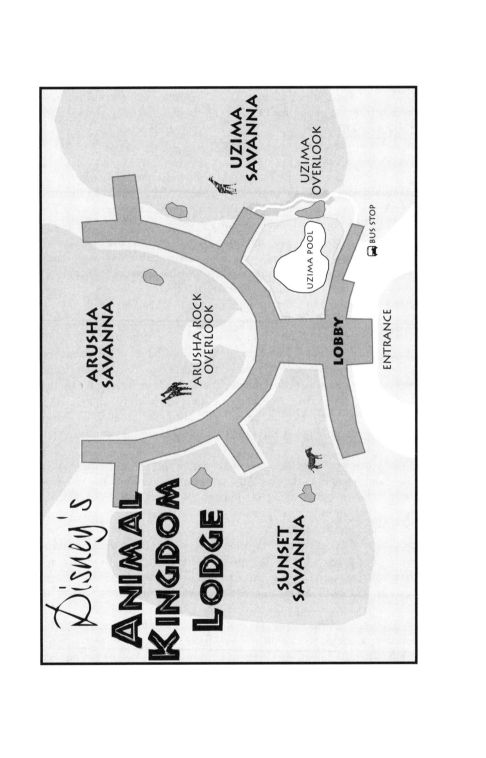

world's most unusual vacation destinations: lodges deep in the wilds of Africa, hidden among the untamed creatures of this vast continent. Their travels brought them to such famous places as Treetops, Mala-Mala, and the Matetsi Lodge. When they returned, their adventures became the inspiration for Disney's most ambitious resort project ever, the Animal Kingdom Lodge. Now, this incredible vision has been realized. What was once merely a dream is now a very real, fantasy oasis of luxury and adventure.

As you approach the Lodge, you'll first glimpse its thatched roof, standing majestically above the surrounding African veldt. As the road winds upward, the low-lying log structure comes briefly into view. The Lodge seems somehow smaller than you might have imagined, but as quickly as it appears, you find yourselves in the cooling shade of its huge, thatched porte cochere. Porters in safari garb are busy whisking away your luggage as you enjoy the first tangible sensation of having arrived someplace truly unique. Through the front entrance, you enter a space far greater and far more stunning than you had expected.

Arriving at the Animal Kingdom Lodge seems both exciting and transporting. Once inside, you discover that what appeared from the outside to be ground level was in fact, the Lodge's third floor. You enter, gazing upon a vast space of hand-carved furnishings, inlaid floors, and exotic African fabrics. Above, herds of antelope carvings "stampede" across countless rows of eucalyptus balcony railings. High above them hang colorful chandeliers fashioned from Zulu battle shields. And far above it all, a huge thatched ceiling is laid over great, arched timbers.

At the far end of this enormous space, you see a soaring wall of glass and beyond it, the vast African savanna. Nearby is the towering mud fireplace known as Ogun's Firepit. The comfortable rockers overlooking the savanna have already attracted other guests contentedly enjoying this inviting space.

After these dizzying first moments, you become aware of even more: a suspension bridge that spans this immense space, vines that appear to cling to the huge expanse of glass, and everywhere the musical sounds of a small stream that bubbles up from the lobby's wellspring and cascades away to places unseen. The exotic aromas of spices, herbs, and a smoky deliciousness stir your senses. You know now that this place is a celebration of all things African: art, culture, and cuisine. Only when costumed cast members from various African nations bid you "Welcome to Disney's Animal Kingdom Lodge," will you suddenly remember where you really are.

Yes, the Animal Kingdom Lodge is easily Disney's most magnificent resort creation. It's an ingenious creation in both architecture and atmosphere, and it's one that has been achieved with great care and an unwavering determination to be true to the source from which it all flows: the great land that is Africa. Everything here tells a story that is rich in the tribal lore of this exotic continent. From fabrics and sculptures to the intricate work of tribal artisans, this is a place that will simply transport you. But the stunning design of the Animal Kingdom Lodge is not its only impressive feature. In fact, it may not even be what's most impressive about it.

This resort is surrounded on three sides by a landscape that has been meticulously created to resemble the savannas of Central Africa. Its rocky outcroppings, water holes, and Yellow Flame trees are merely the backdrop for the nearly two hundred African animals that inhabit it: giraffes, zebra, kudus, wildebeest, and gazelle. Yes, this place is more than a resort, more than a celebration of the mysteries of this great continent. The Animal Kingdom Lodge is alive with the very adventure of Africa.

The footprint of the lodge is the traditional semi-circle of the African "kraal," or village. From the central lobby, hallways called "trails" make their way to lodging areas with names such as Giraffe, Zebra, and Kudu. Even the halls are impressively decorated: Zulu war shields, sconce lighting made of tribal drums, engaging hut-like areas with carved posts and woven *euki* "roofs," and everywhere the patterns and fabrics of Africa. Along these trails, you'll find spacious overlooks of the surrounding savannas. You'll certainly want to explore them all to experience every unique vantage point. It won't take you long to realize that with the Animal Kingdom Lodge, Disney has taken resort theming to a completely new level of realism and adventure.

Rooms at Disney's Animal Kingdom Lodge

Accommodations here at the Lodge range from stunning to startlingly beautiful. Each of the guest rooms is a veritable showcase of African craftsmanship: hand-carved furniture from Zimbabwe, vivid Kuba- and Kente-inspired fabrics, a decorative canopy of mosquito netting, and a balcony that overlooks one of the resort's three wild-animal reserves. Handcrafted headboards tell stories of Africa, such as the butterfly mask design, a tribal African symbol used to call for rain. Decor includes spear-like lamps, handmade baskets, a carved mirror, and subtle, hidden Mickeys. Natural earth hues of henna and rust combine with accents of jewel tones to create an exotic yet restful ambience. The spacious double vanity of each marble bath features a wall covering that charts the ancient trade routes of Africa and every shower-tub enjoys a lavish treatment of patterned tiles.

There are two levels of rooms here at the lodge: deluxe and standard. Standard rooms occupy the lower floors and are about the same

Room Rates as of 2004 for Disney's Animal Kingdom Lodge (prices include taxes)

Accommodation	Value Season	Regular Season	Peak Season	Holiday Season
Standard	$222	$266	$322	$361
Standard Water/Pool	$290	$329	$385	$436
Standard Savanna	$307	$351	$407	$435
Deluxe Water/Pool	$318	$368	$435	$496
Deluxe Savanna	$373	$429	$496	$568
Kilimanjaro Club	$474	$535	$608	$680

size as those at the Wilderness Lodge (344 square feet). Deluxe rooms are a bit larger, about the size found at deluxe resorts such as the Yacht Club (381 square feet).

Although deluxe rooms are on upper floors, don't assume that they provide better views of the animals below. In fact, from what we have seen, balconies on lower floors may make even better places from which to see the wildlife. It's important to note that while most rooms provide views of the wild animal landscapes, some do not. These offer either obstructed views or ones that overlook the front of the resort or the pool.

Luxurious Animal Kingdom Lodge accommodations feature either two queen beds or a single king. Deluxe rooms also have a daybed, providing sleeping arrangements for a fifth guest. There are also 327 rooms with a single queen and bunk beds, an inviting combination for a family visit to Disney's Africa.

Kilimanjaro Club–Animal Kingdom Lodge Concierge Services

If you're the kind of traveler who enjoys this splendid service, you'll certainly relish your stay here. Of the Kilimanjaro Club's fifty-five rooms, fifteen are located on the private-access sixth floor, overlooking either the pool or one of the three wild animal savannas. The remaining rooms are on the fifth floor and enjoy exceptional vistas of wildlife areas. All Kilimanjaro Club rooms feature special amenities such as bathrobes and upgraded toiletries.

The plush concierge lounge is located on a large sixth-floor balcony and provides a stunning view of the lobby below. As concierge guests, you'll enjoy pre-arrival planning that will ensure everything from hard-to-get dining reservations to tickets to La Nouba. And after you arrive, you'll find a staff dedicated to helping you plan every facet of your Disney vacation. Kilimanjaro Club guest privileges include use of the luxurious lounge and day-long offerings of food and drink. Continental breakfast, midday snacks and drinks, afternoon tea, hors d'oeuvres and wine, and evening cordials make this a truly special experience. One thing we especially love here is the Club's automatic espresso machine. Every concierge lounge should have one.

The Kilimanjaro Club also offers its guests the incredible "Sunrise Safari." For about $50 ($25 for ages 3 to 9), you'll be taken to Disney's Animal Kingdom for an early morning Safari experience, with a breakfast in the park (park admission is required). No doubt, this is one of Disney's most exclusive offerings and one not to miss. We suggest that you call to make a reservation for this as soon as your club room reservation is secured. Call the Lodge at (407) 938-3000 and ask for the concierge desk.

Suites at the Animal Kingdom Lodge

Besides lavish theming and luxurious accommodations, suites here at the lodge provide both exceptional views of the wild-animal savannas and Kilimanjaro Club concierge privileges. The Royal Assante is this resort's presidential suite and it is Disney's largest and grandest. Both it and the vice presidential, the Royal Kuba, enjoy circular living rooms with thatched ceilings, fireplaces, and two large bedrooms. Each also features a Jacuzzi tub that provides a vista of the savanna below. Located on the resort's top floor on either side of the lobby's soaring window, these suites are Disney's last word in special and sublime accommodations. A stay in the Royal Assante begins around $2,169 per night.

The Animal Kingdom Lodge also features spacious one- and two-bedroom suites, each of which includes a parlor room with pull-out sofa bed. These are masterpieces of African craftsmanship and charm, and with specially chosen locations throughout the resort, each features an extraordinary view of a wild animal savanna. Any would be the perfect choice for a family visit to the Lodge. For a one-bedroom suite that would accommodate six, prices begin at $708 per night.

Transportation at Disney's Animal Kingdom Lodge

@ To all Disney destinations: by bus

Culinary Adventures at the Animal Kingdom Lodge

At the Lodge, the dinner hour is announced by a chorus of singing African cast members. As they make their way from high in the lobby to the village of restaurants on the ground floor, they will invite you to join them and partake in the exotic offerings of this resort's three unique restaurants.

Jiko ♥♥ is the signature eatery here at the Animal Kingdom Lodge. Its name means "the cooking place," and its cuisine features the fresh and innovative fusion of the many and exciting flavors of Africa. Jiko serves dinner in a stylish and trendy setting of pearlescent mosaics and wrought black iron. Boma is the Lodge's family, buffet-style restaurant. It features a large assortment for both breakfast and dinner. This beautiful eatery enjoys a village-like African decor, a candle-lit ambience, and eight onstage-cooking areas. For more information and greater detail about both Jiko and Boma, see chapter 6.

Of course, the Animal Kingdom Lodge also has an all-day, counter-service restaurant. Mara is named for one of Africa's fast-flowing rivers. With an open bakery and a cartoonish African ambience, it serves up not only the usual Disney fast foods but also a few enticing exotic dishes such as Tandoori chicken pizza and African stew. Animal Kingdom Lodge room service features a variety of delights from all three restaurants, serving from 6 A.M. to midnight each day.

Insider's Secret

The Animal Kingdom Lodge features the largest selection of South African wines anywhere in the world, outside of South Africa.

Lodge kitchens will also prepare an in-room romantic dining experience for two, the Savannah Package (about $100). With twenty-four-hour notice, this wonderful offering includes a lavish meal with wine and dessert, all served in your room or on your balcony, overlooking the wild places of this resort. It's intimate, romantic, and unforgettable.

Animal Kingdom Lodge Lounges

While you're here, you might wish to discover the wines of South Africa. Where the small river that runs from the lobby and cascades to the restaurants below, you'll find Victoria Falls, this resort's stylish and comfortable lounge. Enjoy its varieties of gourmet coffees and teas, international beers, full-service bar, and seemingly endless offerings of South African wines. Decor features drum-like barstools and plush leather seating. Victoria Falls is the perfect place for an aperitif or a nightcap of Africa's Amarula liqueur.

And, while you're enjoying a swim or a little sun, you might want to visit the thatched, poolside bar, Uzima Springs, and partake in its assortment of wines and cooling specialty drinks.

Shopping at the Zawadi Marketplace

This large and bustling marketplace features a stunning assortment of African arts, crafts, and apparel. Disney buyers must have had a lot of fun scouring Africa for this unusual treasure trove of woodcarvings, batiks, jewelry, tapestries, and much, much more. Zawadi's other offerings include a selection of clothing inspired by African tribal dress, an attractive line of Animal Kingdom Lodge logo merchandise, and such sundries as film, suncare products, and snacks. You might even drop in here just to watch African artisans practice their unique crafts. Zawadi Marketplace is more than just a store, it's a cultural encounter.

Special Activities and Recreation at Disney's Animal Kingdom Lodge

In addition to its exceptionally large Uzima Pool, two hot tubs, and a 67-foot water slide, the Animal Kingdom Lodge features an inviting assortment of activities for both adults and youngsters: hands-on arts and crafts, talks with expert animal curators and African cultural representatives, evening bonfires with African storytelling, and scheduled lodge tours. With small art galleries located throughout the resort, you'll want to take yourselves on a self-guided walking tour in search of the Bamileki duck, the Guro mask, or the Kotoko bronze gazelle.

But if you're like us, what you'll most want to see will be the animals. And you won't be disappointed. Enjoy a private "safari" from your own balcony or from one of the many well-chosen overlooks around the resort. After dark, specially Imagineered lighting bathes the savannas in a beautiful "moonglow" that enables guests to view animals late into the evening hours. It's pure magic.

Whether in the early hours of the morning or after the sun has set, you'll also want to venture out onto the savanna, to Arusha Rock, the Lodge's place for close-up animal encounters. Here you'll meet animal experts who will reveal the marvelous mysteries of the Lodge's wild inhabitants. It's both enjoyable and enlightening.

And, if you're "on safari" with your children, you'll want to be sure they enjoy their very own Disney adventure at Simba's Cubhouse children's activity center. While they enjoy dressing up in African costumes and making puppets, the two of you can be off on your African adventure for a romantic evening of fine dining at Jiko.

Recreation at Disney's Animal Kingdom Lodge

- One large swimming pool—Uzima Pool
- Two hot tubs
- Hakuna Matata children's play area

- Simba's Cubhouse children's activity center

- Pumba's Fun & Games video game arcade

- Zahanati fitness center (see page 366)

Our Impressions of the Animal Kingdom Lodge

- Like nothing we've ever seen before! It's awesome, magnificent, transporting, even thrilling. Disney's greatest resort achievement, and one of the greatest resort experiences anywhere.

- If you love Disney resorts, staying here is a must. If you can't stay here, by all means, make dinner reservations at Jiko or Boma (or both!) and come take a look. A crowning achievement. We wonder where can Disney go from here. Even if you are unable to get a room with a savanna view, rest assured. There are many places throughout the resort from which to enjoy the surrounding wildlife.

Recommendations for Disney's Animal Kingdom Lodge

- Reserve a savanna-view room. It's what this magnificent place is all about.

- After you arrive, be sure to check out the Lodge's "newspaper" for the list of activities featured during your visit.

- Don't forget to request the nightly turndown service

Romance at the Animal Kingdom Lodge

- Resort theming ♥♥♥♥

- Room theming ♥♥♥♥

- Breakfast on your balcony ♥♥

- Evening bonfire, storytelling, and watching the animals from Arusha Rock ♥♥♥

- Dinner at Jiko with wine pairing ♥♥

- A late-night hot tub ♥♥♥

- A stay at the Kilimanjaro Club and a "Sunrise Safari" ♥♥♥♥

- The Savanna Package romantic dinner on your balcony ♥♥♥♥

- A late-night glass of DieKraans port at Victoria Falls ♥♥♥

- After-dark, "moonglow" animal viewing from your balcony ♥♥♥

- The Sunset Overlook ♥♥♥

Disney's Coronado Springs Resort

In his quest for the fabled seven cities of Cibola, Spanish conquistador Francisco de Coronado should have come to Florida. While he wouldn't have found the legendary lost cities of gold, he would have discovered eighteen of the most fanciful resorts in the New World, one of which bears his name.

Disney's Coronado Springs features the flavor and architecture of the Southwestern U.S. and Mexico and is set on 125 wooded acres between Disney's MGM Studios and the Animal Kingdom. Spread lazily around Lago Dorado, a picturesque 16-acre lake, Coronado Springs is comprised of three "villages," each a unique taste of the old Southwest. Disney's first moderately priced resort to include a convention center and fine dining, Coronado Springs offers a colorful diversity of resort experiences all wrapped neatly into one.

If you arrive here with just the right amount of imagination, you'll find yourselves journeying to another place and time. The resort's entranceway leads across a small stone bridge and up to the central building's grand and tent-like porte cochere, where you will be welcomed by a costumed staff. This is El Centro, Coronado's hub of activity, and the home of its front desk, guest services, restaurants, shops, and convention center.

The cars and vans of arriving guests seem oddly out of time amid the palms and sun-washed terra cotta. Once inside, you are beneath the lobby's great tiled dome. White clouds float above on a blue painted sky. On the sunburst tile floor of the rotunda, a fountain whispers softly; beyond, through an expanse of glass and across the lake, you see what appears to be the ruins of an ancient Mayan pyramid, peeking above dense vegetation. The magic and mystery of this lost kingdom begin to take hold. The gentle gurgling of water and the sun-drenched atmosphere are Coronado Spring's stock-in-trade. Tile floors, Native American throw rugs, and massive wooden ceiling beams accent this great hacienda. Large chandeliers, tile-framed arches, and Spanish-style ironwork are all accented by splashes of aqua and corals.

Your Coronado Springs odyssey will take you through the varied geographic areas of southwestern North America. From the bustling, city-like Casitas to the coastal Cabanas and on to the arid arroyos of the Ranchos, the trip is both diverse and engaging. Throughout the resort are gaily-colored fountains set amid quiet and shaded plazas. Landscaping is typically Disney: perfect in every detail, relaxing in its ambience, and transporting in its effect. Cacti, palms, and the vegetation of the region all enhance the resort's motif.

The three- and four-story Casitas are adjacent to El Centro and, we think, most ideal for convention guests. Since they are adjacent to the central area, rooms here enjoy the greatest convenience to the

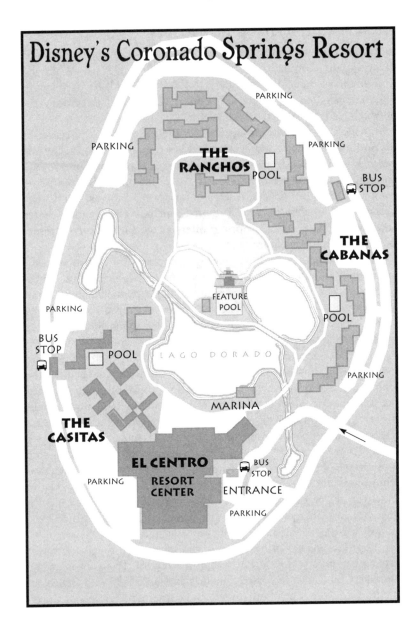

restaurants, shops, and guest services of Disney's Coronado Springs. These large, brightly colored haciendas most resemble a hotel and enjoy an urban and busy ambience. Everywhere, guests come and go through sun-splashed courtyards and flower-filled patios. The detailed architecture and landscaping transport the spirit to another time and place. The rushing waters of ornamental fountains, the palm-shaded plazas, and the iron-crested balconies complete the picture of this little south-of-the-border city.

Across the lake, Coronado Springs takes on yet another mood. Forgotten now is the hustle and bustle of El Centro. Here, a pleasant stroll away, across picturesque footbridges, you'll discover the quiet and enchanting countryside of southwestern North America.

Your journey will take you first to the small rocky cove of Lago Mar, around which are scattered the tin-roofed Cabanas. They are a picturesque celebration of coastal Mexico. Half of the rooms in these two-story, terra cotta bungalows enjoy stunning vistas of the lake, the ruins of the "ancient" pyramid, and at night, the dazzling lights of the central area. Life here in the Cabanas is leisurely and romantic.

Not far away, you'll come across this resort's exciting feature pool, the Dig Site. Here, surrounded by the ruins of a vanished civilization, an "ancient" Mayan pyramid appears only partially unearthed. A tangle of jungle vines seems intent on reclaiming it while water tumbles gently down its steep staircase and into the swimming pool that lies at its base. From somewhere behind, the Jaguar Flume water slide whooshes its riders beneath the steely gaze of a giant jungle cat and into the cool waters below.

In the shadow of this great pyramid lies a unique children's play area. One of its many features is a large sandbox where little archaeologists can dig to uncover Mayan antiquities. Other "excavations" amid these ruins include a large hot tub, arcade, and poolside bar and snack shop, Siesta's. The Dig Site even features a volleyball court and children's wading pond. It is the discovery of the Lost Kingdom of Gold come to life.

Past the Dig Site, you'll enter a small wildlife area. The dense foliage, wooden walkway, and iron lamps are the ideal elements for an evening stroll. Farther along, this mythical journey will take you into the arid regions of the pueblo-style Ranchos. Rocky buttes, cactus gardens, hitching posts, and red tile roofs accent this, the best-themed of Coronado Spring's three villages. This village may be farthest from the central area but it is the one not to miss. Throughout the Ranchos runs a dry and stony riverbed. Add to all of this the Florida sunshine and you'll easily imagine that you are visiting a grand hacienda of Old Mexico.

Each of the three villages has its own uniquely landscaped quiet pool and a network of walkways connects them all to each other, to El Centro, and to the Dig Site. The Esplanade walkway runs around the entire lake. It's perfect for a romantic evening stroll.

Rooms at Disney's Coronado Springs Resort

This is a moderately priced Disney resort, and rooms here are all comparable to other resorts of this category. With 314 square feet, you

Room Rates as of 2004 for Disney's Coronado Springs Resort (prices include taxes)

Accommodation	Value Season	Regular Season	Peak Season	Holiday Season
Standard View	$148	$161	$188	$205
Water View	$165	$177	$216	$233
King Bed	$165	$177	$216	$233

should find them spacious for two and fairly comfortable for a small family. Each has a large vanity with a single sink and the usual shower-tub bathroom. All of the rooms at this resort feature coffeemakers and irons and ironing boards. Refrigerators are available for a small daily charge. There is the usual mix of single king beds and twin double beds. Elevators and both ice and vending machines are conveniently located in every building.

Each of the three villages features its own special decor that has been created to enhance its theme. Rooms at the Casitas are casually formal and accented with turquoise and terra cotta. Bedspreads are a colorful Mexican pattern, and bedstead and armoire are antiqued aqua accented with Mayan sunbursts. Rooms at the Ranchos have a decidedly native motif. Blues, golds, and the triangular patterns of Navajo artistry accentuate these rustic lodgings. Furniture is dark wood and the room decor includes a mirror with hammered metal frame. The ambience of Old Mexico comes alive in the bright and comfortable Cabana rooms. Bedspreads are of reds and golds, while the Spanish-style furnishings are antique gold with brightly painted accents.

Because this resort features a large convention center, it also offers an assortment of suites. The junior suites, VIP suites, and executive suite seem to us, though, to be aimed largely at the convention market.

Transportation and Convenience

Transportation to all Disney World destinations is by bus. There is one bus stop at the central area and another at each of the three village areas. Because of the size of this resort, transportation is a bit slow.

- To all Disney destinations: by bus

- To resort central area: take any theme park–bound bus (after 10 P.M., any Downtown Disney bus) and get off at El Centro

- To return to your room from El Centro, take any Downtown Disney bus

Dining at Coronado Springs

Food choices here are better than at any of the other Disney moderate resorts. Because of the convention trade, Coronado Springs features the upscale Maya Grill with a menu of grilled seafood, steaks, and poultry. You can read more about the Maya Grill on page 332.

Instead of a food court, Coronado Springs has the Pepper Market. This unique restaurant features a festive "marketplace" of open kitchens. Food is prepared to order at nine colorful stands, and all you have to do is decide what you want and have your ticket stamped. Everything we've tried here has been fresh and tasty. The Pepper Market is fun and a good place to eat. It's an amusing version of a Mexican open-air marketplace with an inviting selection of Tex-Mex offerings, including fajitas, tacos, salads, and an overstuffed burrito. There are even burgers, sandwiches, pastas, and pizza as well a kid-friendly station with macaroni and cheese, hot dogs, and chicken fingers. This is not your usual paper-plate-and-plastic-flatware eatery, so expect prices to be a bit higher than at other resort food courts (there's also a 10% service charge, for what, we aren't sure!). The bakery window is open from 6 A.M. to 11 P.M. with a variety of baked goods and specialty coffees, tea, and beer.

La Tienda is Coronado's convenience store, and it features a variety of beverages, sandwiches, fruit, salads, and snacks. It even offers wine and beer. If you're looking for this resort's refillable logo mug, you'll find it here. La Tienda is open from 6 A.M. to midnight.

Coronado Springs also features a limited room service with continental breakfasts, taco and Caesar salads, deli subs, and pizza. At the Dig Site there's Siesta's, the poolside lounge and grill. Here you'll find a selection of specialty drinks as well as fajitas, tortilla wraps, burgers, and hot dogs. It's worth noting that this resort's refillable cup can be filled at either the Pepper Market or at Siesta's, the poolside bar.

Francisco's is this resort's colorful lounge, and it is adjacent to the Pepper Market. It's a nice place to unwind after a day at the parks.

Shops at Coronado Springs

Besides the usual Disney merchandise and resort logo-wear, Panchito's offers a small selection of Southwestern and Mexican artwork and curios. Of course, you'll also find the usual resort selection of sundry items such as film, magazines, snacks, and nonprescription medications.

Recreational Activities at Coronado Springs

- One feature pool area, the Dig Site, with Jaguar water slide
- Hot tub/spa for twenty-two people

- Three quiet pools, one in each area of the resort
- La Vida Health Club and Tanning Salon
- Two video arcades: Jumping Beans and the Iguana Arcade
- Children's wading pool and playground area
- Jogging and walking path (0.9 mile)
- Rental bicycles, paddle boats, kayaks, water mice, and canoes
- Rental "surrey" quadri-cycles are now available at this resort
- Volleyball
- Nature walk in preserved wetlands
- Look for the "Mickey-cacti" at the Ranchos
- Fun photo opportunities around the pool and children's playground

Our Impressions of Coronado Springs

- The central area and the Casitas are where the action is. The Ranchos and Cabanas are much more laid-back and quiet.
- The central area, with restaurants and guest services, is convenient to the Casitas but a bit of a walk from the Cabanas and even a little farther from the Ranchos. The Dig Site is located adjacent to both the Cabanas and the Ranchos and is a bit of a hike from the Casitas. It all seems to balance out.
- Because of the convention trade, this resort seems to be the most adult-oriented of the moderate resorts.

Recommendations for Disney's Coronado Springs Resort

- For a romantic experience, we'd suggest a king bed in either the Ranchos or Cabanas.
- For proximity to the Dig Site, stay in the Ranchos or Cabanas.
- Of the Cabanas, building 9B is most convenient to the central area.
- The Ranchos is the best-themed of the three villages.
- Corner rooms, with windows on two walls, offer more light.

Romance at Coronado Springs

- An evening stroll along the lakeside Esplanade ♥♥♥
- Breakfast in bed ♥♥

@ Late-night hot tub or swim ♥♥

@ Cabana with water view and king bed ♥♥

Disney's All-Star Resorts: Music, Sports, and Movies

The All-Star Resorts are Disney's foray into the budget market. Rooms here are the least expensive on-property and, as you would expect, the All-Star Resorts is one of Disney World's busiest destinations.

Each of the All-Star's three areas carries its lively and colorful themes all the way from landscaping and architecture to the details of room furnishings. The All-Star Resorts feature nearly six thousand rooms.

The road to the All-Star Resorts takes you right past Blizzard Beach, Disney's newest water park. A peek at this fantastic playground will definitely get you in the mood for the bright and comic-strip-like All-Stars. These resorts are larger than life, and we mean a lot larger than life.

The resort buildings here are dwarfed by the sculptures that decorate them. The All-Star Resorts will dazzle you with five-story footballs, soaring surfboards, towering trumpets, mammoth maracas, tremendous toy soldiers, and voluminous Volkswagens. Not for a minute will you forget that you are on vacation and that the theme is fantasy.

Although the three resort areas feature their own overall themes, each is further divided into smaller areas, comprised of two buildings, each with a more specific theme. Our room at All-Star Music was at Jazz Inn, which had a definite New Orleans feel to its fountains, cast-iron benches, and walkways. The railings around the upper-floor walkways are musical scales, appropriately decorated with colorful notes and clefs. Piped-in music around the grounds has a jazz flavor, and the tops of the buildings are edged in silhouettes of musicians. Even our room decor featured jazz accents.

Other areas in All-Star Music are Calypso, Country Fair, Rock Inn, and Broadway Hotel. Each is Imagineered with its own theme from top to bottom. Calypso, for example, is decorated with brightly colored palm leaves; four-story-tall conga drums; and spectacular, rainbow-like marimbas. The music here is the lively beat of the tropics. Taking a walk around this resort is a musical adventure.

Over at All-Star Sports, things are much the same. Which is to say that they are quite different. The theme there is sports, and the areas have names such as Center Court, Hoops Hotel, and Touchdown. The courtyard at Touchdown is arranged like a football stadium, complete with gigantic helmets, a playing field, goal posts, and towering "floodlights." Over at Surf's Up, the landscaping will take you to the seashore. Here,

Disney's ALL-STAR RESORTS

ALL-STAR MOVIES

TOY STORY

FANTASIA

LOVE BUG

101 DALMATIONS

POOL

POOL

LAUNDRY

LAUNDRY

CINEMA HALL

PARKING

PARKING

PARKING

BUS STOP

ALL-STAR MUSIC

MIGHTY DUCKS

POOL

BROADWAY HOTEL

COUNTRY FAIR

LAUNDRY

POOL

ROCK INN

JAZZ INN

CALYPSO

POOL

MELODY HALL

LAUNDRY

BUS STOP

PARKING

PARKING

PARKING

ALL-STAR SPORTS

HOOPS HOTEL

PARKING

CENTER COURT

SURF'S UP!

POOL

LAUNDRY

TOUCHDOWN

HOME RUN HOTEL

POOL

STADIUM HALL

LAUNDRY

BUS STOP

PARKING

the grounds around the pool resemble grass-covered sand dunes. Mounds of pampas grass and thickets of palms complete the picture.

Of course, the theme at All-Star Movies is the cinema. Here, you'll find areas themed after Disney classics: *101 Dalmatians, The Mighty Ducks, Fantasia, Toy Story,* and *The Love Bug.* The Imagineers have added outrageous photo opportunities and other amusing details to "Andy's Bedroom," the children's playground at Movies. There's even a hammock where you can catch some moonbeams.

Music, Sports, and Movies each have a central area with a front desk, guest services, food court, shop, video arcade, and lounge. The central areas are called Melody Hall at Music, Stadium Hall at Sports, and Cinema Hall at Movies.

If you elect to stay at the All-Star Resorts, whether Music, Sports, or Movies, we suggest that you take a stroll around all the properties. There are a lot of wonderful little touches that have been created to delight you. And they will.

Rooms at the All-Star Resorts

There are two basic types of rooms, standard with two double beds and rooms with a single king bed. The king room is also the room equipped for handicapped use. All-Star rooms are on the small side, 260 square feet, which is to say that they are about the same size as most budget motels. The room furnishings are decidedly more Disney than off-property rooms but, by Disney standards, they are pretty modest.

Our king bedroom at Jazz Inn lacked many of the amenities of even the Disney moderately priced resorts. The room decor was festive and modern. The "quilted" bedspread and bathroom wallpaper both featured patterns of jazz musicians, and the drapes were decorated with musical scales. The room furniture is similar throughout the All-Star. Modern, colorful, and cartoon-like, it seemed entertaining.

Each room at the All-Star has a rather small vanity. Our king bedroom had only a shower. Wonderfully designed for the use of those physically challenged, it was very spacious with a handy seat right

Room Rates as of 2004 for Disney's All-Star Resorts (prices include taxes)

Accommodation	Value Season	Regular Season	Peak Season	Holiday Season
Standard view	$86	$110	$122	$127
Preferred View	$97	$122	$133	$138

under the water. The double room has the more conventional shower-tub. King bedrooms each come with a small refrigerator.

Transportation and Convenience

The All-Star resorts have their own Disney bus fleet, and we found service to be quite good—better, in fact, than many other Disney resorts.

@ To all Disney destinations: by bus

Dining at the All-Star Resorts

The End Zone Food Court at Sports, the World Premier Food Court at Movies, and the Intermission Food Court at Music offer a complete array of food for breakfast, lunch, and dinner. All of the food served here is cooked on the premises, and much to our surprise, it was somewhat better than many other Disney food-court offerings.

The dining areas here, like most food courts, are noisy and at peak hours are crowded. Try taking your trays a few steps out to the pool area and eat at a table, under an umbrella. The World Premier Food Court at Movies is the very latest technology in food courts and features changing marquee menus with pictures of special offerings. It's worth a look.

There are several other interesting options for eating at All-Star. One is ordering out. There is a pizza delivery at All-Star, and while this pizza is nothing to write home about, it is decent. The menu also includes beers, wines, salads, and subs. There are also food trucks that drive around during the day, hawking breakfast stuff in the morning and sandwich goodies later.

Lounges at the All-Star Resorts

Each central area has a lounge that serves beers, wines, and specialty drinks, both alcoholic and nonalcoholic. The Singing Spirits Pool Bar is the lounge at Melody Hall; at Sports, it's the Team Spirits Pool Bar; and at Movies, it's Silver Screen Spirits. As their names imply, each is adjacent to the main pool.

Shops at the All-Star Resorts

Sport Goofy Gifts and Sundries is at All-Star Sports, Maestro Mickey's is at All-Star Music, and Donald's Double Feature is at All-Star Movies. Each offers a selection of its own logo merchandise, including the usual Disney character products, sportswear, gifts, souvenirs, sundries, and even a small selection of liquor. Also available is a small offering of magazines, books, and newspapers. And if you are planning to snack in your room, each shop has a modest selection of chips, beverages, and grocery items.

Recreational Activities at the All-Star Resorts

Each of the All-Star Resorts has two pools—one large main pool and one smaller, less centrally located pool. At All-Star Music, the large pool is shaped like a huge guitar. An island in the center features a frolicking gang of sculptured Disney characters who occasionally spray nearby swimmers with jets of water. It is a delightful sight gag. The quiet swimming area at Music is the Piano Pool and is—you guessed it—shaped like a huge piano. At Sports, the main pool is called Surfboard Bay and is located amid the beachside landscaping of Surf's Up. It has a California beach theme. A bit farther away is the quieter swimming area, the Grand Slam Pool. Movies' pool is the Fantasia Pool and is styled after the animated film *Fantasia.* Movies' quiet pool is the Duck Pond. Each main swimming area also has a nice kiddie pool.

Our Impressions of the All-Star Resorts

- $ For the cost-conscious, the All-Star Resorts are an affordable way to stay on-property. Each is a charming and themed Disney resort, albeit a bit spartan and low on the romance scale.

- Many of the rooms are a hike from the parking lots and main buildings. The luggage assistance system is awkward and runs on its own schedule, not yours. A stay here will teach you the real meaning of LUGgage. Plan on carrying your own bags to your room unless you simply cannot. If this is the case, speak with the front desk at check-in.

- All the rooms we've stayed in have been clean and in good repair.

- These are very busy resorts. Quiet moments here are hard to find.

Recommendations for Disney's All-Star Resorts

- At Music, the Calypso area is closest to Melody Hall and is adjacent to the main pool. It is also the noisiest area. Country Fair is the most secluded but it is a hike from the parking area. Rock Inn, Broadway Hotel, and Jazz Inn seemed to be the most convenient, are relatively quiet (for this resort), and are near the quieter pool. We recommend that you request one of these areas if you are staying at All-Star Music.

- At Sports, the busier area is Surf's Up. All other areas seemed quiet by comparison. Touchdown and Home Run Hotel would be our recommendations. Both are convenient to the quieter pool area and to parking.

- ✐ At Movies, Fantasia and 101 Dalmatians will be adjacent to the central Fantasia Pool. Mighty Ducks and The Love Bug will be a bit farther away. All Movie buildings are fairly convenient to parking areas.

- ✐ If you want a quiet room, ask for one near the parking lot.

Romance at the All-Star Resorts

- ✐ Separate room for the kids ♥♥

✹Disney's Wide World of Sports Complex Resorts

This is Disney's newest resort area, and it's home to Disney's Pop Century Resort. Another value accommodation, the Pop Century is located just south of the Caribbean Beach Resort and directly across Osceola Parkway from Disney's Wide World of Sports complex. We wonder what else Disney might have in mind for this area.

✹Disney's Pop Century Resort

As we prepare this edition for publication, the Pop Century is largely complete and scheduled to open sometime in 2003 or 2004. It will be another value resort, similar in most ways to Disney's All-Star Resorts. The resort is divided into two themed areas, the Classic Years, the 1950s to the end of the century, and the Legendary Years, 1900 to mid-century (opening date for this area has not been announced).

Located on 177 acres around Hour Glass Lake, the twenty, four-story Pop Century buildings have 2,880 rooms. Buildings are larger-than-life "time capsules" of twentieth-century popular culture, much of it related to things Disney. Theming includes the fads, dance crazes, and other highlights of the last century. How we lived, how we played, and how we partied are all celebrated with huge, freestanding figures. A towering jukebox, a giant Duncan yo-yo, a huge cell phone, and a gigantic bowling pin are just a few of the landmarks of this recollection of popular American culture. Giant icons and sight gags for the various time periods decorate buildings, pools, and grounds and popular expressions of the day are displayed in huge letters along roof lines: "Get Real!" "Yo!" and "Gnarly Dude." All in all, it's colorful and cartoonish. There is nothing subtle about this place.

Rooms at the Pop Century

Accommodations at the Pop Century are typical of Disney's value resorts: 260 square feet with either two doubles or a single king bed.

Room Rates as of 2004 for Disney's Pop Century Resort

Accommodation	Value Season	Regular Season	Peak Season	Holiday Season
Standard View	$86	$110	$122	$127
Preferred View	$97	$122	$133	$138

Each includes a small table and chairs, small vanity area with sink and separate bathroom, and a 27-inch TV. Though smaller than the 314 square foot Disney moderate resorts, we think these rooms are comfortable and adequate.

Each pair of buildings represents a different decade, and room decor reflects the highlights of that time. Bedspreads, draperies, and wallpaper feature various decades of popular culture.

Transportation at Disney's Pop Century Resort

ℯ Transportation to all Disney destinations: by bus

Dining and Shopping at the Pop Century

The central areas, Classic Hall and Legendary Hall, feature large, open spaces. Each central area includes a shop with Disney merchandise and a selection of sundries; a bar; and a large, state-of-the-art food court. An after-4 P.M. delivery service features pizza, subs, salads, desserts, and wine and beer.

Recreation at Disney's Pop Century Resort

The Classic Years features three large swimming pools, with a central pool called the Hippy Dippy Pool. All swimming areas are fanciful, brightly colored, and complete with the amusing details so typical of Disney. Both Classic Hall and Legendary Hall have a video game arcade, Instant Replay and Fast Forward, and each area also features a children's playground. Memory Lane is the promenade that runs around Hour Glass Lake, and the two resort areas are connected by Generation Gap Bridge.

ℯ Eight swimming pools

ℯ Children's playgrounds

The Downtown Disney Resorts

As big and as much fun as a theme park, Downtown Disney is a happening place, and being near it will provide some real after-dark excitement. Several of the seven non-Disney hotels on Hotel Plaza Boulevard are especially convenient to Downtown Disney. New to this area in 2004 will be Disney's Saratoga Springs Resort & Spa. Located across the lake from Downtown Disney, this resort will be another Disney Vacation Club property and will offer exceptional proximity to Downtown Disney.

Disney's Port Orleans Resort

If you hop a boat at Downtown Disney and head upstream along the "Sassagoula Waterway," you'll find Disney's quaint picture of life on the Ol' Mississippi. On your voyage, you'll first make harbor at Port Orleans Resort French Quarter. This romantic and colorful little city, with its shady, cobbled streets, gaslights, and relaxed Creole ambience, will bring you back in time to walk the streets of Old New Orleans. Farther upriver, you'll discover Port Orleans Resort Riverside. Here, along the quiet banks of the Sassagoula, are stately magnolias, graceful willows, and the grand "old mansions" of Riverside's Magnolia Bend.

A bit farther upstream, you'll find Alligator Bayou. Here, Port Orleans Riverside reflects the rural charm of the bayou. The rustic resort buildings are nestled amid a dense forest of slash pines. Shaded footpaths crisscross in all directions past small ponds and along tiny streams. At night, the crickets "sing" in the bushes, compliments of the Disney Imagineers.

Disney's Port Orleans Resort French Quarter

This lovely resort evokes the ambience of Old New Orleans. The delight begins the moment you pass through the iron entrance gates and onto the tree-lined drive. The Disney artists have been hard at work. The main building is "The Mint," and it's a masterpiece of ornate wrought-iron work and glass. The Mint is the hub of the French Quarter, where you'll find the food court, lounge, front desk, and guest services. Check-in at French Quarter is more fantasy than chore. The vaulted ceilings and iron railings of the Mint more resemble a bank than a hotel lobby, and friendly service is the coin of this realm. The hotel staff is attired in perfect period costume. Not a detail has been missed. The Imagineers have been busy, and the promise of Mardi Gras is everywhere.

The French Quarter grounds are splendidly landscaped, and on our recent stay, we discovered that they have improved with age. A stroll here at night will be relaxing and romantic. The narrow, cobbled streets have names such as Rue d'Blues and Rue d'Baga. The small parks and lovely stone fountains are enchanting. Narrow sidewalks, gaslights, and iron hitching posts combine to create a real sense of neighborhoods in this "old city" on the river.

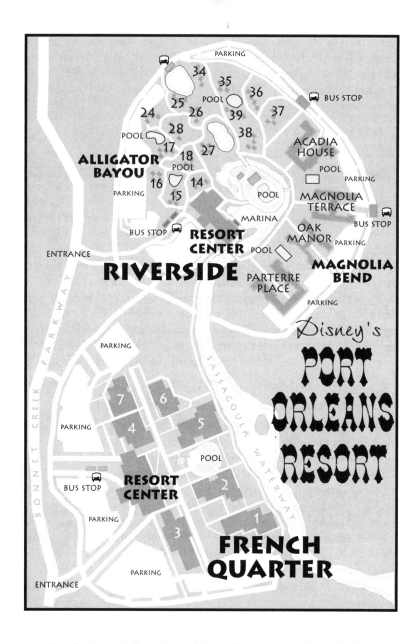

French Quarter's "row houses" have distinct personalities. Each has its own unique yard, surrounded by an iron fence just a bit different than its neighbor's. The quaint charm is convincing. Nothing has been overlooked, and we suggest that you overlook nothing. Spend some time strolling about in the evening. Find a nice bench in a cozy garden and sit awhile.

The swimming pool here is the exciting Doubloon Lagoon. A giant dragon slithers its way through this fantasy playground, forming a water slide with its long and slippery tongue. It's colorful and fun. Don't miss the comical crocodile shower at poolside for a memorable photo opportunity.

The resort's hot tub is located in an enchanting garden near enough to the pool to invite a quick dip but far enough away to keep it fairly quiet. The ivy-covered trellises and beautiful gardens make this a magical spot after dark.

Rooms at Port Orleans Resort French Quarter

The rooms here are typical of the moderately priced Disney resorts. At 314 square feet, they are a bit smaller than those at Disney's luxury resorts are, but we found ours to be spacious and comfortable. Each features a small vanity area, complete with two pedestal sinks and mirrors. Beneath the drapes are genuine wooden Venetian blinds. The antiqued wood furniture, ceiling fan, and formal armoire enhance a sense of the old French Quarter. Our room was just elegant enough to be romantic. One look out the window and onto the French Quarter streets below, and we knew that we were someplace special.

Disney's Port Orleans Resort Riverside

With a bit of the old Disney magic, Riverside is really two unique resorts. The Magnolia Bend area of Riverside recalls the plantations of the Old South. Stately courtyards, charming fountains, and formal gardens re-create the sweeping grandeur of the antebellum South. Resort rooms here are in large mansion-like buildings with winding stairways and imposing columns. The weeping willows and sloping lawns of Magnolia Bend give way to dense thickets of pine and Florida maple at Alligator Bayou. Here, the "weathered" resort buildings are quaint and small. Their tin roofs peek through the treetops. Footpaths seem narrow and winding and the charm is more rustic and homey.

The Sassagoula Steamboat Company is Riverside's central area and with docks, warehouses, and a water-driven mill, it re-creates the Mississippi charm of a bustling riverside port. Disney's penchant for detail is everywhere. Even the bathrooms in the lobby have old-fashioned cisterns and wooden toilet seats.

Check-in will be the beginning of your Riverside adventure. The front desk seems more like a steamship office than a hotel. Piles of battered steamer trunks and the names of exotic ports of call lend a tangible sense of adventure. Reservationists wear the costumes of steamship clerks, and will "book passage" for your trip upriver.

The Sassagoula Steamboat Company is home to the Riverside's restaurants, lounge, general store, and food court. Also located here is guest services. The guest buildings of both Alligator Bayou and Magnolia Bend surround Ol' Man Island, a three-acre water recreation area with pool, playground, spa, and a stocked fishing hole.

Ol' Man Island has one large pool with a short water slide. There are also five quiet pools located around the resort. These are convenient to most rooms, so if you are looking for something a bit more intimate, you're in luck. There's only one hot tub here at Riverside, and we feel that it's not enough. You'll find it right in the middle of things at Ol' Man Island, minimizing peace and quiet.

Rooms at Riverside's Magnolia Bend

Magnolia Bend is made up of four "parishes." With such names as Parterre Place and Acadia House, each is really a large resort building housing more than 250 guest rooms. The feel here is a bit big for our tastes, especially in the standard rooms that look out onto the parking areas. Views from the river side of the complex are infinitely more relaxing and private.

The rooms at both Magnolia Bend and Alligator Bayou are the same general size and shape. With 314 square feet of space, each is adequate and comfortable. Although the rooms at both the Bend and the Bayou are the same dimensions, they are worlds apart in decor. The ambience at Magnolia Bend is definitely more formal. French Provincial furniture, brocade upholstery, and an antiqued, mirrored armoire are suited perfectly to the antebellum grand manor. Each room has a ceiling fan, a small sitting bench, table and chairs, and a spacious and well-lit vanity area. There are two pedestal sinks and each has its own mirror, giving you both a place to get ready for your evening out. Rooms feature either two double beds or one king.

Rooms at Riverside's Alligator Bayou

Alligator Bayou offers much more of a down-home feeling. Instead of four large mansions, the same number of guest rooms is spread out among sixteen rustic and weathered buildings, each housing about sixty rooms. The look here is "backwater cracker" but the ambience translates into something more intimate. The Bayou's buildings are tucked away in a small forest. Each feels a bit hidden and the sensation of being in a large resort is lost.

The Bayou rooms manage an aura of homespun comfort and warmth. The log bedstead frames, patchwork "quilts," and other details give the rooms a feeling of fantasy and fun. Port Orleans room theming is at its best here in Alligator Bayou. Rooms with two double beds in Alligator Bayou also feature a trundle bed, making them Disney's only moderate resort rooms able to accommodate five adults.

Room Rates as of 2004 for Disney's Port Orleans Resort (prices include taxes)

Accommodation	Value Season	Regular Season	Peak Season	Holiday Season
Standard View	$148	$161	$188	$205
Water View	$165	$177	$216	$233
King Bed	$165	$177	$216	$233

Transportation at Disney's Port Orleans Resort

Transportation and convenience at Port Orleans is fairly good. There is one large bus stop in front of the French Quarter and four at various locations around Riverside; buses run every twenty minutes and even more frequently during the busier hours. For Wide World of Sports, Discovery Island, and River Country bus transfers, consult your Transportation Guidemap (available at guest services).

A boat service runs to Pleasure Island and the Downtown Disney Marketplace. The small launches are fun and will take you through parts of Walt Disney World that you'd never have a chance to see otherwise. Don't miss this trip. There's also a shuttle that runs between the French Quarter and Riverside. It operates from 9:00 A.M. to 9:30 P.M., every fifteen minutes.

- ℮ To Downtown Disney: by boat (from 4 P.M. to 11 P.M., every twenty minutes); or by bus
- ℮ To Magic Kingdom, Epcot, Disney-MGM Studios, Animal Kingdom, Typhoon Lagoon, and Blizzard Beach: by bus
- ℮ To BoardWalk: by bus or boat to Downtown Disney and take BoardWalk Resort bus

Dining at Port Orleans

Boatwright's is the table-service restaurant for Port Orleans, and it's located in the central area of Riverside. Boatwright's serves up hearty meals for both breakfast and dinner. The food is pretty good and the portions are generous. For more information about Boatwright's, see page 316.

The Sassagoula Floatworks food court at French Quarter is a warehouse of Mardi Gras props. Giant masks and colorful floats hang from the ceiling and food choices feature a definite New Orleans flair. Its variety of "shops" offer everything from scrambled eggs and muffins to burgers and rotisserie chicken. There's even pasta, subs, and pizza. Don't miss the traditional French Quarter treat, beignets, at the bakeshop.

At Riverside, the food court is the Riverside Mill, and it offers a selection of fast foods for any of the day's meals. Breakfast offerings run the gamut from a muffin or bagel to French toast or eggs. Other meals get a hearty treatment of burgers, barbecued ribs, pizza, and daily Cajun specialties and dinnertime adds a few more entrées and a daily special.

Both food courts are open from 6 A.M. to midnight and at meal times, you're apt to find them crowded and noisy. Our choice for these times has always been to sit at one of the tables outside. Some are well shaded and comfortable, especially those out by the pools.

Another meal or snack alternative at Port Orleans is the Sassagoula Pizza Express, which delivers pizza, salads, beverages, and desserts from 4 P.M. to midnight. A minimum order of $15 is required.

Lounges at Port Orleans

French Quarter and Riverside each have a full-service lounge. At French Quarter, Scat Cat's is adjacent to the lobby and features a large-screen TV. Over at Riverside, you'll find the comfort of River Roost. Its long mahogany bar, leather club chairs, and fireplace make it an inviting place to simply relax or to enjoy a nightcap and the lounge's nightly entertainment. River Roost also serves up a small selection of appetizers and finger foods.

Port Orleans also features two pool bars. Both Mardi Grogs at French Quarter and Muddy Rivers at Riverside serve a variety of nonalcoholic and specialty cocktails from 11 A.M. till dusk. Also on the menu are a small variety of snacks and deli sandwiches.

Shops at Port Orleans Resort

Jackson Square Gifts and Desires at French Quarter and Fulton's General Store at Riverside each offer the usual selection of Disney character merchandise as well as a line of clothes and accessories with Port Orleans logos. Either store also carries the usual assortment of magazines, snacks, beverages, sunscreen, film, and other sundries.

Recreational Activities at Port Orleans Riverside and French Quarter

- Each area features a themed swimming pool with water slide
- Riverside has four additional quiet pools
- Hot tubs (spa) at both
- NEW Evening horse-drawn carriage ride (see chapter 7 for details)
- Boat and bike rentals (at Riverside)
- Surrey quadri-cycle rentals (at Riverside)

@ Walking or jogging paths

@ Video arcade in both

@ Guided fishing, excursions, and stocked fishing hole at Riverside (see page 359 for details)

Our Impressions of Port Orleans Resort French Quarter and Riverside

@ These are beautifully themed resorts, charming in every way. However, on our recent visit to French Quarter, we found our room to be in real need of refurbishing. We have been told that renovation is planned, although no date has been set.

@ Of the moderately priced resorts, we think that Port Orleans French Quarter is the most romantic. After dark, it's simply enchanting.

@ The boat service to Downtown Disney is delightful. It turned our trip into an adventure. It's especially pleasant around sunset.

Recommendations for Disney's Port Orleans Resorts

@ As we go to press, Port Orleans French Quarter has been closed for complete refurbishing. For the reopening date, call central reservations.

@ Avoid the standard parking lot views. When you check-in, ask to get another view.

@ Pool-view rooms at French Quarter are convenient for swimming, but you may find that you've sacrificed peace and quiet.

@ For the sake of convenience, you may wish to request a particular building when you reserve your room at Riverside. Oak Manor would be our choice at Magnolia Bend, and in Alligator Bayou, buildings 14–17 or 27 are our suggestions. All are nearest the central building and Ol' Man Island.

@ Some rooms at Riverside feature a trundle bed ($15 charge per night), providing sleeping accommodations for five.

@ Because Riverside is such a beautiful resort and because we enjoy walking, we prefer the rooms in Alligator Bayou.

Romance at Port Orleans Resort

@ Overall theme ♥♥♥

@ Room with king bed ♥♥

@ The evening horse-drawn carriage ride♥♥

- Doubloon Lagoon at French Quarter ♥♥
- Breakfast at a poolside table ♥
- Long hot-tub soak at day's end ♥♥♥
- Evening stroll from one resort area to the other ♥♥♥
- Late-night swim in a quiet pool at Riverside ♥♥
- Evening carriage ride ♥♥
- Sunset cruise to Downtown Disney ♥♥
- Boat or surrey rental for exploring ♥♥

Disney's Old Key West Resort

Old Key West is part of the Vacation Club, Disney's time-share venture. And since it is also available as a nightly rental, we thought we'd give it a try. We must admit to being a bit skeptical. It seemed large and not particularly close to anything, and it looked like condos. Whatever doubts we had, however, were quickly put to rest when we arrived at our one-bedroom vacation home.

The Key West theme is executed perfectly. The Florida Keys should look this nice. The pastel villas, with their "tin" roofs and gingerbread gables, are scattered in small clusters around the resort grounds.

Landscaping at Old Key West is lush and tropical. The villas are surrounded by dense stands of foliage and flowering trees, providing a feeling of privacy that you will find hard to equal elsewhere in Walt Disney World. Plants are larger than life. If you are from a northern clime, you'll marvel at the variety of greenery, most of which you've probably only seen as potted houseplants. Like much of Walt Disney World, this place is one big garden. Palms, crepe myrtle, blossoming hibiscus, and spider lilies abound. Quaint and narrow Key West streets wander gently among the Florida cracker-style villas. Southern porches, iron streetlamps, and old-fashioned bus stops add the finishing touches to the little taste of Key West created by the Disney Imagineers.

Driving, we followed Old Turtle Pond Road to our villa. We parked a few steps from our front door. Once inside, our curiosity turned to sheer delight. Our villa was not only large but surprisingly beautiful. The ambience was definitely Florida Keys style—open and airy, bright, and casually comfortable. Greeted by a mix of pastels, a splash of florals, and an expanse of open spaces, we hurried from room to room to survey our new abode. Ceiling fans, numerous large windows, and a king-size bed were just the beginnings. The vacation home had a huge living room/kitchen where we found a comfortable chair, love seat, and sofa with queen-size, foldaway bed. Handsome water-

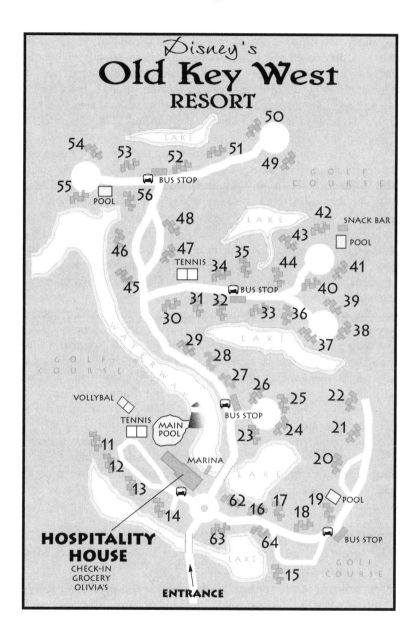

colors of island scenery, silk "tropical plants," and a carved wooden conch combined to give our villa a lived-in, at-home feeling.

The large kitchen opened onto the living room, just like our own house. It featured a large refrigerator, microwave, dishwasher, stove, toaster, coffeemaker, and enough basic culinary gear to cook up whatever we might have cared to. There was even a blender and an electric hand-mixer. In the drawers and cupboards were mixing bowls, quality utensils, and dinner service for eight. With the cloth placemats, terry napkins, and napkin rings provided, we could have entertained. There were even wine glasses. The kitchen and the living room were separated by a tile-topped island that held a large-screen television and VCR. Our expectations were surpassed.

There was also a lovely patio overlooking water. Featured here was another ceiling fan, a table, and chairs. Surrounded by dense growths of tropical plants, it was private and inviting.

The master bedroom of our vacation home was comfortable and beautifully appointed. The king-size bedstead was made of decorative, enameled iron. The floral "quilt" was a wedding-ring pattern, and the armoire (with television) was an antique white. In one corner, a wicker chair and ottoman; in another corner, a glass door that opened onto the tiled patio. This was beginning to look like paradise. And then we entered the bathroom.

We knew that we'd arrived. The Jacuzzi was easily large enough for two. Next to it, louvered doors opened onto the sleeping area. A charming pedestal sink and beautiful tilework tied everything together neatly. As big as the tub was, the bathroom itself was even larger. Adjoining it was yet another room, with toilet, large walk-in shower, and another sink and vanity area. There was even a laundry room, complete with full-size washer and dryer, a small supply of laundry detergent, and iron and ironing board.

What made this place so inviting was its casual elegance. Everything from the beautiful prints to the varnished-wood blinds spoke of quality. It was a completely and beautifully furnished little apartment, a place where almost anyone would be glad to live. A few hours after we'd arrived, we were happily calling it "home."

Accommodations at Old Key West

There are three basic types of lodgings here at Old Key West: the studios, the vacation villas, and the Grand Villas. The studio offers a single room with two queen beds, an outside patio, and a small kitchen with microwave oven, wet bar, and mini-refrigerator. A studio added to our one-bedroom vacation villa would make a two-bedroom vacation villa, able to accommodate eight persons.

The three-bedroom Grand Villa is a two-level townhouse, something quite different altogether. Accommodations are for 12. The master bedroom still has the king bed and Jacuzzi tub, but upstairs are two queen-size beds in one room and two double beds in the other. The

Room Rates as of 2004 for Disney's Old Key West Resort (prices include taxes)

Accommodation	Value Season	Regular Season	Peak Season	Holiday Season
Studio	$256	$283	$317	$411
One-bedroom Villa	$379	$430	$496	$569
Two-bedroom Villa	$534	$624	$758	$864
Three-bedroom Grand Villa	$1,160	$1,293	$1,461	$1,628

fine furnishings of the Grand Villa and its cathedral ceiling create an impressive effect.

Transportation and Convenience

We are pleased to tell you that getting places from Old Key West is relatively easy. To make things even better, the buses follow a schedule, which you'll receive in your check-in packet.

- To Downtown Disney: by boat or bus
- To all other Disney Destinations: by bus
- To central area: internal bus

Dining at Old Key West

There are two counter-service snack shops, Good's Food-To-Go and the Turtle Shack, and one table-service restaurant, Olivia's Cafe. Both Good's and Olivia's are located in the resort's central area, adjacent to the main swimming area. The Turtle Shack is in one of the outlying pool areas. Both fast-food outlets offer a selection of sandwiches and snacks. The poolside bar at the central pool is the Gurgling Suitcase, and it features the usual assortment of wines, beers, and specialty drinks.

Olivia's serves breakfast, lunch, and dinner, offering an intriguing menu of Key West cuisine. It also features a character breakfast on Sunday and Wednesday. Old Key West features room service from Olivia's. For a review of Olivia's see page 334.

Shops at Old Key West

The Conch Flat General Store will be your source for just about everything at Old Key West. There is even a substantial grocery section. Every room comes equipped with a grocery check-off list that you can drop off at the General Store. They'll do the shopping and deliver the goods for a mere buck. Now we're talking vacation.

Recreational Activities at Old Key West

- One themed central pool area with sauna and hot tub
- Three quiet pool areas, one with a hot tub and sauna
- ½-mile biking, jogging, walking path
- Children's playground and kiddie pool
- Marina with rental watercraft
- Bicycle and surrey quadri-cycle rentals
- Tennis, basketball, and volleyball
- Fitness center
- Video game room
- Complimentary videotape library
- In-room massage, by appointment

Our Impressions of Old Key West

- We really like this resort and found it beautiful, well-themed, and relaxing.
- During our visit, transportation to all Disney destinations seemed good.
- Don't miss the pleasant boat ride to Downtown Disney from Old Key West.

Recommendations for Disney's Old Key West

- $ The one-bedroom vacation home is an ideal place for a family, especially during value season when the prices come down.

Romance at Old Key West

- Resort theming ♥♥
- Villa amenities ♥♥♥♥
- Jacuzzi in the vacation homes ♥♥♥♥

Disney's Saratoga Springs Resort & Spa

Coming to Walt Disney World in late Spring of 2004 is Disney's Saratoga Springs Resort & Spa. This new offering from the Disney Vacation Club is now under construction across the lake from Downtown Disney, on the site of what was once the Disney Institute. The town-houses and bungalows of the Institute have been razed to make way for this resort. We weren't able to find out a lot about it, but we'll tell you what we do know.

Disney's Saratoga Springs Resort & Spa will celebrate its name-sake, the historic resort town in upstate New York. At the foot of the Adirondacks, the real Saratoga Springs is steeped in American history. It was here on the battlefields of Saratoga in October 1777 that the tide of the Revolutionary War and the fate of our nation turned. In the late nineteenth century, the quaint town gained notoriety as Americans flocked to its healing mineral springs and to the Saratoga Race Course, the nation's oldest horseracing track.

Summers still bring flocks of tourists to Saratoga Springs, who still enjoy its thoroughbred racing and mineral baths and spas. But tourists also come to savor its gracious, old-world charm, tree-lined streets, op-ulent inns, and historic bed and breakfasts. Disney's celebration of his-toric Saratoga Springs will encompass all of these features.

Boston's architectural firm of Graham Gund (Disney's Coronado Springs and Disney's Vero Beach Resorts) has designed Disney's Saratoga Springs Resort & Spa. It will be a place of quiet beauty, of tur-rets and towers, of arched granite stonework and Victorian gingerbread. We expect its central areas, retail shops, restaurants, and landscaped grounds to pay homage to the history of Saratoga Springs, its horserac-ing, and its famed mineral springs. The Spa at Disney's Saratoga Springs Resort will be central to this theme, as it will be a place where resort guests can indulge themselves in luxurious massages, soothing mineral baths, and other relaxing treatments.

Saratoga Springs Resort & Spa will feature the wonderful (and practical) home-away-from-home accommodations of the Disney Va-cation Club. The 65-acre site will feature twelve campus-style build-ings, each with an upstate New York granite and shingle-style architecture. The resort's 584 units will consist of one-room studios, one- and two-bedroom villas, and lavish Grand Villas with accommo-dations for twelve.

Typical of other recent Vacation Club properties, we expect that each studio will feature a queen bed and sleeper-sofa and a small "kitchen" area with refrigerator, microwave oven, toaster, and cof-feemaker. The larger villas will each have a full kitchen, living room with sleeper-sofa, washer and dryer, whirlpool tub, and one to three bedrooms. Of course, we haven't heard any details about the decor, but we imagine that Team Disney will create accommodations with an eclectic and historic bed and breakfast ambience.

Because of its location, we think that transportation from the resort to the Disney attractions will be by bus. It will also include a pleasant walkway around the lake to the Downtown Disney Marketplace. We hope also to see a shuttle boat to Downtown Disney.

Disney's Saratoga Springs Resort & Spa will feature a rockwork, themed pool with a natural springs–inspired water slide. Recreation will certainly include a state-of-the-art fitness center, clay tennis courts, and championship golf at the Buena Vista Golf Course. And if other Disney Vacation Clubs are any indication, we also expect to see a video arcade and a variety of bike rentals. Disney's Saratoga Springs Resort & Spa room rates are the same as those at Disney's Old Key West Resort. See you there.

The Downtown Disney Resorts on Hotel Plaza Boulevard

These seven hotels lie along Hotel Plaza Boulevard, and while they are not owned or operated by Disney, they do offer an unsurpassed proximity to the excitement of Downtown Disney. The shady and beautifully landscaped boulevard is a place of high-rise towers, and its urban ambience complements the bright lights and excitement of Disney's nighttime destination. At one end of the boulevard is the Downtown Disney Marketplace, and at the other is the Crossroads Shopping Center, about a mile and a half away, where you'll find Gooding's Supermarket (the closest market to Disney World) and a variety of non-Disney shops and chain restaurants.

Money-Saving Tip

Such Internet travel sites as Expedia and Travelocity offer great rates on the hotels on Hotel Plaza Boulevard.

$ Although these hotels do not enjoy the storytelling themes of Disney resorts, they do provide other advantages. First and most important, each of these hotels offers specials, even during the busy summer months.

Room availability is another important feature. If you're making a last-minute trip or are simply unable to find a room in a Disney resort, give Downtown Disney a try. We think that most of these hotels are better than Disney's value resorts, and several are especially nice.

Another plus are the high-rise views. Many of the hotels feature stunning panoramas of Walt Disney World. During our visits, we were able to see as far as the Magic Kingdom and have enjoyed rooms from

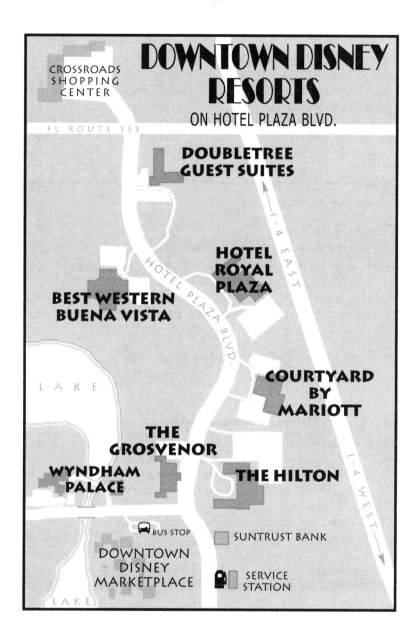

which we were able to watch fireworks shows from all the Disney parks. Generally speaking, these hotels are attractive and well kept. The Wyndham Palace, the Hilton, and the Best Western are all exceptionally nice; we'd rate the others as good accommodations.

Most of the hotels along the boulevard provide space for five guests per room; several accommodate more. Pools and grounds range from good to beautiful, although none begins to approach the likes of Stormalong Bay at the Yacht and Beach Clubs or Doubloon Lagoon at Port Orleans French Quarter.

Each of the hotels has a Disney Store that offers logo merchandise and the full assortment of tickets to all Disney attractions, including Ultimate Park Hopper Passes and E-Ride Nights. The Extra Magic Hour is also featured. We suggest you drop by after check-in and pick up the World Update and a set of the Disney theme park guidemaps so that you can learn what's going on during your visit.

Transportation from Downtown Disney's Hotel Plaza Boulevard

Hotels along the boulevard have their own fleet of white buses, each marked with the purple, red, and yellow logo of Hotel Plaza Boulevard. The Hilton and the Wyndham Palace share buses, while the rest of the fleet serves the remaining hotels. Buses run every thirty minutes (a bit less frequently during the slow seasons).

- To all Disney attractions: by direct bus

- To Downtown Disney: walk, or after 4 P.M., by shuttle service

Wyndham Palace Resort & Spa

The Palace is located directly across the street from Downtown Disney on 27 gardenlike acres and alongside a serene, freshwater lagoon. It is our favorite place to stay at Hotel Plaza, and, like its neighbor the Hilton, the Wyndham Place offers all the luxury, amenities, and services that seasoned travelers like ourselves have come to expect.

Its twenty-seven stories of mirrored balconies make it a distinctive sight even here among the other towers of the boulevard. Fountains, manicured beds of flowering plants, weeping willows, and date palms combine to create a real sense of beauty and relaxation.

We found the lobby to be an elegantly understated mix of handsome carpets, potted palms, expanses of marble, and crystal chandeliers. Our luggage was immediately whisked away by the bell staff, and our check-in took a few brief minutes. We explored the lobby's "library" area, with its stuffed sofas, leather club chairs, and shelves of books. For us, it seemed the perfect place to relax and recap the day or simply to sit and browse our way through the rack of daily newspapers. The view onto the quiet lake behind the resort gave everything a sense of ease and comfort. We had arrived.

Rooms at the Wyndham Palace Resort & Spa

The luxurious guest rooms at the Palace are in one of its four towers, and most feature balconies or patios and either two queen-sized beds or a single king. Our king room was on the twenty-sixth floor of the main tower building. We were drawn immediately to our balcony and to the panorama of Downtown Disney and Epcot. In the distance, we could even see the Magic Kingdom. We were already making plans to catch the fireworks from the balcony later in the evening.

The handsome blonde furnishings included a large desk with a Herman Miller desk chair and an armoire with a large-screen TV. Bedspread, carpets, and upholstery featured tones of deep blue that contrasted well with the pale yellow wall covering and light furniture. A small tree and beautifully framed prints finished the accents for this, our plush new home. There was even a comfortable sitting area with pull-out sleeper sofa and coffee table.

Our bath featured a separate vanity area and the usual shower-tub combination. Plush towels, tile floors, and marble trim gave everything a sense of elegance. All rooms at the Palace feature high-speed (T-1) Internet access, Web-TV, PlayStation, and cordless phones. Other standard amenities include in-room coffee, stocked mini-bars, hairdryer, Golden Door Spa amenities, iron and ironing board, daily newspaper delivery, On-Command Movies, free access for local and calling card calls, and unlimited fitness center use.

There are thirty VIP suites in the tower, some with a kitchen, a living and dining area, and one to five bedrooms. There is also a thirty-six-room Crown Level Concierge floor as well as an eighteen-room Presidential floor that features continental breakfasts, waffle robes lined with terry and velour, matching slippers, bathroom scale, upgraded Golden Door Spa amenities, Sony clock radio with compact disc player—all the comforts of home and then some.

The Palace also has sixty-five EverGreen rooms that offer independent air cleaning systems, filtered water, non-allergic pillows and blankets, and undyed towels and linens.

There are also a hundred suites in the Palace Island Resort Suites building, a short walk away and adjacent to the pool complex on what is known as Recreation Island.

Palace Island Resort suites feature either one or two bedrooms, a balcony or patio, living room with queen sleeper/sofa, microwave oven, refrigerator, mini-bar, coffeemaker, and hairdryer. The area offers unequaled proximity to the resort's tennis court, whirlpool, sauna, sand volleyball court, and pools. The covered walkway from Palace Island to the main building is via a lovely garden path, past the kitchen's herb garden, and across a footbridge that spans part of the lake.

Room Rates for the Wyndham Palace Resort & Spa

Peak season at the Wyndham Palace usually runs from Christmas through Easter, with its value season running from mid-May to early September and the second week of December. Rates for standard guest rooms range from around $110 to more than $155, depending on the season (prices include Florida's 11½% tax). Expect higher rates for preferred views, suites, and concierge level rooms. For reservations, call Disney Central Reservations (407) W-DISNEY (934-7639), (800) WYNDHAM, or (407) 827-3000. $ Also, check the Palace's Web site at www.wyndham.com/hotels/MCOPV/main.wnt for special offers.

Food and Beverages at the Palace

Dining at the Palace features a number of options, all of which are quite good. Add to that the many eateries in nearby Downtown Disney, and dining at the Palace becomes nearly limitless. This hotel's premier eatery is the award-winning Arthur's 27 ♥♥♥. Exquisite continental cuisine combined with a romantic twenty-seventh-floor panorama makes this a place where even the locals come to enjoy a fine meal. Adjacent to the lobby is the Australian-themed Outback Restaurant (no relation to the chain). Featuring a large menu of well-prepared steaks, seafood, and other specialties, the Outback Restaurant enjoys an interesting Australian "bush" motif. For our reviews of both restaurants, see chapter 6.

The Watercress Cafe is the Palace's "all-purpose eatery," and you'll find a good breakfast buffet here each day, or you can order à la carte. Sunday mornings feature a Disney character breakfast. The cafe serves from 6 A.M. to 3 P.M. each day and from 6 P.M. to 10 P.M. each evening. The menu is large and includes a generous number of healthful dishes from the resort's spa cuisine. The Watercress Cafe, located on the first floor, has a casual ambience and lakeside location, which make it an ideal place for any of the day's meals.

The Watercress Pastry Shop & Mini-Market is another place you'll want to know about. Open 6 A.M. to midnight, this pleasant little cafe features another splendid lakeside view as well as a tempting selection of treats: assorted pastries, cookies, and desserts from the Palace's kitchen; espresso and cappuccino; ice cream; and a breakfast featuring bagels, cold cereal, fresh-squeezed orange juice, and more. Picnic lunches are also available. It's the kind of place we'd like to see in every resort.

The Palace's twenty-four-hour room service menu is large. We counted nearly fifty items for breakfast alone, and selections from the resort's spa menu are also available. So while you're staying at the Palace, don't forget to enjoy a breakfast in bed or have a romantic dinner in your room.

Out by the pool, you'll find the Recreation Island Pool Snack Bar. It serves a selection of burgers, sandwiches, and salads from 11 A.M. to 6 P.M., along with a refreshing variety of specialty beverages. There are two lounges at the Palace. The Lobby Lounge is exceptionally comfortable (the "library" is part of it), and in addition to a large selection of cocktails and fine wines, it offers exotic teas, pastries, and canapes. Stop in for your own afternoon high tea. Adjacent to Arthur's is the Top of the Palace ♥♥♥, which features piano entertainment Wednesday through Saturday nights as well as an extraordinary wine list.

Of course, no resort of this caliber would be complete without a nightclub, and here it is: the Laughing Kookaburra Good Time Bar. "The Kook" features spirited music and dancing and is the place to go for an evening of fun.

Wyndham Palace Shops

On the ground-floor level of the lobby is a Disney gift and sundries shop and nearby, W. H. Smith's, which features quality men's and women's resort wear and Wyndham Palace logo merchandise. The Spa Boutique also features its large variety of Pevonia Botanica spa and health products and Wyndham Palace logo merchandise.

The Spa at Wyndham Palace

Our experiences at the Spa were nothing short of blissful. This world-class, European-style spa features a sublime selection of body treatments, massages, whirlpool baths, wet and dry saunas, a lap pool, and a state-of-the-art fitness center. It even has a full-service hair salon. We urge you to take some time to pamper yourselves here. It's what vacations are all about. For more details, see page 349.

Services Available at Wyndham Palace Resort & Spa

- Full bell service
- Valet parking ($10 overnight)
- Twenty-four-hour room service
- Nine restaurants and lounges
- Concierge desk
- Childcare programs and babysitting
- Car rental desk
- European-style spa
- Full-service hair salon
- Laundry service

Recreational Activities at Wyndham Palace Resort & Spa

- Three heated swimming pools
- Whirlpool tub
- Sauna
- Three lighted tennis courts (complimentary)
- Tee times at the Disney golf courses
- Sand volleyball court
- Video arcade
- State-of-the-art fitness center
- Children's playground
- Pool concierge service provides CD players, cooling spritzes, and reading materials while you relax poolside

Our Impressions of Wyndham Palace Resort & Spa

- It's a beautiful and luxurious hotel.
- This is the place to stay if you want to be near Downtown Disney.

Recommendations for the Wyndham Palace Resort & Spa

- Get a room high up in the tower with an Epcot view.
- $ Check the Palace's Web site for special discounts (www.wyndham palaceresort.com).

Romance at Wyndham Palace Resort & Spa

- The Spa ♥♥♥
- Breakfast in bed ♥♥♥
- Dining at Arthur's 27 ♥♥♥
- Evening stroll to Downtown Disney ♥♥
- Tower room with Epcot view ♥♥
- Daily free champagne toast at the Top of the Palace lounge ♥♥♥
- Nightcap at the Top of the Palace ♥♥♥

The Hilton

The very name of this resort has come to be synonymous with fine lodgings. This is an award-winning, Four-Diamond hotel with an impressive list of amenities. The grand marble lobby is vibrant and exciting. From one end to the other, it encompasses a world of shops and restaurants, a sports bar, and even a twenty-four-hour market and deli. Large saltwater aquariums decorate the area behind the front desk and teem with brightly colored and exotic tropical fish. Service at the Hilton is so good that if you simply stand here for a few minutes, someone is bound to ask if you need something.

The Hilton is located directly across the street from the Downtown Disney Marketplace, and it is one of the boulevard's most outstanding travel destinations. It boasts a sophisticated tropical theme, which is carried elegantly from its lush gardens to its comfortable rooms. All rooms at the Hilton have enjoyed a recent refurbishing and feel luxurious and new. With either two double beds or a single king, each standard room features a small sitting area, perfect for in-room dining. Furniture is a honey maple tone and room decor features restful earth tones of rust and beige. A carved apple lamp and table with game-board top lend an elegant touch of whimsy.

All rooms feature well-stocked mini-bars, cable TV with pay-per-view movies, high-speed Internet access, twin vanities, hairdryer, and iron and ironing board.

The Hilton's Executive Level rooms can be found on the exclusive ninth and tenth floors and feature this hotel's concierge service. Our room on this level was large and luxurious. As Tower guests, we happily enjoyed the comfortable private lounge, plush bathrobes, continental breakfasts, and beverages and snacks served throughout the day. Our comings and goings were made all the easier by a well-trained desk staff that seemed only too happy to fulfill our every wish.

Room Rates at the Hilton

The peak season at the Hilton is the winter tourist season of January to March. Value season is June through August, and during the rest of the year, prices vary widely, based on availability. During the summer value season, expect rooms to cost around $179, and during the busiest season, around $385 per night (prices include Florida 11½% taxes). For reservations, call (800) 782-4414 or visit the Hilton's Web site at www.hilton-wdwv.com.

Food and Beverages at the Hilton

The Hilton boasts a large selection of restaurants and lounges, even for a resort of its size. Finn's Grill is its premier dining place, and each night it offers a different all-you-can-eat special as well as a large menu of à la carte items. Specialties here are seafood and steaks; on the night of our visit, the special was barbecued ribs. Nearby is Covington Mill, which features buffet and à la carte breakfasts as well as a varied lunch selection. It all comes from the Hilton's large kitchen, which includes everything from homemade potato chips to a tantalizing selection of desserts. Covington Mill enjoys a quaint, New England, back-porch theme and is a pleasant place to enjoy any meal. It also features a Sunday Disney character breakfast.

Mug's is this resort's gourmet coffee shop. Drop by to enjoy a pastry, a cappuccino, or an aperitif. Nearby, there's live jazz in the evenings. It is a cozy and comfortable spot. Next door to Mug's is the Mainstreet Market, where you'll find everything from desserts and deli selections to wines, Ben and Jerry's ice cream, and a formidable selection of snacks, twenty-four hours a day.

At the other end of the lobby is John T's lounge, which features large-screen TVs, sandwiches and snacks, and a full-service bar. The Hilton also offers its guests Benihana, the well-known Japanese steakhouse and sushi bar. There's even more: Rum Largo is the poolside bar and cafe, the perfect place for a refreshing tropical concoction or a light lunch. And of course, at the Hilton you'll find complete twenty-four-hour room service. All in all, it's an outstanding selection of quality choices. However, if you prefer to go out for the evening, the fine restaurants and clubs of Downtown Disney are just a stroll away.

Shops at the Hilton

If you get the munchies or are looking for a snack to take to your room, Mainstreet Market is sure to have something for you. On the Green features a classy assortment of men's and women's resort sportswear, with an emphasis on golf, and there is also a small jewelry shop and eyewear store. If you want to do some really serious shopping, the Downtown Disney Marketplace is right across the street.

Services Available at the Hilton

- Twenty-four-hour concierge service
- Valet parking
- Full bell service
- Valet and coin-operated laundries
- In-house car rentals

Recreational Activities at the Hilton

- Two heated swimming pools and children's play pool in a beautiful garden area
- Two charming and secluded tropical hot tubs

@ Preferred tee times for Disney golf

@ Nautilus health club

@ Championship volleyball court

@ Video arcade

Our Impressions of the Hilton

@ This is an excellent hotel with outstanding service. It's a great place to stay in the Downtown Disney area.

@ None of the guest rooms at the Hilton have balconies.

@ There is a good selection of restaurants.

@ It's the closest hotel to Downtown Disney.

Romance at the Hilton

@ Evening hot tub ♥♥♥

@ A Tower room ♥♥

@ Stroll to Downtown Disney ♥♥

@ Breakfast in bed ♥♥♥

Grosvenor Resort

Pronounced "grove-nor," this nineteen-story hotel is one of the nearest to Downtown Disney and features a pleasant British-colonial theme. Throughout its spacious lobby, cooling shades of green, wicker chairs, and comfortable sofas abound. There's a constant flow of guests through here, heading for all destinations Disney and otherwise.

The large grounds of the Grosvenor most certainly set it apart from the others along the boulevard. Located on 13 beautifully land-scaped acres, the Grosvenor features two quiet, lakeside garden pools. Here amid the hubbub of Downtown Disney is an area that is surprisingly serene and marvelously restful. After a morning at the parks, you'll want to get your batteries recharged here for a night on the town.

Rooms at the Grosvenor are located either in the high-rise tower building or in one of its two garden wings. Tower rooms boast an impressive view of Downtown Disney or Lake Buena Vista. Garden wing rooms overlook either the parking lot and Hotel Plaza Boulevard or the garden and pool areas. Rooms feature either two doubles or a single king (rollaway beds and cribs are available). Room amenities include refrigerators and coffeemakers with complimentary coffee. The Grosvenor's new room furnishings are of light wood and include a large dresser, desk, and television armoire, and bedspreads are of pastel floral designs.

Room Rates at the Grosvenor Resort

Standard rooms at the Grosvenor begin around $110 to $184 per night, depending on the season (prices include Florida's 11½% taxes). **$** Specials and last-minute discounts throughout the year can lower these rates to around $92 a night or less. We suggest you call to see what is available. For the best and other special offers, check the hotel's Web site at www.grosvenorresort.com, or call Grosvenor reservations at (800) 624-4109.

Food and Beverages at the Grosvenor Resort

The Grosvenor makes more of an effort than any hotel along the plaza to give itself something of a theme, and you'll find it most evident in its eateries and lounges. Baskervilles is the hotel's premier restaurant, and it features an authentic Sherlock Holmes museum and re-creation of the famous 221B Baker Street. This eatery's specialty is its prime rib buffet, and on Saturday evenings there is the MurderWatch Mystery Theater dinner show. Baskervilles serves breakfast, lunch, and dinner with à la carte menus and features a Disney character breakfast with Inspector Goofy and Sleuth Pluto on Tuesdays, Thursdays, and Sundays. Right next door is Moriarty's Pub. Drop in here before dinner for a cocktail or later for a nightcap. Remember to ask if there is live entertainment here during your visit.

You won't likely miss Crumpet's Cafe in the lobby. Open twenty-four hours, Crumpet's is just the place to grab a quick snack and drink before you head off to your day of park adventures. Also located in the lobby is Cricket's Lounge, which has large-screen sporting events and a full-service bar with light snacks.

And of course, you'll find Barnacle's poolside with snacks, sandwiches, and beverages. During the busy season, there may even be live entertainment here, too.

Services Available at the Grosvenor Resort

- Valet parking ($8 daily)
- Valet and dry cleaning services
- Coin-operated laundry facilities
- In-house car rental
- Video camera and cell phone rentals
- ATM
- Childcare arrangements

Recreational Activities at the Grosvenor Resort

- Two heated pools and hot tub
- Two complimentary lighted tennis courts
- Electronic game room
- Basketball, volleyball, and shuffleboard courts
- Children's play pool and playground
- Fitness center
- Golf arrangements
- Lakeside gazebo

Our Impression of the Grosvenor Resort

- A comfortable resort that is virtually across the street from Downtown Disney.
- Room rates here can be attractive, indeed.
- Many tower rooms feature astounding views of Downtown Disney. There are no balconies at the Grosvenor.

Romance at the Grosvenor Resort

- An evening stroll to Downtown Disney ♥♥

Courtyard by Marriott

This familiar name in hotels enjoys a solid reputation for comfortable and well-furnished accommodations. This fourteen-story, atrium-style hotel features glass elevators and a tropical-theme lobby. Colors are bright and airy, and upper-floor rooms offer panoramas of Downtown Disney and nearby Lake Buena Vista.

Our fourteenth-floor room commanded a stunning view of Downtown Disney, and in the distance, we could see both Epcot and the Magic Kingdom. Spacious and comfortable, our guest room featured fabrics of green, burnt orange, and yellow. The bedspread was a tropical jungle print, and the club chairs in our small but comfortable sitting area were a warm blue. With a large balcony and king bed, we quickly made ourselves at home.

Guest rooms are either in the fourteen-story tower building or in the adjacent wing that overlooks the pool or I-4. Most rooms feature balconies. Ground-floor, pool-view rooms at the Marriott are beautiful and offer both patios and a real convenience to the pool and hot tub. These "courtyard" rooms are less expensive than upper-floor tower rooms and would come with our recommendation. Most rooms feature twin queen beds, but there are a few single kings. With a rollaway bed, each room can accommodate up to five persons. All rooms feature pay-per-view movies, iron and ironing board, television with Nintendo gaming, complimentary coffeemaker (with coffee), hairdryer, and high-speed Internet access ($10 per day).

Room Rates at the Courtyard by Marriott

Rates for guestrooms range from $105 to $244, depending on the season (prices include Florida's 11½% taxes). Standard view here at the Courtyard by Marriott means rooms in the back of the hotel, overlooking I-4.

Reservations can be made through Disney Central Reservations (407) W-DISNEY (934-7639) or through the Marriott at (800) 223-9930. For the best prices, visit the hotel's Web site at www.courtyard orlando.com.

Food and Beverages at the Courtyard by Marriott

Even with all your comings and goings to Disney, you can find good food at the Marriott for any of the day's meals. The Courtyard Cafe and Grille is the main eatery, and it features either à la carte or buffet breakfasts and a variety of dinner entrées. The Village Deli, which features Pizza Hut pizza, sandwiches, and frozen yogurt, is another place you'll want to know about. We enjoyed a continental breakfast in the atrium lobby at the 2GO Bar, which had a nice selection of pastries, muffins, cold cereals, and Barney's coffee. 2GO also has a variety of snacks and beverages.

The Tipsy Parrot Lounge is right in the great lobby and features a full-service bar and snacks. Poolside is the seasonal Tiki Bar. All in all, you'll find an ample supply of food and beverages.

Services Available at the Courtyard by Marriott

- Free parking
- Car rental desk in lobby
- Guest laundry and valet service

Recreational Activities at the Courtyard by Marriott

- Two outdoor, heated swimming pools
- Children's pool
- Quiet hot tub

- Exercise room

- Video game room

- Use of all Disney golf courses and tennis courts at the Grand Floridian

Our Impressions of the Courtyard by Marriott

- This is a quality yet fairly ordinary hotel. Rooms are spacious and comfortable. Most rooms have balconies.

- Off-season rooms here can be a real bargain.

- Upper-floor rooms can feature great views.

Recommendations for Courtyard by Marriott

- Ground-floor, pool-view courtyard rooms are especially nice.

Hotel Royal Plaza

The Royal Plaza enjoys something of a touch of Old Bermuda. Its bright and airy tiled lobby expresses a relaxing touch of the tropics. White expanses of wall that soar to high ceilings, wrought-iron accents, large potted palms, and bellpersons in starched-white uniforms and epaulets bring this theme together handsomely.

The 394 guest rooms are either in the sixteen-floor Tower building or in the two-story Lanai building adjacent to the pool. Rooms are bright and colorful and feature pastel tropical fish bedspreads. Toiletries from Bath & Body Works come standard—a nice touch.

Rooms feature either two doubles or a single king, a pull-out sleeper/sofa, coffeemaker with complimentary coffee, and either a small balcony or patio. The large Tower rooms offer a big tub, which can easily accommodate two. During our Hotel Royal Plaza visit, we were able to stay in one of our favorite rooms, the Executive King. This spacious two-room suite features a comfortable living room with pull-out queen sofa, a dining area, desk, and armoire with large-screen TV and video player. Our cozy king bedroom had a large TV and small sitting area. There were even dimmers on the lights

All Royal Plaza baths feature a small vanity area, which we found to be quite adequate. If you're visiting Disney with kids, we happily recommend the Executive King. Several of these rooms even feature whirlpool tubs.

Another nice room here is the ground-floor, pool-view Lanai room. Though a bit smaller than a Tower room, each features a private poolside patio.

Room Rates at Hotel Royal Plaza

$ The value season runs pretty much like the Disney resorts, but expect to find exceptionally good rates in the first week of June, all of September, and early October. Standard room rates run from $99 nightly to around $200, depending on the season (prices include Florida's 11½% taxes). For reservations, we suggest that you call this hotel's reservation desk at (800) 248-7890 or visit their Web site at www.royalplaza.com.

Food and Beverages at the Hotel Royal Plaza

Giraffe's is this hotel's main restaurant, and it features each of the day's meals à la carte as well as buffet breakfasts. The ambience is tropical, with potted plants, varnished wood floors, and colorful accents. The Giraffe Lounge features a daily happy hour with darts and a pool table. Nearby is the "Marketessin." This little shop is something of a market and something of a deli. It features an interesting assortment of snacks, sandwiches, beverages, and desserts. It's just the place for a light meal or to cure a case of the munchies.

Sip's Poolbar is a pleasant gazebo right alongside the swimming area. It features a selection of refreshing tropical specialty drinks and snacks.

Services Available at the Hotel Royal Plaza

- Valet parking ($8)
- Bell service
- Coin-operated laundry and valet service
- Room service until 11 P.M.

Recreational Activities at the Hotel Royal Plaza

- Large heated pool
- Fitness center with whirlpool tub
- Four lighted tennis courts
- Video arcade
- Tee times at the Disney golf courses

Our Impressions of the Hotel Royal Plaza

- The rooms are tropical, pleasant, and quite comfortable. Except for the Lanai rooms, balconies at Hotel Royal Plaza are very small. Due to the proximity of I-4, the pool area here is quite noisy.
- $ This hotel can be a good value.

Romance at the Hotel Royal Plaza

❧ One of this resort's Romance packages ♥♥

❧ A (family) visit in an Executive King room ♥♥

Best Western Lake Buena Vista Resort

This hotel is an eighteen-story high-rise and affords stunning views of Disney and Lake Buena Vista. It is located on a small and woodsy lot adjacent to the lake, and its pool and garden areas are exceptionally quiet. The bright and airy lobby enjoys a pleasant and tropical theme.

Rooms at the Lake Buena Vista Resort are undergoing an impressive refurbishing and upgrading during 2003. Floral spreads of muted purple, green, and beige lend each room a contemporary and classy look. All rooms feature balconies with a small table and chairs. There are a choice of three views: Disney, lake, or Orlando. All were pleasant enough, though we found both the lake and Disney views to be quite special, especially after dark. It is worth noting that the higher the room, the better the view.

There are four large, two-bedroom suites on the eighteenth floor of the Best Western, and with a rate around $340 per night, each seems something of a bargain. In addition to two spacious bedrooms and a comfortable living room, each suite also features a very nice enclosed porch with skylight. It is bright, airy, and one of the most unique features we've seen in any room at Walt Disney World. One of these would make a great romance destination or would provide ample space for a small family. If you are interested in one of these beautiful suites, we advise that you reserve early.

All rooms and suites include coffeemaker and complimentary coffee and tea, as well as a hairdryer, small vanity area, and the usual shower-tub combination. Accommodations feature either double queens or a single king bed with pull-out sleeper/sofa. All rooms can accommodate four guests (five with a $15 per night rollaway bed). Other amenities include iron and ironing board, pay-per-view movies, and Nintendo television gaming.

Room Rates at the Best Western Lake Buena Vista Resort

Room rates range from $95 to $188, depending on the season (prices include 11½% Florida taxes). Best Western adds a $5-per-day resort fee that includes all local telephone calls and use of its fitness center. $ To get the best possible rate during your visit, we suggest visiting the hotel's Web site at www.orlandoresorthotel.com or calling the hotel's reservation number at (800) 348-3765.

Food and Beverages at Best Western
Lake Buena Vista Resort

Trader's is the Best Western's all-purpose restaurant, and it features a breakfast buffet and à la carte dinner with a Caribbean flair. Steaks and seafood are the specialties of the house, and Trader's features a pleasant garden ambience and an even more beautiful dining porch. For a quick snack or light meal, you'll be happy with the Parakeet Cafe and its homemade doughnuts, croissandwiches, and pizza. There's even a nice "breakfast pizza." This resort also has a 7 A.M. to midnight room service.

Flamingo Cove is the hotel's lounge, found in the lobby, adjacent to Trader's. During the day, Flamingo Cove serves sandwiches, salads, and burgers. Toppers Night Club on the eighteenth floor is currently closed, but we are told that it will be reinvented and reopened sometime during 2003.

Services Available at Best Western
Lake Buena Vista Resort

- Convenient self-parking
- Room service from 7 A.M. to midnight
- Baby-sitting services

Recreational Activities at Best Western
Lake Buena Vista Resort

- Heated pool and garden sundeck
- Kiddie pool
- Children's playground
- Video game room
- Small fitness center

Our Impressions of Best Western
Lake Buena Vista Resort

- The rooms are pleasant, with many good views. It's a reasonable place to stay near Disney.
- This resort is a bit farther than most from Downtown Disney.

Romance at the Best Western
Lake Buena Vista Resort

- King bed with Disney or lake view ♥
- Best Western suite ♥♥

DoubleTree Guest Suites Resort

Our stay here began with warm chocolate chip cookies. A nice beginning. Next to the front desk, we noticed another nice touch: kids check-in. While parents are getting registered, so are the kids. A cute sign-in book and small gift pack make this a special moment for everyone. There are other special things about this hotel, too. Most notable is that the DoubleTree is the only all-suite resort on-property at Disney. The 229 lodgings in the seven-story DoubleTree are all spacious multiroom, one- and two-bedroom suites.

When we arrived in our room on the seventh floor, we were impressed by all the space. The large living room featured a dining area and a comfortable sitting area with pull-out queen bed. With television, wet bar, and a desk, we immediately set up shop. Our bedroom featured a king bed, but other suites are available with twin doubles. The bath and vanity areas were spacious and practical. There was even another TV in the bedroom. We definitely enjoyed all of the space.

Suites at the DoubleTree are whimsical and bright. Room decor is colorful and fun, featuring burgundy, blues, and greens. Each room includes a coffeemaker and complimentary coffee and tea, wet bar with refrigerator and microwave oven, hairdryer, iron and ironing board, and video player with on-demand gaming. Accommodations at the DoubleTree are most certainly large enough for a family and will provide the privacy that a single hotel room simply cannot. We made breakfast an in-room affair by dropping in at Streamer's Market (in the lobby) and buying milk and cold cereal. It made our first meal of the day both affordable and what we're used to eating.

Room Rates at DoubleTree Guest Suites Resort

Rates for the DoubleTree's one-bedroom suites range from a bargain $144 to around $278, depending on the season (prices include 11½% Florida taxes). The DoubleTree also offers a variety of seasonal and special packages. $ Discounts for both AAA and AARP are quite good. For reservations, phone DoubleTree at (800) 222-TREE (8733) or Disney Central Reservations (407) W-DISNEY (934-7639). For discounted suites and other special offers, visit the DoubleTree's Web site at www.doubletreeguestsuites.com.

Food and Beverages at DoubleTree Guest Suites Resort

Streamer's is the restaurant at DoubleTree. Adjacent to the atrium-style lobby, this eatery offers a breakfast buffet and an à la carte dinner menu. DoubleTree also has a tropical poolside snack bar and lounge, and for those wishing to do for themselves, there's Streamer's Market. This little store features a great selection of drinks, snacks, and groceries. Using

Streamer's Market and your suite's microwave and refrigerator can add up to some real savings, particularly at breakfast. DoubleTree also has a Starbuck's coffee cart in the lobby.

Services Available at DoubleTree Guest Suites Resort

- Coin-operated laundry and dry cleaning service
- Budget car rental desk in lobby
- Kids check-in desk and childcare services
- Nightly turndown, by request
- Bed boards

Recreational Activities at DoubleTree Guest Suites Resort

- Heated, tropical pool with pool bar and snack area
- Hot tub
- Complimentary fitness center
- Two lighted tennis courts
- Children's playground
- Volleyball court
- Jogging trail
- Video game room
- Preferred tee times at Disney golf courses

Our Impressions of DoubleTree Guest Suites Resort

- These are very spacious accommodations for the money. Comfortable, but not luxurious. Decor is pleasant and colorful, and all suites are bright and fresh.
- A bit longer walk to Downtown Disney than some other hotels here on the boulevard, but it's also closer to the Crossroads Shopping Plaza.
- I-4 traffic makes the pool area fairly noisy.

Recommendations for Doubletree Guest Suites

- $ Off-season rates can make this place ideal for a small family.

Romance at DoubleTree Guest Suites Resort

- Having your own private bedroom ♥♥
- Letting your kids enjoy DoubleTree's "Kids Theater" while you enjoy a quiet dinner together ♥

The Disney Cruise Line

The Disney Cruise Line delivers all of what we most love about Walt Disney World: lavish accommodations, innovative dining, romantic nightlife, and unique entertainment, all sprinkled with a bit of Disney magic. We found even more to enjoy on our Disney cruises: enchanting nights at sea, pampering spa treatments, and an unforgettable day along the sparkling sands of Disney's private island paradise, Castaway Cay.

The Ships: *The Magic* and *The Wonder*

The Disney Cruise Line has two ships, the Disney Magic and the Disney Wonder. Both vessels were constructed in the same Italian shipyard and both enjoy the same classic lines. While their beautiful design recalls the golden age of ocean liners, these ships are state-of-the-art from stem to stern.

Although both ships are identical in overall design, each enjoys its own unique decor. The Disney Magic features the vibrant colors and echoing geometric patterns of Art Deco, while the Wonder's Art Nouveau is one of elegant and intricate patterns of curving lines. We noticed the differences mostly in the details of the common areas, such as the artwork, chandeliers, and carpets of the atria and restaurants.

The Cruises

The Disney Cruise Line offers a variety of cruises and "land/sea" packages. All cruises depart from and return to the beautiful Disney Cruise Line terminal at Port Canaveral.

The Wonder cruises the Bahamas with alternating three- and four-night cruises. The three-night cruises spend a day in Nassau and a day at Castaway Cay. The four-night cruises also visit Nassau and Castaway Cay, but alternate with a visit to Grand Bahama Island one week, and a day at sea the next. You can also book a seven-night "land/sea adventure" and enjoy either a three- or four-night cruise with the rest of the seven days on a Walt Disney World vacation.

The Magic's seven-night cruises are to the eastern or western Caribbean. The eastern Caribbean itinerary includes St. Maarten and St. Thomas in the Virgin Islands and Castaway Cay, while the western Caribbean cruise stops at Key West, Grand Cayman, Cozumel, and Castaway Cay.

Disney's Castaway Cay

Whatever cruise you're on, you'll spend a day on beautiful Castaway Cay, Disney's private island in the Bahamas. We simply loved its pristine sand beaches, water sports, snorkeling, and relaxation Bahamas-style.

The island offered rental sailboats, bikes, kayaks, paddleboats, rafts, and even parasailing. Family activities include nature hikes and beach games. Scattered along the shores of the bay, are several tropical bars and a restaurant that features an island barbecue.

On the other side of the island, we discovered Serenity Bay, Disney's adults-only beach. What we found here were open-air massage cabanas, a tropical fruit and beverage bar, and a kind of peace and plenty rare even in vacation paradises. The only complaint we've ever heard about Castaway Cay is that people simply wanted to stay longer.

Helpful Hint

Make your Castaway Cay massage reservations as soon as you board ship in Florida.

Shore Excursions

The variety of shore excursions offered on the Disney cruises is far too large to list here. Snorkeling, kayaking, sailing, golf, horseback riding, and an inviting array of tours and adventures are just a few of the many offerings. We suggest you gather this information before you sail, so that you'll be prepared to make your reservations early.

Accommodations

Both ships offer the same variety of accommodations with similar decor. Nautical prints of reds, whites, and blues and the golden glow of hand-crafted pearwood cabinetry combine to create a rich and classy feeling. Even the most modest stateroom offers spacious closets and numerous drawers. It's important to note that staterooms aboard the Disney cruise ships are 25 percent larger than cruise industry standards.

But most important is that every stateroom provides the quality that we have come to expect from Team Disney. Each is beautiful, comfortable, well furnished, and complete with the signature Disney details. Every stateroom features satellite TV and a hairdryer, and most feature something altogether new for cruise ships, a "split bath." This means one bath with a vanity and shower/tub, and another with vanity and toilet. It's perfect for a couple or a family.

Staterooms are either outside (with ocean view) or inside (no ocean view). Three out of four staterooms feature ocean views and nearly half of those have private verandahs. There are two types of inside staterooms: the standard (184 square feet) and the deluxe (214 square feet with split bath). Outside staterooms include the deluxe ocean view (with large porthole), deluxe stateroom with navigator's verandah ♥♥ (enclosed balcony with partially obstructed view), and deluxe stateroom with verandah ♥♥♥ (268 square feet and an open and spacious verandah). Both ships also feature one and two-bedroom suites ♥♥♥♥ and a Royal Suite ♥♥♥♥. All suites have verandahs and feature concierge service.

Dining on the Disney Cruise Ships

The Disney Cruise Line delivers unique cruise ship dining. There are three themed restaurants onboard each ship, and passengers and their service staff enjoy a different one each night. The Animator's Palate is featured on both ships. This amusing restaurant and its wait staff all appear in black and white at the beginning of the meal but gradually, everything comes alive with colors. The creative cuisine features such selections as parmesan-crusted veal chops and roast chicken stuffed with crabmeat. Another restaurant featured on both ships is the brightly colored Parrot Cay, serving fresh fish, meats, fruits, and vegetables, all prepared with a real taste of the tropics.

The French flair and classic dining room of Lumiere's is found on the Magic. Aboard the Wonder is the undersea theme of Triton's, with its specialty of seafood, including sea bass, tuna, and salmon.

> **Helpful Hint**
> Make your reservations for Palo as soon as you get aboard in Florida.

There's a fourth restaurant on both ships also, the adults-only Palo ♥♥♥ . This beautiful and romantic dining features the best food you will find aboard ship.

Both ships feature themed buffet eateries (Topsider Buffet on Magic and Beach Blanket Buffet on Wonder) that serve breakfast, lunch, and a light dinner. And atop the pool deck, you'll find Pluto's (hot) Dog House and Pinocchio's Pizzeria. There's even an ice cream shop and stateroom dining at no extra charge. Room service, however, is extra.

In addition to the usual meal offerings is an inviting assortment of other food "events." Seven-day cruises feature the Captain's Gala Dinner, "It's a Small World Dinner," the Disney Master Chef's Series, High Tea, a champagne brunch, Tea with Wendy Darling, and more. The Bahama cruises offer a late-night buffet deck party in Nassau and, on the four-night cruise, the Disney Master Chef's Series.

Shipboard Entertainment

There's so much to do aboard the Disney cruise ships that we can't describe it all in detail. The center of the galaxy of entertainment is the Walt Disney Theater, which presents a different, family-oriented Broadway-style show each evening. And for movie lovers, the beautiful Buena Vista Theater screens first-run movies from the various Disney studios.

Each ship also offers its own nightclub "district." On board Magic, it's Beat Street, and onboard Wonder, it's called Route 66. Each area includes three different clubs, with a variety of entertainment from rock 'n' roll to stand-up comedy. And each ship features an ESPN Skybox Sports Club in one of its smokestacks.

Later in the evening, we enjoyed the mellow jazz of Sessions on board Magic and the vintage tunes of the Cadillac Lounge onboard Wonder.

Children's Cruise Activities

When it comes to children's programming, each ship has almost an entire deck and a total of fifty counselors devoted solely to supervised children's activities. There are three unique areas, each designed to provide age-specific adventures for children: Oceaneer Club (ages 3 to 8), Oceaneer Lab (ages 9 to 12), and Common Grounds, a coffeehouse for teens. Children's activities on Disney cruise ships are so great that the rest of the industry is struggling to keep up. Good luck to them.

Onboard Recreation and the Vista Spa and Salon

In addition to three pools (one for adults only), each ship has several hot tubs and an on-deck sports area featuring volleyball, basketball, badminton, shuffleboard, and Ping-Pong. There's a quarter-mile jogging and walking course as well as a state-of-the-art Cybex fitness center.

Also on board each is a beautiful Vista Spa and Salon ♥♥♥, which features a sublime variety of treatments from around the world. Enjoy hydrotherapy, massages, aromatherapy, saunas, whirlpools, and the marvelous Tropical Rain Shower. This is a place you'll not want to miss.

Onboard Shopping

Each ship has a tax-free gift shop, which features liquor, leather goods, jewelry, and gifts. And, as you might imagine, several shops on board each ship are dedicated to character and logo merchandise, toys and novelties, and men's and women's apparel.

How Much It Costs

Price is based on what cruise you select, the type of stateroom you choose, and where on the ship it is located. There are so many variations that we suggest you contact a travel agent or the Disney Cruise Line to determine what cruise best fits your desires. Know that the cruise price includes shipboard accommodations, entertainment aboardship, and all meals as well as snacks and ice cream. A land/sea adventure would add resort accommodations at WDW and admission to all Disney attractions (meals at Walt Disney World are not included). Here's what is not included onboard ship: spa or salon visits, shore excursions, sightseeing and meals ashore, phone calls, video games, Internet usage, alcoholic beverages, and soft drinks other than those served with meals. You can also expect to pay gratuities, transfers, and any taxes and fees imposed at the various ports of call, including U.S. Customs arrival and departure taxes.

We urge you to learn more about a Disney cruise by visiting www.disneycruise.com or calling (888) 325-2500. Below is a list of a few sample prices, just to give you an idea of how much things cost. The prices are per couple; include gratuities, port charges, and transfers; and are for early booking during value season:

- 7-night cruise, inside deluxe stateroom: $2,250 per couple

- 7-night land/sea adventure, WDW moderate resort and inside stateroom: about $2,200 per couple

- 7-night cruise, outside stateroom with navigator's verandah: about $2,850 per couple

- 7-night land/sea adventure, outside stateroom with navigator's verandah and deluxe resort at WDW: about $2,800 per couple

- 3-night cruise, inside deluxe stateroom: $1,300 (4 nights are $1,530) per couple

- 4-night cruise, outside stateroom with navigator's verandah: $1,900 per couple

Cruising with a family? For a 7-night cruise and for each child (or extra adult), add to the above prices about $275 for children under 3, $570 for ages 3 to 12, and $770 for over 12. For a 4-night cruise, $208/ $453/$499 (prices include gratuities, taxes, transfers, and port charges).

Money-Saving Tip

Discounts for Disney cruises are available simply by booking early and through AAA and discount clubs such as BJs, Costco, and Sam's Club.

Romance On Board the Disney Cruise Ships

- A deluxe stateroom with verandah ♥♥♥♥

- A romantic dinner at Palo ♥♥♥

- The Surial Bath for two at the Vista Spa ♥♥♥

- ❦ Massage on the beach at Castaway Cay ♥♥♥

- ❦ Breakfast in bed or on your verandah ♥♥♥

Our Impressions of the Disney Cruise Experience

- ❦ Our cruises aboard the Magic and the Wonder were memorable experiences. We enjoyed the food very much. Our evening meal at Triton's was superb. We had such a good time we'd love to take another Disney cruise. We even went to a wine-tasting party at Palo's. All in all, we're happy to report that this is a first-class cruise experience. Bon Voyage!

- ❦ Both the ships and Castaway Cay are simply far too beautiful to describe in the limited space we have here.

- ❦ Staterooms are exceptionally comfortable, quiet, and beautiful.

- ❦ Onboard children's activities are by far the best of any ships that sail the seas.

Our Recommendations for the Disney Cruise Line

- ❦ $ The best discounts can be had simply by booking early.

- ❦ The three-day cruise seems to us like too little time on the ship.

- ❦ The Disney Cruise Line offers a variety of honeymoons and wedding packages. For more details, see chapter 8.

PART 2

What to Do Once You Get There

CHAPTER

3

Getting Started

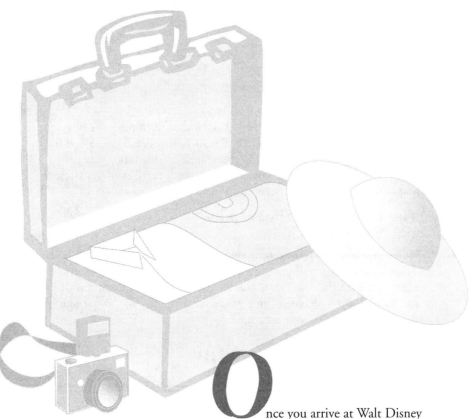

Once you arrive at Walt Disney World and settle in at your resort, you'll want to rush out the door and start your Disney adventure right away. Well, not quite. We think it's wise first to get a handle on what's happening at Disney during your visit, to know how you're going to get where it is you want to go, and to think about what it is you want to rush off to see. So take a few minutes now to learn some of the basics you'll need at Walt Disney World.

Getting Up-to-Speed on WDW

First, you'll need to bring yourselves up-to-speed on what will be happening during your visit. Things change constantly at Disney. Not so much the big things like new resorts or theme parks, but smaller things like show times, which attractions may not be running, and a large assortment of seasonal variables like park hours and special events. There are two useful tools for learning what will be happening during your visit, and you can get them both when you check in to your resort.

The World Update

At check-in, be sure you get this Walt Disney World general information pamphlet. It provides the most current information on park hours, special events, new attractions, and the latest on the Extra Magic Hour and *FASTPASS*. Look it over carefully and carry it with you for reference.

The Guidemaps

Available for every Disney attraction (including such places as Blizzard Beach, Downtown Disney, and the Epcot Resort Area), these colorful maps will be your guides to rides, shows, rest rooms, shops, and restaurants. The guidemaps are available at the guest services of your resort and at the entrance of every Disney theme park.

The Theme Park Times Guide and New Information

When you arrive at your resort, you'll want to pick up an *All Four Parks Times Guide*. This will give you the hours of the shows and entertainment in all four of the theme parks. Know that each theme park also has its own more-detailed times guide, and you'll want to get one of these when your first visit each park.

Getting Around at WDW

Walt Disney World is a big place. Getting around its nearly 50 square miles will be something that you'll want to get good at, and it won't be hard. There are many ways to get around Disney and from buses to boats, you should find yourselves enjoying your "World" travels. Transportation from each of the Disney resorts to the various Disney attractions varies from resort to resort and we told you about each resort's transportation options in chapter 2. In this section, we'll give you a brief overview of ways to get around Disney.

Fun Fact

With nearly 300 buses and 970 drivers, Disney's is the third largest bus fleet in Florida.

Parking

If you're driving to the theme parks, keep in mind that parking costs $7 ($8 for an RV or camper). Once parked, you'll be ferried to the front entrance of the park by one of the Walt Disney World trams. Parking for annual pass holders and for Disney resort guests is free.

The Transportation Guidemap

This map and chart will give you all the information you'll need to successfully navigate your way around "The World." It will provide every option, be it bus, boat, or monorail, to and from every Disney resort and attraction. Pick up one of these at guest services and keep it with you during your travels. It will save time and keep you from getting lost.

Disney Bus Service

Bus service is the mainstay of transportation at Walt Disney World. Buses run to and from all Disney resorts to all Disney attractions from one hour prior to opening to two hours after closing. Bus transportation is probably the most complained-about thing at Walt Disney World, and we'll admit that on occasion, we've had a modest number of delays. As we go to press with this book, Team Disney is trying out some new things to make bus transportation better. One of them is "Bus on Demand," a program that tries to identify slow-ups and to re-route buses to deal with them. We see Disney making a real effort to improve their bus service (278 buses and nearly 1,000 drivers).

The Disney Fleet

If you enjoy a pleasant outdoor trip, there is nothing like a boat ride. Dozens of watercraft ply the waters of Disney World, and as Disney resort guests you'll be free to use all of them. From the dock at the Magic Kingdom, boats arrive and depart for the Ticket and Transportation Center (TTC), Wilderness Lodge, the Grand Floridian and Polynesian Resorts, and Fort Wilderness. At Epcot's Showcase Plaza, catch a launch across the lagoon to either Germany or Morocco. At Epcot's International Gateway, Friendship water taxis carry passengers to the BoardWalk, the Yacht and the Beach Clubs, the Swan and the Dolphin, and on to Disney-MGM Studios.

Downtown Disney is located on Lake Buena Vista, which connects to a series of waterways. Here, watercraft leave for trips up the Sassagoula Waterway to Port Orleans and Old Key West. There's even a water taxi that connects the West Side with the Downtown Marketplace.

The Famous Disney Monorail

There are three monorail spurs at Walt Disney World running on nearly 14 miles of elevated track. Two spurs circle the Seven Seas Lagoon. The express carries "day guests" to the Magic Kingdom from the TTC; the local, for Disney resort guests, makes stops at the TTC and at all three resorts around the lagoon. The third monorail line runs from the TTC to Epcot. This monorail line is long and scenic, but crowded in the early morning hours when Magic Kingdom resort guests flock to Epcot.

Insider's Secret

You can ride in the front of the monorail with the driver. Ask at the loading platform at your resort.

Traveling to Other Disney Resorts

You'll likely want to visit other Disney resorts to dine or perhaps just to look around. If you have a car, driving will be the easiest way to go. Pick up a map of Walt Disney World at guest services and follow the large purple and red signs.

If you don't have a car, you can take the bus. Simply catch one from your resort to any theme park and then switch buses to one going to the resort you're headed for. After the parks close, you'll have to use Downtown Disney for switching buses. Here, buses run to and from all Disney resorts into the wee hours of the morning.

Making Some Important Decisions

Before you rush off to begin your Disney adventure, we urge you to make a few decisions about what you most want to see and do during your visit. As we've said, there's far too much at Walt Disney World to see in any single visit (even if you were staying for weeks!). So, it's important that you have at least some idea of what you must see. We're not suggesting that you plan every moment of your vacation, but simply give it an overall shape.

Take a few minutes to sit down with the guidemaps and World Update, look at park operating hours and the times and days of special events, and rough-out your Disney journey. Don't overplan. Leave enough room for spontaneity, surprise discoveries, and changes of heart. Okay, now you can head out.

The Attractions

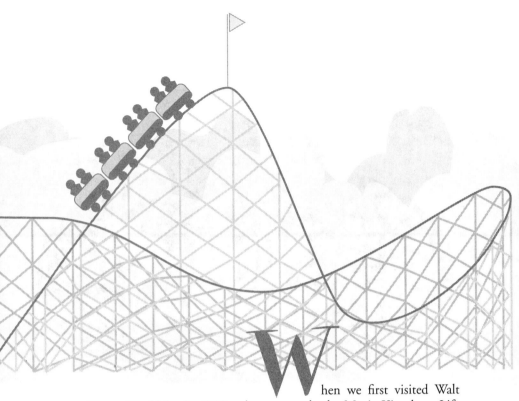

When we first visited Walt Disney World in the 1970s, there was only the Magic Kingdom. Life used to be so simple. In two or three days, we could see it all and still have time to enjoy a few encores. How times have changed. These days, with four major theme parks (and much, much more), we'd have to visit for a month to even see most of it. Too bad that isn't practical.

Today, with the sheer size of Disney, you have to pick and choose what you are going to do. This chapter is intended to help you do just that. We'll provide a good idea of what there is to see and do at the theme parks so that you can decide what you must see and what you won't mind missing. This kind of planning is necessary to help you avoid wasting precious (and expensive) vacation time. Remember that most first-time visitors to Walt Disney World are shocked to see how big it is and how much there is to do.

We promise not to ramble on about Dumbo the Flying Elephant. Our plan is to provide you with just enough information to make informed decisions without spoiling the excitement of discovery, which is one of the greatest pleasures of Disney. We urge you to keep an open mind when it comes to all Disney attractions. Sure, you're eager to "ride the big ones," but in our experience it's sometimes that small and unsung attraction that you'll remember long after the thrill of Test Track has faded.

We'll let you know which attractions we think should not be missed, which might be too intense for young ones, and even which ones might strike you as particularly romantic. We'll also tell you lots more, from how to avoid long lines, to how to get the most out of dining, shopping, and getting around the parks. We'll do everything we can to help make your visit to the Disney theme parks what it should be: a fun vacation.

Setting a Practical Pace

Resist the urge to spend all day in any theme park. During the midday hours, the parks all become terribly crowded. It's a good time to duck out and head back to your resort for lunch, a few hours rest, or even a nap. Go swimming, take a boat ride, or enjoy some of Disney's other recreational offerings (see chapter 7). If your hotel is off-property, see a movie or shop at Downtown Disney, visit a water park, or have lunch in one of the Disney resorts. Whatever you do, escape the madness of the theme parks for at least a few hours at midday and return later in the day.

Disney's *FASTPASS*

We believe that Disney's *FASTPASS* is one of the most significant Disney innovations ever. It has, in fact, revolutionized the waiting game for the popular theme park attractions.

Basically, it works like this: Say you want to ride the Tower of Terror at Disney-MGM Studios. To avoid waiting in a line that would typically be an hour long, you can stroll up to the *FASTPASS* distribution area in front of the attraction, run your park pass through the machine, and receive a special pass for the ride (you'll also get your park ticket back).

This new pass will specify an hour-long time period during which you can return to the Tower of Terror's *FASTPASS* entrance and get right in. So instead of wasting an hour in line, you're free to spend it at other attractions, shopping, or whatever.

There is, however, one ground rule to the *FASTPASS*. You can only get a *FASTPASS* for a second attraction after the first *FASTPASS* time has expired or after a time printed on the pass, whichever comes first. Not all attractions feature *FASTPASS*, just Disney's busiest and some only on busy days.

FASTPASS Tips

The real trick to using the *FASTPASS* is to get one as soon as you arrive in each new area of a park. Once you have it, you'll be free to explore until your window of opportunity arrives. It makes sense to get your *FASTPASS* for the attractions with the longest lines and then see the attractions with shorter (or no) lines Be sure to check your theme park guidemaps to see if any new attractions have been added to *FASTPASS.*

@ If you arrive at a park early, get a *FASTPASS* for one busy attraction, then ride another popular attraction, and then return to use the *FASTPASS* a little while later.

@ Check the tip board when you first arrive to see which attractions necessitate a *FASTPASS.*

@ Another early-morning trick: To visit a popular attraction twice, grab a *FASTPASS* on your way in, ride the attraction without the *FASTPASS,* and return later with your *FASTPASS* to ride again.

@ Get a FASTPASS for the busiest attraction first. The most popular attractions can actually run out.

What You'll Find at Every Theme Park

All the parks have certain things in common:

@ **The Theme Park Guidemap and Times Guide and New Information**   From water parks to theme parks (even the Epcot Resort Area), each of the Disney attractions has its own guidemap. On each you will find rides, shows, parade routes, first aid, ATMs, phones, rest rooms, restaurants, and just about anything you require. In addition, each of the four theme parks has a Times Guide that includes the day's show times and, if applicable, any limited opening hours for attractions and restaurants. Together, these will be your most important tools for visiting any attraction. Pick them up at your resort's guest services when you arrive or at the entrance gates to the theme parks, and use them to familiarize yourselves with the Disney attractions.

@ **Tip Board**   Each theme park has this information board that will tell you about its special events, wait times, and which of the attractions might be closed.

@ **Ticket Booths**   At the entrance to every theme park, there are ticket booths where you can purchase the entire variety of Disney admission tickets and passes, except for the Ultimate Hopper Pass.

@ **Guest Services**   A guest relations desk is located near the entrance of each park. Cast members here will be able to make resort reservations and priority seating arrangements for Disney restaurants. Guest relations also serves as a lost and found area and foreign currency exchange.

@ **Rentals**   Strollers, wheelchairs, and electric convenience vehicles (ECVs) are available at the entrance to every park. Single strollers or wheelchairs cost $8 per day, double strollers, where available, are $15, and ECVs are $30. Some deposits apply.

Storage lockers are also located near the entrance of each theme park. If you purchase something and don't want to lug it around all day, a locker will come in handy. Lockers are also useful for storing rain gear, jackets, and sweaters that you might need later in the day. Locker rental fees are about $5 a day plus a $2 key deposit.

@ **Miscellaneous Necessities**   Rest rooms, telephones, and ATMs can all be found near the entrance to each park.

@ **Lost and Found**   Every park has a "same-day" lost and found department. At the end of the day, everything goes to "Lost and Found Central" at the kennel near the Ticket and Transportation Center (near the Magic Kingdom). Its phone number is (407) 824-4245.

@ **Theme Park Childcare Centers**   These centers provide areas for changing diapers as well as rocking chairs for feeding and play areas for older siblings. Each center also has a small offering of diapers and other childcare products. Use your theme park guidemap to find the location of each.

@ **The Extra Magic Hour**   This valuable perk is for Disney resort guests only; if you're staying in a Disney resort, make good use of it. The Extra Magic Hour allows you into a different (and specified) theme park each day, one hour before the general public. Only select attractions are up and running, and these may vary. Check the World Update to see which. The Extra Magic Hour schedule is:

The Magic Kingdom: Sundays and Thursdays

Epcot: Wednesdays

Disney-MGM Studios: Tuesdays and Saturdays

The Animal Kingdom: Mondays and Fridays

@ **Character Greeting Places**   Team Disney has really increased the number of characters appearing in the theme parks. There are designated areas in the parks for meeting the Disney characters (see your guidemaps for locations). If you're traveling with kids, they'll certainly wish to meet Mickey and his friends, and you'll want to take advantage of these heart-warming photo opportunities. If your kids are interested, the characters will happily sign autographs. Disney autograph books are available almost everywhere in the parks.

@ **Character Photos Are Not Just for Kids!** Cast members are available at every character greeting place to snap a photo (with your camera) of the two of you or of your entire family. These will be your most memorable pictures. Trust us.

@ **"Attraction-Action" Photos** You'll automatically be photographed just at the most exciting moment in several theme park attractions. After the ride ends, you can see your photo and purchase it if you like. Cost is around $10. One of our most cherished Disney photos was taken on Splash Mountain. You'll find others at Test Track (Epcot); DINOSAUR (Animal Kingdom); Rock 'n' Roller Coaster and The Twilight Zone Tower of Terror (Disney-MGM); and Teamboat Springs (Blizzard Beach).

Eating in the Theme Parks

Let us warn you, food in the Disney theme parks is expensive. Although prices are definitely higher than similar style restaurants in the outside world, we think servings at Disney are usually a little larger, and quality is a little better. For our take on eating at Walt Disney World, see chapter 6, and for an overview of what to expect to spend on various meals at Walt Disney World, see page 301.

Our Theme Parks Tips

@ Get an early start. This is the most important advice we can give you about seeing the parks. The first few hours in any park are the least crowded, and lines are shortest. Make use of this time to see the popular attractions that will have long lines by mid-morning. Most people arrive between 10 A.M. and 11 A.M. Get there before they do.

@ If you wish to eat in a theme park table-service restaurant, be sure to make priority seating arrangements ahead of time. This is especially true for dinner. See page 302 to learn about making Disney dinner "reservations."

@ Almost every attraction has a sign telling how long the wait will be for that attraction. Use that information to avoid wasting time in line.

- To avoid wasting time standing in lines, use *FASTPASS*.

- The busiest days in each park are that park's Extra Magic Hour days. Most Disney resort guests arrive early and stay all day. Avoid this. Come early, but as soon as it begins to get crowded, head over to one of the other, less crowded theme parks or back to your resort for rest or recreation.

- If you are waiting for a scheduled show, ask the cast member who patrols the line if you'll make it into the next show or the one after that.

- Try arriving at one of the parks an hour or so before closing time. You may feel like salmon heading upriver, but you'll be amazed at how much you can see while most people are leaving.

- A good time to take in the busiest rides or shows is during a parade or a fireworks show that you may have already seen. Check guidemaps for parade routes, so you won't be caught on the wrong side.

- Travel light. Avoid carrying lots of camera gear, large purses, or anything else that will weigh you down. Additional bag-checking security gates (and a second line to get through) are now fixtures at Walt Disney World. For those without bags, there is a faster express entrance.

- "The Kid Swap." If you're visiting with a youngster who's too short or too young for a particular ride, Disney has devised a method that allows you both to ride without him, just not at the same time. While one of you "babysits" at the boarding area, the other enjoys the attraction. Afterward, you'll switch. Simply get in line as usual and when you arrive at the boarding area for the ride, ask a cast member what to do.

Other Things to Know About

- **Disney's 100 Years of Magic**   Although officially ended, some of the events may continue during the coming year. We can't tell you for how long, but we expect to see the following during 2003 and possibly into 2004: Illuminations: Reflections of Earth at Epcot, Mickey's Jammin' Jungle Parade at the Animal Kingdom, and MGM's Stars and Cars Motorparade.

- **Character Photos**   All the theme parks feature roving photographers who will take your photo in front of a castle or other landmark and, while processing it, will enhance it with Disney characters. We have some terrific Character Photos. Ask the photographer where you can pick up the picture and get there before the end of the day to avoid a long line. Picture prices begin around $13.

- **Pin Trading** This began with the Millennium Celebration, and it has been so successful that it will probably continue for the next millennium. Every Disney area has a pin trading station and there are information sessions scheduled each day. Check your guidemap for locations and times.

- **Discover the Stories Behind the Magic Kiosks** These interactive kiosks reveal the magic and stories behind the creation of the Disney theme parks. You'll find one in each theme park. Check the guidemap for location.

- **E-Mail Disney Greetings** At several places around Disney, you'll be able to send free e-mail photo-postcards to friends and family back home. Here's where you'll find them: In Future World at Epcot at Innoventions West, at Imagination's Imageworks, and at the Wonderland Cafe at DisneyQuest (Downtown Disney). They are a nice touch, so be sure to jot down a few e-mail addresses before you leave home and carry them with you.

- **Free Package Delivery** Disney resort guests can purchase merchandise in any of the Disney parks and have it delivered to their resort rooms for free. It's a good way to travel light, but remember that this is a "next-day" service.

The Magic Kingdom

No matter how many times we visit the Magic Kingdom, we are always surprised by its beauty. It's easy to think of it only in terms of attractions, parades, and fireworks, but the Magic Kingdom *is* magical. The fantasy architecture and meticulous gardens are a fairy tale of loveliness. The Magic Kingdom typifies what is so wonderful about all the Disney parks. They are much more than a bunch of rides and shows. They are perfect masterpieces of storytelling. Everything you will see has a tale to tell, from shops and rides, to shows and restaurants.

Children tend to think of the Magic Kingdom as the best part of Disney, which often leads adults to think that it is largely for children. While there are many child-oriented attractions here, don't assume that the child in you won't enjoy them.

The Magic Kingdom is made up of seven different areas, all of which surround the central area in front of Cinderella Castle: Main Street USA, Adventureland, Frontierland, Liberty Square, Fantasyland, Mickey's Toontown Fair, and Tomorrowland.

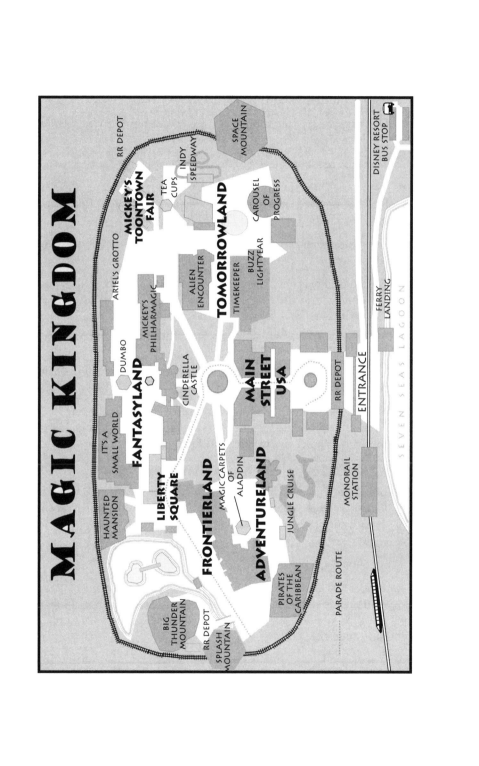

MAGIC KINGDOM

RR DEPOT

SPACE MOUNTAIN

INDY SPEEDWAY

TEA CUPS

MICKEY'S TOONTOWN FAIR

ARIEL'S GROTTO

CAROUSEL OF PROGRESS

TOMORROWLAND

ALIEN ENCOUNTER

BUZZ LIGHTYEAR

MICKEY'S PHILHARMAGIC

TIMEKEEPER

DUMBO

FANTASYLAND

CINDERELLA CASTLE

IT'S A SMALL WORLD

MAIN STREET USA

LIBERTY SQUARE

MAGIC CARPETS OF ALADDIN

HAUNTED MANSION

FRONTIERLAND

JUNGLE CRUISE

RR DEPOT

ADVENTURELAND

ENTRANCE

BIG THUNDER MOUNTAIN

PIRATES OF THE CARIBBEAN

MONORAIL STATION

RR DEPOT

SPLASH MOUNTAIN

PARADE ROUTE

FERRY LANDING

DISNEY RESORT BUS STOP

SEVEN SEAS LAGOON

Magic Kingdom Tips

- The most important thing to know about this theme park is that it is always the busiest part of Walt Disney World.

- Don't try to see it all in one day. In fact, don't even try to spend a whole day here.

- Make the best possible use of *FASTPASS*. You'll need it here.

- If you are interested in seeing the big-name attractions (Splash, Space, Thunder Mountain, etc.), make them your first effort. Start early. Make good use of *FASTPASS*.

- The Extra Magic Hour at the Magic Kingdom is on Sundays and Thursdays.

- E-Ride Nights is for Disney resort guests only. For about $13, you get admission to the Magic Kingdom after closing on select dates (always during busy seasons and not around Christmas), to ride nine of the park's most popular attractions. It's a great deal. See page 50 for other requirements.

- There's one Magic Kingdom tip board located at the end of Main Street and another in Tomorrowland.

- Need help planning your trip? There's a AAA counter in Main Street's Town Square Exposition Hall. You can get Triptiks, maps, tour books, hotel reservations, and more.

Tips for Eating at the Magic Kingdom

- Breakfast choices at the Magic Kingdom: Tony's Town Square, Cinderella's Royal Table, The Crystal Palace, and the coffee cart in Town Square.

- For our sensibilities, Tony's Town Square is our favorite MK restaurant.

- Cinderella's Royal Table ♥♥♥ has an interesting menu of good food. It's romantic and beautiful. Priority seating is an absolute must for families, but couples might be able to get in with only a short wait. Ask.

- The Crystal Palace offers character buffets and many interesting dishes. It's a very good choice for families and for salad lovers.

- Plaza Restaurant and Liberty Tree Tavern both have good sandwiches and pleasant dining areas.

Magic Kingdom Restaurants

Restaurant	Location	Price	Fare	Service	Our Comments
Tony's Town Square*	Main Street	$$	Italian	Table service B/L/D	Nice restaurant, good food. See page 340.
Plaza Restaurant*	Main Street	$	Grilled deli sandwiches, burgers, ice cream	Table service L/D	Restful, good food. See page 335.
Crystal Palace*	Main Street	$$	Large character buffets	Counter service B/L/D	Good food. See page 323.
Casey's Corner	Main Street	$	Hot dogs, fries	Counter service L/D	The usual
El Pirata y el Perico	Adventureland	$	Tacos, chili, hot dogs	Counter service L/D	Not-so-great fast food
Pecos Bill's Cafe	Frontierland	$	Burgers, sandwiches, wraps	Counter service L/D	Good topping bar
Liberty Tree Tavern*	Liberty Square	$$	Sandwiches, buffet dinner	Table service L/D	Decent food. See page 330.
Columbia Harbor House	Liberty Square	$	Seafood, chowder, chicken	Counter service L/D	Mostly fried food
Cinderella's Royal Table*	Fantasyland	$$	Buffet character breakfast; varied menu for lunch, dinner	Table service B/L/D	Good food. See page 321.
Pinocchio Village Haus	Fantasyland	$	Burgers, dogs, sandwiches	Counter service L/D	Good topping bar
Cosmic Ray's Cafe	Tomorrowland	$	Burgers, chicken, soup, sandwiches	Counter service L/D	Typical fast food
The Plaza Pavilion	Tomorrowland	$	Pizza, stacked sandwiches, fried chicken	Counter service L/D	More fast food

B/L/D: Breakfast/Lunch/Dinner; $ most entrées less than $10. $$ most entrées less than $25. $$$ most entrées more than $25

*See chapter 6 for our reviews of these restaurants

- Pecos Bill's has an especially good topping bar.

- The Columbia Harbor House has the best fast-food vegetarian selection.

- If you want to escape the crowds for a quiet lunch, take the boat from near the park's entrance to the wonderful Kona Cafe at the Polynesian or to the Grand Floridian Cafe.

- For more eating tips, see chapter 6.

Magic Kingdom Special Events and Entertainment

The Share A Dream Come True Parade

This lively parade features life-size snow globes, colorful floats, plenty of Disney characters, and the music we have come to love. Check your Magic Kingdom times guide for showtimes and find a viewing place along the parade route (along Main Street and through Frontierland) at least thirty minutes ahead of time.

SpectroMagic ♥♥♥

This not-to-miss musical parade features floats and Disney characters aglow with more than 600,000 miniature lights. The costumes are stunning. Our favorites are the dragonflies. After this, parades may never seem the same. SpectroMagic doesn't happen every day, so check your Magic Kingdom times guide to see when you can catch this parade. Be certain to arrive early to stake out a good viewing spot. For more details, see page 282. *Note:* We have heard recent rumors that the Main Street Electric Parade will be returning during 2003 or 2004 and will replace SpectroMagic.

Time-Saving Tip

During busy times and on holidays, Spectro Magic may run twice. Wait for the less-crowded second showing.

Fantasy in the Sky Fireworks

This fireworks spectacular is set to the music of the Magic Kingdom attractions and is this park's "good night" wish to visitors. It's pure Disney magic! Check your guidemap times guide to see which nights during your visit it occurs. Viewing is best along Main Street, but it can get very crowded there. For more details, see page 281.

Magic Kingdom Live Entertainment

You never know what live entertainment you'll find at the Magic Kingdom, but on any given day, you can be sure there'll be a lot. The

Times Guide insert to the Magic Kingdom guidemap will be your ticket to finding what suits your taste. With luck, you might catch the Main Street Philharmonic, the Dapper Dans barbershop quartet, or the ragtime pianist at Casey's Corner, to mention only a few. And at the Castle Forecourt Stage in front of Cinderella Castle is the daily Cinderella's Surprise Celebration, featuring more than two dozen Disney characters in a musical show. Stick around after the show for photo opportunities.

The "Sword in the Stone" is another bit of entertainment in Fantasyland, and it even includes park guests in its cute drama about King Arthur. It's fun to watch and even more fun to be part of.

Shopping in the Magic Kingdom

In recent years, we've seen many of the more interesting Disney merchandise shops give way to the usual character stuff. We guess this is just what people want to buy. We still have a few favorites though, and these include Ye Old Christmas Shop in Liberty Square and Sir Mickey's in Fantasyland. One of the Magic Kingdom's most unique shops is the Kings Gallery in the castle. It features a unique assortment of Disney collectibles and jewelry, as well as costumes and swords. But if you're simply looking for something to proclaim, "I've been to Disney," you won't have any trouble finding it here in the Magic Kingdom.

Main Street USA

Main Street's assortment of shops and restaurants is a fantasy re-creation of Walt Disney's hometown, Merseline, Missouri. The charming Victorian architecture and ornate gingerbread evoke a period of Americana that we can otherwise only imagine.

Main Street opens thirty minutes before the rest of the park, so if you arrive early enough, we suggest you spend some time browsing the shops and enjoying the art and architecture. If the park is already open when you arrive, forge on and make good use of the early hours to see the park's most popular attractions and return here later.

Walt Disney World Railroad

This is a real steam-powered railway that huffs and puffs its way around the borders of the Magic Kingdom. These authentic old trains were found by Disney in Mexico, hauling sugar in the Yucatan. The ride takes a bit over twenty minutes and is an entertaining way to get a good overall view of the park. There are three stations, one on Main Street, one in Frontierland, and the other at Mickey's Toontown Fair. All aboard!

Harmony Barber Shop (at a new location)

Yes, there's actually an old-time barbershop here on Main Street and if you time it just right, Disney's barbershop quartet, the Dapper Dans, might serenade you during a cut or trim. Rick enjoyed this once and found it memorable.

Transportation on Main Street USA

More a novelty than a means of transportation, Main Street's trolley, horseless carriage, and fire engine make the trip up and down the avenue. While this can be fun, it's rarely worth the usually long wait in line.

The Town Square Exposition Hall

Drop in here for some neat photo opportunities, Disney videos and DVDs, and a mini-theater that plays continuous early Disney classic cartoons.

Adventureland

Before the Animal Kingdom, Adventureland seemed a bit more exotic. But we still enjoy this area's superb assortment of rides and shows, and its unique architecture and scenery. From Africa to Arabia to the Caribbean, there's plenty of adventure to be found here.

The Swiss Family Treehouse

- Walk-through exhibit, with plenty of stairs

- Takes about 30 minutes

- Line can move slowly

Take a stroll through the tree-top home of this famous family of castaways and enjoy the amusing "coconut technology." The huge tree is man-made and features 80,000 vinyl leaves. Before the Animal Kingdom's Tree of Life, it seemed much more impressive.

INTERESTING, but not enough to make it worth a long wait

TIPS: Try this attraction when the line is short. Don't attempt this one with cranky kids if there is a long wait.

The Magic Carpets of Aladdin

- Midway-type ride

- Lasts 1½ minutes

- Line moves slowly

This ride is the same type as Dumbo the Flying Elephant, but instead of elephants, it features flying carpets, whimsical water-spewing camels, and a huge Genie's bottle.

For youngsters and the young at heart.

The Enchanted Tiki Room (Under New Management)

- Sit-down show
- Lasts 9 minutes
- Line moves fairly quickly to fill theater

One of the Magic Kingdom's oldest attractions, this show was updated several years ago. It now enjoys an entertaining new storyline as Iago, the obnoxious parrot from the feature film *Aladdin,* takes over. His promise to bring the show up-to-date becomes an amusing disaster. It's especially good if you're familiar with the old show.

QUITE GOOD, entertaining, and a nice cool place to relax—particularly good for young children.

TIP: If you get into the pre-show, you'll make it into the next show.

The Jungle Cruise FASTPASS

- Boat ride
- Lasts 10 minutes
- Line moves slowly

This boat ride through Africa (and India) is one of the Magic Kingdom's signature attractions. It's loaded with gags and audio-animatronic animals and each boat's pilot gives the ride his or her own unique brand of groan-a-minute humor. We once rode at night, in a misty rain. It was memorable.

EXCELLENT, especially at night—don't miss it.

Shrunken Ned's Junior Jungle Boats

- Remote-controlled boats
- Lasts about 5 minutes, costs $1

Pilot your own tiny, radio-controlled jungle boat through a watery obstacle course that includes shrunken heads and a flaming volcano.

OK, especially for kids—miss this one without worrying.

Pirates of the Caribbean

- Boat ride
- Lasts 8 minutes
- Line moves quickly

This classic Disney attraction is one of the best the Magic Kingdom has to offer. It's a boat ride through a Caribbean town that is being plundered by a gang of fun-loving pirates. The special effects and audio-animatronics are some of Disney's finest despite the age of this attraction. If you've been on this one before, look for how Disney has made this ride more "politically correct:" the pirates no longer chase the women but are chased by them!

EXCELLENT, not to be missed.

TIP: This ride may be too intense for very young children.

Frontierland

This land's western street looks like it's right out of the movies and it boasts several outstanding rides, lots of shopping, a few good shows, and even a shooting arcade.

Splash Mountain FASTPASS

- Water-flume ride, riders must be at least 40 inches tall
- Lasts 10 minutes
- Long waits are typical here; arrive early or get a *FASTPASS*

We never tire of this ride. It is well done from top (and that's five stories!) to bottom. Beautiful sets, characters we know and love, amusing scenery, catchy music, and some real thrills. This attraction has it all. WARNING: You might get sprinkled with water.

EXCELLENT, not to be missed.

TIPS: Get here as soon as the park opens or get a *FASTPASS*. Don't forget to stop at Splashdown Photos after the ride to see your picture, taken at the moment of the great plunge. We got one of our favorite Disney pictures here. Prices begin around $13.

Big Thunder Mountain Railroad FASTPASS

- Mild roller coaster, riders must be at least 40 inches tall
- Lasts 3 minutes
- Line moves quickly

This is one of those attractions that you can do over and over, seeing new things every time. This "runaway" mining train careens through an old-time mining camp, with thrills, fun, sight gags, and great special effects.

EXCELLENT, not to be missed.

TIPS: Pick-up a *FASTPASS* for Splash Mountain first-thing then go ride Thunder Mountain. Try it a second time after dark, too.

Country Bear Jamboree

- Audio-animatronic show
- Lasts 17 minutes
- Line moves slowly

This charming and corny show features bears that sing, dance, and generally horse around. It is entertaining, and we recommend it.

GOOD, especially for children.

TIPS: Try this one during a parade or fireworks show. It has a special Christmas version.

The Frontierland Shootin' Arcade

@ Electronic shooting arcade

@ Costs 50 cents

@ Line (if there is one) moves slowly

If you're visiting with a young boy, be sure to bring him by here for some real shootin'. It's every boy's dream (grown-up boys included).

GOOD, if you like this sort of thing.

TIP: Take a look at the retooled Hawken rifles. A little bit of history.

Raft Ride to Tom Sawyer Island
(open during busier times only)

@ Walk-through playground, closes at dusk

@ No time limit

@ Line for raft trip moves slowly

This raft trip to a small island may not be high on our list of things to see, but it isn't such a bad place to bring an overactive child. It's basically an island-playground, complete with caves, a fort, and lots of places to explore and run around.

Mostly for kids and not too bad for tired parents, either.

Liberty Square

This beautiful square is a small slice of Revolutionary War Americana. Central to it is the Liberty Tree, complete with its thirteen lanterns representing the original states. This "father oak" was moved here from another location at Disney World. Acorns from it have grown more than five hundred new oaks around Walt Disney World.

Liberty Square is home to some outstanding attractions, several boat rides, some shops, and several restaurants.

Liberty Square Riverboat

@ Boat ride

@ Lasts 15 minutes

@ Line moves quickly

This magnificent re-creation of a paddle-wheel steamer was built on Disney property. The ride makes a short loop on Frontierland's River of the Americas and provides a relaxing view of the attractions along it. This riverboat is propelled by a real steam engine along an underwater track.

GOOD, pleasant, can be cool and restful.

TIP: Try queuing up just when the boat arrives, as it can hold virtually everyone waiting.

Country Character Roundup

- Live character show

- See times guide for show times

This is yet another incarnation for the Diamond Horseshoe Saloon location. We hear that this interactive character encounter will feature Woody, Jessie the Cowgirl, and Bullseye the Horse.

REAL DISNEY FUN, especially good for kids

The Hall of Presidents

- Audio-animatronic show

- Lasts 25 minutes

- Line moves quickly

This slow-moving attraction features a robotic array of U.S. presidents. The technology is dated, but if you're a history buff, you'll probably enjoy it.

INTERESTING, with good audio-animatronics.

TIP: Tired? This attraction features a sit-down, air-conditioned escape. Shows start on the hour and half hour.

The Haunted Mansion FASTPASS

- Low-speed ride in sit-down "cars"

- Lasts 9 minutes

- Line moves slowly

We don't want to tell you much about this except to say that it is more fun than scary (and not really very scary). We'll leave the rest a surprise.

EXCELLENT, do not miss.

TIPS: May be frightening for very young children. Use *FASTPASS* for this popular attraction.

Liberty Square Portrait Gallery

This shady pavilion features artists ready to draw your caricature or portrait. These are quite good and make a long-lasting and classy souvenir of your Disney trip. Prices begin around $17.

Fantasyland

Cinderella Castle marks the entrance to Fantasyland. For us, it is a magical and romantic sight. Inside the castle is a beautifully themed restaurant, Cinderella's Royal Table, and inside Fantasyland are many of the rides and attractions that young children will most enjoy. There are restaurants, character encounters, and more.

Cinderella's Golden Carrousel♥

- ℮ Merry-go-round
- ℮ Ride lasts 2 minutes
- ℮ Line moves slowly

This beautiful old carousel was built in 1917, when "handmade" really meant something. There's something romantically nostalgic about this ride. It's a little trip back in time to both childhood and to another, more magical era.

QUITE GOOD, more fun and romantic than you might think.

TIPS: Almost always open for the Extra Magic Hour. Ask a cast member to snap a picture of you.

"It's a Small World"

- ℮ Boat ride
- ℮ Lasts 10 minutes
- ℮ Line moves quickly

This pleasant and upbeat musical boat ride was created for the 1965 New York World's Fair. The music is catchy and it will get you in the mood for Fantasyland.

QUITE GOOD and cool and relaxing, too.

Mickey's PhilharMagic

- ℮ 3-D movie (and more)
- ℮ Line moves to fill theater

This movie and special effects show brings 3-D cinema to the Magic Kingdom, and we hear it will attempt to out-do both Honey, I Shrunk the Audience and It's Tough to Be a Bug. The storyline has Donald Duck commandeering Mickey's orchestra. The 150-foot-wide screen is the largest at Walt Disney World and will change size during the show.

VERY ENTERTAINING; a real family attraction.

Peter Pan's Flight FASTPASS, Snow White's Scary Adventure, and The Many Adventures of Winnie the Pooh FASTPASS

- Low-speed rides
- Each lasts 2 to 3 minutes
- Lines move slowly

We put these three rides together because they are so much alike. Despite the fact that these are basically kiddie rides, you might find them fun. Snow White has been redesigned due to complaints that it was too frightening for younger children. It may still be too scary for some very young children.

OK, especially if you have small children.

TIP: The waits can be long. Both Peter Pan and Winnie the Pooh feature *FASTPASS*. Use it.

Dumbo the Flying Elephant

- Midway-type ride
- Lasts less than 2 minutes
- Line moves very slowly

This is one attraction that all small children simply must ride on. As you would expect, lines here are long, and there's little else to do but tough it out.

A MUST FOR YOUNG CHILDREN.

TIP: Catch this one early. It's usually open for the Extra Magic Hour.

Mad Tea Party

- Spinning midway-type ride
- Lasts 2 minutes
- Line moves slowly

The speed of rotation of these twirling teacups can be controlled by the riders. Usually though, this is a rather mild ride, aimed mostly at younger children.

OK; can be fun, especially if you enjoy feeling dizzy.
TIP: Usually open for the Extra Magic Hour.
WARNING: Not for those prone to motion sickness.

Ariel's Grotto and Fantasyland Character Festival

@ Playground and character encounters

@ Linger as long as you wish

@ Lines here can get long

These areas consist of interactive fountains and scenes from The Little Mermaid. Our grandkids loved them. There's even a cave where children can meet Ariel and another area nearby with more Disney characters. Cute and good photo opportunities, too.
GOOD, for kids.

Fairytale Garden

@ Storytelling show with character encounters

@ Seats for about twenty guests

@ Usually a short line for photos

This area features "Storytime with Belle" and other Disney characters. Afterward, your children can meet them and you can get some good photos.
TIP: Check your guidemap times guide for show times.

Mickey's Toontown Fair

If you're coming to Disney with small children, this is one place you'll want to visit. This three-dimensional, cartoon-like village features the homes of both Mickey and Minnie Mouse as well as a small country fair. There's even a kiddie roller coaster, the Barnstormer (minimum height is 35 inches). It's a must for small children, so set aside half a day to bring yours here. Attractions include Goofy's Wiseacre Farm, Donald's Boat, and a meeting with The Mouse himself. There's also Toon Park, Pete's Garage, and the Toontown Hall of Fame. We suggest that you arrive early. And if you are traveling without young ones, simply take a quick look.

Tomorrowland

Despite an interesting retro–Jules Verne makeover several years ago, Tomorrowland still reminds us of a carnival midway. But it's fun to look at, and it's home to several good attractions.

The ExtraTERRORestrial Alien Encounter

- Special-effects show (not a ride); minimum height is 44 inches
- Lasts 20 minutes
- Line moves quickly

This attraction got off to a bad start when Michael Eisner, Disney's CEO, rode it during a test run. "Not scary enough," he declared, and it was back to the drawing boards for "Alien." The plot involves a botched attempt at intergalactic tele-transportation and an escaped alien monster. Much of the show is in total darkness. The stuff of nightmares (teens will love it).

KIND OF CREEPY and not that entertaining.

WARNING: Far too intense for children under 10 years of age.

NOTE: A persistant rumor suggests that sometime in 2004, Aliens will shut down and have its storyline altered to revolve around the character "Stitch" from the Disney animated film, *Lilo and Stitch*.

Space Mountain FASTPASS

- High-speed roller coaster ride; riders must be at least 44 inches tall
- Lasts 3 minutes
- Line moves quickly

This roller coaster inside a planetarium is one of Disney World's most popular attractions. It's fast and fairly rough.

EXCELLENT, if you like this type of ride.

TIPS: Usually open for the Extra Magic Hour. Get here early or pick up a *FASTPASS*.

WARNING: May be too intense for younger children.

Buzz Lightyear's Space Ranger Spin FASTPASS

- Slow-moving, interactive ride
- Lasts 6 minutes
- Line moves pretty quickly

This special-effects attraction features a train-like conveyor of space cars in which you get to shoot at space villains and score points.

LOTS OF FUN, especially for competitive adults.

The Timekeeper (sometimes open, sometimes not)

- Film and audio-animatronic show
- Lasts 15 minutes
- Line moves quickly to fill large theater

This 360-degree film is narrated by a wild and hilarious Robin Williams robot. The story involves time travel, H. G. Wells, Jules Verne, and some great cinematography and special effects.

QUITE GOOD, don't miss it if it is open

Tomorrowland Arcade

- Video and game arcade
- Waste as much time here as you wish
- No lines, although games can get busy

We wonder why so many kids would pay to visit the Magic Kingdom and then spend their time (and more money) here. Lots of great games, but bring lots of dollar bills. It isn't free.

FOR VIDEO GAMERS, see DisneyQuest at Downtown Disney (page 274) for something far more exciting.

Tomorrowland Transit Authority

- Gentle tram ride
- Lasts 10 minutes
- Line moves very quickly

This is the old WED–Way People Mover, renamed. This was the world's first "MAG–LEV" (linear induction) train constructed for public use.

INTERESTING, but not memorable.

TIP: If you want to see the inside of Space Mountain without riding it, this is the way to do it.

Astro Orbiter

- Midway-type ride
- Lasts about 2 minutes
- Long lines move very slowly

This is a recycled version of the old StarJets ride. It will give you a good view of Tomorrowland. Definitely mild.

OK, more interesting to look at than to ride on.

Carousel of Progress (open only at busier times)

- Show with revolving seating (11 A.M. to 5 P.M.)
- Lasts 20 minutes
- Line moves quickly

This audio-animatronic show demonstrates how technology has impacted our homes over the last century.

Magic Kingdom Best of the Best

Big Thunder Mountain

The Haunted Mansion

The Jungle Cruise

Pirates of the Caribbean

SpectroMagic Light Parade ♥♥♥

Splash Mountain and Splash Mountain photo ♥

Fantasy in the Sky Fireworks ♥♥

Space Mountain

INTERESTING and entertaining.

TIP: Try this show when the other attractions are busy.

Tomorrowland Indy Speedway

@ Miniature raceway, drivers must be at least 52 inches tall

@ Lasts about 5 minutes

@ Line moves slowly

This is a short raceway with small, motorized go-karts. The pace is slow, and a runner-track restricts steering to prevent collisions. Very popular with children, especially those whose mean parents won't let them drive the family car.

OK, a children's ride.

Epcot

The Disney theme parks are like children. Each is different, and very much a unique creation. While the Magic Kingdom celebrates the child in each of us, Epcot salutes the achievements and cultural diversities of humankind. It is a place of science and technology, of travel and discovery, and of course, of excitement and entertainment. It is "the happiest place on earth" for curious minds.

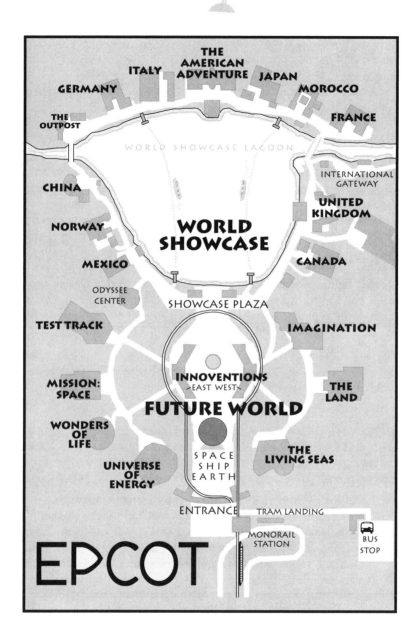

From interactive displays of the latest trends in technology to one of the world's largest saltwater aquariums, Epcot has more than just a little something for everyone. Great rides, wonderful films, an agricultural tour, fine dining, visits to distant lands, and unique international entertainment are all capped off each evening by a thundering laser light and fireworks show perfectly synchronized to music. These are just a few of the treats that await you at this park, where the real theme is discovery.

As if all this wasn't enough, Epcot also features an ever-changing panoply of seasonal celebrations. We think that the Epcot Fall Food and Wine Festival (mid-October to mid-November) is one of the most romantic things to do in any theme park and our favorite time to visit this park. We also enjoy the Spring Flower and Garden Festival (late April to early June) and the World Music Concert Series (June–September). There are international celebrations too, including Chinese New Year (January), Bastille Day (July), and Germany's Oktoberfest. For more information and the dates of these special offerings, contact Disney Information at (407) 824-4321.

Leave a Legacy

Located right inside the front entrance to Epcot is this Disney program. For $35 for a single-person image ($38 for two-person), guests can have their photos taken, etched into a metal plate, and mounted on one of a series of marble monoliths here in Epcot's courtyard. The idea is "to show you were there."

Money-Saving Tip

Get a 10 percent discount on Leave a Legacy with an annual pass.

Epcot Tips

- Epcot has two different areas, each with different operating hours. Future World usually opens around 9 A.M. and usually closes at 7 P.M. and the World Showcase opens at 11 A.M. and closes after IllumiNations, at either 9 P.M. or 10 P.M., depending on the season. However, it seems to us that a number of Future World attractions remain open until 9 P.M.

- The Extra Magic Hour at Epcot is on Wednesdays.

- *FASTPASS* attractions at Epcot are Test Track, Living with the Land, Maelstrom, "Honey, I Shrunk the Audience," and we expect, Mission: Space, when it opens.

- Test Track is easily Epcot's most popular attraction and on busy days *FASTPASS*es are gone by noon. If you want to ride it, make it your *very* first effort. As soon as you arrive at Epcot, either get a

FASTPASS or get in line. *Note:* We expect pretty much the same for Mission: Space.

e Future World is least busy before 10:30 A.M. and again in late afternoon, as the crowds move into the World Showcase. The hour or two before Future World closes is usually a good time to visit.

e The World Showcase is least crowded during the first few hours after opening at 11 A.M.

e Try splitting up your Epcot tour. Spend one morning at Future World, and then do something fun at your resort. Another day, spend the morning around the pool or sleep in and get to Epcot just in time for the opening of the World Showcase.

e The Epcot tip board is located in Innoventions Plaza.

e If you're visiting with kids, don't miss the many "Kidcot Funstops" around the World Showcase. These areas provide hands-on arts and crafts fun for your children and are well supervised by Disney cast members. They open at 1 P.M.

Tips for Eating at Epcot

e If you're at Epcot and hungry for breakfast, Fountain View Espresso and Bakery (Innoventions Plaza), Pure and Simple (Wonders of Life), the Sunshine Season Food Fair (The Land), and Akershus in Norway are your choices. Priority seating arrangements are needed. See page 302 for details.

e In recent years, the restaurants around the World Showcase have gotten much better, though most are still not up to the standards set by such places as the California Grill or Flying Fish. This considered, our favorites are the Coral Reef, Le Cellier, Marrakesh, and Akershus. For entertainment, we recommend Coral Reef (the fish), Marrakesh ♥♥, the Biergarten, and L'Originale Alfredo di Roma Ristorante. Mexico's San Angel Inn ♥♥♥ is beautiful and one of the most romantic restaurants at Disney. See what more we have to say about these restaurants in chapter 6.

e The Coral Reef Restaurant is Epcot's premier dining destination. Priority seating arrangements are a must for either lunch or dinner. For more information, see chapter 6.

e Akershus now features the Princess Storybook Breakfast with the Disney Princesses. Belle, Snow White, Jasmine, Mary Poppins, and Sleeping Beauty are all at this buffett. Hours are 8:30 A.M. to 10:30 A.M., and priority seating is a must. Call (407) WDW-DINE.

@ We suggest lunching here at Epcot and having dinner elsewhere. Pretty much the same food served at dinner is less expensive at lunchtime.

@ Between France and the United Kingdom, you can walk through the International Gateway to the Epcot resort area, where fine eateries are numerous. Some of our favorites there are the Flying Fish Cafe and Spoodles (BoardWalk), Palio (the Swan), and Shula's Steakhouse (the Dolphin). For more about these restaurants, see chapter 6.

@ The table-service restaurants at Epcot are almost always crowded. We highly recommend making priority seating arrangements, especially for dinner and definitely during the busier seasons. In the park, you can make "reservations" at Epcot Guest Relations in Future World, the Epcot tip board at Innoventions Plaza, and at any payphone by dialing *88.

@ If you find yourselves in Epcot, hungry and without priority seating, Norway's Akershus, China's Nine Dragons, and Morocco's Marrakesh are the restaurants most likely to be able to accommodate you.

Future World

If you've been thinking this area is in need of updating, we've been hearing lots of rumors about new attractions here. With the end of AT & T sponsorship of Spaceship Earth, rumor has it that the geosphere is going to be converted into a coaster, with a time travel theme. What will happen to the Global Neighborhood, we don't know. Another persistant rumor is that Epcot will get a "Soarin' Over…" attraction, similar to the one at Disney's California Adventure. These new attractions, we hear, will depend on how well this year's opening of Mission: Space goes. We expect to see some real changes here in Epcot during 2005.

Spaceship Earth

@ Slow ride

@ Lasts about 15 minutes

@ Line moves quickly

This attraction features a comfortable, sit-down journey that spirals up through Epcot's seventeen-story geosphere. Along the way, elaborate scenes sketch the history of communications, from cave drawings to digital communications. Featured are life-like robotics, outstanding sets, special effects, and an interesting narrative by British actor Jeremy Irons.

EXCELLENT, one of Future World's best attractions—don't miss it.

TIP: This ride is usually open for the Extra Magic Hour.

Epcot Future World Restaurants

Restaurant	Location	Price	Fare	Service	Our Comments
Coral Reef*	The Living Seas	$$$	Seafood, beef, poultry	Table Service L/D	Great dining. See page 322.
Electric Umbrella	Innoventions Plaza	$	Burgers, hot dogs, chicken sandwich	Counter service L/D	The usual fast food
Garden Grill	The Land	$$	Family-style character meals	Table service L/D	Pretty good food
Pure and Simple	Wonders of Life	$	waffles, salads, sandwiches, vegetarian	Counter service B/L/D	Pretty good food
Sunshine Season Food Fair	The Land	$	Food court: many offerings	Counter service B/L/D	Typical fast food

B/L/D: Breakfast/Lunch/Dinner
$ most entrées less than $10
$$ most entrées less than $25
$$$ most entrées more than $25
*See chapter 6 for our reviews of these restaurants.

After the park opens to the public, this is the first place the entering crowds go, and it quickly becomes busy. If the line is long, save it for later when there is no line.

Global Neighborhood

This pavilion features a variety of hands-on exhibits that demonstrate new and unusual telephone technologies. Call a friend on a family telephone or a storytelling phone (both accept credit cards). Some exhibits are free, such as paddle games and the voice command entertainment center.

INTERESTING, but an easy one to pass by, especially if it's crowded.

Innoventions, East and West

Journey "The Road to Tomorrow" and get your hands on the latest innovations in technology and see what the future holds. The fourteen interactive areas include video games of the future, displays of new technology, and Internet hook-ups.

VERY GOOD, definitely worth a visit, especially if you are interested in this stuff.

TIP: This area gets very busy, but we've seen it less crowded late in the day, especially during IllumiNations.

The Fountain of Nations Water Ballet

At first glance, this fountain appears pretty unexceptional. But just wait around. This is a classic example of how Disney takes the ordinary and turns it into something very entertaining. At various times throughout the park's hours, the music and water frolic together in perfect and playful synchronicity. Make a real effort to see this "performance." You'll never look at fountains the same way again.

TIP: Unfortunately, due to wind and weather considerations, there is no set schedule for this wonderful "show."

Innoventions Plaza After Dark

At night, the pavement here takes on an entirely new personality. With fiber-optic lights embedded in the ground at various places around the plaza, this place is very cool. Don't forget to drop by for a look.

TIP: Check out the talking water fountain near the Land Pavilion.

Ice Station Cool

Here's a cool attraction, and we mean this literally. The station's soft drink machines feature eight carbonated beverages that Coca-Cola produces for other countries. There's a watermelon soda from China and something strange from Italy called "Beverly." All are free, refreshing, and fun. There's also some nice Coke logo merchandise for sale.

AN EPCOT GEM. Don't miss this one.

Universe of Energy Pavilion

Ellen's Energy Adventure

- ℯ Slow ride and show
- ℯ Lasts about 45 minutes
- ℯ Line moves slowly; shows start every 17 minutes

This isn't one of Disney's most exciting attractions, but it's entertaining. It features comedian Ellen DeGeneres in a nightmare version of "Jeopardy," during which she appears with Jamie Lee Curtis, Bill Nye the Science Guy, and Alex Trebek. The show includes film, special effects, and large, audio-animatronic dinosaurs. It is clever and funny.

ENTERTAINING, with pretty good special effects.

Wonders of Life Pavilion

This is a fun place with lots to see and do: a ride, a show, a movie, shopping, some hands- (and feet-) on exhibits, and even a restaurant. Pure & Simple features a better-than-average selection of salads and sandwiches.

Body Wars

- ℯ Simulated thrill ride, riders must be at least 40 inches tall
- ℯ Lasts 5 minutes
- ℯ Line moves quickly

This adventure utilizes the same type of "flight simulator" used for Star Tours at Disney-MGM. It doesn't really go anywhere, but with tilting and bucking movements perfectly synchronized to a film playing in the front of the car, it creates the illusion of speed and motion. The story involves a rescue mission into a human body aboard a miniaturized, microscopic "inner-space ship." It's very entertaining.

EXCELLENT, DON'T MISS IT. A bit bumpy.

WARNING: Body Wars is not for people prone to motion sickness.

The Making of Me ♥♥

- ℯ Film
- ℯ Shows every 15 minutes
- ℯ Line moves very slowly

This cute film about "where we come from" features Martin Short. It's both humorous and touching.

EXCELLENT, not to be missed.

TIPS: The theater is small and the lines can get long. Make an effort to see it early, or wait until later in the day.

Cranium Command

℮ Show

℮ Lasts 18 minutes

℮ Line moves to fill theater

Another of our favorites, this show features audio-animatronics, animation, and special effects. Throw away your preconceptions about this attraction and see it. It is what Disney does best.

EXCELLENT, another not-to-be-missed attraction.

TIPS: In all but the busiest of times, the wait for this show should not be much of a factor. Don't miss the pre-show, which "sets up" the show.

Goofy About Health

℮ Show

℮ Lasts 15 minutes

This low-key multi-screen show features Goofy getting wise about fitness and health.

OK, for children but otherwise, pass it by.

Hands-On Activities at Wonders of Life

℮ Various displays and exhibits

℮ No set time limits

℮ Lines move slowly

The Wonders of Life pavilion is full of exhibits that involve your participation. Have your golf swing analyzed or hop on to a video exercycle and see the sights. There are lots of things to do that are fun and informative. Don't miss the Sensory Funhouse.

GOOD TO VERY GOOD; don't pass by this area unless it's too crowded.

Live Entertainment at Wonders of Life   At various times throughout the day, the Anacomical Players ad-lib their way through audience-participation skits about staying healthy. This can be funny.

Mission: Space

Get ready for another big Disney adventure attraction. Presented by Compaq Computers, this "ride" will feature a simulated space adventure, from lift-off from earth to weightlessness in space. Set decades in the future, guests will be transported to the International Space Training Center, where they will face simulated challenges similar to those encountered by real astronauts working in space. This neat pavilion looks like the solar system, with giant, colorful planets in orbit around its futuristic, curved structure.

DEFINITELY ONE NOT TO MISS.

TIP: We expect that this attraction will have both *FASTPASS* and a minimum height requirement, as yet unannounced.

Test Track FASTPASS

@ High-speed thrill ride, riders must be 40 inches tall

@ Lasts 5 minutes

@ Line moves slowly, waits can be very long

Test Track is designed to simulate a facility designed for testing automobile performance. At 65 miles per hour, it's the fastest ride at Disney (Space Mountain goes only 28 mph). This interesting ride has one particularly thrilling moment at the end: a tightly banked turn at 60+ miles per hour.

VERY GOOD, one brief thrill.

TIP: Get here first thing after opening or get a *FASTPASS* early. This is one of Epcot's most popular attractions.

Dream Chaser

@ Video simulator

@ Lasts 5 minutes

@ Line moves slowly to accommodate twenty "riders"

Located at the exit of Test Track, this ride is supposed to feature the future of auto design. We didn't think so. Maybe kids would like it better than we did, but there's a drawback: the attraction doesn't function fully for children.

DISAPPOINTING, not worth much of a wait

The Living Seas Pavilion

Despite this pavilion's age, it's still interesting. Everything here revolves around its six-million-gallon saltwater aquarium (the sixth largest in the world). Even this pavilion's seafood restaurant, the Coral Reef, offers a stunning underwater seascape, as well as outstanding seafood.

The pavilion's attraction area involves a trip to the "underwater research station," Sea Base Alpha. During this rather dated "adventure," you'll enjoy breathtaking underwater glimpses of some of this pavilion's

2,000 sea creatures as well as some interactive and hands-on experiences. There is a particularly good dive-suit photo op here. This pavilion also features a gift shop with some nice, sea-related stuff. Don't skip the pre-show film.

Live Entertainment at the Living Seas   Check at Sea Base Alpha for the schedule of the underwater dolphin show and for divers feeding fish.

The Land Pavilion

Even if agriculture isn't high on your list of exciting subjects, you'll find this area entertaining. While this isn't our favorite pavilion, it still manages to provide a pleasant ride, many places to eat, a stirring film, an audio-animatronic show, an interesting greenhouse tour, and a display of the ⭐NEW modern agricultural techniques that bring food to our tables. For kids, you'll want to know about Nestle's Junior Chef area, where kids make their own chocolate chip cookies, and the Garden Grill's afternoon ice cream social with Mickey and friends (see page 307 for details).

Living with the Land *FASTPASS*
- ❡ Boat ride

- ❡ Lasts 14 minutes

- ❡ Line moves very quickly

This cool and pleasant boat ride takes you through the history of agriculture and into its future. Its sets and special effects are memorable.
EXCELLENT, not to be missed. Great for all ages.

Food Rocks
- ❡ Audio-animatronic show

- ❡ Lasts 15 minutes

- ❡ Line moves to fill theater

This show features a whole kitchen full of rockin' 'n' rollin' fruits and vegetables. The tunes here are classic rock, singing the praises of good nutrition.
GOOD, and cute too.
TIP: Waits here never seem long.

The Circle of Life
- ❡ Film

- ❡ Lasts 20 minutes

- ❡ Line moves to fill theater

The theme of this beautiful film is ecology, and stars Simba, Timon, and Pumbaa from *The Lion King*. The message is inspiring and upbeat and the cinematography is outstanding.

GOOD.

TIPS: This theater seats more than four hundred. Check for times at the entrance and ask a cast member if you'll make it into the next show or the one after that.

Behind the Seeds—A Guided Greenhouse Tour

@ Walking tour

@ Lasts 45 minutes

@ By reservation only, $8 per person ($6 for children)

This interesting tour will take you through the experimental greenhouses of The Land, where you will see the latest in agriculture techniques. The tours are conducted by real "agriculturists" and are very popular.

QUITE GOOD.

TIP: Make your reservations inside the pavilion, at the small kiosk near the entrance to Food Rocks.

Imagination! Pavilion

This pavilion features one of Disney World's most entertaining attractions, a marvelous interactive playground, and some very entertaining fountains.

NEW Journey into Imagination with Figment

@ Slow ride

@ Line moves quickly

This attraction has experienced several re-inventions in the past few years. Now with the return of Figment, we think it is no longer the disappointment it once was.

GOOD, but if you have to omit something, this could be it.

Image Works—A Sensory Playground and More   You can enter this area either after the ride or from a side doorway. While Imageworks features a variety of image creation areas that cost money (making labels with your picture or character-enhanced photos), it also has some very entertaining things to do that are free. Our favorite is the "Figment's Melody Makers," where you can create music by waving your hands. It's neat. There are also several computers that will take your picture and send it out as a free e-mail postcard. Very nice, indeed.

GOOD, particularly the e-mail and Melody Makers. Bring $5 bills if you are looking to buy stuff.

"Honey, I Shrunk the Audience" *FASTPASS*

- 3-D film and more

- Lasts 25 minutes

- Line moves to fill theater

We love to bring people here who haven't seen it. Part film and part . . . well, we won't give away the surprises, but we will tell you that it features Rick Moranis as Professor Wayne Szelinski of Disney's feature film, *Honey, I Shrunk the Kids*. This production is more fun than a barrel of . . . oops, we won't tell you that either. Oh, and don't miss the pre-show.

EXCELLENT, what you came here for—don't dare miss this show.

TIPS: Get a *FASTPASS* and play around in Imageworks while you wait.

WARNING: Might be too intense for very young children or people who have phobias about . . . sorry, we can't give this away either.

The Shops of Future World

Disney merchandise seems to get better every year, and we'll admit to a wardrobe of embroidered character clothing. You'll find this and much more at the shops of Future World. MouseGear has all things Mickey plus an impressive selection of caps, backpacks, and gifts. For film and two-hour processing, drop by the Camera Center near the entrance to Spaceship Earth. Even though you might not be looking to buy, you'll certainly want to see the original creations in the Art of Disney.

Each of the pavilions in Future World has a shop and most of them are interesting. We particularly like the shop at The Living Seas (aquatic stuff), at The Land (kitchen and garden merchandise), and at Wonders of Life (Disney sports apparel). Other shops peddle automotive merchandise (Test Track), and film and cameras (Imagination!).

Future World Entertainment

There's some good live entertainment here. During the summer months, school bands and musical groups from across the country perform at a stage behind Innoventions West. At other times of year, the stage by the fountain features special guest performers.

Our favorite Future World performers are the Kristos. This mesmerizing slow-motion acrobatic team (and their unusual costumes) is worth seeing. Check your Epcot guidemap for performance times. Also here are the JAMMitors, an offbeat group that plays instruments that seem better suited for cleaning up Epcot than making music. Check your guidemap times guide for showtimes.

Future World's Best-of-the-Best List

Mission: Space (Coming 2003)

Space Ship Earth

Body Wars

Cranium Command

Test Track

Living with the Land

"Honey, I Shrunk the Audience"

The Fountain of Nations Water Ballet

The World Showcase

We never seem to tire of this part of Walt Disney World. Something of a world's fair, the World Showcase is a large, freshwater lagoon surrounded by the pavilions of eleven nations. Each of these "countries" has been created with meticulous care and is authentic in every way possible. Savor the sublime tranquility of a Japanese garden or enjoy the quaintness of a cobbled Norwegian village. From the narrow, winding streets of Morocco to China's intricate Temple of Heaven, the Disney art and architecture bring each country magically to life.

Landscaping plays a vital role here and the World Showcase is a veritable gardener's dream. From Canada's formal flower garden to the tropical jungles of Mexico, a serious effort has been made to present a horticultural sampling of each land. With such attention paid to detail, it is easy to get the sense of a Bavarian village or a Chinese marketplace.

But there's more to this place than a bunch of pretty faces. Each nation offers an exhibit or show of some sort, and two feature rides. All of the countries have shops filled with their arts and crafts, and some even feature outstanding film travelogues.

To make this experience more inviting, each country offers a sampling of its cuisine. The World Showcase is a place of restaurants, cafes, and street vendors. Enjoy a sidewalk cafe in Morocco, an elegant dinner in France, or simply pick up an Italian pastry or a *kaki gori* ice cone along the promenade. Your choices are many and inviting.

We urge you to take your time and speak with the cast members of the various countries, many of whom are native to the lands they represent. Each country also features live performers. Enjoy an Alpine trio,

Chinese acrobats, or Canadian bagpipers. Every nation has its own unique offerings and you'll find the schedule in the Epcot guidemap and posted along the promenade in each country. Take the time to see them.

At day's end, you'll surely want to enjoy IllumiNations, Epcot's wonderful fireworks show synchronized to music. It's dramatic and thrilling and will be the quintessential finale to your day at Epcot. Check your times guide for showtimes.

On our tour of the World Showcase, we'll take you clockwise around the lagoon, beginning at Showcase Plaza near Future World. We won't give you every detail about what you'll find along the way, just enough information to help you make your own discoveries. Spend time in each of the countries, find a shady bench, relax a while, and enjoy the feeling of being in a foreign land. Explore every nook and alleyway. You never know what you'll find. We happily spend endless hours here, strolling around the lagoon, browsing the shops, and enjoying the sights, sounds, and tastes of the World Showcase. For us, the World Showcase is Disney's most romantic theme park.

Money-Saving Tip

Get a 10 percent discount at the World Showcase restaurants with an annual pass or annual premium pass.

Showcase Plaza

This area is the gateway to the World Showcase. Its two shops, Port of Entry and Disney Traders, offer the usual collection of Disney and Epcot logo merchandise as well as a variety of gifts and film supplies. Behind them on the lake are the landing docks for Epcot's two Friendship launches, which make regular passages across the lagoon to either Germany or Morocco.

There's a character greeting area right along the lagoon. It's a great spot to mingle with the Disney characters and get some great photos.

Mexico

Old Mexico comes to life at this pavilion where a Mayan pyramid towers above a dense, tropical jungle and the rhythms of mariachi fill the courtyard. Inside this "ancient" structure is the bustling Plaza de Los Amigos where merchants peddle their brightly colored wares: baskets, pottery, silver and turquoise, straw hats, piñatas, and much, much more. When you're finished browsing here, you might want to enjoy a meal or snack at Mexico's stunning San Angel Inn Restaurante ♥♥♥.

Set along the banks of El Rio del Tiempo (The River of Time), this beautiful restaurant enjoys an atmosphere unique even here at Walt

Disney World. Beneath a moonlit sky, you can enjoy the culinary delights of Mexico under the watchful gaze of a smoldering volcano. It's memorable and romantic. For more about it, see page 337.

On the sidewalk outside the pavilion is the Cantina de San Angel, with its small but south-of-the-border menu. Relax and have a Mexican beer while you enjoy one of the musical groups that perform here throughout the day or get here early to view IllumiNations. There's even a kiosk on the promenade that serves frozen margaritas.

TIP: Don't miss the art exhibit just inside the pyramid.

El Rio del Tiempo (The River of Time)
- Boat ride

- Lasts 6 minutes

- Line moves very quickly

A pleasant watery tour of Mexico, past and present. This moonlit journey reminds us of "It's a Small World."

GOOD, try not to miss it.

Live Entertainment in Old Mexico   Two outstanding groups perform here, one a musical group, Mariachi Cobre, and the other a costumed band of storytellers. Not exactly a performer, you might also find the glassblower inside this pavilion to be entertaining. We did.

Norway

This charming and picturesque pavilion seems more like a small village than a theme park. Its cobbled town square, sod-roofed huts, and stone buildings make it an inviting stop along your Epcot world tour. Norway is home to one of our favorite shops, the Puffin's Roost. It boasts a quality selection of Scandinavian merchandise.

"Anchored" next to this pavilion is a children's playground created out of a replica Viking ship. With nets, a slide, and a large deck, it's a great place for little Vikings to play.

Inside Norway's miniature replica of Akershus Castle is a restaurant that serves a wonderful and authentic Norwegian buffet. See page 313 for our review. Across the cobbled street, you'll find Kringla Bakeri Og Kafe and its interesting selection of open-faced sandwiches, pastries, and Ringnes beer.

The Stav Kirke
- Architectural display with indoor exhibit

- Stay as long as you wish

- We've never seen a line here

This is Norway's picturesque stave church. It's charming to look at and always features an interesting Norwegian cultural exhibit. We've seen some interesting stuff here (a miniature display of polar exploration, several years ago), so step inside and see what's here during your visit.

Maelstrom *FASTPASS*
@ Boat ride and film

@ Lasts 10 minutes

@ Line moves quickly

This voyage aboard a Viking ship is well done and even has a moment of excitement. The post-ride film travelogue is outstanding.

EXCELLENT, don't be afraid of the thrill and don't miss this ride and film.

TIP: Get here early before there is a big line or see it just before IllumiNations.

Live Entertainment in Norway　　Featured here in the cobbled square is usually a Norwegian folk group. Check performance times in your Epcot times guide and arrive early.

China

The striking Temple of Heaven takes center stage at Disney's China and it is a marvel of intricate and colorful detail. Inside is an all-new 360-degree travel film that features many areas of China rarely seen in the West. Next door is a changing exhibit of art and artifacts from China. Take a look to see what's on display during your visit.

China features a beautiful sit-down restaurant, The Nine Dragons, as well as the counter-service Lotus Blossom Cafe. For more information about The Nine Dragons, see page 332. Shopping at China's Yong Feng Shangdian bazaar is outstanding. From teapots to embroidered silk pajamas, and from hand-loomed carpets to intricate porcelain, this is the largest collection of imported goods at Epcot and all of it is intriguing.

We love to find a shady bench in the garden and enjoy the exotic melodies of China and the beauty of its ponds and flowering plants. Music and landscaping come together here to make this a restful retreat. ♥

NEW Reflections of China
@ Film

@ Lasts about 20 minutes

@ Line moves to fill theater

This all-new 360-degree film was shot in 2002 and features an updated look at China, its cities, its scenic wonders, and its people.

EXCELLENT, don't miss it.

TIPS: Check at the door for the time of the next show and browse until a few minutes before it begins. The theater will almost always accommodate everyone waiting.

China's Live Entertainment   Chinese acrobatics are featured in the courtyard and, sometimes, a solo flutist. Both are good. Check your Epcot guidemap to ensure your timely arrival.

The Outpost

This African set features the Cool Post's fresh fruit, gourmet ice cream, draft beer, and a selection of snacks and non-alcoholic beverages. You'll enjoy the theming here, especially on a hot summer day. Village Traders is a nice little shop that offers a variety of interesting hand-made goods from Africa. It's worth a look.

Live Entertainment at the Outpost   This area also features the wonderful African storytellers and drummers, Orisi Risi. Grab a drum and sit in on this fun.

Germany

Browse in the square here while the musicians are performing, and you'll feel as though you're in a travel documentary. Gayle's sister, Gineen, and her husband have spent a lot of time in Germany (Jimmy was stationed there), and they take great delight at this little taste of Germany.

The main attraction in this charming bit of Bavaria is the pavilion's restaurant, The Biergarten, which features a large buffet and the kind of entertainment you'd find in a German beer hall. The food is okay, and the entertainment is fun. For more information, see page 315. The six quaint shops of this pavilion offer a large variety of handcrafted German merchandise: cuckoo clocks, glass and porcelain, and beautiful toys. There's even a wine cellar with daily wine tastings.

Disney's Germany also offers a small counter-service eatery, Sommerfest. It features bratwurst, a daily chef's special, a ham sandwich, pretzels, and beer.

The Romantic Railway   A miniature version of the train that runs from Füssen to Würzburg, this marvel features not only a beautiful set of trains but also a meticulously-created countryside. It's another of our Epcot favorites.

OUTSTANDING, don't pass it by

Germany's Live Entertainment   Check your times guide for the performances of Oktoberfest Musikanten and the Alpine Trio. These two groups play in both the restaurant and the pavilion's courtyard.

Italy

From the Doge's Palace and St. Mark's Square, to the charming "villa" overlooking the lagoon, this pavilion is a colorful taste of Italy. Shops brimming with chocolates, cookies, pastas, olive oils, and Italian wines are just the beginning. There are street vendors selling pastries, espresso, and gelato as well as one of the most popular restaurants along the World Showcase. While L'Originale Alfredo di Roma Ristorante isn't the very best Italian food at Disney, the entertainment makes it lively and fun. For more information and what we think of this restaurant, see page 330.

Food isn't quite everything here in Disney's Italy. Its three shops offer a selection of leather goods, silk ties, and hand-blown Venetian glass.

Italy's Live Entertainment   In and around the square are the imaginative Character Masquerade artists and Imaginum—a statue act. Although they don't really perform (they mostly appear), their costumes are fantastic and they will happily pose with you for photographs.

The American Adventure

This is the host pavilion of the World Showcase and it features a show, a shop, and in its cavernous rotunda, some outstanding paintings by famous American artists. Across the courtyard is an open-air theater, which features live entertainment throughout the day.

The Liberty Inn restaurant serves up the usual Disney burgers, hot dogs, and chicken sandwiches. Unremarkable by our standards, it always seems busy. One nice thing about the Inn is its shady patio.

This pavilion's shop features a selection of USA logo merchandise and apparel as well as an assortment of patriotic gifts.

The American Adventure

 @ Audio-animatronic show

 @ Lasts 30 minutes

 @ Line moves to fill theater

This patriotic journey through American history is narrated by a robotic "Mark Twain." It is interesting and even stirring.

QUITE GOOD, especially for history buffs.

The America Gardens Theatre

ℚ Open-air theater

ℚ Live entertainment throughout the afternoon and evening

Entertainment is the focus of this outdoor amphitheater, often with college bands or musical groups, and sometimes, even big-name entertainers appear here. Riverdance has performed here in the past, and throughout the year the theater showcases celebrations of jazz, swing, and just about every kind of music you can think of. During the Spring Flower & Garden Show, there's the nostalgic rock tunes of Flower Power, at Christmastime this area features the Candlelight Processional, and during the Fall Food & Wine Festival, an assortment of international artists perform. Be sure to check your Epcot guidemap to see what's happening here during your visit.

Live Entertainment at the American Adventure   Besides the American Gardens Theater, this pavilion features the Spirit of America Fife & Drum Corps. In revolutionary war uniforms, they play and march along the promenade in front of the pavilion. Inside the rotunda, are both the Voices of America, an a cappella chorus performing traditional American ballads, and a group of jazz singers, American Vibe. Both are worth seeing. Check your Epcot times guide for times.

Japan

This lovely pavilion celebrates the serene and stunning beauty of Japan. The Goju-No-Tu pagoda marks its place along the promenade and Japan's "oyster" encrusted torii gate is a landmark along the rocky shore of the lagoon.

One of our favorites here in Disney's Japan is the beautiful garden ♥ area behind the pagoda. It's a wonderful place to enjoy a few quiet moments. We also like the Bijutsu-Kan Gallery at the rear of the pavilion. Exhibits here always provide a fascinating insight into Japanese culture. Don't miss it.

Mitsukoshi Department Store is large and brimming with merchandise from Japan. Bonsai, unusual toys, lacquered bowls, kimonos, and a thousand other items make for some great browsing, even if you aren't interested in buying. Food plays a prominent role here too, with three restaurants and a lounge. Tempura Kiku is Japan's tempura bar and one of our favorite choices for lunch. It is small and quiet. The Teppanyaki Dining Room features grill-tables where performance chefs prepare your dinner with sizzle and flair. Japan is also home to the Yakitori House, a delightful and authentic Japanese fast-food restaurant with a lovely garden dining area. The Matsu No Ma Lounge, a full-service bar, offers a variety of specialty drinks, sake, and a selection of Japanese finger foods including sushi and Kabuki beef.

Live Entertainment in Japan   A Japanese drum group, Matsuriza, has been performing here for many years. Storytellers and various other artists seem to come and go. Check your guidemap times guide to see who's appearing during your visit.

Morocco

Of all the countries at Epcot, Morocco seems to best capture the feeling of a foreign land. Along its winding, narrow streets and shops, you might forget that you are at Disney World. Fruit trees, irrigated gardens, and elaborate tilework all bring a real sense of authenticity to Disney's Morocco. The lively festival of musicians and dancers that appear regularly in the courtyard only serves to make it seem even more exotic.

Tons of handcrafted tiles were imported to create the Chellah Minaret and Bab Boujouloud, the gateway to the ancient city of Fez. Within the walls of this village is a gallery of Moroccan art and a meditation area.

The shops here are especially interesting. All things Moroccan are offered in this bazaar: jewelry, carpets, kaftans, brassware, leather goods, and more. Prices are fairly reasonable.

Morocco features one of our favorite Epcot restaurants, Restaurant Marrakesh ♥♥. This exotic eatery boasts a menu of Moroccan cuisine and live entertainment at both lunch and dinner. With a shady patio right along the promenade, the Tangierine Cafe delivers some interesting and tasty treats from the Middle East. It's another of our favorites. For our review of Restaurant Marrakesh, see page 331.

Moroccan Live Entertainment   Musicians and a traditional Moroccan belly dancer perform throughout the day at Restaurant Marrakesh. In the courtyard, you'll want to see the musical group, Mo'Rockin, with its electric adaptations of traditional Moroccan melodies. They're quite good, though as is usual for Disney, rather loud.

France

It's easy to imagine we're strolling along the banks of the River Seine here in Disney's France. Small boats and artists' easels dot the water's edge, while the Eiffel Tower rises in the distance above the beautiful fountain and mansard roofs of the city. It is not quite Paris, but it certainly has the flavor.

The emphasis here is on cuisine and the pavilion features two good restaurants and a patisserie that serves fruit, sandwiches, quiche, and of course, French pastries. For more information about the two restaurants, Les Chefs de France and Bistro de Paris, see chapter 6.

Browse the French marketplace for wine (and wine tasting), kitchen accessories, perfumes and aromatherapy products, gargoyle souvenirs, and a very nice assortment of Impressionistic art apparel.

Impressions de France ♥♥

℮ Film

℮ Lasts 20 minutes

℮ Line moves to fill theater

This film is beautiful, romantic, and unforgettable, and you'll find the theater a cool and comfortable place to rest your weary feet. Need we say more?

EXCELLENT, NOT TO BE MISSED.

TIPS: Ask at the door for the next show time. If there is no crowd, browse until just before it begins.

Sidewalk Artisans de Paris   Along the lagoon, artists are at work. Some do sketches, some create chalk portraits, and yet others will snip your silhouette. One of these will make a much better souvenir than a photo in front of the geosphere. Prices begin around $17.

Live Entertainment in Disney's France   Lately, entertainment here in France has featured a mime and other assorted street performers.

The United Kingdom

Disney's United Kingdom is charming and picturesque. From Tudor storefronts to the lovely thatched-roofed cottage of Anne Hathaway, this pavilion provides a hearty taste of this island kingdom. We enjoy its decorative gardens, its gas street lamps, and the stately façade of Hampton Court

Shopping is UK's strong suit, and we particularly enjoy its Scottish woolens, English china, and the flavorful assortment of teas. There's more, including British sports apparel, candies, family crests, and some very unusual chess sets. Be sure to explore every area of this pavilion, especially the lovely garden in front of Anne Hathaway's cottage.

If pubs are central to your visit to Britain, you won't be disappointed here. The Rose & Crown Pub offers all the atmosphere necessary to savor a pint of ale or stout. For a real English dinner, there's the lovely Rose & Crown Dining Room. In the mood for fish and chips? Try either the walk-up window of Harry Ramsden's (on the promenade) or the pub.

Epcot Around the World Showcase Restaurants

Restaurant	Location	Price	Fare	Service	Our Comments
Biergarten*	Germany	$$	German buffet	Table service L/D	Large buffet, food is good to quite good; see page 315
Bistro de Paris*	France	$$$	Elegant French cuisine	Table service D	Food is just OK; see page 316
Boulangerie Pâtisserie	France	$	Quiche, desserts, fruit salads, salads	Counter Service L/D	Pretty good
Cantina de San Angel	Mexico	$	Mexican	Counter service L/D	OK Mexican fast food, burritos, tacos and more
Harry Ramsden Fish & Chips	United Kingdom	$	Fried fish and chips	Counter Service L/D	Very popular; small portions
Kringla Bakeri Og Kafe	Norway	$	Open sandwiches, pastries	Counter service L/D	Some interesting stuff here
Le Cellier Steakhouse*	Canada	$$	Steaks, seafood	Table service L/D	Quite good; see page 329
Chefs de France*	France	$$	French cuisine	Table service L/D	Food is pretty good; see page 320
L'Originale Alfredo di Roma Ristorante*	Italy	$$	Italian	Table service L/D	Varied menu, OK food; see page 330
Lotus Blossom Cafe	China	$	Chinese	Counter service L/D	Mediocre Cantonese food
Matsu No Ma Lounge	Japan	$	Japanese, sushi	Table service L/D	OK sushi; great atmosphere and view
Teppanyaki Dining Room*	Japan	$$	Steak, chicken	Table service L/D	Much like Benihana; food is good; see page 340

Epcot Around the World Showcase Restaurants
(continued)

Restaurant	Location	Price	Fare	Service	Our Comments
Nine Dragons*	China	$$	Chinese	Table service L/D	Chinese cuisine, served à la carte; see page 332
Restaurant Akershus*	Norway	$$	Scandinavian buffet	Table service B/L/D	Big spread, good food; we like this place; see page 313
Restaurant Marrakesh*	Morocco	$$	Moroccan	Table service L/D	Exotic and good; see page 331
Rose and Crown*	United Kingdom	$$	British	Table service L/D	English standards; see page 336
San Angel Inn Restaurante*	Mexico	$$	Mexican	Table service L/D	Stunning restaurant, food is OK; see page 337
Sommerfest	Germany	$	Sausage, sandwiches, soup	Counter service L/D	Good sausage; serves beer
Tangierine Cafe*	Morocco	$	Moroccan	Counter service L/D	Exotic fast food, pretty good, too
Tempura Kiku*	Japan	$$	Tempura and sushi	Table service L/D	Quiet and small, good food; a gem; see page 339
Yakitori House*	Japan	$	Japanese chicken, beef noodles	Counter service L/D	Interesting, nice garden dining area

B/L/D: Breakfast/Lunch/Dinner
$ Most entrées less than $15
$$ Most entrées less than $25
$$$ Most entrées more than $25
$$$$ Expensive, most entrées over $30
*See chapter 6 for our reviews of these restaurants.

World Showcase Best-of-the-Best List

Norway's *Maelstrom* ride and film

China's *Reflections of China* film

Impressions de France film ♥♥

O Canada! film followed by a stroll through Canada's
mountains and gardens

Japan's garden and Bijutsu-Kan Gallery exhibits

Morocco's winding streets, shops, and street entertainment

British Invasion rock band in UK garden

IllumiNations

Romance Around the World Showcase

The Epcot Fall Food & Wine Festival ♥♥♥

Dining at Bistro de Paris Restaurant ♥♥♥

A meal at San Angel Inn Restaurant ♥♥♥

The Japanese Garden ♥

Lunch or dinner at Restaurant Marrakesh ♥♥

The Breathless IllumiNations Cruise
(see page 356 for details) ♥♥♥♥

A sketch by a sidewalk artisan in France ♥

Impressions de France film ♥♥

A meal at Alfredo's outside cafe ♥♥

Live Entertainment in the United Kingdom   There's a lot of music and fun going on here. The British Invasion serves up the "golden age of British rock 'n' roll" with hits from the Beatles, Dave Clark Five, and Gerry and the Pacemakers. At the Rose & Crown Pub, you might find pianist Pam Brody. In the pavilion's courtyard, troupes of comic performers and Scottish bagpipers perform. Check your times guide for performance times.

Canada

There's a lot we like about Disney's Canada: the rocky mountain landscape of British Columbia, Quebec's impressive Chateau Frontenac, and an exciting film travelogue are just a few. Totem poles, fir trees, log cabins, and the flowering perfection of Victoria gardens are some of the other realistic elements that bring to Disney a little bit of each of Canada's ten provinces. This pavilion even has its own thundering waterfall. The Northwest Mercantile has maple syrup and a selection of trendy Canadian sports apparel. La Boutique des Provinces has a nice line of Anne of Green Gables dolls, Canadian bath products, and decorative ceramics.

Food offerings mean Le Cellier Steakhouse, Canada's full-service restaurant and one of our World Showcase favorites. It's a nice, quiet place to enjoy a good meal. See page 329 for our take on this restaurant.

O Canada!

- Film
- Lasts 20 minutes
- Line moves to fill theater

This is a 360-degree film, and like the one in China, you'll stand during the presentation. All travel films should be this exciting.

VERY GOOD, no reason to miss this one.

TIP: If it seems particularly crowded, ask one of the attendants if you'll make it into the next show.

Live Entertainment in Canada   Canada's outdoor stage features Off Kilter, a group that plays an interesting rock interpretation of Celtic music. Check your times guide for times and other performers who appear regularly along the Canadian promenade.

Disney-MGM Studios

The pointed cap from the sorcerer's apprentice in *Fantasia* towers over the Studios and is this park's focus: the magic of the movies.

Like all Disney theme parks, Disney-MGM Studios is more than a bunch of rides and shows. It is itself something of a movie set. Along its palm-lined avenues are art deco storefronts, old trolley cables, bus benches, period billboards, and vintage cars. It's Disney's zany vision of 1930s Hollywood. Cast-iron street lamps, fireplugs, and oddball "residents" bring to life this delightful fantasy of a place that never really was.

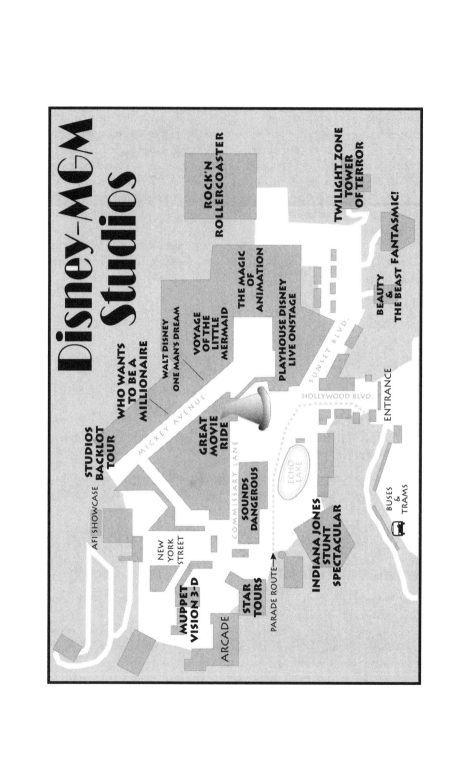

We've always loved strolling along the avenues here, lazily enjoying the park's landscaping and amusing architecture. And while this park is home to several of Disney's best rides, what we like best about it is its engaging variety of shows. Here at Disney-MGM Studios are more than a dozen delightful Disney performances, from Beauty and The Beast stage show to the incredible Fantasmic!

Disney-MGM Tips

@ Disney-MGM Extra Magic Hour is on Tuesdays and Saturdays.

@ With all the shows here, you'll certainly need the guidemap times guide to get a handle on when everything happens.

@ The Studios' main tip board is at Hollywood Junction, and there's a second one on the New York Set.

@ This is a small park, and it quickly becomes crowded. In the past, long waits have been typical, but with the introduction of *FASTPASS,* you should be able to ride many of the attractions without much of a wait. See page 197 for our tips for getting the most out of *FASTPASS.*

@ *FASTPASS* attractions include Indiana Jones, Rock 'n' Roller Coaster, The Twilight Zone Tower of Terror, Star Tours, Voyage of the Little Mermaid, and Who Wants to Be a Millionaire—Play It.

Tips for Eating at Disney-MGM Studios

@ Looking for breakfast at the Studios? Here are your options: Hollywood & Vine Cafeteria, ABC Commissary, and, for lighter fare, Starring Rolls Bakery.

@ The table-service restaurants are always busy. Make priority seating arrangements in the morning or plan to eat fast food. Either call from your room or visit the window at Hollywood Junction, near the tip board.

@ For good food and lots of fun, our choice is the 50's Prime Time Café. This is a place we love to bring people.

@ For an early lunch, try the Backlot Express or the ABC Commissary. They're usually open by 11 A.M. The ABC Commissary features everything from cheeseburgers to a good stir-fry.

@ For fine dining, try The Hollywood Brown Derby ♥♥♥. The Derby takes reservations for as late as 7:20 P.M. We highly recommend eating late and then walking out through the empty park.

Disney-MGM Studios Restaurants

Restaurant	Price	Fare	Service	Our Comments
ABC Commissary	$	International sandwiches, chicken, fish	Counter service B/L/D	Full hot or continental breakfast; fairly good, especially the noodles
Backlot Express	$	Burgers, sandwiches, salads	Counter service L/D	Opens early
Catalina Eddie's	$	Pizza, salads	Counter service L/D	California-style pizza
50's Prime Time Café*	$$	Large home-style menu	Full service L/D	Good food & fun (see our review, page 324)
Hollywood & Vine*	$$	Large character buffet	Buffet service B/L/D	Good food and fun (see our review, page 327)
Hollywood Brown Derby*	$$	Steaks, seafood, salads	Full service L/D	Quite good, fine dining (see our review, page 327)
Mama Melrose's Ristorante Italiano*	$$	Italian and Californian cuisine	Full service L/D	Quite good (see our review, page 331)
Rosie's All-American Cafe	$	Burgers, sandwiches	Counter service L/D	The usual Disney fast food, soups, and salads
Sci-Fi Dine-In Theater*	$$	Large menu: entrée, sandwiches	Full service L/D	Good and fun, too (see our review, page 337)

Disney-MGM Studios Restaurants *(continued)*

Restaurant	Price	Fare	Service	Our Comments
Starring Rolls	$	Pastries, muffins	Counter service B/snacks	Continental breakfast, good snacks; coffee, tea, cocoa, milk
Sunset Ranch Market	$	Turkey legs, hot dogs	Counter service L/D	Some interesting fast food here
Toy Story Pizza Planet	$	Pizza and salads	Counter service L/D	Pizza kids will like; we didn't

B/L/D: Breakfast/Lunch/Dinner
$ Most entrées less than $10
$$ Most entrées less than $25
*See chapter 6 for our reviews of these restaurants.

❧ The Fantasmic! Dinner "package" will provide a meal at one of the park's table-service restaurants (currently Mama Melrose's Ristorante Italiano, Hollywood & Vine, or the Brown Derby) and give you guaranteed seating at Fantasmic! Prices begin around $25 ($12 for ages 3 to 9), depending on your choice of restaurant (there's no charge for the show). During busy times, this dinner can save you an hour or more in line waiting for seats. You can spend it eating dinner, instead. Reservations can be made through Central Reservations dining or at either Disney-MGM Studios or the guest services of any Disney resort. Be forewarned that same-day reservations are hard to get, so plan ahead.

The Shops of Disney-MGM Studios

There are more than twenty shops at the Studios, and you'll find everything from character merchandise and movie memorabilia to artwork and baby clothes. Sid Cahuenga's One-of-a-Kind is one of Disney's most unique shops and features real movie memorabilia. For more offbeat browsing, try Tower Shop at the Tower of Terror or Tatooine Traders at Star Tours. For books and such, check out Writer's Stop, which is also a nice coffee shop. Other stores include Stage 1 Company Store for baby stuff and one of our favorites, the Animation Gallery.

The Rides of Disney-MGM Studios

If you've come here looking for rides, you'll find two of Disney's best: one is a roller coaster and the other, an out-of-control elevator. Along with these, you'll also enjoy an interesting assortment of other attractions that either go somewhere, or seem to.

Rock 'n' Roller Coaster Starring Aerosmith FASTPASS

❧ Special-effects coaster with 3 inversions; riders must be at least 48 inches tall

❧ Line moves slowly

❧ Ride lasts 3 minutes

You might like this even if you don't particularly like roller coasters. It's remarkably smooth and since it's indoors, there's no sensation of height (otherwise, Rick wouldn't get on it!). The story will have you "hitting the road" with the rock group Aerosmith. The coaster is fun, and every twist and turn is perfectly synchronized to a soundtrack that blasts each car through 120 speakers.

OVER THE TOP FUN.

TIPS: Get here early (usually open for Extra Magic Hour) or get a *FASTPASS* (or both). This ride can run out of *FASTPASS*es early in the day. And after your ride, don't forget to check out the picture of yourselves taken along the way.

The Twilight Zone Tower of Terror FASTPASS

- Special-effects thrill ride; minimum height for riders is 40 inches

- Lasts 10 minutes

- Line moves slowly

If being taken to the top of a thirteen-story building in an elevator and being dropped repeatedly to ground level sounds like fun, this ride is for you. If you haven't been here in the past few years, you'll find that Tower has been "improved" with visual, auditory, and olfactory (smell) special effects. It now allows the ride's computer to produce an ever-changing variety of drop sequences. Ghostly apparitions and more drops make this even scarier than it already was. Get ready to scream.

EXCELLENT, if the plunge doesn't frighten you off.

TIPS: A VERY popular attraction. Get here early (it's almost always open for the Extra Magic Hour), or use *FASTPASS*. After the ride, look for your photo taken at the moment of the big drop.

WARNING: During busy times this attraction can run out of *FASTPASS*es.

Star Tours FASTPASS

- Simulated thrill ride, with some bumps; riders must be at least 40 inches tall

- Lasts 10 minutes

- Line moves quickly

Like its "sister" ride, Body Wars in Epcot, this attraction doesn't really go anywhere, but creates a very convincing sensation of speeding through the galaxy in an out-of-control spaceship. The story is funny and the effects are thrilling.

EXCELLENT, do not miss.

TIPS: Usually open for Extra Magic Hour. Lines are usually not too bad; if they are, use *FASTPASS*.

WARNING: Not suitable for persons prone to motion sickness.

The Great Movie Ride

- Slow "train" ride

- Lasts 22 minutes

- Line moves very quickly

This ride takes you through a series of movie scene re-creations. The sets, audio-animatronics, and special effects are all worth seeing again and again. There is even a "live show" staged along the way. (Actually, there are two different versions of the show, shown to alternating cars.)

EXCELLENT, do not miss.

TIP: Parts of this ride may be too intense for very young children.

Disney-MGM Studios Backlot Tour

- @ Tram tour with a thrill
- @ Lasts 35 minutes
- @ Line moves quickly

During this tour you'll see some of the working areas of this real studio, a neat prop yard, and more. There's even some fiery special effects excitement, as the tram gets caught in "Catastrophe Canyon."

VERY GOOD, don't miss it.

TIP: May be too intense for very young children

The Shows of Disney-MGM Studios

You'd expect a park whose theme is the movies and television to have some really great shows, and you won't be disappointed here. This park is a real Oscar winner. Two shows are no longer featured at MGM: Disney's Doug Live! and The Hunchback of Notre Dame—A Musical Adventure. At press time, no replacements had been announced. Check your guidemap and times information guide to find out what may have arrived.

Who Wants to Be a Millionaire—Play It! FASTPASS

- @ A sit-down, soundstage show
- @ Lasts about 30 minutes
- @ 600-seat theater

Sorry, there's no $1,000,000 prize at this attraction, where contestants are selected from park guests and everyone in the audience has a "fast finger" button to get in on the competition. However, the show features prizes and surprises. Much more fun than we expected.

VERY ENTERTAINING, don't miss it.

Indiana Jones Epic Stunt Spectacular FASTPASS

- @ Live show
- @ Lasts 30 minutes
- @ Line moves quickly to fill large amphitheater

The sets and stunts here are executed on a truly grand scale. Fiery explosions, high-flying acrobatics, and a fiery truck wreck are just a few of its many stunts. It's surprising, exciting, and funny, too. One great show!

EXCELLENT, do not miss.

TIP: The theater is very large, and if you won't make it into the next show, get a *FASTPASS*.

Beauty and the Beast—Live on Stage ♥♥

- @ Live show
- @ Lasts 30 minutes
- @ Line moves to fill theater

This is a charming, live version of the Disney classic film (abbreviated, of course). The costumes, sets, and performances are memorable, and we think the music is the very best of any Disney animated feature.

EXCELLENT, even stirring, do not miss.

TIPS: The 1,500-seat Theater of the Stars will accommodate virtually everyone in line. The amphitheater is large, and all of the seats provide a reasonably good view of the stage. Seating begins thirty minutes prior to each show. Check for show times.

Fantasmic!

- @ Nighttime special effects and music show
- @ Lasts 25 minutes: one show nightly, two during busy months
- @ May be cancelled in the event of bad weather
- @ Line moves to fill 8,500-seat theater, seating begins 2 hours prior to show

This show surprised even us. We don't want to tell you much about it, except that it lives up to its name. The theater has been designed especially for this show and there are no bad seats. Expect to see Mickey Mouse, fireworks, special effects, and song and dance. Nobody does this sort of thing better than Disney, and this is one of Disney's best.

OUTSTANDING, not to be missed.

TIPS: If you sit close to the front, you may get sprayed with water. Get here early during busy times or better yet, make plans for the Fantasmic! Dinner (see page 248).

WARNING: May be too intense for very small children.

Time-Saving Tip

Get reserved seating for Fantasmic! by dining in one of this park's restaurants and avoid a wait in line. It doesn't even cost extra. See page 248 for details.

Jim Henson's MuppetVision 3-D

- Film and more
- Lasts 25 minutes
- Line moves quickly to fill large pre-show area, then theater

This is a very funny 3-D movie with many unexpected special effects. Every time we see this, we see things we'd never noticed before.

EXCELLENT, not to be missed.

TIPS: The line here seems to come and go with the flow of people from nearby attractions such as Indiana Jones. Try it at various times throughout the day when there isn't much of a line. Don't miss the engaging pre-show.

WARNING: Loud noises may frighten young children.

The Magic of Disney Animation

- Film and walking tour
- Lasts about 35 minutes
- Line moves quickly

The unlikely duo of Robin Williams and Walter Cronkite join forces for a hilarious film introduction to this tour of the Disney animators' working studio areas. Afterward, a memorable film of animation clips from Disney classics. Take your time in the outstanding gallery as you exit the tour.

EXCELLENT, don't miss this.

Voyage of The Little Mermaid FASTPASS

- Live musical show
- Lasts 17 minutes
- Line moves slowly to fill theater

Don't mistake this show as something for kids only. It features live action, puppetry, good music, and stunning visual effects.

EXCELLENT, do not miss.

TIP: Forget the long lines here and get a *FASTPASS*.

Sounds Dangerous

- Film and sound effects show
- Lasts 12 minutes
- Line moves slowly to fill theater

This show stars Drew Carey and is designed to demonstrate sound effects but, for us, failed to either do that or be very entertaining. We liked the original Chevy Chase show here better than any of its many replacements.

OK, cute, but not terribly entertaining. Skip this one if you wish.

WARNING: Seven minutes of this show are in total darkness. May be too much for small children.

✷ Playhouse Disney – Live Onstage!

@ Live 20-minute show

@ Line moves to fill theater

At Soundstage 5 in the Animation Courtyard, this live musical show features characters from a variety of the Disney kiddie television shows. A cute and heartwarming performance, but one for the younger set.

GOOD FOR YOUNGSTERS, otherwise pass it by.

Boulevard "Streetmosphere"

Along the main avenues of the Studios are the wacky residents of Disney's Hollywood. Dressed in costumes so strange they defy description, these characters "perform" mostly during the afternoon hours, staging comical sketches and interacting with park guests. Make an effort to catch their pranks and even to get involved. We think that this special level of entertainment is what makes the Disney parks the best anywhere. Some great photo opportunities, too.

Disney-MGM's Other Attractions

These attractions don't fit so neatly into our categories, but you'll surely wish to see them.

Disney Stars and Cars Motorparade

This parade features classic cars in regalia inspired by the characters of classic Disney stories. Music, song and dance, and Disney characters make it a not-to-miss special event. Check your Studios times guide for times.

VERY GOOD, worth seeing, especially for kids.

TIP: Find a good viewing spot at least thirty minutes before the parade. See page 244 for our map and the parade route.

Walt Disney: One Man's Dream

@ Walk-through 25-minute show

This multisensory experience chronicles the creation of the Disney empire, from dream to realization. It's hard to imagine anyone not enjoying this interesting stuff.

VERY GOOD, not to miss.

"New York" Street Set

ℯ Walk-through

ℯ No time limit

This façade and forced perspective view of New York will demonstrate why movies appear real when they aren't. Disney's New York includes crazy character entertainment, occasional music, some shopping (at "Yous Guys Moychendise"), some food, and a storefront where you can have your picture put on a magazine cover (everyone's dream when they come to the big city!). Along the way, you can even get your face painted. Don't forget to snap a few photos of your visit to the "Big Apple."
INTERESTING.

American Film Institute Showcase

ℯ Walk-through at the end of the Backlot Tour

ℯ No time limit

This interesting exhibit features real costumes, props, and set pieces from numerous films and television productions, past and present. On our last visit, we saw the 20-foot long Mission to Mars spaceship and other neat stuff.
QUITE GOOD, especially if you love movies.
TIP: You don't have to go on the tour to see this exhibit. Just fight your way in the back door near Studio Catering.

"Honey, I Shrunk the Kids" Movie Set Adventure

ℯ Playground for children age 4 and older

ℯ No time limit

ℯ Line moves very slowly

This is a playground where objects are much larger than usual. Much, much larger. Everything is "rubberized" for safety.
FUN FOR SMALL CHILDREN, otherwise pass it by.

Insider's Secret

FOR *FUN* DINING at Disney-MGM Studios: 50's Prime Time Café and Sci-Fi Dine-In Theater Restaurant. FOR *FINE* DINING at Disney-MGM Studios, The Hollywood Brown Derby. (See chapter 6 for more information about these restaurants.)

Disney-MGM Studios Best-of-the-Best List

Disney-MGM Studios Backlot Tour

Rock 'n' Roller Coaster

Beauty and the Beast—Live on Stage

The Great Movie Ride

Indiana Jones Epic Stunt Spectacular

The Magic of Disney Animation

Jim Henson's MuppetVision 3-D

Star Tours

The Twilight Zone Tower of Terror

Voyage of The Little Mermaid

Fantasmic!

Romance at Disney-MGM Studios

Beauty and the Beast—Live on Stage ♥♥

The Hollywood Brown Derby Restaurant ♥♥♥

Fantasmic! Dinner at Brown Derby ♥♥

Disney's Toy Story Pizza Planet Arcade

Bring along some change (or better yet, plenty of dollar bills) to this video arcade. If this is the kind of thing you really like, we suggest you save it for DisneyQuest, the final word in virtual entertainment (see page 274 for details).

Disney's Animal Kingdom

For our sensibilities, the Animal Kingdom provides a unique breed of Disney magic. Not so much a place of over-the-top rides and Disney characters, the Animal Kingdom is more a zoo and botanical garden. It is a land of sights, sounds, and moods, and these elements are all magically mingled with the exotic fragrances of tropical foliage and exciting

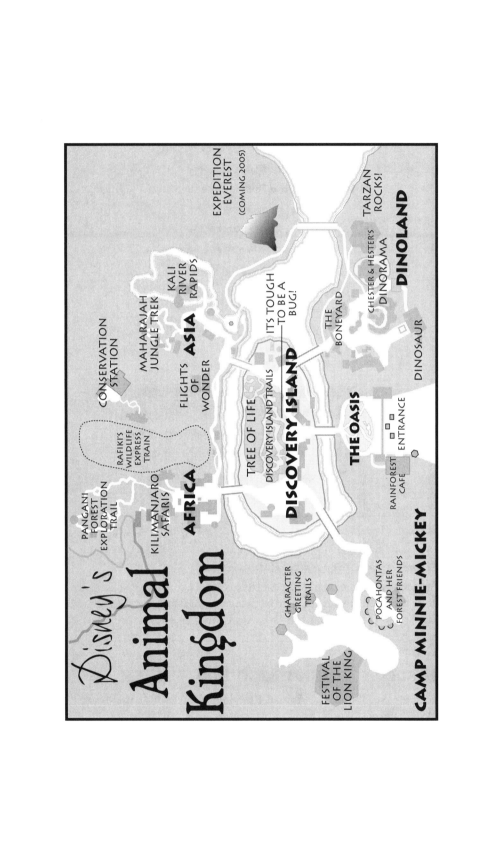

encounters with creatures both wild and imagined. The Animal Kingdom also delivers an important message about conservation, a message vital to our children and to the generations to come. The Animal Kingdom is a land of adventure and discovery, and it is a place where the imagination of Disney has gone wild.

But we don't want to confuse you. This is still a Disney theme park, and that means excitement. You'll definitely find those over-the-top rides and wonderful shows you've come to expect from Disney, but they are simply not the focus of this park. The riotous Kali River Rapids raft adventure, Mickey's Jammin' Jungle Parade, and the music and acrobatics of the Festival of the Lion King are just a few of the not-to-miss attractions you'll find here. There are others.

For us, the real heart of Disney's Animal Kingdom is its creatures and their habitats. From the African savanna to the jungles of Thailand and the rain forests of Indonesia, the Animal Kingdom takes theme parks someplace altogether new. From the whimsical fantasy of Discovery Island to the stunning realism of Asia and Africa, the Animal Kingdom is a land of enchanting beauty and engaging details. It is a place where you'll find adventure and discovery around every corner. It is, indeed, a unique species of theme park and, we think, one of Disney's grandest creations.

Animal Kingdom Tips

@ The Extra Magic Hour at the Animal Kingdom is on Mondays and Fridays.

@ *FASTPASS* attractions here at the Animal Kingdom include Kilimanjaro Safaris, Kali River Rapids, Dinosaur, and Primeval Whirl.

@ Except for the large animal habitats, this is a relatively small park. When it gets crowded, it feels very crowded.

@ We recommend you arrive early, but another good time to visit this park is during the two hours just before it closes. Be sure to stay late to catch some especially beautiful effects around the Tree of Life ♥♥♥.

@ Festival of the Lion King is one of the best live shows ever at Walt Disney World. Lines get so long here in the afternoon that you may not make it inside. Try to see it in the morning.

@ For the live stage shows, arrive 30 minutes before performance time.

@ Check the tip board on Discovery Island for show times, waits, closures, and special events.

- If you're interested in learning more about the foliage and creatures of this theme park, pick up a *Field Guide to Disney's Animal Kingdom at Wonders of the Wild*. It will tell you not only what plants and animals are here, but also where you can find them.

- Throughout this park, you'll find a variety of talented live performers, from African drummers to music of the Andes. They appear around the park without any apparent schedule. Keep your ears open.

- Hate those hand dryers that don't dry your hands? Check out the Xlerator hand dryers in several of the bathrooms. These things blow at nearly 160 miles an hour and really do the job!

Tips for Eating at the Animal Kingdom

- Except for the Rainforest Cafe, all restaurants at the Animal Kingdom are counter-service.

- Breakfast choices include Rainforest Cafe and the character breakfast at Restaurantosaurus.

- Our favorite is Tusker House Restaurant, and it's a surprisingly good value. In good weather, eat on the patio behind the restaurant.

- There's a good topping bar for sandwiches at Restaurantosaurus.

The Lay of the Land

Whether you arrive by car or by bus, you'll wonder where they've hidden this park. There are no castle spires, no towering metallic spheres. Here at the entrance plaza, you'll find only a small cluster of buildings surrounded by a dense thicket of tropical greenery. On one side is a rocky waterfall and behind it is the Rainforest Cafe. It's a wild place to eat.

Once through the turnstiles, you'll enter The Oasis, the beginning of your Animal Kingdom adventure and something of an introduction to this park. Beyond it, a footbridge will take you across the Discovery River and into the six unique lands of the Animal Kingdom: Discovery Island, Africa, Rafiki's Planet Watch, Asia, Dinoland U.S.A., and Camp Minnie-Mickey.

The Oasis

This cool and lush tropical garden is really the park's foyer. Along its winding paths and amid its exotic foliage, you'll discover a variety of interesting plants and creatures. Anteaters, spoonbills, and military macaws are just a few. Hanging lanterns, stone escarpments, and the ever-present music of running water make this a tempting place to

Disney's Animal Kingdom Restaurants

Restaurant	Location	Price	Fare	Service	Our Comments
Chakranadi Chicken Shop	Asia	$	Asian specialties: pot stickers, skewered peanut chicken	Window service L/D portions	Tasty but greasy, small
Flame Tree Barbecue	Discovery Island	$	Barbecued ribs and sandwiches	Counter service L/D	OK barbecue; nice seating areas along water
Mr. Kamal's Burgers	Asia	$	Burgers, fries, drinks	Window service L/D	Decent burger, nice patio
Pizzafari	Discovery Island	$	Pizza, pasta, sandwiches	Counter service L/D	Mediocre pizza, OK sandwiches; tasty veggie sandwich
Rainforest Cafe*	Front gate	$$	Large menu, varied dishes	Table service: B/L/D	Noisy fun, pretty good food; see page 336
Restaurantosaurus	Dinoland	$	Character breakfast buffet, then hamburgers, hot dogs, chicken nuggets	Counter service B/L/D	Good breakfast; good topping bar for sandwiches and burgers
Tusker House Restaurant	Africa	$	Rotisserie chicken, sandwiches	Counter service B/L/D	Our favorite AK restaurant

B/L/D: Breakfast/Lunch/Dinner
$ most entrées less than $10
$$ most entrées less than $25
*See chapter 6 for our reviews of these restaurants.

linger. If this is your first visit to the Animal Kingdom, we suggest you press on and return later to enjoy it at a more leisurely pace.

Discovery Island

As you emerge from the shade of The Oasis, you'll get your first glimpse of the Animal Kingdom's stunning centerpiece, the Tree of Life. This creation celebrates Earth's diversity of life and towers fourteen stories above Discovery Island, with a leafy canopy that spans nearly 200 feet. But as you approach this towering marvel, you'll become aware of its most intriguing feature.

Carved into its massive trunk and limbs and into its winding roots are the intricate images of more than three hundred of Earth's creatures. Amid this swirling tapestry are mammals, reptiles, fish, birds, and insects. It's the living legacy of our planet and it is a mesmerizing sight. You'll want to stand in its shadow and see how many of the creatures you can find. The Tree of Life is certainly one of Disney's most impressive creations.

Discovery Island is the hub of the Animal Kingdom. It is a brightly colored fantasy land of playful creature-architecture and imagery and it is the place to find many of the park's shops and eateries, each of which enjoys its own unique animal theme. The Flame Tree Barbecue, for example, features predators and their prey. Even the island's bathrooms get in on the theming (don't miss the beautiful gecko tiles in Pizzafari's restrooms!). The Disney Imagineers must have had a lot of fun creating this place! We suggest you take the time to look it all over and to enjoy the delightful details.

Shops and restaurants are not the only things you'll find here on Discovery Island. There are also several outstanding attractions.

The Tree of Life

- A landmark display
- No time limit
- No real line

The structure underneath this amazing creation is a deep-sea oil rig. The Tree of Life is thrilling from a distance and even more so up close. Look carefully—not all the creatures are meant to be easily seen. In the trunk is a theater that features It's Tough to Be a Bug!

VERY GOOD, even breathtaking.

TIP: There are two perfect picture spots for the Tree of Life: one across the street from Island Mercantile and the other across the river, between Africa and Asia. Ask a cast member to take your photo.

It's Tough to Be a Bug! FASTPASS *(during busy times only)*

- 3-D film and much, much more

- Lasts 8 minutes

- Line moves slowly to fill 430-seat theater

This wild and zany movie (and more) is flat-out, over-the-top Disney fun. It's the next generation of Muppet-Vision 4-D (Disney-MGM) and "Honey, I Shrunk the Audience" (Epcot). Don't let anyone give away its many surprises and, whatever you do, don't miss it.

OUTSTANDING. Disney at its very best. One of our Disney favorites.

WARNING: Probably too intense for very young children and for people with bug phobias or who are easily frightened.

Discovery Island Trails ♥♥

- Self-guided walking tour

- No set time

- No real line

At the foot of the Tree of Life is a garden of exotic plants, small ponds, and waterfalls. Along its winding paths you will encounter a variety of fascinating creatures such as otters, lemurs, and kangaroos. Take your time here to enjoy its many hidden pleasures.

OUTSTANDING, do not miss.

TIP: Try to see this when it is not crowded and be sure to visit just before the park closes, around sunset ♥♥♥.

Mickey's Jammin' Jungle Parade

This colorful and raucus parade was created especially for the Animal Kingdom. It features jungle rhythms, terrific costumes, and great floats. It's our favorite Disney parade. Check your Animal Kingdom times guide for starting times.

The Shops of Discovery Island

An entire flock of new merchandise has been created for the Animal Kingdom, and much of it is quite engaging. From safari hats to rubber dinos, there's a mammoth selection. Wonders of the Wild features a herd of gifts, which include candles, books, luxury bath products, and Mickey gear. Don't miss the marvelous carved and painted ostrich eggs.

If you're looking for Animal Kingdom souvenirs, stampede over to Island Mercantile for T-shirts, caps, mugs, and just about anything you can imagine featuring this park's logo. It's also the place for pin trading and gourmet chocolate candies.

Shopping for kids? Creature Comforts has everything for your little ones, including some great little character costumes and some loveable stuffed animals. On the other side of the island, you'll find Beastly Bazaar's offbeat offering of surf and island apparel.

Africa

You'll feel positively transported by the exotic architecture of Africa's Harambe Village: strange turrets, thatched roofs, shady verandahs, and gnarly stone walls, all of it slowly crumbling under the relentless equatorial sun. Nearby, the abandoned ramparts of Fort Harambe stand quiet guard over this bustling African town.

Harambe's narrow main street is lined with date palms, jacarandas, and blossoming yellow trumpet trees. At the far end of the village, the old man baobab tree, "Mzee Mbuyo," peeks his head above a cluster of thatched huts, eyeing the throngs of passing visitors.

Excitement and adventure are in the air here at Harambe. This village lies at the edge of a great wildlife preserve and it is the place where you'll embark on your Disney safari adventure. A visit here will also include a delightful wildlife trail, shops, a restaurant and bakery, and some interesting cultural encounters.

Kilimanjaro Safaris FASTPASS

- Bumpy truck ride through the African savanna
- Lasts about 20 minutes
- Line moves fairly quickly to load 32-passenger trucks

Open-sided safari trucks will take you through a land that looks and feels like an African savanna and is teeming with wildlife of every sort: rhinos, hippos, okapis, cheetahs, and much more. You never know what you'll see, but it's sure to be different every time. The Safari features a story, which delivers this park's message of global conservation.

OUTSTANDING, not to be missed, our Animal Kingdom favorite.

TIPS: Get a *FASTPASS* for this attraction. There are plenty of animals to be seen throughout the day. Don't forget to bring plenty of film. Binoculars will also come in handy.

Pangani Forest Exploration Trail ♥♥

- ⅜-mile-long self-guided walking tour
- Lasts about 30 minutes or as long as you wish to take
- No real lines here

This trail is really a well-disguised zoo and botanical garden. It's one of two such attractions here at the Animal Kingdom (the other is the Maharaja Jungle Trek in Asia) and is definitely one of the things we most love about this park. Along this trail you'll experience up-close encounters with animals too small or too shy to be seen from the safari trucks: giant African bullfrogs, dik diks, and meerkats. Cast members are available to tell you more about what you're seeing. There's an underwater hippo viewing area, a stroll-through aviary, and several gorilla habitats.

OUTSTANDING, one of our favorites, not to be missed.

TIPS: Sometimes crowded early in the day; wait until later. Wheelchairs or electric convenience vehicles are easily accommodated along this trail, and there are numerous places to sit and rest. Take your time exploring this place—there's more to see than meets the eye. This is especially nice very late in the day. It's the perfect place to spend time while you're waiting for your *FASTPASS* appointment at the safari.

Rafiki's Planet Watch

- 1.2-mile railroad loop with midway visit to several large exhibits
- Medium-length walk from train to Conservation Station
- Takes at least 45 minutes or as long as you wish

You'll start with a short ride on the Eastern Star Railway, a marvelous replica of the type of British steam engine that was used in India around the turn of the twentieth century. After disembarking, you'll continue on by foot to Conservation Station. Midway along the trail is Habitat Habit, where you can learn about sharing your backyard ecosystem with its wild inhabitants.

Conservation Station itself provides a fascinating look behind the scenes at how this park feeds and cares for its animal residents. It also delivers this park's powerful message about global conservation. Don't miss the many interactive exhibits and live creatures.

Just outside is Affection Section, an animal petting zoo. Nearby there's a souvenir shop and a food wagon with a daily special. All in all, it's interesting and engaging. Don't miss the baby elephant hand-wash at the Affection Section.

Helpful Hint

Don't miss the "Song of the Rainforest" at Conservation Station.

OUTSTANDING, an interesting exhibit and a real must for children.

TIP: Save this one for when the more popular attractions are crowded or while you're waiting for your *FASTPASS* appointment.

Harambe School

You'll find this "attraction" in the open area in front of Kilimanjaro Safaris. "Class" times are posted and they involve discussions with some of the native Africans who work here at the park. This is particularly good for children.

Animal Face Painting

Kids just seem to love having their faces painted to look like a variety of creatures. Prices range from $6 to $15.

Shopping in Africa

Harambe's Mombasa Marketplace/Ziwani Traders has an assortment of "native African" Disney merchandise that makes it our favorite shop here at the Animal Kingdom. A variety of masks, carved creatures, and unusual jewelry make this place worth a visit. It's also the best place in the park for safari-themed apparel, commemorative Animal Kingdom collector's merchandise, and African decor.

Across the street is Duka La Filimu, Harambe's place for film and photo accessories. And at Conservation Station is Out of the Wild, which features conservation-themed apparel, soaps and lotions, and a small variety of gifts.

Asia

The ornate, red-brick Asia Bridge will magically transport you from Discovery Island to the rain forests of India. Along the road to the village of Anandapur, the jungle slowly reclaims the ruins of an ancient stone temple. The melodic rhythms of the East embrace you as you approach the village where you find small shops, rice paddies, and grazing banteng. Winding paths lead through fragrant gardens of jasmine and bamboo and past ancient fountains and pagodas, now inhabited by lazy gibbons snoozing amid the ruins.

This is about as captivating a landscape as the Disney Imagineers have ever created and you'll discover one adventure after another here in Disney's Asia. A bird show, a white-water raft adventure, a nature walk, shops, food and much more await you.

Team Disney has recently announced that a new adventure attraction is coming to the Animal Kingdom. At 200 feet tall, Expedition Everest will tower above Asia and will take guests on a trip aboard an old mountain railway destined for the foot of Everest. During the ride, guests will discover the fearsome legend of the yeti. This high-speed, coaster-like ride will open in 2005.

Flights of Wonder

- ℮ Live bird show

- ℮ Lasts 25 minutes

- ℮ Lines move to fill 700-seat Asia Warehouse Theater

This entertaining show provides some amusing encounters with a variety of winged creatures. At the same time, it also teaches about some of their more humorous habits. Owls, hawks, cranes, and nearly 20 other species of feathered performers are featured.

OUTSTANDING, a "bird-brained" show that's worth seeing.

TIPS: Check your times guide for show times and arrive a few minutes early to guarantee yourselves a seat.

Kali River Rapids FASTPASS

- ℮ A short white-water raft adventure. You *will* get wet; passengers must be at least 38 inches tall

- ℮ Lines are long but move quickly

- ℮ Lasts about 4 minutes

This riotous adventure focuses on the threat to the world's rain forests by loggers. Ten-person rafts zoom down the raging Chakranadi River, through foaming rapids, past ruined temples, and into a blazing forest. The raft ride is bumpy fun and the special effects are good. Knowing that at least one person on the raft gets soaked adds an interesting dimension to this attraction: Who will it be?

OUTSTANDING, great fun and not to be missed.

TIPS: To avoid getting wet, bring along your Mickey Mouse rain poncho and watch out for the elephants at the end of the ride! Avoid this ride in particularly cool weather.

Maharaja Jungle Trek

- ℮ ⅜-mile self-guided walking tour

- ℮ Set your own pace, plenty of nice benches.

This beautiful trek will take you into the dense jungles and the ancient ruins of the Maharaja's palace. Along the way, you'll encounter Bengal tigers, giant Komodo dragons, fruit bats (Gayle's favorite), and Malayan tapirs. Sit awhile in the aviary and watch the many exotic birds. Take the time to speak with this area's curators, who are very knowledgeable about the plants and animals found along the trek.

OUTSTANDING; a memorable zoo and garden experience, don't miss it.

TIP: Get here either early or late to experience the beauty without the distraction of crowds.

Shopping in Asia

Shopping here in Disney's Asia features some particularly nice Asian merchandise. Some of the Asia logo clothing is exceptionally good. Mandala Gifts is a great place to browse for interesting imports from the Far East and right across the avenue you'll find a hut that peddles oysters with pearls in them and a variety of pearl jewelry.

Dinoland U.S.A.

The gateway to this whimsical land is the Oldengate Bridge, a reconstruction of the bones of a 40-foot brachiosaurus. There's a lot of fun to be had here. Dinoland delivers a thrill ride, a rock 'n' roll stage show, a children's playground, and a comical band of "archaeologists" that add some wacky "dino-mosphere" to your visit. "Dino-dining" includes Restaurantosaurus, one of our favorites at Animal Kingdom.

The Boneyard

- Playground and exhibit, rubberized for safety

- Take as long as you like

- Lines rarely get long

If you're visiting with little ones, you'll want to drop in here for slides, nets, a maze of "dinosaur remains," and a terrific sandbox. It has all been created to keep your kids busy and also to teach them a thing or two about dinosaurs.

VERY GOOD PLAYGROUND.

Tarzan Rocks!

- 30-minute live musical stage show

- Line moves to fill 1,500-seat theater

This high-energy performance features the musical highlights of Disney's animated feature film Tarzan. It is something of a fusion of rock 'n' roll and the usual Disney entertainment. Outrageous costumes, in-line-skating stunts, and audience participation are all part of the show.

GOOD but loud. We prefer Festival of the Lion King.

TIP: Check Adventurer's Guide for show times.

Dinosaur FASTPASS

- A vehicular adventure (and a bit rough); riders must be at least 40 inches tall
- 10-minute pre-show, ride lasts 3½ minutes
- Expect long lines that move slowly; a perfect place to use the *FASTPASS*

This ride features the same type of cars used on the Indiana Jones ride at Disneyland. Hop aboard, and you'll time-trip back to the age of dinosaurs to bring back a live iguanodon before a gigantic asteroid crashes to earth. This ride is fun, exciting, loud, and frequently quite dark. If you like this sort of attraction, here's one not to miss.

WILD AND EXCITING, great special effects.

TIP: Too intense for very young children or people with motion sickness.

Triceratop Spin

- Spinning midway ride, four guests per "dino"
- Lasts about 2 minutes
- Lines might get long

This ride is just like the Dumbo ride, only with dinosaurs instead of elephants. Here the dinos spin around a giant toy top that opens to reveal a dinosaur.

OK, mostly for kids

Primeval Whirl FASTPASS

- Family roller coaster: riders must be 48 inches tall
- Lasts about 4 minutes
- Lines get long; you'll need *FASTPASS* here.

This roller coaster features spinning cars that make their way through wild curves and short drops. Really quite mild compared with "real" roller coasters, but loads of fun, nonetheless.

FUN, especially with kids.

Fossil Fun Games This midway features a variety of carnival games, each executed with a dinosaur theme. The games are fun, and if you are a winner, the prizes make good souvenirs. Games cost around $2.

Cretaceous Trail

- Walk through a garden area
- Takes a few minutes
- Expect no lines here

This short stroll passes through a garden of plants and creatures that are the surviving descendants of the age of dinosaurs. There are monkey puzzle trees, Norfolk Island pines, Chinese alligators, magnolias, and a variety of unusual palms and ferns. The trail features one of the world's largest collection of cycads.

INTERESTING, with some nice places to sit and listen to the birds and dinosaurs.

Shopping in Dinoland

For some great shopping, get to Chester & Hester's Dinosaur Treasures for its going-out-of-existence sale. Hats, bags, film, and disposable cameras. Don't miss the signs out front.

Camp Minnie-Mickey

Camp Minnie-Mickey is an inviting landscape of stone bridges, gurgling brooks, and split-rail fences. In fact, it seems more like the Adirondacks than darkest Africa. If you're visiting with children, you'll want to bring them here to meet Minnie, Mickey, Pluto, and Goofy. It's also teeming with Disney characters from *The Jungle Book* and *The Lion King*. It's one of the best places at Walt Disney World for character greetings (expect some long lines, too).

Although most of Camp Minnie-Mickey is dedicated to character encounters and photo opportunities, it does feature two live performances, one of which is outstanding. Whether you are here with children or without them, make sure you catch the Festival of the Lion King. We think it's one of Walt Disney World's best live shows.

TIP: This is the perfect opportunity to get some great photos of yourselves with the Disney characters, especially Minnie and Mickey who appear in safari gear. This may seem silly now, but you'll thank us later.

Festival of the Lion King

- ℮ Live, musical stage show
- ℮ Lasts 25 minutes
- ℮ Lines move to fill 1,000-seat theater

This terrific show features outstanding musical performances, giant floats, unforgettable costumes, singing, dancing, and show-stopping acrobatics. The large, circular theater literally comes alive with this, one of the all-time greatest of Disney stage productions.

OUTSTANDING, don't miss this great show.

TIPS: Check your guidemap for show times and get to an early one. Afternoon shows are hard to get into.

Animal Kingdom Best of the Best

Kilimanjaro Safari

It's Tough to Be a Bug!

Discovery Island Trails

Pangani Forest Exploration Trail

Maharaja Jungle Trek

Kali River Rapids

Festival of the Lion King

Dinosaur

The Romance of the Animal Kingdom

**Pangani Forest Exploration Trail and
Maharaja Jungle Trek ♥♥**

**A sunset stroll along the
Discovery Island Trails ♥♥**

**A late-afternoon treat at the
Tamu Tamu patio ♥♥**

A late-day ♥

**The African music at the Dawa Bar
(usually after 4 P.M.) ♥♥**

Pocahontas and Her Forest Friends

- ℮ Live musical show
- ℮ Lasts 12 minutes
- ℮ Line moves slowly to fill 350-seat theater

The shady Grandmother Willow's Grove is the setting for this entertaining drama that stars Pocahontas, Grandmother Willow, and a forest of wild creatures. Real turtles, rabbits, skunks, an armadillo, and a boa constrictor all have roles in this story of the search for "the great protector," the animal who alone can save the forest.

OK, but really for younger children. Miss this one if you have to.

TIPS: Shows are frequent. Check your Adventurer's Guide for show times.

The Disney Water Parks: Blizzard Beach and Typhoon Lagoon

There are two water parks at Walt Disney World, but only one important thing to know about them: They are really fanciful little theme parks. Each features a unique story line, and each has been carefully crafted with Disney's imaginative flair for details and humor. Of course there's more at these fun places than just cute stories. Both Typhoon Lagoon and Blizzard Beach feature over-the-top slides, wild raft rides, and thundering wave pools.

What You'll Need to Know About the Disney Water Parks

Admission to all water parks is included in the Ultimate Park Hopper and Park Hopper Plus Passes and also with the Premium Annual Pass. One-day admission to either Typhoon Lagoon or Blizzard Beach is about $33 ($27 for children).

Both parks suffer from the same problem: too many people. At peak times and especially weekends, you may find yourselves spending more time in line than having fun. Here are a few ways to avoid the crowds:

- Arrive early. Get there thirty minutes before the park opens, and use the first few hours for the slides and rafts. Save the lazy tubing, swimming, and surfing for later.

- Arrive late. During the summer months, the water parks stay open later. Arrive around 4 P.M., when the crowds are starting to thin out. In the summer, the very late afternoon is cooler, and the sun is kinder.

- Try a water park when the weather is "less than ideal." The water is heated to 80 degrees at each, and, in inclement weather, it may be brisk, but the park will be all but empty.

- Arrive right after an afternoon thundershower. The rain will have driven the crowds away.

Getting to the Disney Water Parks

From the Disney resorts, transportation to both water parks is by bus. If you're driving, both Typhoon Lagoon and Blizzard Beach have large parking areas near their entrances.

More Water Park Tips

- The hours of the water parks vary with the seasons. Check with guest services or the World Update for the operating hours. They may be closed due to inclement weather.

@ During the hot and busy summer months, both Blizzard Beach and Typhoon Lagoon can get so busy that they reach capacity after a few hours and close until later in the day, when guests begin to leave. Either get there before opening or go later in the day.

@ Towels are available as rentals ($1), so consider bringing ones from your resort room. Wear shoes or flip-flops. For women, one-piece bathing suits are best for the slides. There are changing rooms and showers, but, if you like, you can simply wear your suit or wear it under your clothing to avoid having to change. Clothes with rivets are not allowed.

@ Don't forget sunscreen. The Florida sun is dangerous, especially on an overcast day. Remember that a sunburn hurts, and you don't want to spend your romantic Disney vacation being too sore to be touched. We recommend that you wear light T-shirts to protect yourselves from the sun.

@ Leave jewelry and watches back in your room. This stuff tends to fall off. No personal swim gear is allowed, including masks, fins, rafts, and floats. Life vests and tubes are available at no cost.

@ As soon as the park opens, stake out some lounge chairs. Some spots are in the shade, and some are not. Take your pick and deposit a few of your things on enough chairs to provide each of you with one. If you don't, someone else will claim them.

@ Rental lockers are available at all of the water parks. If you have valuables with you, such as a camera or a purse, you can't leave them lying around. This may be Walt Disney World, but it is still planet Earth. Small lockers are $7; large are $9, plus a $2 deposit.

@ If someone in your party isn't up to the slides, there are always the tamer attractions and soaking up some of Florida's famous sunshine on a sand beach.

@ These places will make you thirsty. Both Blizzard Beach and Typhoon Lagoon offer a $10 thermal souvenir cup with free refills all day. It's a nice cup and a very sensible deal. Try sharing one cup.

Blizzard Beach

This park is Rick's favorite, but we both really love the slides here, and with nearly twenty of them, that's a lot to enjoy. We also love the park's goofy sight gags. From Alpine lodges to "melting icicles," this is one very fun place to be. Blizzard Beach tells a tall tale, and it does so with a real sense of humor.

Blizzard Beach, so the story goes, is the result of a freak winter storm that froze this part of Disney World. Work began immediately on a ski resort but before completion, temperatures returned to normal and hopes for a Disney ski complex melted away. About to call it quits, the resort operators realized that the melting snow and ice would make the perfect water park. So, what had once been ski slopes and bobsled runs were hastily converted into some of the wildest and wackiest water slides anywhere.

Insider's Secret

Blizzard Beach is usually closed for maintenance during January and February.

The Attractions of Blizzard Beach

Chair Lift   One-way transportation to top of Mt. Gushmore. Minimum height requirement 32 inches. Don't waste time in line here early in day. Use the stairs and save it for later.

Summit Plummet   A nearly vertical, 120-foot, 50-mile per hour water slide. The park's biggest thrill. Not for the meek (and that includes us!). Minimum height requirement is 48 inches.

Teamboat Springs   Six-person raft ride: long, wet, and loads of fun. Get your picture, which is taken on the way down.

The Slush Gusher   A fast and thrilling body slide. A good alternative to Summit Plummet. Minimum height requirement is 48 inches.

Runoff Rapids   Our favorite. Three wild inner tube runs; go single or double. (Get tubes at the bottom.)

Cross Country Creek   Take a long and lazy tube ride around the park. Lots to enjoy along the way. Don't miss it.

Melt Away Bay   Into body surfing? Try these waves, made by Disney.

Toboggan Racers   Eight-lane slide competition. (Pick up mats at the top.) Tame.

Snow Stormers   Switch-back "slalom" run. (Pick up mats at the top.) Mildly exciting.

Downhill Double Dipper   Side-by-side racing tubes. Minimum height requirement is 48 inches.

Tike's Peak   A compete kiddy water park with slides, pools, and fountains. Will keep kids busy for endless hours. For children 48 inches tall or shorter.

Ski Patrol Training Camp   An area designed especially for pre-teens. Features comical challenges and hours of fun.

Shopping at Blizzard Beach

Beach Haus provides one of the park's most outrageous sight gags and some surprisingly good shopping: unique bathing gear, sunglasses, sports apparel, and logo merchandise. Also available here is film, sunscreen, and footwear.

Food and Beverages at Blizzard Beach (All Counter Service, All Meals Less Than $10)

Lottawatta Lodge	Chicken wraps, burgers, pizza, salad
Avalunch	Hot dogs, pork sandwich, ice cream
The Warming Hut	Hot dogs, sandwiches, ice cream
The Cooling Hut	Soft drinks, sno-cones, ice cream
The Polar Pub	Adult beverages and spirits

Blizzard Beach Tips

- Blizzard Beach now features "Walk-Around Photos." Have your picture taken on the raft ride or somewhere else in the park, and pick it up later near the front gate. Cost is around $13, and it makes a very nice souvenir.

- If the park gets too crowded, go play miniature golf at Winter Summerland, just outside the turnstiles of Blizzard Beach (for more information, see page 354).

Typhoon Lagoon

The lush, tropical foliage of this park makes it Gayle's favorite. Every detail of this delightful place tells the fanciful tale of a storm-ravaged fishing village. With buildings leaning this way and that, and water everywhere, Typhoon Lagoon is a prank of a water park. But it's also a place of beauty, one that's dense with tropical palms and sweet with the exotic fragrances of flowering plants.

While you'll certainly enjoy the beauty and the amusing effects, there's definitely more to Typhoon Lagoon than a cute story and some nifty props. Its 42 acres are jam-packed with fun: body slides, raft rides, and a rumbling surf pool with five-foot waves. If you've come for thrills, you'll find them here.

Insider's Secret

Typhoon Lagoon is usually closed for maintenance sometime during November and December.

The Attractions of Typhoon Lagoon

Humunga Kowabunga   A triple-lane, 214-foot, high-speed water slide. Just the right amount of excitement. Minimum height requirement is 48 inches.

Storm Slides   Three 300-foot body slides. One of Typhoon's best.

Mayday, Gang Plank, Keelhaul Falls   Three whitewater raft rides. Do them all.

Castaway Creek   A laid-back, forty-five-minute tube "cruise." Great sight gags along the way. One of our favorites.

Ketchakiddie Creek   A complete little water park for youngsters ages 2 to 6. Must be under 48 inches tall.

Body Slides   Body slides for children. Must be under 5 feet tall.

Shark Reef   Snorkel this saltwater pool and check out the sea life. Gear provided. (Brrr, it's cold!)

Typhoon Lagoon Surf Pool   Great body surfing on manufactured surf. Wet fun for good swimmers.

Mt. Mayday Trail   This footpath leads to the top of Mt. Mayday and affords a nice view of the park.

Typhoon Lagoon's Learn-to-Surf Program   See page 348 for details about these special surfing classes, held in the morning, before the park opens.

Shopping at Typhoon Lagoon

Singapore Sal's is Typhoon's shop and it features an amusing selection of souvenirs, toys, logo merchandise, and beach apparel as well as such sundries as sunscreen and film.

Food and Beverages at Typhoon Lagoon: (All Counter Service, All Meals Less Than $10)

Typhoon Tilly's	Sandwiches, salads, ice cream
The Leaning Palms	Burgers, pizza, sandwiches, snacks, ice cream, beverages
Let's Go Slurpin'	Soft drinks, beer, wine coolers, snacks
Surf Doggies	Hot dogs, turkey legs
Lowtide Lou's	Snacks and sodas

DisneyQuest

It always amazes us how few people we talk to have been to Disney-Quest. This place is a lot of fun and one of our Disney World favorites. DisneyQuest is nothing less than a large, indoor theme park; one that combines the storytelling of Disney with the latest in interactive technologies. The result is a unique assortment of virtual challenges and adventures, all of which sport the trademark Disney penchant for perfection.

What we like best about DisneyQuest, though, is that unlike home computer and video games, which typically mean one person playing alone, much of the high-tech excitement of DisneyQuest is virtual rides and games that people play *together*. From our own experiences here, we know this makes for much more fun.

> **Helpful Hint**
>
> Try not to bring loads of stuff to DisneyQuest. It will get in the way. If you have to, there's a free "baggage" check-in area on the ground floor.

Day-long admission to DisneyQuest is $33 ($27 for kids ages 3 to 9). Admission is included in the Ultimate Park Hopper Pass and the Premium Annual Pass. There's also a DisneyQuest Annual Pass (see page 16).

Hours of operation are usually 10:30 A.M. to midnight, but vary on weekends, during slow periods, and during holidays.

TIP: Give yourselves at least half a day for DisneyQuest.

When to Go to DisneyQuest

This is important. When this place is crowded, it's not fun. You'll spend most of your time standing around waiting in lines. So, we strongly suggest that you take the following advice seriously.

- *Never* visit on a rainy day. Better to go to a theme park and get wet.

- Avoid weekends and holidays

- Be there when it opens and make good use of the first few hours

Getting to DisneyQuest

DisneyQuest is located at Downtown Disney's West Side, and buses run all day from the Disney resorts and from the Ticket and Transportation Center near the Magic Kingdom. If you're driving, parking during the day can be done easily in the West Side's large lot.

Finding Your Way Around DisneyQuest

DisneyQuest is made up of four different areas: Create Zone, Explore Zone, Score Zone, and Replay Zone. Each zone features its own unique interactive games and adventures. Also here in DisneyQuest's 100,000-square-foot home are two restaurants and a shop. Be sure to pick up a guidemap to help you find your way around.

Explore Zone

In this area, your favorite Disney stories become adventures you can participate in.

Pirates of the Caribbean: Battle for Buccaneer Gold (up to six people) Must be 35 inches tall for this attraction. You and your crew battle pirates aboard a surround screen, virtual, 3-D world, complete with cannons, unexpected obstacles, and real ship's movement. Your score determines the ending. This may be our Disney World favorite attraction. Don't miss it.

Insider's Secret

You don't have to steer the ship at DisneyQuest's Pirates of the Caribbean. Just man the guns and rack up points.

Virtual Jungle Cruise (up to four people) Paddle a real rubber raft along a virtual river of time (with real special effects), frantically avoiding volcanoes, earthquakes, and hungry dinosaurs. This adventure will be different every time you take it.

Aladdin's Magic Carpet Ride Put on a virtual reality helmet for a realistic simulation of flight. It's also a challenging game and one of DQ's best!

Treasure of the Incas Take the wheel of a remote-controlled, video-equipped Land Rover and search for lost treasure in a network of real caves. Confusing, slow, and not up to the other attractions here.

Create Zone

An "Imagineering" studio where powerful computers provide the means for making what you imagine come true. Except for Cyber Space Mountain, most of this area is for the younger set.

Radio Disney SongMaker Up to six guests can create their own song using the latest in sound technologies. Choose from more than twenty musical styles and create your own lyrics. Cut a CD, design the label, and have it ready for purchase in minutes. Make a happy birthday song for someone you know. CD costs $10. Making the song is free.

Cyber Space Mountain (two-person adventure, minimum height is 51 inches)   Computer-design your own roller coaster and then ride it in a 360-degree, roll-and-pitch simulator. An original attraction and a great ride by any standards.

Animation Academy   Learn the secrets of Disney animation in this thirty-minute hands-on computer class.

Sid's Create-a-Toy (for kids)   Design your own bizarre toy from a computer menu of strange parts and then take it home ($10).

Magic Mirror   Give yourselves a very unusual makeover on one of the computers at this attraction (you can buy a picture of it for $5).

Living Easels   Create a painting of color and movement using a computer. Mostly for kids. A print of your creation is $5.

Score Zone

This is DisneyQuest's "competition city": a place for games and doing battle with virtual foes.

Ride the Comix! (up to six players)   Go sword-to-sword with comic book super-villains in this virtual-reality-helmet adventure. Great fun.

Invasion! An ExtraTerrorestrial Alien Encounter (up to four participants on a 360-degree, high-action mission)   Rescue Earth colonists under attack while piloting a planetary walker. Who thinks of this great stuff?

Mighty Duck's Pinball Slam (many players)   A life-size pinball machine and you're the ball! Terrific fun and good exercise, too.

Replay Zone

Take a trip back in time to enjoy some classic games with a futuristic twist.

Buzz Lightyear's AstroBlaster (two players per car)   Must be 51 inches tall for this attraction. Bumper cars with an attitude and a "gunner." This is wild fun.

Underground Arcade and Daytona USA   A treasure trove of arcade games both old and new: cars, motorcycles, air hockey, shooting ranges, a great flight simulator, and much, much more. We could spend a whole day just in this area alone. Play on the games in these areas are included in DisneyQuest admission.

Midway on the Moon   Because the games in this small area provide prizes for winners, they cost money to play.

Food at DisneyQuest

We hear that food offerings at DisneyQuest are undergoing a change and that the Cheesecake Factory is on the way out. One suggested replacement is the ESPN Zone. Whatever happens, know that a variety of food will certainly be available here. Just what it's going to be, we can't say at this time.

Tips for DisneyQuest

- To avoid the crowds, get to DisneyQuest early. Many of the rides are fun, but they are even more fun the second or third time around, after you've learned the rules of the game and begin to get good at playing. This is especially true for the Score Zone games.

- Mondays, Tuesdays, and Wednesdays are generally DisneyQuest's slowest days.

- During inclement weather, DisneyQuest is at its busiest. Avoid DisneyQuest on rainy days, weekends, and holidays.

Money-Saving Tip

DisneyQuest is the perfect place to fill in a last morning at Disney and it will save you nearly $20 per person over theme park admission.

CHAPTER

5

Disney
After Dark

Disney after dark used to be pretty sleepy. At most, we could have dinner out, catch IllumiNations, or maybe the Magic Kingdom would be open late. There just wasn't a lot to do after the sun went down. We're happy to tell you that nightlife has come to Walt Disney World and in a big, big way. There's now so much happening at Disney after the sun goes down that your problem will more likely be one of fitting it all in rather than finding something to do.

The epicenter of Walt Disney World's galaxy of evening entertainment is Downtown Disney. You could fill up a week of nights taking in its clubs, restaurants, and shops. But we wouldn't want you to miss the BoardWalk, either. It's one of our favorite evening Disney destinations. There's even more than this, and we'll give you the complete picture of Disney nights in this chapter.

The Theme Parks After Dark

If you're visiting during the holidays, peak season, or during the busy summer season, you'll find the theme parks open later and running at full throttle. The Magic Kingdom may be open as late as midnight, Epcot and Disney-MGM until 10 P.M., and even the Animal Kingdom might be operating beyond the twilight hours. There will be nighttime parades and fireworks shows and occasional special events and parties, such as Mickey's Very Merry Christmas Party and a Fourth of July celebration.

Magic Kingdom E-Ride Nights

Available only to Disney resort guests with multi-day passes (includes any Hopper Pass, Annual Pass, or Florida Resident Seasonal Pass), this will get you into the Magic Kingdom after the park closes to the public. You'll experience nine of the park's biggest attractions: Space, Splash, and Thunder Mountains, Pirates of the Caribbean, Alien Encounter, AstroOrbiter, Country Bear Jamboree, Haunted Mansion, and Buzz Lightyear's Space Ranger Spin. Participating attractions may vary.

Insider's Secret

E-Ride Nights gets you into the Magic Kingdom after closing to take on its nine best attractions with super-short lines.

E-Ride Nights tickets are available on select nights during the busy seasons (not at Christmas time) and can be purchased at guest services at any Disney resort for about $13 per person. It's a great deal and a great night of fun. Tickets are limited and lines are super short. So, rest up during the day and take advantage of this terrific opportunity.

Fireworks and Other After-Dark Spectaculars

These wonderful nighttime events occur on various days and at different times throughout the year. We suggest that you check all theme park guidemaps and the World Update early in your visit to find out if they are scheduled during your visit.

- **IllumiNations: Reflections of Earth** This spectacular event lights up the skies of Epcot every night year-round. This laser and fireworks show is set perfectly to music and is a Disney event you simply must experience. There are numerous spots along the lagoon from which to watch the show, and we suggest that you arrive early to get yours. Our favorite vantage points include the bridge between the United Kingdom and France, and the bridge near Mexico. Do your best to avoid being downwind of the show, unless you like smoke.

- **Fantasy in the Sky** ♥♥ Another fireworks show set to music. It takes place just before closing at the Magic Kingdom. The most symmetrical view of the show is from Main Street, but you can avoid the crowds at Mickey's Toontown, where at the end of the show, you can hop aboard a train to ride to the Main Street Depot for an easy exit. An especially romantic viewing place is on one of the swings along the beach at the Polynesian Resort. ♥♥♥

@ **SpectroMagic Light Parade ♥♥♥**   This nighttime parade features hundreds of thousands of lights, fiber-optic illuminations, floats, and music. It's a beautiful and memorable event you should not miss. After this, parades will never be the same. It's worth mentioning that we've heard a rumor that the Main Street Electric Parade is returning to the Magic Kingdom after its run in Disneyland Paris. This is another fine nighttime parade and, if it returns, will likely replace SpectroMagic.

@ **Fantasmic!**   This spectacular evening show comes alive in a specially designed stadium-theater at Disney-MGM Studios. It features live action, music, special effects, fireworks, and animated films projected on walls of water. There is one show per evening; two during busier times of the year. Plan to see it. See page 248 for the Fantasmic! Dinner package.

@ **The Electric Water Pageant on the Seven Seas Lagoon ♥♥**   This floating musical parade features a continuously changing array of lights on barges towed around the lagoon. It happens around 9 P.M. each evening, depending on your location. We like this a lot, not because it is exciting but because of the viewing possibilities. A lagoon-view room at any of the resorts on the lake, including the Wilderness Lodge, will provide a memorable experience. Here are a few of our other favorite locations: from the beaches at the Grand Floridian, the Polynesian, or Fort Wilderness; from the beaches behind either garden wing at the Contemporary; from Sunset Point at the Poly; and from almost anywhere along the Walk Around the World path on the lagoon.

@ **Fireworks Cruises ♥♥♥**   You can rent a variety of boats (driver included) to view either Epcot's IllumiNations or Fantasy in the Sky fireworks at the Magic Kingdom. Order refreshments if you wish, and be prepared for a memorable experience. We think a fireworks cruise for IllumiNations is the best. See page 356 for details.

Downtown Disney

Once upon a time, there was the Disney Village Marketplace. Then Disney added the clubs and restaurants of Pleasure Island. Next came the fabulous West Side, and the whole area became known as "Downtown Disney." This remarkable place brings a whole new level of entertainment and excitement to Walt Disney World. Its 120 acres feature unique shopping, movie going, and some of the biggest names in dining

Downtown Disney

PARKING

BUS STOP

VALET PARKING

CIRQUE DU SOLEIL

DISNEYQUEST

VIRGIN RECORDS

WEST SIDE

AMC 24

HOUSE OF BLUES

WOLFGANG PUCK

BONGOS

WETZEL'S PRETZELS

PLANET HOLLYWOOD

PARKING

LAKE BUENA VISTA

SHUTTLE BOAT

ADVENTURER'S CLUB

ROCK 'N ROLL BEACHCLUB

BET SOUNDSTAGE

WEST SIDE STAGE

PLEASURE ISLAND

8TRAX

COMEDY WAREHOUSE

MANNEQUINS

RAINFOREST CAFE

CAP'N JACK'S

MARINA

FULTON'S CRABHOUSE

JAZZ COMPANY

BUS STOP

WOLFGANG PUCK EXPRESS

MARKETPLACE

GHIRADELLI

WORLD OF DISNEY

VALET PARKING

PARKING

BUS STOP

PARKING

PARKING

and entertainment: Planet Hollywood, House of Blues, Wolfgang Puck, and the mesmerizing Cirque du Soleil, to mention only a few.

Downtown Disney is made up of three distinctly different lakeside areas. The Marketplace is the Downtown's shopping mecca and it features unique shops as well as interesting places for food and snacks. Pleasure Island is Downtown Disney's place for nightclubs and late-nightlife. It doesn't begin to hit its stride until after 10 P.M. Be forewarned that after 7 P.M., Pleasure Island charges admission (see page 15 for details).

The West Side is Downtown Disney's powerhouse of entertainment and dining. There's no charge to enter, and you'll find great food, great entertainment, and unique shopping. We highly recommend at least one visit here during your Disney vacation.

Getting to Downtown Disney

Transportation to Downtown Disney from the Disney resorts is easy. Buses run all day long and into the wee hours (most of the clubs stay open until 2 A.M.). There are three bus stops in the Downtown area, one at each of the three areas. Resort buses stop first at the Marketplace, then at Pleasure Island, and last at the West Side.

If you're staying at one of the hotels on nearby Hotel Plaza, you'll be just a stroll away, or after 6 P.M., you can use this area's bus service. If you're driving, there are large parking lots in all three Downtown areas, but as the evening wears on, finding a parking space becomes a challenge. There's also valet parking from 5:30 P.M. to 2:00 A.M. at both Pleasure Island and the West Side. Cost is $6 plus gratuity.

Helpful Hint
You can also visit Downtown Disney during the day. See a movie, browse the shops, and enjoy a meal. Marketplace shops open at 9:30 A.M. and those on the West Side, at 10:30 A.M.. Most restaurants are not crowded at lunchtime.

If you're staying at Old Key West or Port Orleans, there are shuttle boats that make the trip along the beautiful canals of Lake Buena Vista, from 10:30 A.M. to 11:30 P.M. (9:40 P.M. for Old Key West). They're convenient and the voyage is pleasant, especially around sunset.

Finding Your Way Around Downtown Disney

All three Downtown areas are connected by walkways and bridges. There's even a water taxi that runs from Cap'n Jack's at the Marketplace to the House of Blues on the West Side (and back) from 6:30 P.M. to 12:30 A.M. It's a pleasant trip, but then again, so is the walk.

If you don't feel like hoofing it, you can bus (in one direction only) along the bus stops of Downtown Disney. To return to your resort, simply hop aboard your resort bus at any of the three stops.

Downtown Disney Tips

@ Don't forget to pick up a Downtown Disney guidemap at your resort and look it over before you go. It will tell you where everything is and what's happening there during your visit. (Guidemaps are also available at Downtown Disney.)

@ The restaurants of Downtown Disney usually get very crowded in the evening hours. We strongly urge you to make priority seating arrangements ahead of time. See page 302 for more information about how to do this.

@ If you're going to be consuming alcohol, use a designated driver: Take the bus.

The Downtown Disney Marketplace

Whether you're looking for souvenirs or gifts, or you just enjoy browsing, you'll want to visit this colorful lakeside village of shops and restaurants. Besides the world's largest Disney Store, you'll find nearly two dozen other interesting shopping opportunities and a smart selection of places to enjoy a meal or simply savor something sweet.

Money-Saving Tip

Save money on select merchandise at The World of Disney with the themepark annual pass.

Shopping at the Marketplace

With so many neat stores here, you're bound to find something you'll want. Here are some of our favorite Marketplace shops:

@ **The World of Disney** No trip to Walt Disney World is complete without a visit to the largest Disney store on the planet. From sleepwear to kitchen accessories, you'll find items here you never knew existed.

@ **NEW Basin**   This recent addition to the Marketplace features a variety of soaps, bath gels, shampoos, and bath salts. There's even an interactive area where you can try some of them out.

@ **NEW Disney's Wonderful World of Memories**   This new store offers a collection of Disney books, albums, scrapbook supplies, stationery, pens, postcards, and much more.

@ **The Art of Disney**   Loaded with limited-edition animation art and Disney collectibles. It's a great place to browse.

@ **Disney at Home**   This shop features a collection of unique character items for bedroom and bath. Some of this is real "hidden Mickey" kind of stuff and quite nice too. One of our favorites.

@ **Team Mickey's Athletic Club**   This is the place for a cap, a golf shirt, or any other Disney character sports apparel or accessories. Drop in to see this store's little character stadium.

@ **Gourmet Pantry**   This shop has an interesting offering of Disney character culinary gadgets and housewares. It's also a good place to pick up basic grocery items such as milk, cereal, and bread or even a picnic lunch. The real treasure here, though, is its bakery and deli, which is a very nice place for a snack, lunch, or a light dinner.

@ **Disney's Days of Christmas**   This wonderful shop features year-round Christmas ornaments and decorations. This is not just character stuff; you'll also find some extraordinary, non-Disney Christmas treasures here as well.

Food and Snacks at Downtown Disney Marketplace

This place has interesting food, unique snacks, and what we think is the world's greatest ice cream cone. All around the Marketplace are a variety of vendor carts offering beverages and snacks. For our reviews of the Rainforest Cafe, Fulton's Crab House, Cap'n Jack's, and Wolfgang Puck Express, see chapter 6.

@ **Wolfgang Puck Express**   For our tastes, this is the best fast food at Disney (or anywhere else for that matter), although admittedly more expensive than a burger or hot dog. The pizzas and salads are memorable. The Express is open from 11 A.M. to 11 P.M.

@ **Rainforest Cafe**   This is a wild place to eat and offers a large menu of exciting dishes. The only downside is that it gets extremely busy and doesn't take reservations. Try an early or a mid-afternoon lunch. The cafe is open from 10:30 A.M. to 11 P.M.

@ **Fulton's Crab House** This pricey seafood restaurant is located on a "replica" of a Mississippi riverboat. It has a huge menu and serves both lunch and dinner. Our experiences here have been good.

@ **Gourmet Pantry** The deli and bakery here offers a tasty selection of sandwiches, salads, and baked goods. There's even a pleasant outdoor patio with tables and chairs. It's a great place for a quality lunch, and the prices seem reasonable for the quality delivered.

@ **Cap'n Jack's Restaurant** This pleasant little restaurant is right on the water and features a nautical ambience and modest menu. Cap'n Jack's is open from 11:30 A.M. to 10:30 P.M.

@ **Cap'n Jack's Margarita Bar** Nice outdoor, on-the-water bar.

@ **Ghirardelli Soda Fountain and Chocolate Shop** We admit it. It's impossible for us to walk by without wanting a wonderful ice cream creation. Our excuse for working our way through the menu here is "research." Let yours be "vacation." The chocolate-covered, rolled-in-almonds ice cream cone is a sublime experience—easily the best ice cream cone we've ever had. Ask for it. It's no longer on the menu.

@ **McDonald's: Ronald's Fun House** This is a showcase McDonald's, designed especially for Disney. It's like being inside a great big Happy Meal! The cuisine here is the usual McDonald's fare, and it's open from 8:30 A.M. to 3:00 A.M. This McDonald's also includes a retail area with brand apparel and gifts.

Marketplace Entertainment

It's certainly not a theme park, but there's fun to be had here, from speedboats to live entertainment.

@ **Studio M** Did you miss getting a photo of yourselves with Mickey? Here's your second chance with a $30 portfolio of prints. Or maybe you want another character? They're all here along with robot-decorated apparel (that you'll have to see for yourselves!).

@ **The Dock Stage** Check the board here or the Marketplace guest services to see what performances and special events are happening here. During the holidays, this stage features a Christmas pageant.

@ **Cap'n Jack's Marina** Looking for excitement and adventure? Rent a boat. Also offered is a variety of fishing excursions. For more information, see page 359 or call (407) WDW-PLAY (939-0754).

@ **Children's Playground**   Got the kids along? They'll love the Marketplace's giant sandbox, playground, and carousel. The Marketplace also features several amusing fountains and playing in them seems especially attractive for kids. You might want to have yours wear their bathing suits for your Marketplace excursion.

Pleasure Island

The motto of this island of nightclubs is "Carpe P.M." and it fits. If you're looking to "seize the night," this place is filled with bright lights, live bands, music in the street, and rowdy fun. Some people make Pleasure Island a nightly part of their Disney holiday.

All the clubs of Pleasure Island feature full-service bars. "P.I." also serves up a colorful mix of restaurants, shops, a zany carnival midway, street entertainment, and a nightly "New Year's Eve" fireworks celebration. Pleasure Island is nothing less than a small theme park where the theme is adult, nighttime entertainment.

Admission is $22 (including tax) for a single night's admission (for an additional $5, you can add another five nights). Pleasure Island admission is included in both Park Hopper Plus and Ultimate Park Hopper passes as well as the Premium Annual Pass. There is also a Pleasure Island Annual Pass (see page 15 for more information). Pleasure Island is open nightly from 7 P.M. to 2 A.M. Visitors must be at least 18 years of age or be accompanied by an adult.

A word of warning: This place is loud, and we mean LOUD. There is music everywhere, in the clubs and in the streets, and most of it is at volumes we feel are a bit over-the-top.

Several Pleasure Island clubs offer entertainment that will not assault your ears, and we'll note those as ear friendly with ♪♪. If Pleasure Island doesn't sound like your cup of tea, we're sure you'll find lots to do in the other (free) areas of Downtown Disney.

Motion

This high-energy dance club features DJs and top-40 tunes from the past few decades. It has a large dance floor, several bars, and special-effects lighting. Like most of the clubs here at Pleasure Island, this one is quite loud.

Rock 'n' Roll Beach Club

Before we discovered swing, we used to come here to dance. The lights, special effects, and the melodies reflect hit music from the 1960s to the present. Once it gets cranked up, the dance floor fills up. The bands here always seem good, both instrumentally and vocally.

♫ *Pleasure Island Jazz Company*

The tables at this small club are arranged around a stage that features good jazz. Even though it's a bit on the loud side, this is one of our favorite Pleasure Island destinations. Check your Downtown Disney guidemap for show times.

♫ *The Adventurer's Club*

This place doesn't even remotely resemble the other clubs of Pleasure Island. It seems like a stuffy, British gentleman's club of the 1930s, and its variety of rooms are packed to the ceilings with sight gags and strange collectibles. For entertainment, a zany troupe of actors performs and interacts with guests throughout the evening. This place is definitely fun, and it's the only club at Pleasure Island where you can actually meet people and enjoy conversation.

♫ *The Comedy Warehouse*

This is Pleasure Island's most popular club and features improvisational comedy. Of course, the humor is clean and harmless (vulgarities are not part of this or any other Disney show). Occasionally, a well-known comic may appear, in which case an additional admission may be charged. There are five or six shows nightly and long lines are usual. Check your Downtown Disney guidemap for show times.

Helpful Hint

Where's *FASTPASS* when you need it? Try the first show of the night at the Comedy Warehouse for the shortest wait.

BET SoundStage Club

This stylish club features a large dance floor and state-of-the-art multimedia display. The club showcases the best of rhythm and blues and hip-hop with an interactive deejay. Patrons of BET must be at least 21 years of age.

Mannequins Dance Palace

The main dance floor is a large turntable, and the decorative mannequins are all garbed in strange attire. All this and the contemporary music make this the place for the younger crowd. Mannequins requires patrons to be 21 years of age or older.

8 Trax

The DJ here plays the music of the 1970s and 1980s. We're not sure what we were listening to back then, but it wasn't this stuff. Still, the sound system is impressive, and the ambience, multilevel dance floor, and special effects are futuristic. This may be your idea of nostalgic tunes.

Pleasure Island's West End Stage: Bring in the New Year

Every night at 11:45, the countdown begins for Pleasure Island's "New Year's Eve" celebration. It features the multimedia Explosion Dancers, fireworks and special effects, loud music, and confetti cannons. It all centers around the West End Stage, where live bands perform all evening long. It's a lot of fun.

Eating at Pleasure Island

There are three restaurants here at Pleasure Island: the northern Italian cuisine of Portobello Yacht Club, Fulton's Crab House, and Planet Hollywood. Our experiences at Planet Hollywood have been spotty at best. It's entertaining, but we'd have to tell you not to go expecting good food. We will however, recommend a meal at either Portobello or Fulton's. For our reviews, see chapter 6.

If you're looking for a quick bite or a fairly good sandwich, try the Missing Link Sausage Company or the variety of snack and beverage vendors around the island. You'll find pizza, gyros, and lots more. For sweets, there's D-Zertz, with ice creams, frozen yogurt, and specialty coffees.

The Shops of Pleasure Island

The small variety of Pleasure Island shops feature some unusual stuff. Our favorite is Suspended Animation with its collection of Disney animation cels, limited-edition lithographs, and Disney collectibles. There are also several interesting clothing stores, Changing Attitudes and Mouse House. DTV features Disney merchandise, and Reel Finds, music and film memorabilia. Another amusing stop is SuperStar Studios, where you can get your picture on the "cover" of a magazine. If only fame were this easy! It's a great souvenir.

Downtown Disney's West Side

For us, the West Side is Disney's premier evening destination. From dining and shopping to live entertainment, there's so much here to satisfy your curiosity that you might wish to visit more than once. To get your bearings, see our map of Downtown Disney on page 283.

AMC Pleasure Island 24 Theaters

This cinema complex is state-of-the-art in every way, and with twenty-four screens, there's bound to be something that interests you. Sixteen of the theaters have plush, stadium-style seating and "love seats" with high backs and arm rests that lift up. Another eight auditoriums feature extra-wide theater rockers, and two have balconies. Every theater at the AMC has digital sound, and just about every recent release is here. For information and ticket reservation, call (407) 298-4488.

Cirque du Soleil: La Nouba ♥♥♥

Not quite a circus and not really a ballet, this mesmerizing performance is a little of both and a lot of acrobatics, original music, and special effects. We've heard it described as an "avant-garde circus," but after seeing it, we now know how impossible it is to describe. We can only say that we've now seen it twice (with goose bumps both times) and feel haunted by its beauty. It is an electrifying tour de force of imagination and creativity, and something we encourage you strongly to see.

Twice nightly, Tuesday through Saturday, the seventy-two-member Cirque troupe takes to the custom-designed, $50 million stage to perform its magical ninety-minute show, which features unique costumes, incredible music (through 1,500 speakers), and breathtaking performances. Shows are at 6 P.M. and 9 P.M. and tickets begin at $76.68 for adults and $46.86 for ages 3 to 9 (prices include tax). Category one seating is $87.33/52.19. We'll admit this seemed expensive before we saw the show. Afterward, it seemed worth it. For tickets and information, call (407) 939-7600.

Also located in this unique theater is the Cirque du Soleil Boutique, which features clothing based on the exciting costumes of the performers and a variety of unique gifts.

Virgin Megastore

We strolled in here one afternoon and after several hours, had to force ourselves to move on. This huge store features three hundred CD listening stations and the best collection of music we've ever seen. There are also twenty video/DVD viewing-stations for previewing movies. The Megastore sells books and software and occasionally even features big-name stars on a hydraulic stage over the store's main entrance. This is a record (and video) store like no other.

There's also a delightful espresso bar that features the coffee of Seattle's Torrefazione Italia and a selection of extravagant desserts and pastries.

House of Blues

Amid all the glitz and glitter of Downtown Disney, a rusty old water tank towers over the ramshackle buildings of the House of Blues. But inside, this place resembles a museum of African American folk art. Everything here is decorated, and we mean everything. Not just another theme restaurant, this eatery serves up both a mouthwatering Mississippi Delta cuisine and, on its small stage, soulful blues. There's even a store here that sells blues CDs and a line of House of Blues logo clothing and merchandise. (For our review of the House of Blues restaurant, see page 327.)

One of our favorite places at Downtown Disney is here at the House of Blues: the Voodoo Garden ♥♥♥. This lovely area is behind the restaurant and overlooks the lake. At night, it's quiet, romantic, and a little slice of the "Big Easy." In good weather, the Voodoo Garden features both a porch where you can order food and a comfortable garden area for drinks and appetizers.

The House of Blues Concert Hall

Right next door to the restaurant is the House of Blues Concert Hall. There's a concert here every night and occasionally, you might even find a performer of star magnitude. Swing, soul, rock, and rhythm and blues: You never know what you'll get here. To avoid arriving at Disney only to discover that a concert you'd like to attend is sold out, we suggest that you call the House of Blues ticket box office a month before your visit to find out who's playing during your visit. You can then purchase tickets over the phone: (407) 934-BLUE (2583).

The House of Blues Gospel Brunch

Every Sunday, there's a down-home brunch buffet featuring omelets, boiled shrimp, grits, roast beef, ham, and a large variety of other dishes. It's all tasty homestyle cookin'. Afterward, roll up your sleeves for an hour of live gospel music. It's great fun and maybe even a cultural experience. If you are interested (and we highly recommend it), call the box office at least a week in advance to book your tickets. There are two brunches each Sunday, at 10:30 A.M. and 1:00 P.M. Cost is $30 per adult and $15 for children ages 4 to 12 (prices include tax). Kids ages 3 and under are free.

Bongos Cuban Cafe

Owned by superstar Gloria Estefan, this dazzling nightclub brings to Disney the excitement of Miami's South Beach and the sizzle and spice of cuisine Cubano. The three-story Bongos pineapple has become the symbol for the excitement of the entire West Side. Inside, you will find a tropical decor that brings to mind the era of splashy nightspots, when the tango and cha cha reigned supreme. Featured here on Fridays and Saturdays are the hot Latin rhythms of Caliente and on Sundays, a DJ. This is a fun place to spend the evening eating, dancing, and romancing. For our review of the food at Bongos, see page 317.

Wolfgang Puck Cafe

This stylish place is really four restaurants in one, and we love them all. On the avenue is the sidewalk seating of the Wolfgang Puck Express. Drop in to enjoy a quick bite of pizza, rotisserie chicken, a salad, or pasta. Inside, enjoy B's Bar (and some exceptional sushi) or the downstairs cafe with its offerings of pizzas, salads, and pasta entrées. In the evening, take the trip upstairs to the elegant dining room for the California cuisine that has made Wolfgang Puck one of the world's most renowned chefs. This is Downtown Disney's best food and any of these "restaurants" is worth the trip. We've never been disappointed with anything we've eaten here. For our reviews and more information about the Wolfgang Puck restaurants, see page 342.

Planet Hollywood

This well-known restaurant is really something to look at, both inside and out. Inside you'll find some of the world's most valuable movie and television memorabilia. The interesting menu features unusual pastas, pizzas, a variety of vegetarian offerings, and Arnold Schwarzenegger's mother's apple strudel.

TIP: This place gets especially busy. Arrive early for lunch or dinner.

Wetzels Pretzels

We guess pretzels must be pretty popular, because here's a store that specializes in them. Fresh every thirty minutes, the sixty-three pretzel varieties includes cheese, cinnamon, and the popular butter and salt pretzel. Also on the Wetzel menu are pretzel-wrapped hotdogs, fresh-squeezed lemonade, and frozen granitas.

Hoypoloi

If you are looking for a one-of-a-kind gift, this shop has some very neat stuff. Most of Hoypoloi's merchandise has been created by artisans from around the United States, and the rest includes unique furniture, light sculptures, and decorative accessories.

Downtown Disney Best of the Best

Cirque du Soleil's La Nouba

DisneyQuest: Pirates of the Caribbean

Most interesting shop: Hoypoloi

Best club on Pleasure Island: P. I. Jazz Club

Best oddball entertainment: Adventurer's Club

Best ice cream cone: Ghirardelli

Best fast food: Wolfgang Puck Express

Best moderately priced meal: Wolfgang Puck Cafe

Best fine dining: Wolfgang Puck Cafe Dining Room

Starabilias

Here's a place not to miss. Starabilias features more than a thousand pieces of original memorabilia from film and music. Browsing among the autographed photos and real Hollywood costumes is fun, but what we like best is the large collection of restored coin-operated machines and antique furnishings. There's much more, and all of it is ridiculously expensive but great to look at. Starabilias also features a more affordable line of nostalgic gift and novelty items.

Magnetron

Luckily, we have a stainless steel refrigerator, or Rick would spend a fortune here. This is heaven for refrigerator magnet lovers and its 20,000 magnets sing, dance, light up, and glow in the dark. Rick's favorite is the fried-chicken magnet.

The Guitar Gallery

This shop is almost a museum for famous guitars. But there's stuff to buy here too, including guitar accessories, books, videos, musically themed clothing, and of course, guitars. Prices range from $199 to $25,000.

Mickey's Groove

Just when we thought we'd seen every conceivable bit of Mickey Mouse merchandise along comes this shop, full of what else but "groovy"

Mickey stuff. Trendy nail polish, brightly colored wigs, and lots of perfect gifts for Generation Xers.

Other Shops of the West Side

There are other shops here, and you might find some of them suit your interests. **NEW** Another new addition to Downtown's West Side is Magic Masters, a magic shop for beginner and expert alike. The Planet Hollywood Store peddles the merchandise of its mother company, while the Candy Cauldron features a show kitchen, more than two hundred delectable sweets, and a dungeon-like atmosphere. Sosa Family Cigars sells an assortment of premium cigars and humidors, all in a re-creation of the founder's living room. (We're not making this stuff up!) Looking for the latest designer sunglasses? Check out Celebrity Eyeworks Studio. It's a shades superstore.

Disney's BoardWalk Promenade

More than just a resort, Disney's BoardWalk is also a 1930s "seaside" promenade of nighttime entertainment: shops, restaurants, clubs, amusements, dancing, and sidewalk performers. It's one of Disney's after-dark hot spots, and we suggest you not miss it.

Getting to the BoardWalk

If you are staying in one of the Epcot deluxe resorts, you'll be just a pleasant stroll away. If you are staying in one of the other Disney resorts, getting here will involve a trip to Downtown Disney and then hopping a bus to the BoardWalk. If you are driving in, know that there is a large self-parking lot at the BoardWalk, and valet parking is also available after 6 P.M. for $6 (plus gratuity).

The BoardWalk is also a short walk from the World Showcase at Epcot. Simply exit through the International Gateway (between Great Britain and France) and take a left across the bridge. You can't miss it. There's no admission to the BoardWalk.

Dining and Shopping Along the Promenade

Food is definitely one of the BoardWalk's strong suits. Begin your evening here with priority seating arrangements in one of the Board-Walk's restaurants: The Flying Fish Cafe ♥♥, the Mediterranean cuisine of Spoodles, the ESPN Club, or the Big River Grille & Brewing

Works. All are good choices. For details about these restaurants, see chapter 6. There's also a window and sidewalk tables for pizza from Spoodles and sidewalk carts peddling a variety of foods, from hot dogs to chicken fingers.

After dinner, stroll the BoardWalk Promenade and nosh a dessert at BoardWalk Bakery, a pastry and coffee at the coffee cart, or enjoy an ice cream at Seashore Sweets.

Browsing is good along the Promenade, particularly the beautiful works of internationally renowned artists in the Wyland Gallery. For more ordinary Disney merchandise, visit Thimbles and Threads for the latest Disney designer fashions or venture into ESPN Club for unique sports apparel.

BoardWalk Entertainment

The BoardWalk is definitely a place for entertainment, and there's enough here to keep you busy into the wee hours: fortune tellers, portrait artists, jugglers, face painters, a small arcade of carnival games, and the BoardWalk Buskers, a couple of off-beat, juggler-musicians who joke around and perform.

One of our favorite things at Disney is to rent a surrey quadri-cycle. Riding around the lake on one of these four-wheeled bicycle/carriages is a lot of fun. These carriages can accommodate up to six persons.

Also along the BoardWalk are several good nightspots.

☺ **Atlantic Dance** ♥♥♥　This stylish dance club features live bands on weekends and DJs on other nights. The focus here is on hit music from the 1980s and 1990s. Atlantic Dance features a full-service bar with specialty drinks and a small assortment of finger foods. It is open Tuesday through Saturday from 9 P.M. to 2 A.M. nightly for those 21 and older.

☺ **Jellyroll's**　This neighborhood-style bar showcases the music and antics of its dueling pianists, who match wits each evening from 7 P.M. to 2 A.M. There's singing, playing, and lots of rowdy fun. Jelly's has a full bar, and we suggest that you give this place a try. It might surprise you.

☺ **ESPN Club**　Besides good food and a bar, this club is heaven for sports lovers. There are more than seventy video monitors, with satellite feeds covering sporting events worldwide. Select what interests you with your own controls. There are scoreboards, live interviews, Internet terminals, state-of-the-art video games, and more than you can think of when it comes to sports input. There's also a theater-size video array featuring special sporting events. It is the place to go for the big game or championship boxing match (cover charges apply for some events).

@ **Big River Grille & Brewing Works**   In addition to its pub menu, Big River makes its own beers and ales. Drop in for a sampler of the day's brewing. The atmosphere is interesting, the brews and food are good, and the tables outside on the promenade are particularly pleasant ♥♥ when the weather is good.

@ **The BelleVue Room**   Located in the BoardWalk Inn, this quiet lounge ♥♥ features a full-service bar with variety flights of single-malt scotch, small-batch bourbons, and Grand Marniers. Its decor will take you back to the 1920s and 1930s; vintage radios play old-time shows. It even has a beautiful outside balcony overlooking the BoardWalk Green.

Resort Hopping

If you've never seen the Disney resorts, let us suggest a tour of these magical creations. Don't miss the award-winning lobby of the Wilderness Lodge and those at both the Grand Floridian and the Animal Kingdom Lodge. Other charming resorts include the Polynesian, Port Orleans, and Coronado Springs. To "resort hop," simply go to Downtown Disney and hop aboard a bus going to the resort you'd like to visit.

While you're making the rounds at the Disney resorts, you might want to discover their interesting themed lounges. They are quiet and romantic places, and most offer interesting selections of appetizers and hors d'oeuvres. Try skipping dinner and going lounge hopping in search of tasty treats. Some of our favorite spots are the Crew's Cup at the Yacht Club, the Territory Lounge at the Wilderness Lodge, Kimonos at the Swan, Victoria Falls at the Animal Kingdom Lodge, and the California Grill Lounge at the Contemporary. There are others, and we'll leave them for you to discover.

Resort hopping is especially fun during the weeks between Thanksgiving and Christmas, when the lobbies of the resorts are decked out in all their Christmas finery. Arrive at the right moment and you might discover Christmas carolers, storytellers, a chorus of bell ringers, or a tree-lighting ceremony. Check with your resort's guest services for a schedule of events.

The Romance of Disney Nights

- The Chef's Table at Wolfgang Puck Cafe (upstairs dining room) ♥♥

- A private carriage ride at Port Orleans Riverside ♥♥

- Watching the Magic Kingdom fireworks or the Electric Water Pageant from one of the swings on the beach at the Grand Floridian or the Polynesian ♥♥♥♥

- Dining at Portobello Yacht Club, followed by an evening out at Downtown Disney ♥♥

- Pleasure Island fireworks from Wolfgang's dining room or Bongos' upstairs patio ♥♥

- "Resort hopping" at Christmastime to see the decorations and tree-lighting ceremonies ♥♥

- Watching IllumiNations from the second-floor outside balcony of Atlantic Dance ♥♥

- The Voodoo Garden at House of Blues (in good weather only) ♥♥♥

- A flight of Grand Marnier at BoardWalk's BelleVue Room ♥♥♥

- A fireworks cruise ♥♥♥

- Musical entertainment any evening at the Grand Floridian Resort ♥

- The Luau at the Polynesian Resort ♥

- A moonlight stroll along the Seven Seas Lagoon (time it to pass the Polynesian's Luau during the show!) ♥♥

- Cirque du Soleil's La Nouba ♥♥

- Having a hot tub when you come back from an evening out ♥♥♥

CHAPTER

6

Dining at
Walt Disney
World®

After a decade of more Disney trips than we can count, we find ourselves savoring our Disney meals more than ever. And for good reason, too. Over the years, food at Walt Disney World has steadily improved and we're talking not just about the fancy places but about food everywhere, across Disney's entire spectrum of restaurants.

Today we find menus that more reflect modern tastes: fresher, tastier, and less-processed foods, salads, lighter fare, and a modest variety of vegetarian offerings. Even the cornerstones of Disney fast food, the humble hamburger and hot dog, now enjoy interesting topping bars and overall improved quality. While we once cautioned readers about table-service restaurants in the theme parks, this is no longer the case. Although dining in the parks is not up to the lofty standards of Disney resort restaurants, on the whole, it is quite good.

Besides the food, we also enjoy the food experience at Disney. From Tusker House at the Animal Kingdom to 'Ohana at the Polynesian, restaurants at Disney do more than simply provide food, they entertain. These are fun places that each tell a story, and they are an integral part of the overall Disney experience. Whether you're enjoying the Mississippi ambience of Boatwright's or savoring the Scandinavian specialties of Restaurant Akershus, you'll find a story to go along with almost every dining experience.

Just about the only complaint we hear about Disney food, both fast and fine, regards its cost. Anyway you cut it, meals at Disney seem more expensive than what you'll find in the world outside and this seems especially true if you are used to eating out in a rural area. While we think that much of the food is a little better than places outside Disney, there's just no escaping the cost factor. This is one of the realities of a Walt Disney World vacation and something you should plan on. See page 28 for our suggestions on allowing for meals during your Disney vacation and see our overview of meal expenses below.

Insider's Secret

There are over 100 certified sommeliers (wine stewards) at Walt Disney World.

The Disney World of Eating

With more than two hundred places serving meals at Walt Disney World, the variety of places to eat is mind-boggling. Disney restaurants run the gamut from a hot dog at Casey's Corner in the Magic Kingdom

Quick View of Disney Average Food and Beverage Prices

Meal and Type of Restaurant	Adult	Child
Counter-Service Continental Breakfast*	$6.00	$4.00
Counter-Service Full Breakfast*	$10.00	$4.00
Table-Service Continental Breakfast*	$7.00	$4.00
Table-Service Full Breakfast*	$12.00	$5.00
Buffet Breakfast*	$15.00	$8.00
Character Buffet Breakfast*	$15.00	$11.00
Counter-Service Lunch	$8.00	$5.00
Table-Service Lunch (sandwiches, burgers)	$11.00	$6.00
Table-Service Lunch (full hot meal)	$16.00	$7.00
Buffet Lunch	$15.00	$6.00
Character Buffet Lunch	$19.00	$10.50
Counter-Service Dinner	$8.00	$5.00
Table-Service Moderate Dinner	$20.00	$10.00
Table-Service Deluxe Dinner	$26.00	$11.00
Table-Service Premium Dinner	$31.00+	$12.00
Character Dinner	$23.50	$13.00

*Adult breakfasts include entrée, juice, and coffee; other meals include entrée and one beverage. Most appetizers cost around $8.50.
For desserts, expect to spend another $4 for counter service, $7 to $10 for table service.
Beer or wine $4.50 (counter service) and $5.00 and $9.00 (table service); mixed drinks $7.50.
All prices include tax and tip, where applicable, and all prices reflect average menu prices.

to the 5-Diamond elegance of Victoria & Albert's at Disney's Grand Floridian Resort. Between these two extremes lies a lot of territory and a great many choices.

This brings us to what this chapter is all about: to help you get the most enjoyment out of your Disney food experience, to better understand your choices, and to have at least some notion of what's available and what it's going to cost. See our chart of basic food and beverage expenses on page 301.

We'll give you some budget eating tips and we'll also tell you about character meals, dinner shows, and fine dining at Disney. We'll even point out a few of our favorite fast-food places. And, of course, this chapter will also include our reviews of the many and varied dining experiences at Walt Disney World.

Making "Reservations"

Dinner reservations at Walt Disney World are known as "priority seating arrangements." What this means is that you will make the usual "reservations" and when you arrive at the restaurant, you'll get the next available table. This usually involves a short wait.

Most restaurants (including those at the Swan and Dolphin) accept priority seating arrangements 60 days in advance. Call (407) WDW-DINE (407-934-3463) or Central Reservations at (407) W-DISNEY (934-7639). Once at Walt Disney World, arrangements for meals can be made by dialing 55 from your Disney room telephone or 88 from any pay phone, or by using the video telephone kiosks located throughout Walt Disney World. You can also make priority seating arrangements at the guest services of any resort or theme park. Here are some important things to know about Disney priority seating arrangements:

- During busy seasons and at the theme parks, priority seating arrangements are a *must*. Make them and arrive a few minutes early.

- Theme park restaurants will take same-day reservations at the door. Make them early in the day.

- Priority seating arrangements are a must for all character meals, dinner shows, and dining after 7 P.M.

- If you're running late, priority seating will be held for fifteen minutes. If you're going to be later than this, call and let them know.

- Most resort guest services have "mini-menu cards" from many Disney restaurants. Look them over, then have guest services make your priority seating arrangements.

@ Dinner time with no reservations? If there are only two of you, there's a pretty good chance you can get a table after only a short wait. Just stroll in and ask.

@ Priority seating for character breakfasts can be made up to 120 days in advance, depending on the restaurant.

Dining Tricks and Budget Tips

Over the years, we've learned to be creative with our approach to the pleasures of dining at Walt Disney World. Here are some of our ideas.

Our Tips for Breakfast

@ Virtually all table-service restaurants and room service will fix anything you desire. To get what you really want, just ask for it.

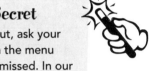

Insider's Secret

When dining out, ask your server what on the menu should not be missed. In our experience, this is usually very good advice.

@ Watch out for food courts if you are in a hurry for breakfast. During the usual breakfast hours, they are very crowded and you could find yourself standing in line for eggs instead of the Rock 'n' Roller Coaster. Try having breakfast earlier or later. Most food courts start serving at 6 A.M.

@ Enjoy a poolside breakfast ♥. Pick up your breakfast at the food court and find a nice shady table on a patio or out by the pool.

@ $ Fix your own breakfast. Get a refrigerator from housekeeping ($10 a day at most resorts), and make a simple breakfast right in your room. Ingredients and supplies can be found either at the Gourmet Pantry at the Downtown Disney Marketplace or nearby at Gooding's at the Crossroads Plaza.

@ For luxury and convenience, try room service and breakfast in bed ♥♥♥♥. It's only a little more expensive and will leave you feeling wonderfully pampered. You might also get off to an earlier start.

Our Tips for Lunch

@ $ Eat your big meal of the day for lunch. It's usually the same food that's served at dinner, only cheaper. This is especially true at Epcot's World Showcase.

@ Have some appetizers for lunch. Pick a fancy restaurant and share ♥.

- Room service ♥♥♥. Need we say more?

- Avoid the crowds and have an early lunch, as soon as places begin to serve, usually 11:30 A.M.

- Have a breakfast buffet for brunch. These are usually character meals and offer many foods appropriate for midday dining. Most usually serve until 11:30 A.M.

Our Tips for Dinner

- **$** Share a meal at one of the pricier dining spots. Try sharing a salad, an appetizer, a dessert, and one or two entrées. We do this frequently.

- At most of the fine restaurants at Disney, the chefs or wine stewards have selected wines that are well paired with the entrées of the evening, or ask your server what wine will go best with your meal.

- Pull out all the stops at least once during your vacation. Dress up and go someplace extravagant ♥♥♥.

- At the deluxe resorts, try in-room dining ♥♥♥.

Helpful Hint
You can usually order anything from any restaurant at your resort, even if it's not on the room-service menu.

$ Enjoy a Meal in a Lounge

Many of the lounges around Disney feature appetizers and foods from restaurants adjacent to them. Lounges at Walt Disney World are not what you find in the outside world. Often, they are quiet, comfortable, and quite intimate. For a lunch or a light meal, eating in a lounge can be a good choice. Some even feature live entertainment. The Matsu No Ma Lounge in Epcot, the Crew's Cup at the Yacht Club, the Territory Lounge at the Wilderness Lodge, and the California Grill bar are just a few of your choices.

Special Dietary Needs

If you have special dietary requirements or are simply selective about what you eat, you'll be happy to hear that Disney really makes an effort to accommodate diets of every kind. It is easy to find lowfat meals and a host of more healthful and lighter meals. Such foods are everywhere, from counter-service eateries to the most elegant gourmet dining spots. Fast-food outlets are even offering fruit as an option to french fries. Many restuarants at Disney feature at least one vegetarian item. Some offer several. Walt Disney World has become committed to satisfying the dietary needs of virtually every guest.

To test this commitment, we brought Aunt June and Uncle Jake to Walt Disney World. These folks are on a no-fat, vegetarian diet. No fat, no nuts, no olives, no cheese, and no fish. If you are wondering what that leaves, we can tell you how surprised we were at what the chefs of Disney created. By notifying the kitchens when we made our reservations, Jake and June enjoyed dinners created especially for them. From

Insider's Secret

The best places for vegetarian dining: Jiko and Spoodles

cold melon soup to grilled vegetables and couscous, each entrée was handcrafted. After a few meals, we were saying, "We'll have whatever they're having." To say that the kitchens went out of their way for Jake and June would be an understatement. For kosher requirements, twenty-four-hour notice is needed. Except for Jiko and Boma at the Animal Kingdom Lodge, kosher foods arrive at Walt Disney World prepared and frozen. With twenty-four-hour notice at these restaurants, you'll get a kosher meal prepared fresh.

Dining with Children

Restaurants of all kinds at Disney expect children, and there are reasonably priced kids' menus everywhere except for Victoria & Albert's, Shula's, and Arthur's 27. Team Disney really knows what kids like. Children's menus typically feature hamburgers, hot dogs, macaroni and cheese, and a variety of finger foods such as chicken nuggets and pizza. If you don't see what your child wants, ask for it. They'll be happy to fix it.

Buffets, though pricey, are a good choice for children. The variety of foods is so great that even the fussiest of eaters is certain to find something appetizing. Most buffets include "kids' stations," which feature foods with kid appeal. And being able to *see* the food before they make their selection reduces the surprise factor for kids. More than once, one of ours would order from a menu and when the food arrived, would declare, "That looks gross!" For restaurants that we think are particularly good choices for children, look for our "Kid Friendly" restaurants, marked by a ☺.

Of course, if you want to step out without your kids, there are plenty of options for giving them their own Disney adventure while the two of you enjoy your night on the town. For childcare options, see page 36.

Disney Character Meals

These delightful experiences are usually buffets. Disney characters make the rounds during mealtime, visiting each table. Not just for kids, character meals are fun and provide great photo opportunities. Priority seating arrangements for these meals are a must, especially during busy times. Please note that character appearances are particularly subject to change.

Insider's Secret

NEW For character dining, dine with Cinderella and her storybook friends at 1900 Park Fare or visit Restaurant Akershus in Norway for the Princess Breakfast.

Where to Have Character Breakfasts

- Akershus, Epcot's Norway, the Disney Princess Breakfast with Belle, Jasmin, Sleeping Beauty and more

- Baskervilles, The Grosvenor (Tuesday, Thursday, and Saturday) with Inspector Goofy and Sleuth Pluto

- Cape May Cafe, the Beach Club, with Goofy's Beach Club Character Breakfast

- Chef Mickey's Buffet, the Contemporary, with Mickey, Goofy, and friends

- Cinderella's Royal Table, Magic Kingdom, with Cinderella and storybook friends

- Covington Mills, the Hilton (Sunday), with Minnie, Pluto, and Donald

- Crystal Palace, Magic Kingdom, with Winnie the Pooh and friends

- Garden Grove Cafe, the Swan (Saturday)

- Hollywood & Vine, Disney-MGM Studios, with Goofy, Minnie, and Pluto

- 1900 Park Fare, the Grand Floridian, with Mary Poppins and Alice in Wonderland

- 'Ohana, the Polynesian, with Mickey, Goofy, and Chip and Dale
- Restaurantosaurus, Animal Kingdom, with Safari Mickey, Donald, and Goofy
- Watercress Cafe, Wyndham Palace (Sunday)

Where to Have Character Lunches
- Crystal Palace, Magic Kingdom, with Winnie the Pooh, Tigger, and friends
- Garden Grill, The Land, Epcot, with Farmer Mickey and Chip and Dale
- Hollywood & Vine, Disney-MGM Studios, with Goofy, Minnie, and Pluto

Where to Have Character Dinners
- Chef Mickey's Buffet, the Contemporary, with Mickey, Goofy, and friends
- Crystal Palace, Magic Kingdom, with Winnie the Pooh and friends
- Garden Grill, The Land, Epcot, with Farmer Mickey and Chip and Dale
- Gulliver's Grill, the Swan (except Monday and Friday), with Lion King characters and Goofy
- Liberty Tree Tavern, Magic Kingdom, with Minnie, Chip and Dale, and Goofy
- 1900 Park Fare, the Grand Floridian, with Cinderella and storybook friends

The Garden Grill Ice Cream Social with Mickey and Friends

This delightful party begins every day at 3:00, 3:10, and 3:20 P.M. at Epcot's Living with the Land Pavilion. It features ice cream and cookies and a visit with the Mouse himself. Cost is $6.99 per person and arrangments should be be made in advance by calling (407) WDW-DINE (939-3463).

Dinner Shows

If you're looking for an evening of food and entertainment, a Walt Disney World dinner show is just the ticket. We suggest that you set aside some time for a dinner show and make arrangements when you book your room or before you begin your vacation. Call (407) WDW-DINE (939-3463). Tickets for both the Luau and the Hoop-Dee-Doo Review can be made up to two years in advance. Let this be a warning.

The Polynesian Luau

The new show features performers from a variety of South Sea islands and a story about a girl returning to her island after being away. There is hula dancing, fire dancing, and the music of the South Seas. The touching show feels like a village gathering.

You'll be seated at long tables and fed endless amounts of appetizers, roasted chicken, Island Pork, fried rice, and sauteed vegetables. Beer and wine are included and the food is okay. Non-meat entrées are available upon request.

Adults, $48; children (ages 3 to 11), $25; children under 3, no charge. There are two shows nightly (5:15 P.M. and 8:00 P.M.), Tuesday through Saturday. Prices include tax and gratuity.

This show is a lot of fun and a good choice for couples with or without kids. It's even romantic ♥♥.

The Hoop-Dee-Doo Musical Revue

This saloon-style show has been a regular at Fort Wilderness for many years. It's very popular, and tickets don't come easily. Pioneer Hall, the setting for the Hoop-Dee-Doo, is an amusing re-creation of an Old West dance hall, complete with velvet curtains, rough-hewn beams, and saloon-like tables and chairs.

The cuisine is country cooking: barbecued ribs, fried chicken, salad, bread, corn on the cob, baked beans, and strawberry shortcake. Beverages include beer and wine. The show is memorable—a delight of song, dance, and corny laughs—and the food is pretty good. The performers are talented and their timing is flawless. This is not sophisticated entertainment, mind you, but good, wholesome Disney fun.

Adults, $48; children (ages 3 to 11), $25. There are three shows nightly (5:00 P.M., 7:15 P.M., and 9:00 P.M.). Prices include tax and gratuity.

TIP: Transportation to and from this show is tricky. Check with your guest services.

Mickey's Backyard Barbecue

Offered seasonally on Tuesday and Thursday evenings from March through November, this picnic-table feast features live country music, Disney character fun, and a hearty selection of backyard favorites: chicken, burgers, hot dogs, ribs, corn bread, barbecue beans, and lots more. There's even beer and wine, and it's all surprisingly good. If you enjoy this kind of thing (or especially if you've never tried anything like it), we recommend you give it a go. Reservations are required and can be arranged through Disney dining reservations at (407) WDW-DINE (939-3463). Adults, $39; children (ages 3 to 11), $25. Prices include tax and gratuity.

The House of Blues Gospel Brunch

Although this is not a Disney production, it is one of our favorites. The brunch features a bayou-inspired, home-cooked buffet of shrimp, roast beef, ham, jambalaya, and much more. Following the repast is a lively hour of gospel music and song. We found it uplifting and fun. For complete details, see page 292.

MurderWatch Mystery Theater

Presented on Saturday nights in Baskervilles at the Grosvenor, this show features music and drama during a prime rib buffet. Guests participate in two nightly shows. Adults, $42.54; children, $13.79. For reservations, call (800) 624-4109. Prices include tax and gratuity.

A Bit of Dinner Entertainment

If you are looking for a bit of entertainment during dinner instead of a production, you can choose from among a number of restaurants that feature live dinner entertainment.

- Hollywood Brown Derby at Disney-MGM ♥: a pianist in the evenings
- House of Blues at Downtown Disney: blues performer after 11 P.M.
- Coral Reef at Epcot: watch the fish and divers
- L'Originale Alfredo di Roma Ristorante at Epcot: a group of musicians and singers
- Palio at the Swan ♥♥♥: strolling violinist or guitarist (or both), Tuesday through Saturday only
- Restaurant Marrakesh at Epcot ♥♥: Moroccan musicians and belly dancer, for lunch and dinner
- Victoria & Albert's at the Grand Floridian ♥♥♥♥: a harpist
- The Biergarten at Epcot: beer hall entertainment during lunch and dinner
- Bongos at Downtown Disney: live Latin rhythms after 10:30 P.M., Fridays and Saturdays

Not Your Usual Dinner Shows

The following restaurants do not feature song or dance during dinner. The talented performing artists at these restaurants are their chefs and the stages are their kitchens.

- @ Both the California Grill and the Flying Fish feature "performance kitchens" with counter seating. At either, chat with the chefs and enjoy watching them work. At the Grill, try our regular seats at Yoshi's sushi bar (if we're not there).

- @ Victoria & Albert's Chef's Table is much more than a fine show. Here in the kitchen of award-winning Chef Scott Hunnel, you will be wined and dined to your tastes by a world-class culinary team. We promise you an unequalled dining experience. With wine pairing, prix fixe dinner is $160 per person; without wine pairing, $115. Arrangements for this can be made six months in advance by calling Disney Group Dining at (407) 939-7707. For more about "V & A's," see page 341.

- @ The Chef's Table at Wolfgang Puck is for lovers of fine food and wine. Not really a special table, this wonderful service will have you catered to by chefs, wait staff, and wine steward at your own table during a casual and unforgettable evening of wining, dining, and excitement. It's a real dining experience. $65 per person, with wine pairing an additional $35. For more information about this, one of our favorite restaurants, see page 344.

The Epcot Fall Food & Wine Festival

This is one of our favorite Disney events, and it runs from mid-October to mid-November. The World Showcase is the focus for this festival, and it features numerous kiosks around the lagoon, each offering a variety of appetizer-sized foods from around the world. Other kiosks serve wines and beers. The food is cooked on the spot and is surpisingly good. It is a rare opportunity to sample such an array of good food.

This past year, we enjoyed such tasty treats as grilled salmon, sushi, sesame noodles, and sublime mussels with ginger broth. We visited shops that sold everything from wine and cookbooks, to olive oil and kitchen accessories. We think that strolling around the lagoon and savoring this festival is one of the most romantic things we've done recently at Disney.

Know, too, that this festival includes special sit-down dinners, by reservation only. Because these dinners feature guest chefs, interesting menus, and exceptional wines, priority seating arrangements go very quickly. If you are planning to visit this event, we urge you to inquire about what is available and make your arrangements early. Call (407) WDW-DINE (939-3463).

TIP: The November weeks of the Epcot Food & Wine Festival are value season.

$ Disney Fast Food

Fast food seems an inevitable part of a Disney vacation. While burgers and hot dogs are still the cornerstone of Disney counter-service restaurants, most menus also include tortilla wraps, salads, interesting sandwiches, and even turkey burgers. Topping bars that range from basic to elaborate are another welcome addition. We especially like Restaurantosaurus at the Animal Kingdom and Pecos Bill's in the Magic Kingdom.

Here are some of our favorites for fast-food at Walt Disney World:

- Wolfgang Puck Express at Downtown Disney's West Side and Marketplace (everything here is wonderful and under $10)

- Pecos Bill's at the Magic Kingdom

- Tusker House and Restaurantosaurus at the Animal Kingdom

- Pure & Simple (Wonders of Life) at Epcot Future World (interesting sandwiches)

- Kringla Bakery (Norway) and Yakitori House (Japan) Epcot World Showcase

- ABC Commissary and Backlot Express at Disney-MGM Studios

- Food courts at the All-Star Resorts, especially at All-Star Movies

- Pepper Market at Coronado Springs Resort: Disney's best food court

- Beaches and Cream at Disney's Beach Club Resort

- Turkey leg carts in all the theme parks

Fine Dining at Walt Disney World

Disney is a great place for fine dining. Here are our favorites:

- Jiko at the Animal Kingdom Lodge

- Shula's Steakhouse at the Dolphin

- California Grill at the Contemporary

℮ Flying Fish at BoardWalk

℮ Wolfgang Puck Upstairs Dining Room at Downtown Disney

℮ Victoria & Albert's at the Grand Floridian

℮ The Coral Reef at the Living Seas, Epcot

℮ Arthur's 27 at Wyndham Palace

℮ Citricos at the Grand Floridian

Restaurants of Walt Disney World

We don't take surveys to come up with our ratings. We don't poll other diners or our readers, and we don't consult with other restaurant reviewers. We just eat everywhere, some places more than once, and some places many times. While we look for good food, we also consider consistency, and when we don't find it, we factor it into our ratings. These are not all of Disney's eateries, just those we feel are worthy of mention.

Know that menus change from time to time. Such is the way of good restaurants. Some of our favorite dishes may have given way to new creations. Quality and service vary too, one of the unfortunate realities when it comes to dining out. Generally, we find the service at Disney eateries to be exceptionally good. The following section should give you a good idea of what each restaurant is like and how good the food is.

In this section, we'll use the following symbols and ratings:

❗ Those restaurants we think are an exceptionally good value

☺ Those that are particularly good choices for dining with children

🆕 Those restaurants that are new since our last edition

★ OK food, simply not memorable. This is the kind of food that leaves you satisfied but that you won't go home talking about.

★★ Quite good. You'd happily eat here again, especially if the price is right.

★★★ Very good food, well prepared, even creatively conceived. A find, indeed, especially if it's moderately priced. The kind of place you'd happily go back to, or send friends to.

★★★★ Outstanding food; it's the stuff of memories: imaginative, perfectly prepared, and artfully presented, the creation of a world-class chef and a first-rate kitchen. This is the kind of place you'd want to *bring* your friends, so you could be with them for their first experience.

$ Inexpensive, most entrées under $10

$$ Moderately priced, most entrées $10 to $20

$$$ Expensive, most entrées $20 to $30

$$$$ Very Expensive, most entrées over $30

**! *Restaurant Akershus* Norway Pavilion, Epcot World Showcase
★★ $$ Character Breakfast, Lunch, and Dinner   ♥**

- Buffet, lunch and dinner

- Norwegian beer, wine, and full-service bar

- Priority seating recommended for dinner

- Atmosphere is quaint and medieval. One of the best lunching places around the World Showcase Lagoon.

Features a Norwegian "koldtbord" buffet as well as hot Scandinavian specialties. The forty tasty items include smoked salmon, herring, meatballs, a daily chef's special, and much more. It's one of the more exotic dining voyages at Epcot, and one of our favorites.

Akershus is Norway's charming re-creation of a medieval fortress and it's just what you'd expect if you were to dine in a castle: high-beamed ceilings; arched, cut-glass windows; and sturdy wooden furnishings. Cast members are young Norwegians dressed in traditional peasant garb. **NEW** Breakfast at Akershus features the Disney Princess Breakfast. See page 306 for details.

***All-Star Cafe*   Disney's Wide World of Sports
★   Sandwiches $, entrées $$**

- Table service, one menu for lunch and dinner

- Atmosphere is noisy and busy; lots to look at

This theme restaurant is owned by a group that includes Tiger Woods, Joe Montana, Wayne Gretzky, and other sports celebrities. Naturally, the theme here is sports, and you'll find different areas of the cafe featuring various sports. There are displays, awards, exhibits, and memorabilia everywhere, from floor to ceiling. There is even a row of booths that look like huge baseball gloves.

We had a small sampling of the menu and found our meal to be tasty and well prepared. The menu features a variety of better-than-average burgers, fresh salads, sandwiches, and pastas. All in all, we'd say that All-Star Cafe food is not memorable, but that the atmosphere and noise are.

Arthur's 27　　　　　　　　**Wyndham Palace Resort & Spa**
★★★★　　$$$　　♥♥♥♥

@　Table service, dinner only

@　Full-service bar with exceptional wine list

@　Reservations recommended: (407) 827-3450

@　Atmosphere is quiet and romantic: the best view at WDW

@　TIP: Valet parking is complimentary for patrons of Arthur's.

This beautiful and romantic restaurant is located atop the twenty-seven-story Wydham Palace Resort & Spa. Sit next to each other on love seats overlooking all of Walt Disney World. When the food begins to arrive, you'll know why we say this is a restaurant that's worth the trip.

The inspired menu of chef Theresa Connors changes with the season to present diners with what's freshest and best in the marketplace. We can't promise what will be on the menu during your visit, but expect to find such dishes as sesame-crusted ahi tuna or pan-seared sea bass with potato leek fondue. From appetizers to desserts, everything seems imaginatively concieved and beautifully presented. We think this is one of Disney World's most romantic dining destinations.

Arthur's 27 features "The Temptation" and "The Excitement," five- and four-course prix fixe meals for $68 and $62, respectively. Either is a great way to enjoy this marvelous and romantic dining place. Ask about Arthur's wine pairing. For reservations, call (407) 827-3450.

! *Artist Point*　　　　　**Disney's Wilderness Lodge Resort**
★★★　　♥♥　　$$$

@　Table service, dinner only

@　Full-service bar, very good wine list from the Pacific Northwest

@　Reservations suggested

@　Atmosphere is woodsy and very pleasant

This handsome restaurant is set amidst the splendor of the magnificent Wilderness Lodge. Inlaid wooden tables and huge canvases of western vistas make this a very pleasant place. Large windows overlook the courtyard and geyser, lending it an ambience of the high-timber country.

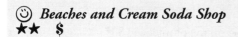

Its menu features the market-driven fare of the Pacific Northwest: seafood, game, poultry, and choice cuts of meat. The Artist Point even features a buffalo steak. The emphasis is on fresh and natural, and the Artist Point's menu changes with the seasons. Our dining experiences here have all been superb and we think it's a particularly good value for Disney fine dining. Their signature cedar-planked salmon is exceptional. Save room for the berry cobbler. If you love wine, try one of Artist Point's "Wine Flights" and sample a real variety.

| ☺ *Beaches and Cream Soda Shop* ★★ $ | **Disney's Beach Club Resort** |

- ✇ Table service with take-out; lunch, light dinner, snacks

- ✇ Reservations not accepted

This fifties-style soda shop is one of our regular haunts when we are at the Beach or the Yacht. For us, a stay at either of these resorts is simply not complete without a swim and a great double-chocolate ice cream soda. Hamburgers and sandwiches are very good, and the hot dogs are Disney's finest. Also a terrific assortment of soda-fountain concoctions. Beaches even has a lime rickey. Nothing elaborate here, just good old American fare and someplace fun to enjoy it.

| *Biergarten* ★★ $$ ♥ | **Germany Pavilion, Epcot World Showcase** |

- ✇ Buffet lunch and dinner

- ✇ Beck's beer and German wines

- ✇ Priority seating advised

- ✇ Atmosphere is well themed, quaint, and fun

The inside of this restaurant feels like an Alpine village square, complete with building facades, waterwheel, and tree. Servers are costumed in Bavarian peasant garb, and you'll find yourselves sitting beer-hall–style at large tables with other guests. It's all quite pleasant, and meals feature live, zany beer-hall entertainment.

The large buffet includes sauerbraten, rotisserie chicken, sausages, wurst salad, and spaetzle, to mention just a few items. Most of the food is good, and the German beer flows in large steins. Overall, a fun and pleasant experience.

Big River Grille & Brewing Works   Disney's BoardWalk
★ $$ Promenade

ⓔ Table-service lunch and dinner

ⓔ Full-service bar and fresh-brewed beers and ales

ⓔ Priority seating not required

ⓔ Atmosphere is an eclectic blend of wood and metal; pleasant patio on the promenade

ⓔ TIP: Try an evening table on the promenade ♥♥

Try a sampler tray of Big River's home-brewed beers and ales. The pub-style menu of this sidewalk cafe features salads, sandwiches, and a small selection of entrées such as char-grilled meatloaf, barbecued ribs, and a grilled catch of the day.

Bistro de Paris   France Pavilion, Epcot World Showcase
★★ $$$$ ♥♥♥

ⓔ Table-service dinner only

ⓔ Good wine list of French wines

ⓔ Priority seating a must

ⓔ Atmosphere is quiet and elegant

As you would expect, the menu here features a sampling of fine French cuisine. This is one of Epcot's most romantic dining destinations, and although it's a tranquil escape from the hubbub of the park, the food falls short of our expectations, especially considering its cost. By all means, dine here if you wish, but don't expect the food to be exceptional.

❗*Boatwright's Dining Hall*   Disney's Port Orleans Riverside
★   Breakfast $/Dinner $$

ⓔ Table service; breakfast, à la carte and buffet; and dinner

ⓔ Bar features a variety of regional beers and fair wine list

ⓔ Priority seating recommended

ⓔ Atmosphere is themed but not unforgettable

This is the only table-service eatery at the large Port Orleans Resort, and it is good, not fancy dining, but hearty fare at a reasonable price.

The setting is a large boat factory with real antique shipwright tools, from giant augers to chisels and mallets. Overhead, you'll see a partially completed keel and framed-out vessel. Boatwright's is decorative and comfortable.

The cuisine has a definite bayou flair. Servings for both breakfast and dinner are large. Order breakfast à la carte or enjoy the large buffet. Dinners range from jambalaya and étouffée to grilled tenderloin and seafood pasta. It's a pleasant place to dine and a fairly good value.

Boma: Flavors of Africa   Disney's Animal Kingdom Lodge
★★★ $$

@ Buffet, breakfast and dinner

@ Very good list of South African wines

@ Priority seating a must

@ Atmosphere is exotic and African (and fairly noisy)

Boma enjoys the theming of an African village and features comfortable seating areas in traditional circular "kraals" made of euki poles. Its eight onstage cooking areas serve up a huge spread of everything from fresh roasted rotisserie chicken to African stews. Specialties include Moroccan seafood salad, corn porridge, prime rib, and pepper steak. Boma's exotic flavors, curries, sambals, chutneys, and the Indian and Asian influences make this a premier dining destination and Disney's most exotic buffet meal.

Bongos Cuban Cafe   The West Side, Downtown Disney
★★   Lunch and Dinner $$ ♥♥

@ Table service, lunch (smaller menu) and dinner, open 11 A.M. to 2 A.M.

@ Two full-service bars

@ Priority seating suggested for dinner

@ Atmosphere is tropical and beautiful

@ Live Latin music Friday and Saturday nights

Bongos is owned by singer Gloria Estefan. The cuisine is decidedly Latin, and the atmosphere recalls the days of splashy supper clubs and Latin rhythms. Inside and out, Bongos recalls Havana of the 1930s and 1940s. Tile mosaics bring scenes of this old city to life, and art deco palms, bamboo curtains, and conga drum barstools import all the exuberance and romance of Old Havana. Bongos is chic, stylish, nostalgic, and fun.

The large menu covers all the bases of Cuban cuisine with such standards as ropa vieja, bistec de Palomilla, steak churrasco, and arroz con pollo. Seafood, steaks, poultry, and sandwiches: Bongos has it all. The menu is large and the food is interesting and well prepared. Dining here can be done downstairs or up, inside or on charming patios ♥♥ outside.

Bongos also brings to Downtown Disney a bit of Miami's Little Havana with its sidewalk cafe window. There are a thousand places like this in Miami, and they are as much a part of the Cuban culture as is the Spanish language. The cafe features a variety of Cuban sandwiches and pastries and, of course, Cafe Cubano. The small seating area is pleasant and right on the avenue.

California Grill   Disney's Contemporary Resort
★★★★ $$$ ♥♥

@ Table service, dinner only

@ Full-service bar; exceptional California wine list

@ Priority seating a must

@ Atmosphere is stylish, high energy, and fairly noisy; features a stunning panorama.

@ TIPS: Have dinner here during the Magic Kingdom's fireworks show or have late-night sushi at the bar. No reservation? Try getting here when it first opens at 6 P.M. Good luck.

California Grill has a new chef, John State, from the Flying Fish Cafe. We're pleased to say that John has brought to the Grill his own superb style of intriguing combinations and intense reductions. Although several of the Grill's standards remain (such as the signature pork tenderloin), Chef State is introducing his own take on California cuisine, and it is most certainly one that we enjoy.

Our recent experience here included a roasted Artic char with rock shrimp risotto and blood orange reduction. We still dream about it. His yellowfin tuna with shiitake mushrooms and spicy somen noodles was another winner. From our openers of sushi and Sonoma goat cheese raviolis with cherry vinaigrette to a warm Valrhona chocolate-banana bread pudding dessert, this was a meal to savor.

No doubt, the team at the California Grill takes great pride in what they do, and you'll see and taste it with every dish. We suggest you ask your server what wine will be the best accompaniment for each course. Oh, and don't forget to save room for dessert!

! ☺ *Cape May Cafe*   Disney's Beach Club Resort
★★   Breakfast $$/Dinner $$

- Table-service buffet, character breakfast, and "clambake" dinner
- Full-service bar
- Priority seating strongly suggested
- Atmosphere is pleasant, though hardly memorable

Mornings feature Goofy's Beach Club character breakfast buffet. The spread is large, and the quality is good. If you can't find something here, they'll be glad to fix it for you.

Dinner at Cape May features a New England-style "clambake" and all-American buffet. We think it's pretty good. While this is not seafood dining at its finest, Cape May offers a moderately priced, all-you-can-eat buffet that includes chicken, shrimp, fish, clams, ribs, and much more. Good food and a good value, too.

Cap'n Jack's Restaurant   The Downtown
★   Lunch $/Dinner $$ ♥   Disney Marketplace

- Table service, lunch and dinner
- Full-service bar
- Reservations not accepted
- Atmosphere is charming, especially if you sit by a window overlooking the water

Cap'n Jack's enjoys a pleasant waterfront location and charming nautical ambience. The food is fairly good, though certainly not fine dining. We'd have to say that Jack's is a good choice for a meal here at Downtown Disney's Marketplace.

☺ *Chef Mickey's Buffet*   Disney's Contemporary Resort
★ $$

- Table-service character buffet, breakfast and dinner
- Wine and beer
- Priority seating a must
- Atmosphere is noisy and fun

Breakfasts at Chef Mickey's feature a spread of egg dishes, pancakes and French toast, breakfast meats, and fruits and cereals. Dinners offer the usual buffet selection of poultry, fish, pastas, and roast beef as well as numerous side dishes and desserts. The food is fair, but you'd be missing the point if you visited Chef Mickey's for that. This is a place for Disney character fun, and it is one of the most popular and lively character meals in the land. It's a great place to eat with kids.

Chefs de France Restaurant   France Pavilion, Epcot
★★   Lunch $$/Dinner $$$ ♥   World Showcase

- Table service, lunch and dinner
- Full-service bar with French wines
- Reservations are a must, unless you arrive before 12:30 P.M. for lunch and 6:00 P.M. for dinner
- Atmosphere is pleasant, especially in the evening

The kitchen and menu at Chefs de France are supervised by three of France's most famous chefs: Roger Verde, Paul Bocuse, and Gaston LeNôtre. This large restaurant features paneled walls, exquisite fixtures, and works of French Impressionist art. Service is impeccable, and tables are dressed with white linens. It is a delightful re-creation of a Parisian restaurant and features a charming glassed-in porch dining room.

    The food at Chefs de France is imaginatively conceived and as well prepared as is possible for the large numbers of guests that are served here. The large and decidedly Gallic menu features classic French fare as well as the innovative cuisines of these three great chefs: grilled salmon, roast breast of duck in orange sauce, and grilled tenderloin of beef are only a few of the many good choices here. From appetizers to soups and salads, we are sure that you'll find something here to enjoy. The lunch menu at Chefs de France features some of the same entrées found at dinner, and we think this is a good value for an Epcot midday meal. Chefs de France features wines paired with each entrée.

☺ *Cinderella's Royal Table* Fantasyland, Magic Kingdom
★★ Breakfast and lunch $$/Dinner $$$ ♥♥♥

- ℮ Table service, breakfast, lunch, and dinner
- ℮ No alcohol (this is the Magic Kingdom!)
- ℮ Atmosphere is beautiful and memorable
- ℮ TIP: Priority seating is an absolute must, but if there are just two of you, you might be able to sneak in after a short wait.

This royal place is located inside the castle, and its ambience is just what you would wish for: a cavernous dining hall, "medieval" tapestries, stained-glass windows, suits of armor, and great tables befit for lords and ladies. Cinderella herself greets diners in the downstairs hall. Yes, this is Disney's premier and most sought-after fantasy dining experience.

The dinner menu features roasted prime rib, roasted chicken on spinach, and a tasty spice-encrusted salmon. These and all accompaniments were acceptably good. The lunch menu includes several of the dinner entrées as well as Major Domo's Pie and a few good sandwiches and salads. Mornings at the castle mean a Cinderella character breakfast.

Cítricos Disney's Grand Floridian Resort
★★★★ $$$ ♥♥♥

- ℮ Table service, dinner only
- ℮ Full-service bar; outstanding wine list
- ℮ Priority seating advised, especially for window seating
- ℮ Atmosphere is beautiful, elegant, romantic, and quiet
- ℮ TIPS: Try the Grand Wine Pairing for $25 per person. Dine during Magic Kingdom fireworks and ask for a table with a view.

This stylish restaurant is the creation of the designer of the California Grill and the Flying Fish. From furnishings and wall sconces to plush carpets and table service, all things are uniquely original creations. Our waitress even wore a broach that was the restaurant's signature curl. Everything is pure Cítricos, and everything is serenely beautiful and more than just a bit romantic. But this award-winning restaurant isn't just another pretty face.

Cítricos' menu is painted from a palette of what is best in the marketplace each day and draws its inspration from Tuscany, Provence, and the Spanish Riviera. Expect such delights as jumbo crabcakes, grilled swordfish, roast duck, rack of lamb, and filet of beef. Our recent meal here was exceptional.

If you are seeking a dining experience that will bring stylish presentations and delicious creations together in a focus that is enchantingly beautiful, with service that is both knowledgeable and faultless, then set your sights on Cítricos.

Concourse Steakhouse   Disney's Contemporary Resort
★★   Breakfast $/Lunch $$/Dinner $$

- Table service, breakfast, lunch, and dinner

- Full-service bar, good wine list

- Priority seating recommended for dinner

- Atmosphere is noisy and modern

- TIP: Get here early and beat the crowds.

For breakfast and lunch, the Concourse Steakhouse offers a well-prepared selection of à la carte standards. Lunches include salads, sandwiches, and a very good burger. While this would not be considered fine dining, it's certainly good food and a good value, too.

Dinners are more upscale. With a menu of seafood, poultry, and good cuts of meat, this restaurant features dishes that are well prepared, well conceived, and handsomely presented. The creamed spinach is memorable. But for the clamor of the Contemporary's noisy Concourse, we would not hesitate to recommend it.

Coral Reef Restaurant   The Living Seas Pavilion, Future
★★★★   Lunch $$/Dinner $$$ ♥♥   World, Epcot

- Table service, lunch and dinner

- Atmosphere is exceptionally nice by the aquarium; can be noisy

- TIPS: Probably the busiest Epcot restaurant. Priority seating is a must. Dine early to avoid the din.

The Coral Reef features an underwater theme, and it's a beautiful and romantic place to dine. The specialty is seafood, and chef Roland Mueller (from Cítricos) has brought a level of food never before enjoyed here. The menu now features a variety of seafood, all of it imagi-

natively conceived and perfectly prepared. The Coral Reef is the only theme park restaurant that we give four stars. *Bon appetit.*

! ☺ ★ *Crystal Palace*   **Main Street USA, Magic Kingdom**
Breakfast and lunch $$ / Dinner $$$

℮ Table-service character buffet, breakfast, lunch, and dinner

℮ Priority seating strongly suggested

We particularly enjoy the beautiful interior of this restaurant as well as its imaginative and tasty lunch and dinner buffets. We expect the menu will change over time, but during our meal we enjoyed a pleasant variety of quality fresh salads and both hot and cold entrées, including a variety of carved meats and fish filets.

★ *Dolphin Fountain*   **The Dolphin**
$

℮ Table service, fifties-style soda shop, open 11 A.M. to 11 P.M.

℮ Atmosphere is loud, bright, and fun; service is slow

"The Golden Oldies" here refer more to the fried foods than to the fifties rock 'n' roll background music. Hot dogs, hamburgers, grilled chicken sandwich, and BLT about sum it up. Toss in a salad, some nachos and fries, and a large selection of soda fountain sweets and ice creams, and you've pretty much described this fun place. This is the Beaches and Cream of the Dolphin. Every resort should have one!

★ *ESPN Club*   **Disney's BoardWalk Promenade**
Sandwiches $, entrées $$

℮ Table service, lunch and dinner (same menu)

℮ Full-service bar; beer on tap

℮ Atmosphere is noisy, like being at a sports event

This full-service restaurant is also a sports/entertainment club. With a 220-seat arena and wall of video monitors showing the most popular sporting events, this is definitely the place to go for the big fight or the playoff game. With more than seventy video monitors and tableside audio controls, a bank of Internet terminals, and state-of-the-art computer games, this is a sports lover's nirvana.

Not just the ultimate in sports entertainment, this place also has an interesting menu of well-prepared standards. Salads, pasta, and a selection of large and tasty sandwiches make ESPN an eating place too: try the grilled chicken, BBQ pork, or the club sandwich. The burger here is good (not to mention huge). Also lots of good finger foods to go with the sporting events and drinks.

! ☺ 50's Prime Time Café   Disney-MGM Studios
★★ $$

@ Table service, same menu for lunch and dinner

@ Full-service bar and lounge

@ Reservations strongly suggested

@ Atmosphere, though not romantic, is memorable and entertaining

This is a good example of how much fun a meal at Disney can be. The Prime Time looks like your "average" American kitchen of the fifties: Formica tables, knotty-pine cupboards, and other authentic "antiques" of the period (our youth!). There's a vintage TV at every table, showing clips from old 1950s sitcoms: *I Love Lucy, My Little Margie, Our Miss Brooks,* and other classics. We took our mothers here once for one of our most memorable Disney experiences.

Servers at the Prime Time are brother or cousin, aunt or uncle, and you'd better keep your elbows off the table! There's lots of fun to be had here, and the food is also quite good though certainly not fine dining. The Prime Time menu features a variety of sandwiches and such 1950s kitchen classics as meat loaf and fried chicken. The dessert menu is particularly entertaining. It's good fun and good food. Oh yes, and you'd better clean your plate if you want dessert!

Flying Fish Cafe   Disney's BoardWalk Promenade
★★★★ $$$ ♥♥

@ Table service, dinner only, from 6 P.M.

@ Full-service bar, outstanding wine list

@ Priority seating a must

This dependably outstanding restaurant is one of our favorites. We've dined here countless times and have rarely been disappointed. Marty Dorf's stylish, 1930s "amusement park" ambience is something you'll have to see for yourselves. It's classy and amusing. Service is outstanding in every way.

Now with new chef Robert Curry, "The Fish" continues to delight us with a market-driven menu that now seems a bit more seafood oriented. We still found the old standbys, a memorable char-crusted New York strip steak and the signature potato-wrapped snapper. But there's much more, including the "Chef's Thunder," each evening's special offerings. This is one place where you'll leave wondering what delights you might have missed. From opening wine to after-dinner port, from starters to desserts, there's a lot to savor here. If you're like us, you'll be planning your next meal at the Flying Fish before you're even out the door.

Fulton's Crab House   Downtown Disney Marketplace
★★★   Lunch $$ /Dinner $$$ to $$$$

- Table-service lunch and dinner
- Full-service bar with a very good wine list
- Priority seating strongly suggested
- Atmosphere is fairly busy and noisy, with nice views from the quarterdeck
- TIP: Try eating on the outside deck.

The specialty of the house is seafood. However, the food lately seems less impressive than on past visits. Still, the fish is very fresh (check out the day's airfare receipts posted in the hallway for the answer) and the assortment is large: Fanny Bay oysters, Alaskan king crab, and Penn Cove mussels are but a few of the offerings on Fulton's huge menu.

☺ *Garden Grill Restaurant*   The Land Pavilion,
★   Lunch $$/Dinner $$$ Future World, Epcot

- Table service, family-style lunch and dinner
- Beer and wine
- Priority seating a must
- Atmosphere is pleasant, although part of the trip is noisy.

Built on a revolving deck, this restaurant transports diners through a scenic part of this pavilion's attraction. Character meals feature Farmer

Mickey and Minnie. Service is family-style, and the food will keep coming as long as you are willing. On our last visit here, we found the food to be good. Hardly fine dining, the lunch and dinner menus included rotisserie chicken, steak, fried fish, and several side dishes. All in all, a very good value.

Garden Grove Cafe/Gulliver's Grill   The Swan
★★   Breakfast and Lunch $ to $$/Dinner $$$

- Table service, breakfast, lunch, and dinner
- Full-service bar with modest wine list
- Priority seating suggested for dinner
- Atmosphere tells a story; pleasant and comfortable

Not really two restaurants, this eatery changes its name at dinner to become Gulliver's Grill. As the Garden Grove Cafe, breakfast offerings include a large buffet of American standards as well as a large menu of morning standards. Lunches feature à la carte salads, sandwiches, and a few entrées.

Dinner at Gulliver's Grill is bit more upscale. Utilizing the story of *Gulliver's Travels,* dinner begins here with a bit of wine poured into cup-size thimbles. It's not long before you realize that the entire restaurant resembles a large birdcage and, like Gulliver, you are inside. The menu is fairly imaginative with a large selection of steaks, poultry, and seafood, and each night you'll also enjoy the option of a different buffet. Service is outstanding, the food is very well prepared, and all in all, it's a very pleasant restaurant experience. Disney characters appear nightly and for breakfasts every Saturday. Sunday mornings feature a champagne brunch.

Grand Floridian Cafe   Disney's Grand Floridian Resort
★★★   Breakfast $/Lunch $$

- Table service, breakfast and lunch
- Full-service bar
- Reservations suggested during peak hours

This charming restaurant is the Grand Floridian's "all-purpose" eatery. Breakfasts include everything from a bagel to a vegetable frittata. Lunches include an impressive array of sandwiches, salads, and a few entrées. This is one of those restaurants that has something for everyone.

Hollywood & Vine
★★ $$

Disney-MGM Studios

℮ Character buffet for breakfast, lunch, dinner

℮ Priority seating for lunch is a must

Although this place features all the fun of a Disney character meal, we're sorry to report that the food is unremarkable. In fact, it's not as good as many other buffet meals here at Disney. Breakfast features all the expected plus frittatas, chocolate French toast, and pancakes. Lunches add a variety of pastas, rotisserie chicken, baked fish, and pot roast. It sounds and even looks better than it tastes. We don't know how they do it.

Hollywood Brown Derby
★★★   Lunch $$/Dinner $$ to $$$ ♥♥

Disney-MGM Studios

℮ Table service, lunch and dinner

℮ Full-service bar, good wine list

℮ Priority seating suggested

℮ TIP: In good weather, ask for a table on the patio.

The Derby is an elegant re-creation of the famous restaurant at Hollywood and Vine. It features the same sketches of 1930s and 1940s celebrities, dark polished woodwork, and potted palms. In the evening, there's a pianist in the handsome sunken dining room. If you arrive early or late for lunch or for dinner, you're likely to find the Derby quiet and wonderfully romantic.

The Derby is an excellent choice for dining at the Studios, either for lunch or dinner. Its ever-changing menu covers all the basics with seafood, chops and steaks, poultry, pasta, and its signature Cobb Salad. From starters to desserts, everything is imaginative and well prepared. It's a good value for both lunch and dinner and an especially nice place to dine.

House of Blues
★★★   Sandwiches $, Entrées $$ ♥ (The Voodoo Garden ♥♥♥)

Downtown Disney West Side

℮ Table service, lunch and dinner (one menu)

℮ Full-service bar, good wine list

℮ Priority seating suggested especially for weekends

℮ TIP: Try the Sunday Gospel Brunch (see page 292).

This pleasing restaurant is a Mississippi roadhouse. Its tin roof and ramshackle exterior hide the unusual and eclectic works of art that virtually cover the interior. From inlaid bottle caps to garish portraits, House of Blues (HOB) features artwork the likes of which you've probably not seen.

The cuisine here is of the bayou, and the large menu is quite interesting. Openers include a tasty seafood gumbo, an ahi tuna salad, Mediterranean calamari, and catfish nuggets. For entrées, you can make the trip from the famous Elwood sandwich to blackened prime rib. Other Delta offerings include shrimp and crawfish étouffée, smoked babyback ribs, Cajun meatloaf, and a good jambalaya. There's much more, and even a classic New Orleans Po'boy. Everything tastes fresh and well prepared.

One of our favorite things about HOB is the Voodoo Garden, behind the restaurant. This porch and garden area is exceptionally beautiful, and after dark, it's pure magic. Having a cocktail or dining here on the porch overlooking the lake is an experience we highly recommend. For more information about the House of Blues, its concerts, Gospel Brunch, and the HOB store, see page 292.

Jiko: The Cooking Place   Disney's Animal Kingdom Lodge
★★★★ $$$ ♥♥♥

@ Table service, dinner only

@ Full-service bar with exceptional South African wine list

@ Priority seating a must

If you're looking for a dining adventure, set your sights on this exceptional dining experience. Jiko's focus is the innovative fusion of the many flavors of Africa, a cuisine that reflects not only countless tribal cultures but also such exotic neighbors as the Middle East, India, and the Far East. And after many years of Colonial rule, even the tastes of Europe are evident in this unique melange of cuisines. Banana leaf–steamed sea bass, oven-roasted Chermoula chicken, and an oak-grilled beef tenderloin are just a few of the unforgettable offerings that come out of chef Anette Grecchi-Gray's kitchen. Jiko features an extraordinary collection of South African wines, many of which are served by the glass. A beautiful decor makes this a modern and stylish eatery. Exceptional food and flawless and knowledgeable service make it one of Disney's premier dining destinations. It is, we think, a not-to-miss dining experience.

Kimonos *The Swan*
★★ $$ ♥♥

@ Table service and sushi bar, dinner only

@ Full-service bar with good sakes

@ Atmosphere is beautiful and romantic

If you are looking for a place to enjoy sushi or tempura and feel like something stunning, quiet, and out of the way, Kimonos is it. This handsome eatery features Japanese lanterns, black-enameled bamboo, plush leather chairs, and hanging kimonos. Offerings of sushi, sashimi, and tempura are quite good. The bar menu also features single-malt scotches, small-batch bourbons, and a variety of sakes. Karaoke is featured later in the evening, and we suggest that you arrive and depart accordingly.

! *Kona Cafe* Disney's Polynesian Resort
★★★ Breakfast and Lunch $/Dinner $$

@ Table service, breakfast, lunch, and dinner

@ Atmosphere is pleasant and stylish

The Kona Cafe enjoys a simple yet elegant tropical theme with fanciful sculpted metalwork and an open pastry kitchen. With a menu of memorable salads, hearty sandwiches, and imaginative entrées, the Kona Cafe has also kept some of its past glories (such as the famous Auntie Kaui's banana-stuffed Tonga Toast). It's an especially good choice for a lunch escape while you are visiting the Magic Kingdom and a particularly good value for an evening of fine dining. Don't miss their wonderful desserts.

Le Cellier Steakhouse Canada Pavilion, Epcot
★★★ Lunch: sandwiches $, entrées $$ / Dinner $$ to $$$

@ Table service, lunch and dinner

@ Beer and wine

@ Priority seating suggested during peak seasons

@ Atmosphere restful and quiet

In our experiences, this is one of the better places to dine along the World Showcase. Compared with many of the other restaurants here, Le Cellier is relatively small and able to create food that does not have the mass-produced feeling that is so common here in the countries of Epcot.

The menu features a selection of grilled steaks and a delicious glazed salmon. Not strong on ambience, Le Cellier is a comfortable, cool, and quiet retreat from the crowds and a very good choice for a meal here at Epcot.

The castle-like dining room of Le Cellier features an inviting selection of aged, corn-fed beef and a variety of seafood, poultry, and even a rack of lamb. There's something here for every taste. We think that the small size of this restaurant explains why the food seems a cut above the other World Showcase eateries. It's a nice place to dine and a good value.

☺ *Liberty Tree Tavern*   Liberty Square, Magic Kingdom
★   Lunch $$ / Dinner $$$

℮ Table service, lunch and buffet, character dinner

℮ Reservations strongly suggested

℮ Atmosphere is pleasant and comfortable

℮ TIPS: Try the Liberty Tree for lunch. If you are looking for a light meal, try splitting one of the large sandwiches.

The decor here is Colonial American and it is done quite well, down to the "hand-hewn" ceiling. The Liberty Tree Tavern is a pleasant and restful place to eat. The food is well prepared but not great. The lunch menu offers a variety of large sandwiches and such entrées as fresh fish, turkey dinner, pot roast, and shrimp and vegetable pasta. The strawberry vinaigrette salad dressing is quite good. The Liberty Tree Tavern is sponsored by Stouffers.

The Character dinner buffet features roasted turkey, carved beef, smoked pork, and accompaniments.

L'Originale Alfredo di Roma Ristorante   Italy Pavilion,
★   Lunch $$ / Dinner $$$ On the patio ♥♥   Epcot

℮ Table service, lunch and dinner

℮ Beer and Italian wines only

℮ Reservations suggested during mealtimes

℮ Restaurant is attractive but crowded and noisy

With a band of entertainers singing and playing during dinner, Alfredo's is an enjoyable place to eat if you don't mind the noise (it can even get noisy on the patio). Featured dishes here are the standards that have become known as Italian cuisine. Fettuccini alfredo, of course, is

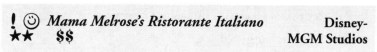

the signature dish but in recent years, Alfredo's has made a real effort to include a wider variety of non-mainstream Italian cuisine. Although we don't find the food here more than merely okay, we do think that a lunch on the patio is particularly pleasant.

! ☺ *Mama Melrose's Ristorante Italiano*   **Disney-**
★★ $$ **MGM Studios**

@ Table service, lunch and dinner

@ Full-service bar with good wine list

@ Reservations strongly suggested

@ Atmosphere is cute and interesting

Mama's features a menu of traditional Italian cuisine. Lunches include a small variety of soups, salads, and wood-fired flatbreads as well as entrées such as eggplant parmesan and linguini with seafood. The evening menu goes further, adding such dishes as veal osso bucco, oak-grilled salmon, and filet of beef.

Restaurant Marrakesh   **Morocco Pavilion,**
★★   Lunch $$/Dinner $$$ ♥♥   **Epcot World Showcase**

@ Table service, lunch and dinner

@ Full-service bar

@ Reservations suggested

@ The atmosphere here is exotic

@ TIPS: For a real taste of Morocco, try either the Marrakesh or Royal Feast.

Restaurant Marrakesh is one of Epcot's most exotic restaurants. Featuring a live belly dancer and musicians at both lunch and dinner, it's one of our favorites. From a selection of couscous dishes to salmon ala Marocaine, chicken kebabs, and roast lamb Meshoui, Marrakesh delivers what so many other World Showcase restaurants merely promise: the exotic and the unique. If you are looking for a dining adventure beyond the usual, don't miss it.

Maya Grill   Disney's Coronado Springs Resort
★★★   Breakfast $$/Dinner $$ to $$$ ♥♥

- Table-service, dinner only
- Full-service bar, good wine list, a great margarita
- Priority seating suggested
- Atmosphere is quiet and understated

The atmosphere here at Maya Grill evokes the ancient Mayan world and its harmony with sun, fire, and water. Built to have the feel of a great stone Mayan temple, the decor is simple, almost spartan. An offering to the gods "burns" on a pedestal under the center of the pyramid-like interior. The menu features an interesting selection of steaks and chops, seafood and poultry. Mornings at Maya Grill feature a typical Disney breakfast buffet.

Narcoossee's   Disney's Grand Floridian Resort
★★★ $$$ to $$$$

- Table service, dinner only
- Full-service bar, very good wine list
- Priority seating recommended for dinner
- Waterfront atmosphere with a pleasant view, but awfully noisy

Fresh seafood is the star here at Narcoossee's. Changing to accommodate what is freshest and best in the marketplace, Narcoossee's serves up a menu of salmon, lobster, halibut, scallops, and crab. If seafood is not your thing, rest assured. Offerings here also include filet mignon, lamb chops, chicken, and vegetarian fare.

Although this restaurant often seems noisy, it offers one of the most beautiful dinner views at Walt Disney World, including views of both fireworks and the Elecric Water Pageant. Try dining early to avoid the din.

Nine Dragons Restaurant   China Pavilion,
★★ $$ ♥   Epcot World Showcase

- Table service, lunch and dinner
- Full-service bar
- Reservations suggested

ℯ A beautiful dining room; quiet and pleasant

ℯ TIPS: Try snacking here on dumplings, if you wish to enjoy the atmosphere. This restaurant is usually not too busy. If you can't get in elsewhere, it's a good choice.

With all of its carved furnishings and beautiful Chinese artwork, Nine Dragons is a lovely place to dine. The food is well prepared and probably better than your neighborhood Chinese restaurant. Offerings include mu shu pork and kung pao chicken. Although most everything here is à la carte, Nine Dragons also features an all-you-care-to-eat lunch and a dinner sampler for two.

☺ *1900 Park Fare*   Disney's Grand Floridian Resort
★★   Breakfast $$/Dinner $$$

ℯ Table service, character buffets, breakfast, and dinner

ℯ Reservations recommended (this place is popular)

ℯ Atmosphere is noisy and gay

ℯ TIP: Bring your camera for some terrific pictures. Ask your server to snap a photo of the two of you with some of the Disney characters.

We think that this an outstanding buffet. Offerings for both breakfast and dinner are large and the quality is surprisingly good. The only drawback is that Park Fare is noisy. First, there's all of the children and characters and then there's Big Bertha, the mechanical organ. If you are looking for peace and quiet, this isn't it. If you are looking for fun and a character meal, we doubt that you'll find a better one than this.

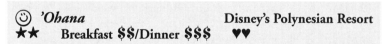

☺ *'Ohana*   Disney's Polynesian Resort
★★   Breakfast $$/Dinner $$$ ♥♥

ℯ Table-service all-you-care-to-eat, breakfast, and dinner

ℯ Full-service bar, Polynesian specialty drinks

ℯ Atmosphere is tropical, sometimes noisy

From bamboo decor to the flaming fire-pit, 'Ohana is steeped in the flavor of the South Seas. Servers bring course after course of roasted meats and shrimp on sword-like skewers. Appetizers, salad, vegetables, and exotic dipping sauces are all quite good. It's a South Seas feast, fit for a Polynesian king.

There is entertainment throughout the evening. Most of it is fun, and with games for kids, it can get quite noisy. 'Ohana is a good choice for dining fun. Mornings at 'Ohana features a family style Disney character breakfast.

Olivia's Cafe   Disney's Old Key West
★   **Breakfast and Lunch $/Dinner $$**

@ Table service, breakfast, lunch, and dinner

@ Full-service bar; good wine list

Key West is the theme here, and Olivia's delivers a colorful and casual atmosphere. For any of the day's meals, the menu is inviting. Dinners feature a hearty selection of steaks, poultry, and seafood. There is also a nice offering of fresh salads and soups. In our experience, however, the food is a little unpredictable.

One drawback to Olivia's is getting there. If you're not staying at Old Key West, you'll need a car or try busing from the Downtown Disney Marketplace or one of the theme parks back to Old Key West.

Outback Restaurant   **Wyndham Palace Resort & Spa**
★★   **$$$**   ♥

@ Table service, dinner only

@ Full-service bar

@ Reservations suggested: (407) 827-3430

Don't confuse this place with the Outback Steakhouse chain. Although both claim an Australian theme, this Outback really delivers. The open-hearth dining area enjoys such touches as a three-story waterfall and a fish pond. Specialties of the house include hearty grilled steaks and giant lobsters. If you can manage to devour one of these three- to six-pound monsters, you'll get a plaque on the wall with your name on it.

The Outback Restaurant menu is large enough to accommodate virtually any taste. From poultry to fish filets, this place has a lot to offer. We found both food and service to be quite good.

Palio   **The Swan**
★★★   **$$$**   ♥♥♥

@ Table service, dinner only

@ Full-service bar

@ Reservations suggested

@ TIPS: If you want to eat for less, order one pizza and one of the more moderately priced entrées. Drop by later in the evening for an espresso or cappuccino and your choice of desserts.

Your meal at Palio will begin with a Boccalino, the traditional "little jug" of wine. This restaurant is easily Disney World's finest for Italian cuisine and if you're dining as a couple, be sure to ask for one of the comfortable booths where you can sit next to each other. Once the strolling violinist (or guitarist) begins, you'll begin to see why we rate this place as an outstanding romantic dining experience. Musicians play Tuesday through Saturday.

Palio is not a spaghetti-and-meatballs Italian restaurant. It's not difficult to eat here for about the same price as most of the Epcot restaurants, and the food at Palio is incomparably superior. Entrées include seafood and spaghettini baked in parchment, ragout of lobster and tortellini, and pork alla Milanese. The osso buco is extraordinary, and we still long for the Risotto con Vongole. The specialty pizzas are small but exceptionally good.

Plaza Restaurant   Main Street USA, Magic Kingdom
★ $

@ Table service, lunch and dinner (same menu)

@ Priority seating suggested

@ Atmosphere is quaint and a pleasant escape

This turn-of-the-century, art nouveau eatery offers a fairly standard menu of well-prepared sandwiches including a Reuben, double-decker roast beef, and grilled turkey. Other tasty offerings include a Southwest chicken salad and a variety of burgers. This is a nice quiet place for lunch.

Portobello Yacht Club   Pleasure Island, Downtown Disney
★★★ Lunch $$/Dinner $$$ ♥ (admission not required)

@ Table service, lunch and dinner

@ Full-service bar, good wine list

@ No reservations accepted

@ Atmosphere is casual; can be noisy at peak hours

@ TIP: If the weather is pleasant, try sitting in the beautiful garden area outside.

Amid all the excitement of the big-name Disney dining spots, here's a restaurant that is too easily overlooked. Portobello is one of our favorite places to eat at Walt Disney World. The menu features a large array of Northern Italian foods, all elegantly prepared. We've never had anything here that we didn't like a lot. We often share an entrée and several appetizers. The gelato cappuccino is one of our very favorite desserts.

☺ *Rainforest Cafe*   The Downtown Disney Marketplace and ★★ Breakfast $/Lunch and Dinner $$ the Animal Kingdom

❧ Table service, breakfast (Animal Kingdom only), lunch and dinner

❧ Full-service bar

❧ Atmosphere is fun, exciting, and very noisy

❧ TIPS: Priority seating is available only at the Animal Kingdom. We advise it. At the Marketplace, avoid mealtimes; try eating before 11:30 A.M. or at 4:30 P.M.

This is one very busy, but very fun place to eat. The smoldering volcano exterior of this restaurant towers above the rest of the Marketplace. At the Animal Kingdom, the Rainforest is hidden behind a 65-foot waterfall. Inside is a dense "rain forest," complete with canopy of trees, periodic thunderstorms, and a host of robotic wildlife that all occasionally come to life. It has the detail and excitement of a theme park attraction. It's a wild place to eat!

Like many theme restaurants, the food is fun but not exceptional. We particularly enjoyed the coconut bread pudding. The Rainforest Cafe at the Animal Kingdom serves breakfast, beginning each morning at 6:30. The menu features some interesting stuff: custom breakfast pizzas, jungle wraps, and our favorite, Rainforest Tonga Toast. There's much more, and it's all unusual and good.

Rose and Crown Pub & Dining Room   United Kingdom, ★★ $$ ♥   World Showcase Epcot

❧ Table service, lunch and dinner

❧ Full-service bar with English ales and beers

❧ Reservations suggested

❧ Atmosphere on the patio is very nice during pleasant weather

❧ TIPS: The lakeside patio is the best place at Epcot to dine while watching IllumiNations.

A pleasant place to eat, especially if the weather is cool enough to dine on the patio overlooking the lagoon. The food here is well prepared and tasty, although nothing here seems particularly memorable (much like real British cuisine). Fish and chips, roast chicken, bangers and mash, and an English pie sampler are among the many offerings.

San Angel Inn Restaurante
★★ $$ ♥♥♥

Mexico Pavilion,
Epcot World Showcase

- ℮ Table service, lunch and dinner

- ℮ Full-service bar with Mexican beer

- ℮ Reservations suggested during busy mealtimes

- ℮ TIP: Try having a cold Mexican beer and some nachos or other appetizer. This way, you'll get to enjoy the atmosphere without having to eat an entire meal.

What a beautiful place this is. It's always nighttime at the San Angel Inn, which is set amid the facade of a quaint Mexican village. The restaurant overlooks the most scenic part of the pavilion's boat ride, where the River of Time passes through a dense and mountainous jungle. Enjoy your meal on the lovely plaza at the river's edge, while a volcano smolders in the distance. It's truly memorable; a charming and romantic spot.

The food here is good, though not memorable. We suggest you try something a bit more exotic. Ask about the daily chef's special.

☺ Sci-Fi Dine-In Theater
★★ $$

Disney-MGM Studios

- ℮ Table service, lunch and dinner

- ℮ Beer and wine

- ℮ Priority seating a must

- ℮ Atmosphere is cute and entertaining

At this popular restaurant, you'll eat in a "convertible" at a drive-in theater that shows nonstop 1950s sci-fi movie previews. In recent years, the food here has improved. Current offerings include some fun sandwiches, pan-seared tuna, and a small variety of pasta entrées. We certainly like this place more than we used to.

Shula's Steak House   Walt Disney World Dolphin
★★★★ $$$ ♥♥♥

℮ Table service, dinner only

℮ Outstanding wine list

℮ Priority seating a must

℮ Atmosphere quiet and beautiful, especially in the back room

℮ TIP: Servings here are huge. Consider sharing, especially if you have no place to bring leftovers.

Shula's was recently declared Orlando's best overall restaurant and best high-end steakhouse. What's more, it can be found on virtually any "top 10 steakhouses of the U.S." list. And for good reason. Shula's serves up steaks of the finest quality, all simply and superbly prepared. Seafood, chops, and prime rib, all without frills and all first-rate. Side dishes are so large that we suggest sharing. Don't miss the sublime potato pancake or the splendid creamed spinach. Our chocolate soufflé dessert was the perfect end to a meal that left us thinking that food just doesn't get any better than this.

If you're looking for an unforgettable dining experience and are especially interested in one that proves that dinner doesn't have to be fancy to be fantastic, Shula's is it. With unsurpassed food, impeccable service, and lovely surroundings, this restaurant doesn't miss a beat. Since there is no children's menu here at Shula's, you might wish to take advantage of two hours of free childcare while you dine (first come, first served). Ask when you make your reservations.

Shutters   Disney's Caribbean Beach Resort
★★★ $$

℮ Table service, dinner only

℮ Small wine list and full bar

Finally, Caribbean Beach has a real restaurant! A bit short on ambience, this eatery makes up for it with a creatively conceived and well-executed menu. Our recent meal here included seafood dumplings, some very tasty grilled shrimp, and a perfectly prepared tuna. From appetizers to desserts, we were very pleased. And when the check arrived, we were even happier. At Shutters' moderate prices, this is a dining experience to recommend.

Spoodles
★★★   Breakfast and Dinner $$
Disney's BoardWalk Pron

- Table service

- Beer and large Mediterranean wine list

- Priority seating for dinner suggested

- Noisy, family-style atmosphere

- TIP: Spoodles is a particularly good choice for vegetarian offerings.

We've always liked this restaurant a lot. Spoodles features a lively and delicious Mediterranean cuisine that includes imaginative wood-fired pizzas, salads, and entrées ranging from delicious stuffed Spanish peppers to Moroccan spiced tuna. We love enjoying Spoodles' "tapas-style," with its wonderful selection of appetizer-sized treats. From arugula salad and Mediterranean dips to grilled lamb and crispy calamari, the great tastes just keep coming.

Breakfast features not only a tasty selection of usual morning favorites, but also some interesting Mediterranean offerings. For our taste, it's the best breakfast menu at Disney. Chef Marianne Hunnel and her team have made this place one of our favorites for breakfast or dinner.

Tempura Kiku
★★ $$ ♥♥
Japan Pavilion, Epcot World Showcase

- Table service, lunch and dinner

- Full-service bar

- Reservations suggested

- Atmosphere is exotic and quiet

If you're at Epcot and looking for an eating adventure, this is a great choice. With fewer than thirty chairs, it is surely the smallest restaurant at Walt Disney World. It consists of three counters surrounding a compact cooking area. Chairs are comfortable, and watching the Japanese chefs practice their skillful art is engaging.

The menu includes a variety of well-prepared tempura, a lightly battered and delicately fried variety of chicken, shrimp, or vegetables. Either may be ordered individually or in a variety of combinations. Other interesting items include sushi, Kabuki beef and a chestnut mousse dessert.

Teppanyaki Dining Room
★★ Lunch $$/Dinner $$$

Japan Pavilion, Epcot
World Showcase

℮ Table service, lunch and dinner

℮ Full-service bar, Kirin beer and sake

℮ Reservations suggested during mealtimes

℮ Atmosphere is Japanese: pleasant and themed

If you have ever eaten at a Benihana's restaurant, then you will know what this experience is all about. Here at Teppanyaki, you sit at tables with other Disney guests. The center of each table is actually a cooking surface, where a Japanese chef will "perform." The chef's deft chopping and slicing skills and some knife-acrobatics are quite impressive. Entrées include shrimp, chicken, beef, and lobster, each sliced or cubed and grilled right in front of you. There are also grilled vegetables and several dipping sauces. The food is good, and the show is entertaining.

☺ *Tony's Town Square Restaurant*
★★ Lunch $$/Dinner $$$

Main Street USA,
Magic Kingdom

℮ Table service, breakfast, lunch, and dinner

℮ Priority seating a must

℮ Atmosphere is pleasant, though noisy when crowded (nearly always)

The theme here is from *Lady and the Tramp,* Disney's classic animated film. The cuisine is Italian and we think it's some of the very best food in the Magic Kingdom. Tony's dinner menu includes sauteed veal medallions, Italian roasted chicken, and a fresh catch of the day. The lunch menu is more limited to a few pasta and salad offerings. Everything here seems fresh and well-seasoned, and we would happily return for lunch or dinner. Try the outside patio in good weather or during a parade.

! *Trail's End Restaurant*
★ Breakfast and Lunch $/Dinner $$

Disney's Fort Wilderness Resort
& Campground

℮ Breakfast, lunch, and dinner: buffet and à la carte

℮ Beer and wine available

This pleasant, log-sided eatery is located near Pioneer Hall at Fort Wilderness and is quite a bargain considering both fare and price. Breakfasts feature a typical Disney buffet while both lunch and dinner buffets include a selection of ribs, fried chicken, pizza, sandwiches, a salad bar, and lots more. These are the lowest buffet prices in the land and the food is pretty decent. After a day at the Magic Kingdom, you might want to hop a boat and come out here for country cookin' with all the fixin's.

Victoria & Albert's   Disney's Grand Floridian Resort
★★★★ $$$$ ♥♥♥♥

@ Table service, dinner only, two seatings: 6 P.M. and 9 P.M.

@ Full-service bar, outstanding wine list

@ Priority seating only: make it when you book your room

@ Victorian charm and elegance come to life, a truly romantic experience

If you are looking for someplace to celebrate something special, a honeymoon, an anniversary, or simply being in love, and you are looking for a dining experience that you will remember for years to come, set your sights on Victoria & Albert's, Orlando's only Five-Diamond restaurant. Victoria & Albert's features a formal dining experience, impeccable service, and the artistry of Chef Scott Hunnel. It is a sublimely romantic experience.

Serving a limited number of guests each evening, Hunnel and his staff meticulously create imaginative and innovative dishes, using only the finest ingredients from the international marketplace: white truffle, Kobe beef, foie gras, caviar, and whatever is freshest and best. Hunnel himself picks herbs each day from his own garden on the grounds of the Grand Floridian. Each dish is served by butler-and-maid serving team "Victoria and Albert," and each is a supremely delicious masterpiece. Be it Alaskan king crab, venison tenderloin, or roasted quail, a meal here will take your dining experiences to a new level.

If you enjoy wine, we urge you to make Victoria & Albert's Royal Wine Pairing part of your dinner. Allow Sommelier Brian Koziol to select a variety of outstanding vintages to enhance each of your courses.

Guests at "V & A's" are served on Royal Doulton china, with Sambonet silver from Italy and Schott-Zwiesel crystal from Germany. During dinner, the serene music of a harpist gently fills the air. Quite literally, this is much more than your usual extraordinary dining experience.

If you desire something supremely special, consider Victoria & Albert's "Chef's Table." This beautifully appointed table is right in the kitchen and is the most sought-after dining destination in Central Florida. The Chef's Table seats only once each evening and is more relaxed than the formal dining room. Our evening there was an unforgettable gastronomic experience. We enjoyed chatting with Chef Hunnel and his team as they prepared meals crafted to our individual tastes. It was an unequalled evening of exceptional food, wonderful wine, and culinary excitement.

Make no mistake about it, Victoria & Albert's is an unforgettable experience. Expensive certainly, but worth the price. What better thing can lovers do than to create such memories?

Victoria & Albert's features a seven-course, prix fixe menu. Cost is $85 per guest and an additional $42 per guest for Royal Wine Pairing. (For more about the Chef's Table, see page 310).

! ☺ **Whispering Canyon Cafe**	Disney's Wilderness
★ Breakfast $/Lunch and Dinner $$	Lodge Resort

@ Table service, buffet, and à la carte breakfast; à la carte lunch and dinner

@ Full-service bar and specialty brews

@ Priority seating recommended

@ Wild West atmosphere is charming, entertaining, and often noisy

@ TIP: There's a cozy little area in the back by the fireplace.

Whispering Canyon's real specialty is meals served family-style. Food arrives in large pans, and it's all-you-care-to-eat. "Sunrise Samplin's" include breakfast skillets of eggs, pan-fried potatoes, breakfast meats, biscuits, waffles, and more. À la carte offerings include fresh fruit platters or light continental fare. "High Noon Offerin's" include a barbecue served family-style: chicken, ribs, fried fish, baked beans, and corn on the cob. Other choices are available à la carte and include chili, salads, smoked prime rib, burgers, grilled chicken, and a sauteed vegetable platter. Whispering Canyon's Canyon Skillet dinner is a big spread: ribs, beef, chicken, turkey leg, trail sausage, and a host of accompaniments. Dinner à la carte offerings include a vegetarian pasta, seafood, grilled meats, and a chef's special of the day. All in all, you get a decent hearty fare for a reasonable price.

! **Wolfgang Puck Cafe**	The West Side, Downtown Disney
★★★ $ to $$	

@ Table service, one menu, lunch and dinner

@ Full-service bar, outstanding wine list

@ Priority seating suggested

@ Atmosphere is lively, artful, and casual with pleasant lakeside patio

"Live, Love, Eat." It's the motto of the Wolfgang Puck Cafe, and it's just one of the things we love about this restaurant. One of the first things to know about Wolfgang's is that it is really four outstanding restaurants in one stylish package. At both Downtown Disney West Side and the Marketplace, you'll find the counter-service "Wolfgang Puck Express." Forget everything you think you know about fast food and read about the Express below. Upstairs is "The Dining Room." It's so good, we'll also cover it separately (see below). Inside and downstairs are both The Cafe and B's Bar, two of our favorite Disney dining destinations.

Besides a full-service bar, B's features the sublime artistry of sushi chef Fuji. Be sure to enjoy some Sho Chiku Bai saki while you order from the large menu of nagiri, sashimi, and maki sushi. Savor it as an appetizer or if you simply can't stop, make a meal of it.

Downstairs, The Cafe offerings include many of the dishes that have made Puck famous. The shrimp BLT club, grilled vegetable sandwich, and Fettuccini Wolf-fredo are just a few. Pizzas are memorable and include spicy shrimp, four cheese, and our personal favorite, the divine smoked-salmon pizza. Don't miss the Mezzaluna Ravioli or the squash soup. But, alas, the truth is that we've never had anything here that we didn't love. If you have an appetite for food that is imaginatively conceived and perfectly prepared, but can't see paying a small fortune for it, get thee to Wolfgang's Cafe. It's one of our favorite places to eat.

! *Wolfgang Puck Express*   **Downtown Disney West Side**
★★ $ **and Marketplace (there are two of them!)**

@ Counter service, lunch and dinner with pleasant patio seating

@ Wine available

We wish this was a coast-to-coast chain so that we could eat in one wherever we went. Simply, this is very good food served over-the-counter. We'd happily eat the Chinois Chicken Salad anytime and the pizzas are in a class by themselves. Have a salad or sandwich for lunch or enjoy the wonderful rosemary rotisserie chicken and garlic-mashed potatoes for dinner. There's more, too, and all of it is so good you'll have to look twice to believe that virtually anything on the menu is under $10. For this kind of quality, it's a real bargain. Here at Disney, it seems underpriced.

Wolfgang Puck Dining Room
★★★★ $$$ ♥♥

The West Side,
Downtown Disney Marketplace

@ Table-service dinner only

@ Full-service bar, exceptional wine list

@ Priority seating a must, especially for the Chef's Table

@ Atmosphere is casual

The market-driven menu here changes daily, so we won't bother to tell you about the heavenly spinach and ricotta ravioli or the unforgettable wild mushroom Napoleon that we enjoyed here. While these superb offerings may no longer be on the menu, we're certain that whatever creations replace them will be equally as memorable. Wolfgang Puck's culinary signature is an innovative marriage of ingredients, and the Dining Room delivers this and more with an ever-changing menu of stunning delights. Make no mistake about it, this is one of Florida's premier dining destinations. It is a place of superb service, exciting cuisine, and sheer eating enjoyment.

If you're looking for a truly exceptional dining experience, you'll want to try "The Chef's Table." During this five-course meal, you'll be doted over by a first-class team of chefs and table staff. Wolfgang's knowledgeable sommelier will present wines carefully selected for each course as you spend this evening of relaxed and casual dining entertainment. Cost for this culinary adventure is $65 per person with an additional $35 per person for wine. It seemed a bargain to us.

Yacht Club Galley
★★   Breakfast $/Lunch $$

Disney's Yacht Club Resort

@ Table service and buffet breakfast, table service lunch and dinner

@ Full-service bar

@ Reservations not required

@ Atmosphere is themed and pleasant

Most of the premium resorts feature an "all-purpose restaurant," which offers an assortment of dishes for the day's meals. We usually find ourselves comparing them all to the Yacht Club Galley. Not a fine dining spot, the Galley serves food that is well prepared, tasty, and reasonably priced. Breakfasts are either à la carte or buffet. Lunches feature a good selection of soups, salads, and sandwiches. In our many stays at the Yacht or the Beach, we have never been disappointed here.

The decor is nautical, with framed displays of knots and glass-encased models of the beautiful old J-Boats of last century's America's Cup races. Salt and pepper shakers resemble small lighthouses. This is a pleasant place to eat—not particularly memorable, but simply nice.

Yachtsman Steakhouse	Disney's Yacht Club Resort
★★★ $$$ to $$$$ ♥♥	

- Table service, dinner only

- Full-service bar

- Reservations suggested after 6:30 P.M.

- Atmosphere is warm and beautiful

From Kansas City strips to porterhouse steaks, there is the perfect cut for every taste here at the Yachtsman. And if steak is not your thing, this restaurant offers a full menu of lamb, pork, poultry, seafood, and pasta. All of it is very good.

The woody, Craftsman-style ambience of the Yachtsman Steakhouse makes it a charming and romantic place to dine. Like the menu, the decor here is simple yet elegant. We highly recommend this restaurant.

Gee, We Didn't Know We Could Do That at Disney World!

If you think Walt Disney World is just a bunch of theme parks, we've got news for you! Even without the theme parks, Walt Disney World would probably still be the "Vacation Capital of the World." Here at Disney, you'll find a luxurious world of pampering spas, a fascinating array of behind-the-scenes tours, and enough sports to satisfy even the most die-hard enthusiast.

Disney's mind-boggling assortment of recreational offerings includes parasailing, waterskiing, surfing, and world-class golf, to mention only a few. Ride a bike or a horse; take a sail or a cruise; fish for bass or take a private carriage ride. You can even take a few laps around the Walt Disney World Speedway at 135 miles per hour. Outside the theme parks, there's a whole other world of Disney magic, and it's one of excitement, discovery, and fun.

This chapter is dedicated to those things you might not have known were available at Walt Disney World. We urge you to mix your theme park adventures with some of this fun and relaxation. It will get you out of the crowds and into more vacation-like settings. We promise it will make for a more leisurely and memorable time. Note that all prices include Florida's 6½ percent sales tax.

Parasailing, Waterskiing, and Jet-Skis at Sammy Duvall's Watersports

Ready for Disney's highest attraction? The Tower of Terror? Not even close. At 199 feet, it's a mere bump in the road compared to parasailing at Sammy Duvall's Watersports. We found floating under a parachute 450 feet above Bay Lake (higher than the Contemporary) to be quiet, peaceful, and beautiful (not to mention thrilling). In fact, our morning soaring over Disney, waterskiing, and tubing with Sammy Duvall was as much fun as we've ever had at Walt Disney World.

A parasailing adventure costs $90.52 for a single and $143.78 for tandem for ten minutes aloft. You'll have more fun than you can imagine and, we can tell you from our own experiences, this is the perfect complement to a theme park vacation. Cost for waterskiing is $85.20 for half an hour or $149.10 per hour for the boat, with five guests max.

NEW This year, Sammy Duvall's has added personal water craft (jet-skis) to really jack up the fun level on the waters of Disney. Cost is $69.23 per half hour, $106.50 per hour. Discounts are available through AAA, Annual Pass, and Disney Vacation Club membership. So, if getting wet and having a great time is your idea of vacation, call Sammy Duvall's to get in on this fun. This franchise is operated by world-caliber instructors who use state-of-the-art equipment to ensure that your watersports activities are both exciting and safe. Reservations are recommended. Call (407) WDW-PLAY (939-0754) or dial 57 on your resort room phone.

Money-Saving Tip

Annual pass holders and Disney Vacation Club members get a 10 percent discount at Sammy Duvall's Watersports.

Learn to Surf at Typhoon Lagoon's Craig Carroll's Surf School

Learn to surf the big ones when they crank up the waves at Typhoon Lagoon. This class includes both dry-land and big-wave instruction before this water park opens. Available to Disney resort guests only, this course is offered on Tuesdays, from 6:30 A.M. to 9:00 A.M., and costs $125 per person. Classes are limited to fourteen. For reservations, call (407) WDW-PLAY (939-7529) or dial 57 on your resort room phone. Students must be at least 8 years old and strong swimmers.

Disney's Ultimate Speed Trip: The Richard Petty Driving Experience

Ready for something much faster than Test Track, where *you* get to drive? At the Disney Speedway, you'll have the choice of riding in a real race car at 145 miles per hour or driving one yourself, at speeds well over 100 miles per hour. Riders must be at least 16 years old and drivers at least 18.

An annual or premium annual pass or Florida residency will provide a 10 percent discount. The three driving programs involve time in the classroom as well as on the track. Plan on spending three to four hours. The ride-along program is currently offered on a walk-in basis, but other offers require reservations. Call the Richard Petty Driving Experience at (800) BE-PETTY (237-3889).

The Richard Petty Driving Experience also has a merchandise shop with logo hats, polo shirts, and T-shirts, as well as an assortment of model race cars and novelties. Chips and sodas are available at the track, but if you plan on being there all day, we suggest having your resort prepare box lunches for you. Prices include tax.

Ride-Along Program

Take a three-lap, 145-mile per hour spin in a two-seater stock car. No reservation necessary, and rides begin at 9 A.M. daily, seven days a week. Cost is $94.77.

Rookie Experience

Take the wheel for eight laps around the track at 125 miles per hour. Cost is $371.69.

The Kings Experience

This is an eighteen-lap, two-session program at 125 miles per hour. Cost is $744.44.

Experience of a Lifetime

This thirty-lap program includes three ten-lap sessions. Cost is $1,276.94. Speeds reached are in excess of 130 miles per hour.

The Spas of Walt Disney World ♥♥♥

After a day in the parks or an afternoon of recreational activity, you'll be ready for this. We guarantee it. One spa treatment was all it took to convince us that this is the stuff of dream vacations. For us, these pampering treatments not only feel great, but they leave us both with an enhanced sense of relaxation and sensuality. From our own experiences, we can tell you that just one treatment will get you both in the perfect mood for your romantic escape. We urge you to consider indulging yourselves, even if for just a short treatment

Walt Disney World is home to three spas, and each has its own specialties and character. All are designed to enrapture guests with a soothing blend of colors, music, and mood, and all three feature steam rooms, whirlpool baths, plush locker rooms, and comfortable lounges. Spa treatments fall loosely into several categories: massage therapies, skin and body treatments, and water therapies. There are many massage techniques: Swedish, shiatsu, reflexology, and sports massage are the most common. Water therapies might mean a hydrotherapy massage, a mineral bath, or an exotic soak. Skin treatments include facials, body masques, seaweed wraps, aromatherapies, and body polishing. There are even hand and foot treatments. These may sound unusual, but all of them relieve tension, leave you feeling utterly pampered, and will bring your senses wonderfully to life. Spa treatments are not just for women. All of the Disney World spas feature wonderful treatments designed for men.

Another feature of spas is the expense. Treatments usually cost from $60 to about $150, depending on choice and length. We think this kind of pampering is what vacations are all about. More than merely self-indulgent, the spa experience is about relieving stress, soothing sore muscles, and promoting well-being. We warn you: once you start, you won't want to stop. This stuff is deliciously habit-forming.

Each of the spas has a health and fitness center with the very latest in exercise equipment. All spas provide a variety of à la carte treatments and day or half-day packages. Gift certificates are available, and knowledgeable reservationists are waiting to help you plan your spa experience.

The Grand Floridian Spa and Health Club

Florida is the theme of this elegant spa, and simply walking in the door will immerse you in the heavenly smells of its custom-formulated, citrus-based spa and skin products. We are hooked on the spa's ruby-red grapefruit bath gel. Comfortable treatment rooms and luxurious lounges, complete with signature robes and slippers, herbal teas, and world-class amenities, make this the perfect addition to the exquisite Grand Floridian resort. Facilities and service here are first-class, and the ambience is exceptionally intimate and personal. This spa is run by Niki Bryan Spas.

Offerings include a couple's massage room ♥♥♥ with romance aromatherapy massages, "My First Facial" for young guests, a gentleman's facial, a Secret Garden Bath, soothing tired-legs treatment, a post-sports package, and an anti-stress collection. There's even a soothing aloe wrap for sunburns. We could spend a whole vacation here. Ask about the spa's Grand Romance Evening for Two, which includes three hours of massage and instruction.

This spa is popular, so make your plans before you arrive at Walt Disney World, especially from Thanksgiving through April. For more information or to reserve your Grand Floridian spa experience, call (407) 824-2332.

The Spa at Disney's Saratoga Springs Resort and Spa

When this spa was originally built for the now-defunct Disney Institute, no expense was spared in creating it. From aerobics pool, gymnasium, and Cybex fitness center to the well-appointed and spacious lounges and treatment rooms, this spa is the very definition of "state of the art." Offering Phytomer beauty products, Sothys skin treatments, and the Aromatherapy Associates line of aromatherapies, this spa knows what it takes to please.

The wonderful "menu" here has such treatments as a half-day men's program, deluxe seaweed program, after-sports body therapy, European facials, French body polish, and aromatherapy hydro-massage.

To get the treatment you desire, we suggest reserving well in advance. For more information or to make arrangements, call The Spa at Disney's Saratoga Springs Resort at (407) 827-4455. Don't forget to inquire about the spa lunch.

The Spa and Fitness Center at the Wyndham Palace

It only follows that this elegant and luxurious hotel, located across the street from Downtown Disney, would offer its guests a full-service, European-style spa. This spa offers not only a line of extraordinary treatments and a modern fitness center, but also a first-class hair salon. This whole package is located in a separate part of the resort and features a private lap pool, outdoor whirlpools, specialized treatment rooms, and a wonderful spa cuisine.

Whether you are looking for herbal body wraps, warm stone massage, relaxing massages, soothing aromatherapies, or rejuvenating facials, you'll find it all here. The Spa at the Wyndham Palace offers the full line of luxurious and natural Pevonia Botanical and EcoCare products. For more information or to arrange your blissful time here, call (800) 827-3200.

Our Recommendations for the Spas of Disney

ℯ Arrive at least thirty minutes early to relax in the spa's steam rooms and whirlpool baths.

ℯ A single treatment will give you the whole day's use of the spa's fitness center.

ℯ Enjoy aromatherapy romance oil massages ♥♥♥♥ together in the couple's treatment room at The Grand Floridian Spa. We suggest you set aside a few hours afterward, too.

ℯ The aromatherapy massage and seaweed facial at The Spa at Disney's Saratoga Springs Resort & Spa are exceptional.

ℯ The Spa at the Wyndham Palace offers some very well-priced packages. Check them out.

ℯ Men: This is not just for women!

ℯ Call to ask for a brochure from each spa to see the full array of treatments.

Hit the Links at Disney for World-Class Golf

No matter how you slice it, Disney world is a golfer's paradise. With 99 holes of championship PGA-level golf and over 20,000 resort rooms, Walt Disney World is the largest golf resort in the world. Disney's six courses present unique challenges to both amateur and professional. There are five eighteen-hole championship courses and Oak Trail, a nine-hole executive course. All are open to the public and, as Disney resort guests, you'll get discounted green fees and preferred tee times.

Green fees at the five championship courses vary by the course and with the three Disney golf seasons. From the beginning of October to mid-January, green fees range from $100 at the Palm or Lake Buena Vista courses to $130 at Osprey Ridge. The most expensive season is from mid-January through May, with green fees ranging from $129 to $174. From May to the end of September is value season. Green fees during these months range from $109 to $144. Green fees at Disney now include a bucket of pre-round practice balls (a $7 value).

$ Disney offers discounts of up to 40 percent for tee times after 10 A.M., with prices ranging from $45 to $65 during value season. A real bargain. There are also after 3 P.M. twilight rates, from $60 to $80 and even further discounted after 3 P.M. rates. Twilight rates, however, do not include the free bucket of practice balls.

$ If you are a Florida resident or a member of the Disney Vacation Club, you can purchase an Annual Golf Membership Badge. For the $50 annual fee, you get play after 10 A.M. on any of the five eighteen-hole Disney courses, for $50 to $70 a round, depending on the season. Good for a year and available at any of the Disney pro shops, this badge is a great deal if you plan to play even twice.

The six Disney courses are located at three different locations around Walt Disney World. Both Osprey Ridge and Eagle Pines can be found at the Bonnet Creek Golf Club, while the Palm, the Magnolia, and Oak Trail are located at Shades of Green. The Lake Buena Vista course is near the Saratoga Springs Resort. Here are the links, rated in order of difficulty by pros of the PGA:

@ Osprey Ridge (6,680 yards, designed by Tom Fazio)—Rated by the pros as the toughest course here at Disney, this course has elevations that are not at all typical of central Florida. Osprey Ridge does not double-back on itself. It just takes off into the woods. Tom Fazio himself considers this one of his best courses.

@ The Palm (6,461 yards, designed by Joe Lee)—The eighteenth hole here has been rated the fourth toughest on the PGA Tour.

@ The Magnolia (6,642 yards, designed by Joe Lee)—This course has the Disney signature "Mousetrap" on its sixth hole. The final round of the Funai Classic is played here.

@ Eagle Pines (6,309 yards, designed by Pete Dye)—This low-profile course features dished instead of crowned fairways. Relatively flat, this course has no grass for rough.

@ Lake Buena Vista (6,268 yards, designed by Joe Lee)—This is a fairly short, wide-open course. Hole 16 is called the "Intimidator."

@ Oak Trail (executive course, 2,913 yards, designed by Joe Lee)—No electric carts are allowed on this course, and golfers are allowed to carry their own bags.

Logistics

Tee times may be reserved up to sixty days in advance by Disney resort guests and thirty days ahead by day guests. These courses are busy during the peak seasons, and we strongly suggest that you arrange your tee times if you want to play early in the day. For tee times and information about any of the six courses, call (407) WDW-PLAY (939-7529), (407) 939-4653, or dial 57 on your resort room phone.

Club and shoe rentals are available at all six courses and are about $55 per round for men's clubs ($45 for women's) and $7 a round for shoes. Rental clubs here are top-of-the-line Titleist.

Insider's Secret

Golf Magazine has rated Osprey Ridge as one of the top 10 resort courses in the U.S.

Transportation to the Disney Golf Courses

Complimentary transportation to any of the Disney golf courses is free from any of the Disney resorts. This does not include the Swan, the Dolphin, and the hotels on Hotel Plaza Boulevard. To make arrangements at a Disney resort, notify Bell Services of your tee times, and they will provide you with a taxi voucher. Try to give them a day's notice.

Our Recommendations for Golf

@ The Funai Classic takes place in mid-October. Guests are advised not to schedule play during this time.

@ Shirts with collars are required at all Disney courses.

@ We suggest that you arrange tee times sixty days in advance, especially from February through Easter.

@ Private golf lessons are available for $50 per half hour. Call WDW-PLAY for details and reservations.

Play Miniature Golf, Disney Style

We didn't think miniature golf would go over well at Disney. How wrong we were. Walt Disney World's first miniature golf attraction was so popular, a second popped up a year later. Of course, these aren't your run-of-the-mill miniature golf courses. They've been created by Disney, and that means they're little masterpieces of theming and entertainment.

Fantasia Gardens and Fantasia Fairways are located right next door to The Swan. Together, these courses provide a total miniature golf experience. One is an amusing bit of fun, the other an innovative and challenging putting course. Both feature comical scenes and bigger-than-life characters from Disney's animated classic, *Fantasia*.

Winter Summerland is Disney's newest miniature course and it's right next door to Blizzard Beach. This zany, elf-sized course features one eighteen-hole course of holiday-themed sun and sand, and another of a wacky, snow-clad Florida.

All courses are open from about 10 A.M. to 11 P.M., depending on the season, and admission is about $10 ($8 for ages 3 to 9). The second round is half price. At each area, you'll find logo merchandise and a small selection of snacks and beverages.

Money-Saving Tip

An Annual Passport will deliver a 50% discount off one admission to Disney miniature golf.

Tennis at Walt Disney World

There are so many tennis courts around Walt Disney World that you might think it's a tennis resort. Located around "The World," you'll have little trouble finding a convenient court. Tennis lessons are available at the Contemporary courts. For information and reservations, call WDW-PLAY (939-7529) or dial 57 on your room phone.

Play on Disney resort courts is free and on a first-come, first-served basis. However, you'll have to bring your own equipment. Most courts are open from 8 A.M. to 6 P.M., and all courts are lighted. Here's what's available:

- ℮ The Contemporary features six hydrogrid clay courts.

- ℮ The Grand Floridian has two clay courts.

- ℮ The Yacht & Beach Clubs have one court.

- ℮ $ Fort Wilderness has two courts, open 8 A.M. to 7 P.M., which are available to all Disney resort guests. Rental racquets are available at the Bike Barn. No reservations.

- ℮ $ Old Key West has two courts, open twenty-four hours. Use is complimentary for registered guests of Old Key West on a first-come, first-serve basis. Rental equipment is available at Hank's.

- ℮ $ The Swan and the Dolphin share four tennis courts. Open from 8 A.M. to 11 P.M. Use is complimentary to guests of these resorts.

- ℮ $ Shades of Green has two tennis courts. Open from dawn until 10 P.M. Use is complimentary for guests of the resort. No reservations.

- ℮ $ The BoardWalk has two courts, open twenty-four hours. Use is free to all BoardWalk guests. Equipment rentals are available at Community Hall.

Take a Fireworks Cruise ♥♥♥♥

Disney offers a variety of boat trips that will take you out on the water to view the evening fireworks show at either Epcot or the Magic Kingdom. These pontoon boat adventures can accommodate up to twelve people. Cost is $127.80 for a fifty-minute voyage with driver, and a variety of food options are available, beginning at $200 for four people (cruise included). Unfortunately, fireworks cruises are so popular that you'll have to pick your date and reserve exactly ninety days ahead by calling (407) WDW-PLAY (939-7529). A credit card guarantee is required and cancellations must be at least twenty-four hours prior to departure time.

Take a "Specialty" Cruise

Disney pontoon boats with drivers are available for picnics, birthdays, anniversaries, family reunions, or just for fun. A birthday cruise, for example, could accommodate up to twelve and includes a cake, nonalcoholic beverages, and party decorations. Cost would be $234.30 and a deposit is required. Cruises can begin as early as noon.

A more extravagant offering is the Grand Floridian's 48-foot luxury motor yacht, The Grand One ♥♥♥♥. Available for daytime crewed charters, for evening dinner cruises, and for fireworks voyages, this classy vessel can accommodate up to sixteen guests at a cost of $350 per hour. This lavish boat would make the perfect setting for a romantic dinner or fireworks cruise. We've even heard of it being used for proposals of marriage.

Reservations for all cruises must be made in advance and cancellations must be made twenty-four hours prior to cruise time. For information and reservations, call (407) WDW-PLAY (939-7529) or dial 57 on your resort room phone. For reservations and more information about The Grand One, call (407) 824-2439.

Take a *Breathless* Cruise ♥♥♥♥

There are a few really special things that you can do on the waters of Disney. The most enchanting is to take a ride aboard Breathless, the Yacht Club's replica 1933 Chris Craft speedboat. With flawless varnishwork and shiny chrome fittings, this classic wooden speedboat belongs to an age long past. A half-hour cruise with driver is $85 for up to five passengers, and for $25 you can enjoy a ten-minute "Breathless Glide." Cruises begin at 2 P.M. and continue into the evening hours. The most memorable Breathless cruise, however, is to IllumiNations. For $190, this beautiful motor yacht ♥♥♥♥ will take you over to the World Showcase Lagoon to view Epcot's nightly fireworks spectacular. Truly romantic and absolutely unforgettable, this is the quintessential experience for any special occasion.

We must warn you that the Breathless IllumiNations cruise has become extremely popular. Decide when you wish to do it and call exactly ninety days in advance of that date. All arrangements for Breathless can be made through (407) WDW-PLAY (939-7529).

Around "The World" by Boat

One of our favorite things to do at Walt Disney World is to go boating. Despite the fact that we have our own little fleet, we simply love boating around Disney. It's fun and gives an interesting perspective on this fabulous place.

A variety of rental craft are available nearly anywhere there's a body of water. Most marina rental areas open at 10 A.M. and stay open until dusk. You don't have to be staying at Disney to use these watercraft.

Marina Rental Locations at Walt Disney World

The Seven Seas Lagoon and Bay Lake:
- The Contemporary
- The Polynesian
- The Grand Floridian
- The Wilderness Lodge
- Fort Wilderness

Lake Buena Vista and its connecting waterways:
- Cap'n Jack's Marina at Downtown Disney Marketplace
- Old Key West
- Port Orleans Riverside

Crescent Lake:
- The Yacht and the Beach Clubs
- The Swan and the Dolphin (swan paddleboats only and not on Crescent Lake)

Barefoot Bay at the Caribbean Beach

Lago Dorado at Disney's Coronado Springs

Watercraft Rental Prices

All boats are not available at all locations. To locate the kind of boat you are interested in, call (407) WDW-PLAY (939-7529). While prices and hourly minimums may vary slightly from marina to marina, the following will give you an idea of what it costs to rent a watercraft:

- Water Mouse (two-person mini "speed" boat): about $23 per half hour, $32 an hour
- Pedal boats, rowboats, and canoes: about $7 per half hour
- Kayaks: $7 to $10 per hour
- Sailboats: about $20 per hour
- Hobie Cats (only at the Polynesian): $24 per half hour
- Canopy boats: $25 per half hour
- Pontoon boats (Flote boats), ten-person: about $37 per half hour

The Captains Plan
and the Family Recreation Plan

These plans are offered at every resort that features boat rentals. The Captains Plan is around $123 and provides four hours of boating for up to five people and even includes certain motorboats. For about $212, the Family Recreation Plan will give up to five guests unlimited use of motorboats, sailboats, and bikes for length of stay. It's a real deal if you are staying for more than a few days and plan to make use of the recreation.

Our Recommendations for Boat Rentals

- The Seven Seas Lagoon and Bay Lake are the best places to rent a boat. Since these two bodies of water connect, they provide the largest area to explore. If you are not staying in one of the resorts here, simply go and rent the boat of your choice at any of the marinas listed at the Seven Seas Lagoon or Bay Lake.

Insider's Secret
With more than five hundred vessels, Walt Disney World has the world's largest fleet of rental boats.

Money-Saving Tip
There is a 15 percent discount on hourly boat rentals with annual pass (does not include recreation plans or specialty cruises).

Biking Around Disney

Not just for exercise, but fun, too. Bikes can be rented at Fort Wilderness, the Wilderness Lodge, Old Key West, Port Orleans Riverside, the BoardWalk, Caribbean Beach, Saratoga Springs, and Coronado Springs. Rates are pretty much the same everywhere, around $8 per hour or $22 a day, and the variety includes men's, women's, children's, tandems, and bicycles with child carriers. Most rental shops open around 10 A.M. and close around sunset.

The BoardWalk, Caribbean Beach, Port Orleans Riverside, Coronado Springs, Wilderness Lodge, and Old Key West offer some really unique biking with their surrey quadri-cycles. These four-wheeled, carriage-like cycles are some of the most fun we've ever had pedaling. Available for two, four, or six persons, rentals start at $18 per half hour. Surrey rentals at the BoardWalk continue late into the evening.

Our Recommendations for Cycling

@ Try one of the surrey quadri-cycles. They're simply too much fun to miss!

@ Rent your bikes at the Wilderness Lodge and ride around the lake to Fort Wilderness. Continue on to the Fort Wilderness Swamp Trail Nature Path for some real scenery.

@ The best biking areas: Old Key West and Wilderness Lodge/Fort Wilderness

☀Private, Evening Horse-Drawn Carriage Ride ♥♥

There are currently two places at Disney for this, Port Orleans Riverside and Fort Wilderness. Carriages can accommodate up to four persons and cost $30 for a thirty-minute ride. We suggest you book ahead by calling (407) WDW-PLAY (939-7529).

Walt Disney World Fishing Excursions

There's something fishy here at Disney. Decades ago, the lakes and waterways of Walt Disney World were stocked with thousands of fingerling bass. Here and throughout central Florida, bass fishing has become world famous, and guided fishing trips are available in a number of places around Disney World. Trips on Bay Lake, Lake Buena Vista, and on Crescent Lake all last two hours, accommodate up to five persons, and cost between $180 and $210, depending on the time of day. Excursions are early morning, mid-morning, and afternoon. Trips include guide, gear, and beverages. Reservations must be made in advance; trips may be canceled due to inclement weather. All fishing excursions are catch-and-release only.

For something simpler, try the Ol' Fishin' Hole at Port Orleans Riverside, cane pole fishing at Captain Jack's Marina in Downtown Disney, or the Coronado Springs for $4 per half hour ($13 for the whole family,) or head out to the Fort Wilderness Bike Barn, rent a cane pole for about $4 a day or a rod and reel for $8 a day, and fish the many waterways there. You can even rent a canoe and make a day of it.

Helpful Hint

Fishing excursions are very popular; be sure to book yours early by calling (407) WDW-PLAY (407-939-7529).

The Grand Floridian Children's Activities (available to any Disney visitor)

Let Your Kids Sail with the Pirates on the Pirate Cruise

Let your kids sail with Disney's pirate crew in search of treasure on the Seven Seas Lagoon. The ninety-minute adventure costs $25 per child and the voyage departs from the Grand Floridian on Mondays, Wednesdays, and Thursdays, 10 A.M. to 12 P.M. Snacks are included. For reservations, call (407) WDW-DINE (939-3463).

Children's Wonderland Tea Party

Hosted by characters from Alice in Wonderland on Monday to Friday, from 1:15 P.M. to 2:30 P.M., this marvelous tea party is for children ages 3 to 10, and includes stories, lunch, and "apple" tea. Cost is $25 per child. For reservations, call (407) WDW-DINE (939-3463).

The Perfectly Princess Tea

This children's tea party takes place at the Grand Floridian and will include tea, snacks, and a visit from one of the Disney princesses (Snow White, Cinderella, Pocahontas, or others). The party includes a beautiful, keepsake princess doll. Hours and price have yet to be announced. For details, call (407) WDW-DINE (939-3463).

Jogging and Walking Around The World

Nearly every resort offers a jogging or walking path. Check with the guest services at your resort for a map. Some of our favorite paths include the ones at the Yacht and Beach Clubs, the Swan and the Dolphin area, the Wilderness Lodge to Fort Wilderness area, the Wilderness Swamp Trail, Port Orleans, and a long circuit around the Polynesian and the Grand Floridian. There are also especially nice paths at Old Key West, Coronado Springs, and the Caribbean Beach as well. Walking and jogging have become national pastimes, and the folks at Disney have been paying attention.

Horsin' Around at Walt Disney World

The Fort Wilderness Trail Ride departs daily from the Tri-Circle-D Ranch Livery and Trail Blaze Corral, located near the parking area to Fort Wilderness. The horses are Arabians and Appaloosas but the pace is very slow. It's really a horseback walk. No galloping is allowed.

Cost is about $34 per person. Children under age 9 are not permitted, and there is a 250-pound weight limit. Reservations are a good idea, especially during the summer months. Call (407) WDW-PLAY (939-7529).

Horseback Riding Tips

@ Wear long pants and don't bring along things such as cameras and pocketbooks. Horses don't have back seats or glove compartments.

@ The ride lasts about forty-five minutes and times vary with the season.

@ For experienced riders, this isn't much of a ride. But novices will enjoy it, perhaps even catching a glimpse of the Fort Wilderness wildlife: deer, birds, and maybe even a gator.

Getting Backstage

Walt Disney World offers a variety of behind-the-scenes tours and interesting programs that are not widely publicized. One will have you exploring the tunnels under the Magic Kingdom and another, swimming with the Dolphins in Epcot's Living Seas. All are entertaining and enlightening. For more details and to arrange this special Disney experience, call (407) WDW-TOUR (939-8687).

Insider's Secret

Reservations should be made at least six weeks in advance, except those for Backstage Magic, which should be made two months in advance.

Money-Saving Tip

Ten percent discounts on Disney tours are given to Annual Pass holders.

Backstage Safari

Go behind the scenes at Disney's Animal Kingdom and see the food-handling areas, nighttime animal houses, and the veterinary hospital during this three-hour walking tour. Sorry, you won't see animals on this tour. $65 per person plus park admission. Monday, Wednesday, Thursday, and Friday.

Backstage Magic

Look behind the scenes at Disney's theme parks during this all-day, seven-hour tour. Explore the Utilidor tunnels under the Magic Kingdom, examine the backstage control systems of rides, visit the Disney repair shop, and much more. Monday through Friday at 9 A.M.; $199 per person. Reservations must be made at least two months in advance. Includes lunch.

Hidden Treasures of World Showcase

This three-and-a-half-hour walking tour explores Epcot in search of its many hidden surprises, architectural curiosities, and art. Offered on Tuesdays and Thursdays; $59 per person plus theme park admission.

Gardens of the World

Offered on Tuesday through Thursday, this three-hour program is an in-depth study of the landscaping and gardens of Epcot. The perfect experience for gardening enthusiasts. $59 per person.

Keys to the Kingdom

Learn the lore, magic, and trivia of the Magic Kingdom on this daily four-and-a-half-hour walking tour. Go backstage, into the tunnel system, and to the Disney wardrobe area. $58 per person, plus theme park admission. Very popular.

Epcot DiveQuest

This daily diving experience will take you into the Living Seas' six-million-gallon aquarium. Swim with turtles, tropical fish, and sharks. $140 per person. Theme park admission not required, but proof of current open water scuba certification is necessary.

Disney's Dolphins in Depth

This three-and-a-half-hour program is available Monday through Friday and is conducted at the Living Seas in Epcot. This hands-on encounter with dolphins costs $150 per person (theme park admission not required). Guests under 18 years of age must be accompanied by an adult.

The Undiscovered Future World

Tour all Future World pavilions during this four-and-a-half-hour walking tour and learn the vision of each, look behind the scenes, visit the Epcot VIP lounge, and get an up-close look at the Epcot marina where fireworks barges are stored. $49 per person; Mondays, Tuesdays, Fridays, and Saturdays.

The Magic Behind Our Steam Trains

Explore Walt's passion for trains and see how the steam trains at Magic Kingdom are prepared for their day's work. A two-hour walking tour. Mondays through Thursdays. Cost is $30 per person and the minimum age is 10 years old.

Disney's Family Magic Tour

Not really a tour, but a scavenger hunt in the Magic Kingdom. Park admission is required for this two-hour walking program. Cost is $25 per guest.

Disney's Yuletide Fantasy

This three-hour program is offered seasonally. Participants "unwrap" the magical themes of Disney yuletide decorations at various locations around "The World." Cost is $59 per person.

Wild by Design

This three hour program focuses on the Animal Kingdom and the creation of its art and architecture. Cost is $58 per person, and theme park admission is also required. A light continental breakfast is included, and guests must be at least 14 years old. The program is offered on Tuesdays, Thursdays, and Fridays.

Disney's Wide World of Sports Complex

The first time we visited this 200-acre sports complex, the mission-style architecture and Florida landscaping made us feel like we were in 1950s Southern California. We had expected throngs of people crowded onto noisy fields and into packed stadiums, but found something completely different.

The pale yellow, tile-roofed buildings of Disney's Wide World of Sports are perfectly placed amid acres of lush green playing fields. Footpaths lined with tall palms crisscross in perfect symmetry from field house to stadium to playing areas. This may be one of the world's state-of-the-art sports facilities, but it's also a place of quiet beauty.

The Wide World of Sports features a huge variety of spectator sports as well as a training facility for amateur and professional athletes. There are also programs for Disney guests, such as the Multi-Sports Experience and a variety of sports training programs that are scheduled throughout the year.

Disney's Wide World of Sports includes a 7,000-seat baseball stadium, a six-court basketball field house, four soccer fields, a softball quadriplex, four youth baseball fields, a track-and-field complex, a velodrome, eleven ISP clay courts, three major league baseball fields, and locker and training facilities for all regimens.

The Wide World of Sports is the spring training home of the Atlanta Braves and home for the O-Rays, Orlando's minor league baseball team. This facility also hosts countless athletic events each year, including the annual WDW Marathon (January), the Cincinnati Bengals Mini-Camp (April), ACC Men and Women's Track and Field Championships, the NFL Quarterback Challenge (May), and major league soccer all-stars (July). There are championship events in nearly every sport for both amateur and collegiate athletics, everything from martial arts and lacrosse to fast pitch softball.

Helpful Hint

Spend your last morning at the All-Sports Experience and save paying for a full day's theme park admission.

The Multi-Sports Experience

This "training camp" is open only when there is an event going on at Wide World of Sports. It is designed to help participants sharpen their skills in virtually every popular sport: football, basketball, baseball, softball, hockey, and soccer. From place kicking to pitching, this fun place has a lot to offer anyone who likes to participate in sports.

Disney's Wide World of Sports and the Multi-Sports Experience are open only when there are events scheduled. To find out what is happeing during your visit, call (407) 828-FANS (3267) or check the complex's Web site at www .disneyworldsports.com.

Helpful Hint

To find out what sports events are featured at Disney Wide World of Sports Complex during your visit, visit their Web site at www .disneyworldsports.com.

All-Star Cafe

Wide World of Sports is also home to this sports-themed restaurant. The menu features a selection of salads, sandwiches, and burgers. For more information, see page 313.

Getting to the Wide World of Sports

If you're driving, you'll need a map to find this place (available at guest services in your resort), which is located right off of the Osceola Parkway in the south-central part of Disney World. If you are a guest in one of the Disney resorts, just take a bus from Disney-MGM Studios.

Admission to Disney's Wide World of Sports

General admission to Disney Wide World of Sports costs around $10 ($8 for children) and is included in both the Ultimate Park Hopper Pass and Premium Annual Passes. Admission to special events such as Atlanta Braves or O-Ray games is not included.

Other Sports Offerings Around Walt Disney World

Some of the Disney resorts feature special sports that are not found elsewhere.

- ℮ Basketball: Old Key West, Fort Wilderness, Contemporary, and the Swan and the Dolphin

- ℮ Croquet: the Yacht and Beach Clubs, the BoardWalk

- ℮ Volleyball: Caribbean Beach, Typhoon Lagoon, Beach Club, Contemporary, Coronado Springs, Wilderness Lodge, Swan & Dolphin, Old Key West

- ℮ Horseshoes: Fort Wilderness

Keeping Fit at Disney

@ The Fitness Center at the Saratoga Springs Resort and Spa is in a class by itself. Along with the luxurious spa facilities, guests here are treated to Cybex equipment that is still in development: video exercise games, computerized training gear, and a weight room. A day of access to this fitness center is complimentary if you are having a spa treatment. Day guests and Disney resort guests pay $15 per day, $35 for length of stay, and $50 for family length of stay. For information, call (407) 827-4455.

@ Wyndham Palace Spa and Fitness Center is another superb facility. This facility features Life Fitness and Reebok equipment, and one-on-one training. Reebok Sky Walkers and Life Fitness Entertainment Cycles are highlighted. Palace guests may use the facilities for free and non-Palace guests pay $20 daily. For details, call (407) 827-3200.

@ The health centers at the Grand Floridian, Yacht and Beach Clubs, BoardWalk, Contemporary, Animal Kingdom Lodge, The Villas at the Wilderness Lodge, and Coronado Springs are all operated by Niki Bryan Spas. At the Grand Floridian is the Grand Floridian Spa; at Yacht and Beach Clubs, you'll find the Ship Shape Health Club; at BoardWalk it's Muscles and Bustles; at the Contemporary, it's the Olympiad Health Club; at the Animal Kingdom, you'll find Zahanati Fitness Center; at Wilderness Lodge, it's Sturdy Branches; and there's La Vida Health Club at Coronado. These clubs are available to all Disney resort guests at a cost of $15 per day, $25 for individual length of stay, and $45 for family length of stay. Massages are available by appointment only, and all clubs have the latest in Nautilus and LifeCycle equipment. Personal training is by appointment, and tanning beds are available at BoardWalk, Coronado Springs, and the Contemporary. Only the Grand Floridian Spa, the Ship Shape Health Club, and Zahanati Fitness Center feature an indoor hot tub and sauna. For more information, call (407) 824-2332 (Grand Floridian Spa); (407) 934-3256 (Ship Shape Health Club); (407) 939-2370 (Muscles and Bustles); (407) 824-3410 (Olympiad Health Club); (407) 938-3000 (Zahanati Fitness Center); (407) 938-4222 (Sturdy Branches); and (407) 939-3030 (La Vida Health Club).

@ Body by Jake is the Dolphin's health club. With a complete selection of Polaris equipment, a coed Jacuzzi, saunas, an array of personal training, massages, and water aerobics, Jake's is a complete fitness center, available at no cost for all guests of the Dolphin. Hours vary seasonally.

@ The Health Club at the Swan is a modern facility with exercise equipment, Sprint weight systems, and a sauna. Use of this facility is complimentary with a stay at the Swan.

@ R.E.S.T. Fitness Center at Old Key West offers a fairly complete exercise room, and use of it is complimentary to guests and club members. Facilities include a coed steam room, whirlpool bath, and Nautilus equipment.

@ Shades of Green and all of the hotels along Hotel Plaza (except the Best Western) have fitness rooms with a variety of exercise equipment. All are available to resort guests of each hotel.

$ Hunt for Bargain Character Merchandise

This isn't exactly at Walt Disney World, but if you have access to a car, you'll certainly be interested in the discount Disney merchandise (mostly clothing) available at the Character Warehouse and at Character Premier. These two Disney stores are located in Belz Outlet Center in Orlando, and sell last year's character and logo merchandise at bargain prices. Items that sold last year for $36 might be found here for $15. You never know what you'll find, but at these prices, you're sure to see something.

To get there, take I-4 East (to Orlando) to International Drive. Take a left at the light and follow International Drive to the end. Look for Mall #2, with two towers, for the Character Warehouse. Character Premier is next door, in Mall #1.

The Disney Vacation Club: Own a Piece of Walt Disney World

Love Disney so much you'd like to own a little piece of it? The Disney Vacation Club provides the perfect opportunity. To become a member, you first purchase a real-estate interest in the club. This provides a yearly allotment of points, which you can use for a vacation in any of the club's Walt Disney World properties (or many of the Disney resorts, if you prefer). You can also choose to vacation at a selection of first-class accommodations around the world.

Disney Vacation Club members get some inviting priveleges at the Walt Disney World Resort, among them 10 percent discount on admission, free video rentals, free use of health and fitness centers, and a discount on such Disney recreation as golf and boat and bike rentals. The club's 70,000 members rave about the Disney Vacation Club and say it's a great deal for any family that takes regular vacations, especially ones at Walt Disney World. We'd have to agree: It looks awfully inviting.

For more information, call (800) 500-3990, stop by one of the many Disney Vacation Club desks (there's one at every resort and every theme park) throughout Walt Disney World, or visit the club's Web site at www.DisneyVacationClub.com.

CHAPTER

8

Love at Walt Disney World®

Proposals, Anniversaries,
Weddings, and Honeymoons

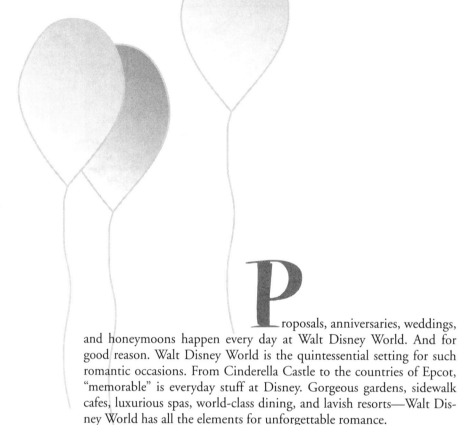

P roposals, anniversaries, weddings, and honeymoons happen every day at Walt Disney World. And for good reason. Walt Disney World is the quintessential setting for such romantic occasions. From Cinderella Castle to the countries of Epcot, "memorable" is everyday stuff at Disney. Gorgeous gardens, sidewalk cafes, luxurious spas, world-class dining, and lavish resorts—Walt Disney World has all the elements for unforgettable romance.

Proposing Marriage at WDW

There's something wonderfully romantic about the Cinderella fairy tale: magic spells, glass slippers, love, a handsome prince, a beautiful princess. It's the stuff that dreams are made of, and when it comes to popping the question, it's an enchantment that many find irresistible. If you are interested in proposing marriage at Walt Disney World, read on to find out what's offered. We also give you a few hints about doing it all yourself. And if you're hoping that someone in your life might have a special question to ask you, this might be a good time to mark this page and pass it to the someone you love. Sometimes a little hint is all that's needed.

Presentations: Gifts of a Lifetime

Gifts of a Lifetime is not a Disney service, but this small company is able to stage engagements almost anywhere at Walt Disney World.

Their events are especially imaginative and are custom-crafted to suit your wishes. Perhaps you'd like to stroll the beach at sunset and "find" a treasure map that leads you both to a buried chest. Inside, you discover a declaration of love and a ring. Other engagements we've heard about include scavenger hunts, a surprise "award" at a dinner show, and a glass slipper and ring "found" at Cinderella's Wishing Well in the Magic Kingdom. Gifts of a Lifetime is dedicated to creating special events that are innovative and fun. Prices begin around $275. To make inquiries or arrangements, call (407) 909-0593 or visit www.giftsofal-ifetime.com on the Internet.

Doing It on Your Own

Of course, you can simply bring the one you love to Disney and propose wherever you wish: amid the flower gardens of Canada, by the fireside at Victoria & Albert's, or even on the Twilight Zone Tower of Terror, if that is your heart's desire. Your choices are many, and you can easily create your own plan and arrange all the details yourself. Stage a special surprise in your room by arranging it with room service at any deluxe resort or with the Disney Florist (407-827-3505) at any other resort. If you stay in concierge at one of the Disney resorts, phone the concierge desk before you arrive and ask for help in planning a special, memorable moment.

Or make arrangements with one of Disney's more romantic restau-rants to propose after a special meal (we don't, however, recommend hiding the ring in a chocolate mousse!). Our choices for especially ro-mantic restaurants are Victoria & Albert's, Cítricos, Bistro de Paris, Cin-derella's Royal Table, Shula's Steakhouse, and Arthur's 27. Call (407) WDW-DINE (939-3463) to make arrangements.

Other options include the Romance Dinner package at the Grand Floridian (see page 75) or the Savannah dinner package at the Animal Kingdom Lodge (see page 134). Both options provide a memorable moment for a proposal. Another fine choice is a private fireworks cruise (see page 356) or a cruise aboard the Grand Floridian's Grand One motor yacht (call 407-824-2439 to make arrangements).

Anniversaries and Vow Renewals

Walt Disney World is also a magical place for anniversaries. There's so much romance at Disney that we've written this book about it. If you'd like to have your own celebration, room service at any deluxe resort will be happy to provide decorations and a host of surprises from chocolate treats to chilled champagne. All this can be planned stealthily and before you arrive.

Walt Disney World Florists (407-827-3505) can deliver roses, champagne or wine, custom designed baskets, and a host of other specialty gifts and decorations to any Disney resort room, whenever you wish. The possibilities are limitless. Another anniversary choice is one of Disney's Fairy Tale Honeymoons. Not strictly for honeymooners, these are "romance packages," and any one of them is a perfect choice for your anniversary celebration. For details, see Disney's Honeymoon Offerings later in this chapter.

Hint of Romance

When you reserve your room and again when you check in, be *sure* to mention that you are celebrating your anniversary. Also mention it when you're dining out. We've had some memorable anniversary delights at both the resorts and restaurants of Disney.

For a really special anniversary, you may be interested in renewing your marriage vows. Reaffirming love and commitment seems especially wonderful here at Walt Disney World, where the theme parks add a touch of fun to the Disney world of romance, recreation, and fine dining. Disney's Fairy Tale Weddings offers three vow renewal packages: the Deluxe Intimate Vow Renewal, the Deluxe Premium Vow Renewal, and the Vow Renewal at Sea. These packages are basically the same as the Intimate Wedding packages but offer ceremonies for vow renewals. For more details and prices, see Intimate Weddings, later in this chapter.

Hint of Romance

Whatever your anniversary or vow renewal wishes, let the folks at Disney's Fairy Tale Weddings help you plan an unforgettable occasion: (407) 828-3400.

Disney Fairy Tale Weddings

A wedding is more than just a ceremony. It is theater, it is dining, and it is entertainment. Who, then, could possibly craft a more perfect wedding celebration than Disney? And what place could possibly be better than the fabulous Walt Disney World Resort in which to celebrate the most important day of your life? From rehearsal dinner to guest accommodations, the scope of what is available at Walt Disney World promises a special and memorable event for everyone.

Over the years that we've been writing this book, we've gotten to know the folks at Disney's Fairy Tale Weddings. Of their many impressive talents (and there are many), we are most taken with their dedication to making each and every wedding a uniquely personal creation. They are determined not simply to *meet* your expectations but to *exceed* them. From small and intimate ceremonies to lavish wedding extravaganzas, Disney's Fairy Tale Weddings specialists have the talent, the imagination, the resources, and the commitment to create something even beyond your dreams.

There are two basic Fairy Tale Weddings: the Intimate Wedding and the Custom Wedding. Intimate Weddings are small. Allowing a maximum of eight guests, Intimate Weddings are elegant and beautiful. The Intimate Wedding package includes not only a complete wedding ceremony but also a Fairy Tale honeymoon at one of the wonderful Disney resorts.

Weddings with more than eight guests fall into the next category, Custom Weddings. Facilities, reception, and accommodations become important factors in an affair that can include as many people as you wish and that can be as simple or as lavish as you desire. A Custom Wedding is individually created to reflect your style, your tastes, and your imagination.

Disney's Wedding Pavilion

Whatever type of wedding you prefer, you'll have the option to have your ceremony in the beautiful and lavish Wedding Pavilion. Like a Victorian summer house, this charming glass-enclosed pavilion has been designed and decorated for only one purpose: to be the perfect location for your storybook wedding. Its gabled roofs, sloping turrets, and intricately carved hearts and cupids make it enchanting and unforgettable. Not a detail has been overlooked. Behind the altar, a stained-glass window perfectly frames Cinderella Castle. Sound, lighting, and every possible camera angle has been carefully calculated into this formula for the perfect wedding.

Disney's Fairy Tale Intimate Weddings

These charming affairs are designed for the wedding couple and up to eight additional guests. (If you desire to have more than eight guests, you'll have to contact Disney's Fairy Tale Weddings.)

Having attended a number of Disney's Fairy Tale Intimate Weddings, we can tell you that each reflects thoughtful planning and the personal touches of both bride and groom. Of the ceremonies we witnessed, one was in the morning, three were in the afternoon, and another was late in the day, just before sunset. One couple arrived by horse-drawn coach; another in Disney's vintage, white, 1929 Cadillac motorcar. Others simply arrived on foot. One wedding had a handful of guests, three others had eight, and one simply involved the bride and groom, an officiant, and several attendants.

Music at one ceremony featured a flutist; at the others, a violinist performed. Tunes varied from "When You Wish upon a Star" to the more traditional songs. At the end of several ceremonies, Mickey, in top hat and tails, and Minnie, in a sparkling evening gown, arrived for the serving of the cake and the champagne toasts. Some weddings were videotaped, and all were well photographed. The guests were thrilled at the perfection of the events, and so were we.

The Intimate Wedding offers variety and enhancements enough to ensure a ceremony that is uniquely yours. Special intimate wedding options include a ride in Cinderella's Glass Coach, Disney characters at your reception, and a variety of photographic packages. Every Intimate Wedding package includes these "Twelve Magical Amenities:"

- Luxurious accommodations for two, for four or more nights, in one of the following Disney resorts: BoardWalk Inn, Polynesian, Grand Floridian, Yacht or Beach Club, Wilderness Lodge, the Animal Kingdom Lodge, or one of the Disney moderate resorts, Caribbean Beach or Port Orleans Riverside.

- Unlimited admission to all Walt Disney World attractions for length of package

- An on-site wedding coordinator

- Officiant to perform the wedding ceremony

- Choice of fresh flower bouquet for bride and boutonniere for the groom

- A violinist for ceremony and cake-cutting reception for outdoor ceremonies (Premium Intimate Weddings provides an organist at the ceremony and a violinist at the cake-cutting reception.)

- Wedding reception, including elegant two-tier wedding cake with keepsake cake topper and one bottle of Fairy Tale Cuvee for the toast, served by host/hostess

- Special wedding gift

- Special wedding certificate signed by Mickey and Minnie

- Four hours of limousine service to and from the wedding ceremony/reception and the resort hotel

@ One romance tote bag filled with special treats for the bride and groom

@ Unlimited use of Walt Disney World transportation system

The Deluxe Intimate Wedding package includes all of these amenities, plus a choice of wedding location. Enjoy your intimate ceremony at Sea Breeze Pointe on Crescent Lake at the BoardWalk, the wedding gazebo in the garden at the Yacht Club, Sunset Pointe overlooking the Seven Seas Lagoon at the Polynesian Resort, or the Sunrise Terrace overlooking Bay Lake at the Wilderness Lodge. Each location is uniquely memorable. Prices for an Intimate Wedding, with bride and groom staying at Disney's Caribbean Beach Resort, begins at around $3,000 (price includes tax). A four-night intimate wedding with a stay at the Wilderness Lodge costs about $3,370 per couple. Of course, other resorts and additional days are available at varying additional cost.

A Premium Intimate Wedding package includes all the amenities mentioned previously, plus a ceremony at the Disney Wedding Pavilion, a wedding cake and champagne toast at the Grand Floridian Resort, and an organist for the wedding ceremony. A four-night, five-day Premium Intimate Wedding package at the Wilderness Lodge costs around $4,200.

Adding the Uncharted Magic of the Disney Cruise Line

To make your wedding even more memorable, just add water. This, of course, means the fabulous Disney Cruise Line. If you wish to make this great cruise experience part of your wedding, your choices are either to have an Intimate Wedding at Walt Disney World and then honeymoon aboard one of the Disney cruise ships or to sail aboard the Disney cruise ship and have your wedding on Disney's private island, Castaway Cay.

The Intimate Wedding at Sea includes an on-site wedding coordinator to assist with the wedding ceremony, the cake and champagne toast, concierge service onboard to assist with booking shore excursions and spa appointments (the actual excursions and spa treatments are not included in the package), an officiant to perform the wedding ceremony, fresh flower bouquet for bride and boutonniere for groom, a cake and champagne reception served by host or hostess, a solo musician for your ceremony, confirmed dinner for two on ceremony night at Palo, a keepsake wedding certificate, a special wedding gift, champagne and strawberries delivered to your stateroom, and a complimentary 8 × 10 photo taken during your cruise.

Prices for this unforgettable wedding package begin around $4,000 per couple for a three-night cruise. Four- and seven-night cruises and upgraded staterooms are available at varying additional costs. Any wedding guests would, of course, have to come along as passengers on this wonderful wedding cruise.

Planning Your Disney's Fairy Tale Intimate Wedding

As you can see, there are numerous and tempting options for a Disney's Fairy Tale Wedding. You'll want to begin your Intimate Wedding odyssey at least six weeks in advance by calling Disney's Fairy Tale Weddings at (407) 828-3400. If you wish to have a larger and grander wedding than this, your choice would be a Fairy Tale Custom Wedding.

Disney's Fairy Tale Custom Weddings

A Custom Wedding is the unique interpretation of your wishes. Every step of the way, you work with your wedding planning team to create a ceremony and reception that perfectly reflects your tastes and imagination. Disney's legendary magic touch enhance every detail of this important event, from award-winning floral arrangements to lavish entertainment and special effects. Whether you desire a simple ceremony at Disney's Wedding Pavilion or imagine an over-the-top wedding celebration in the courtyard of Cinderella Castle, your choices are virtually limitless. Whether you wish to arrive in Cinderella's glass coach or take your entire wedding party by boat to your sumptuous reception, a Disney Wedding specialist can make it all happen, just as you wish. From Disney characters to fireworks, the sky's the limit.

In addition to having a truly magical Disney wedding and reception, you'll find other good reasons for having a Disney Fairy Tale wedding. With a team of specialists arranging all the details, you'll be free to focus yourselves on making all the fun decisions. The resources available to Disney's Fairy Tale Weddings seem nearly limitless. Disney's Fairy Tale Weddings can provide specially-priced Disney resort stays, special theme park admission for your wedding guests, complete transportations services, photography and videography, an extraordinary choice of floral arrangements, food and beverages, and entertainment, and even professional cosmotologists.

You'll be free to enjoy it all rather than spending your time fretting about the small stuff. Who better to trust with this important day than the people whose job it is to make every dream come true? Your guests will also be able to enjoy their own special Walt Disney World adventure. Staying in one of the fabulous Disney resorts, they will enjoy not only your special event, but also the attractions and excitement of Walt Disney World. It will be an event that everyone will remember.

A Basic Disney Fairy Tale Custom Wedding

Even Disney's "simplest" wedding is a traditional masterpiece: a ceremony in Disney's beautiful wedding pavilion, classic floral bouquets and boutonnieres for the wedding party, a unity candle arrangement for the ceremony, a cocktail reception and sit-down gourmet dinner in one of the beautiful Disney resort ballrooms, classic wedding centerpieces, and a magnificent wedding cake and champagne toast. Also included is a six-hour classic photographic package, open bar throughout the entire event, a disc jockey, transportation for all guests to and from their Disney resorts, and a limousine for the bride and groom. For a hundred guests, the total cost for such a special event would begin around $20,000. Not outrageous at all, considering that this is about the average cost of a wedding in the United States.

Of course, more lavish weddings could include a horse-drawn carriage, a glass slipper and ring, more luxurious floral decorations, a more elaborate reception and dinner, or even a live orchestra. From theme parks to Disney characters, the only limitation imposed upon your Fairy Tale Wedding is what you wish to spend.

Enjoy a candlelit ceremony with trumpeting heralds or a thundering display of fireworks. A bridesmaid's tea party with the Mad Hatter or a calypso-style rehearsal beach party? Have a fantasy wedding in a fog-shrouded forest lit by thousands of twinkling lights or a union amid the 1940s seashore charm of Disney's BoardWalk, complete with a retro-style celebration in the fabulous Art Deco Atlantic Dance Hall. From a New Orleans jazz group to live stage productions, you will have at your wishes every resource of this, the world's most fabulous vacation destination.

The Guidelines for a Disney
Fairy Tale Custom Wedding

If you already have a budget in mind, the Disney wedding specialists can give you a good idea of what a wedding in that price range might include. The Classic Wedding we've outlined previously should give you a good starting point. There are several other sample weddings, the Premium and the Lavish, each featuring more amenities and requiring larger budgets. Your Disney wedding specialist can provide this information.

Disney's Fairy Tale Weddings require certain minimum expenditures, and although these do vary with the seasons of Disney and are subject to change, you'll generally find that a minimum expenditure of $10,000 is required for wedding events from Friday through Sunday, and $7,500 for events Monday through Thursday. The following expenses apply toward reaching (or exceeding) these minimums: food and beverages, music, decor, flowers, photographic services, hair and makeup, special transportation, spa services, ceremony site fees, and any other service exclusively for the wedding.

Another important guideline is a minimum food and beverage expenditure of about $95 per guest (includes service charges and tax) for functions beginning before 2 P.M. and $125 per guest (includes service charges and tax) for events beginning after 2 P.M. Remember that this will apply toward your overall minimum expenditure.

Theme park locations have their own minimum expenditures, with Magic Kingdom events beginning around $42,000. You should also know that based on your estimated number of guests, you must guarantee a minimum number of room nights at the Disney resorts.

Some Custom Wedding "Extras"

Here are a few extras that you'll get with your Disney Fairy Tale Custom Wedding:

@ A complimentary room for your first special night together (suite upgrades may be extra)

@ Discounted rooms at the Disney resorts for wedding guests

@ Specifically priced passes to the Disney attractions offered to your guests

Planning Your Disney Fairy Tale Custom Wedding

Begin your wedding plans at least a year in advance. You'll have many wonderful decisions to make, from cuisine to wedding favors. Take your time and enjoy it all. You'll be free to tour a variety of special locations, sample menus, and everything from invitations to table linens. The Disney dream-makers will also need time to guarantee your locations, establish a working budget, and book rooms for your guests. The wedding specialists at Disney will do whatever it takes to make your wedding dream a reality. It's a promise they make, and it's been a promise they've kept for more than 17,000 weddings since 1991, no two of which have been exactly the same. To begin your wedding plans, call Disney's Fairy Tale Weddings at (407) 828-3400.

Other Weddings at WDW

There are a few options to a Disney Fairy Tale Wedding, but none offer anything like that of Disney. Arrangements can be made for weddings at The Wyndham Palace Resort and Spa, both Swan and Dolphin, The Grosvenor, and Shades of Green. For more information, contact any of these resorts.

Honeymooning at Walt Disney World

Walt Disney World is the number one honeymoon destination in the world. In fact, few vacation destinations anywhere can rival Walt Disney World when it comes to its diversity of romance, relaxation, and entertainment. Make your own plans following our suggestions or choose one of Disney's Fairy Tale Weddings romantic options for honeymooners (or for any couple simply wishing to add something special to their getaway).

Planning Your Own Disney Honeymoon

Throughout this book we have provided suggestions to make your Disney vacation more romantic. From unforgettable resort rooms and sublime dining experiences to exciting nightlife and unique recreation, Disney World offers enough memories for a dozen honeymoons. Here are a few more suggestions for making your honeymoon at Walt Disney World all that it should be:

- When you make your reservation, inform the reservationist that it is your honeymoon. Most resorts will deliver a small gift to your room. Free upgrades to nicer rooms are not unheard of, but only during value season, when those rooms may be vacant. Try asking at check-in.

- The Ultimate Park Hopper Pass is a good deal and will give you the freedom to hop parks and see whatever you like, whenever you want. It provides unlimited admission to all Disney attractions, including DisneyQuest.

- Have your own Disney-themed romance basket delivered to your room. Call Walt Disney World Florists at (407) 827-3505 to make arrangements.

- Make your own arrangements for a photographic session with Disney Photographic Services at (407) 827-5029.

- Pick up a pair of Mickey and Minnie, bride and groom hats and wear them. This will be a flag for all Disney cast members to give you special treatment. And they will. These hats are currently only available at the gift shop at the Grand Floridian Resort.

A Concierge Honeymoon ♥♥♥

Concierge rooms are expensive, but they still cost less than the all-inclusive packages. They include upgraded room amenities, continental breakfasts, day-long snacking, and afternoon-to-evening wines and cordials (for more details, see page 54). This is a level of pampering perfect for a honeymoon. Disney World concierge services are offered at the following resorts (prices are for value season and include the appropriate 11½ percent Florida taxes):

- The Polynesian concierge, from $435 nightly
- The Yacht Club or Beach Club concierge, from $474 nightly
- The Grand Floridian concierge, from $652 nightly
- Grand Floridian Honeymoon, from $664 nightly
- The BoardWalk Inn, Innkeepers Club, from $474 nightly
- Wilderness Lodge Honeymoon concierge, from $402 nightly
- The Animal Kingdom Lodge concierge, from $474 nightly

Disney's Honeymoon Offerings

Disney's Fairy Tale Weddings offers a small assortment of romantic packages. The Dream Maker Romance can be added to any Walt Disney World vacation package. For complete details, see page 21. Other honeymoon offerings introduce the Disney Cruise Line.

The Disney Cruise Line Land & Sea Romance Plan

This package includes a three- or four-night stay at a select Walt Disney World resort and a three- or four-night cruise to the Bahamas and to Disney's Castaway Cay.

Included in the Walt Disney World portion of the package:

- An Ultimate Hopper Pass that includes admission to all four Disney theme parks, the two water parks, DisneyQuest, and more.
- A private, 30-minute horse-drawn carriage ride, with champagne
- Choice of two of the following Romance Plan features:

   Dinner for two at a select Disney signature restaurant (does not include alcohol)

   Couples spa treatment (requires two choices)

   Professional photographic session in Magic Kingdom (requires two choices)

   Admission to Cirque du Soleil La Nouba

The Disney Cruise Line portion of the package includes:

- One romance package delivered to stateroom
- Fresh flowers delivered to stateroom
- One-hour massage (one per person)

Including gratuities, port taxes, and transportation and baggage transfers, the cost for a seven-night land-and-sea Disney Cruise Line Romance Plan at a deluxe resort at Walt Disney World (does not include Grand Floridian Resort) and Deluxe Stateroom with Navigaotor's verandah begins around $3,400 per couple, depending on sailing date.

The Disney Cruise Line Romantic Escape

This package features a seven-night Caribbean cruise (eastern or western), including a day at Disney's Castaway Cay. This package includes:

- Romance basket delivered to stateroom

- Fresh flowers for stateroom

- One-hour massage (one per person)

Including gratuities, port taxes, and transportation and baggage transfers, the cost for a seven-night Disney Cruise Line Romantic Escape in a Deluxe Stateroom with Navigator's Verandah begins around $3,140 per couple, depending on sailing date.

Our Honeymoon Recommendations

- There's nothing quite so special on your honeymoon as a suite. When you make your honeymoon reservations, ask about one of Disney's romantic suites. Our favorite is the Honeymoon Turret Suite at the Grand Floridian (room number 4321). ♥♥♥♥

- If you can afford the Platinum Plan, go for it. It's a special and romantic experience that you'll remember always. It's expensive, but remember that this is your honeymoon. If you can't spoil yourselves now, just when can you?

- For Disney honeymoon package reservations, call (800) 370-6009.

- The package prices we have quoted are for standard-view rooms during value season. Because this is your honeymoon, we urge you to get the best view you can. The truth is that standard-view rooms just don't provide the magic of looking at Cinderella Castle or even a beautiful garden. There is a time for a standard room, and there is a time for something special.

- Don't forget to request a king bed when you make your reservations, and don't forget to mention that it's your honeymoon.

- For honeymooners, we especially recommend these romantic resorts:

The Grand Floridian
The Animal Kingdom Lodge

The Yacht and the Beach Clubs
The Polynesian
The Caribbean Beach Resort
The Wilderness Lodge
The BoardWalk Inn

℮ Here are some of our favorite romantic resort rooms:

Lagoon-view rooms at the Grand Floridian or the Polynesian
Any concierge service room, especially the Grand Floridian
Deluxe savannah view room at the Animal Kingdom Lodge
One of the four honeymoon rooms at the Wilderness Lodge
The honeymoon Turret suite at the Grand Floridian
The Premier King View room at the Dolphin
Upper-floor Epcot-view room at the Beach Club
One-bedroom villa at the BoardWalk Villas or Beach Club Villas
A king bed, "attic" room at the Grand Floridian
A suite at Shades of Green

℮ If money is no object, the following are absolutely lavish suites:

The Yellowstone, Wilderness Lodge
The Commodore, the Yacht Club
Garden King (one-bedroom) suite, Tonga, the Polynesian
Royal Asante or Royal Kuba suites, the Animal Kingdom Lodge

℮ Disney's Vero Beach Resort is only a few hours away from Walt
Disney World and provides a serious getaway following your Walt
Disney World adventure. There's not a lot to do down there, but
that's the point, isn't it? For more information, call Disney Central
Reservations at (407) 934-7639.

PART 3

Universal Orlando: Another Kind of Theme Park Adventure

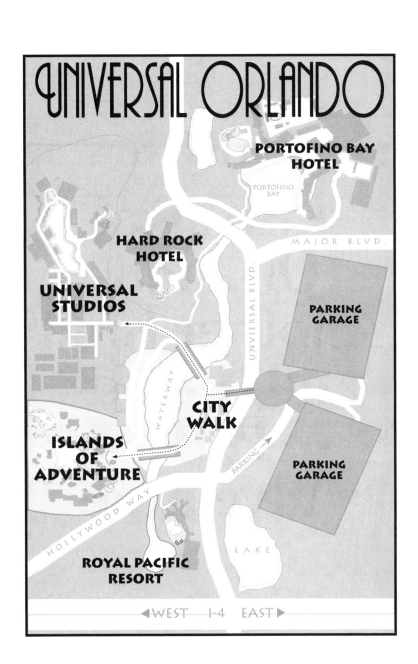

CHAPTER

9

Getting
Ready for
Your

Universal
Orlando
Getaway

While we love theme parks, we also feel that for couples (with or without kids), this kind of fun needs to be part of a bigger picture, one that includes memorable accommodations, great food, and exciting nightlife. With three luxury hotels that offer unique advantages to guests, Universal Orlando features all this and more. Don't come to Universal expecting a Disney-wannabee. Universal Orlando is out there on its own, blazing an original path in theme park attractions.

Less nostalgic and not so warm and fuzzy as WDW, Universal Orlando is more of an in-your-face kind of fun. Adrenalin-pumping roller coasters and pulse-pounding thrill rides give Universal an edginess that you just won't get with Mickey. This is definitely *another kind* of theme park adventure.

Making Universal Orlando Part of Your Central Florida Vacation

You won't need weeks to see all of Universal Orlando. Sure, there's plenty to see and do, but you should be able to accomplish it in two or three days. It's a super destination for a short vacation.

What's New at Universal Orlando for 2003–2004

Theme parks are ever-changing things: The old must make way for the new. What's new in 2003 is the wonderful Royal Pacific Resort, Universal's moderately-priced Loews Hotel (read more about it later in this chapter). New attractions in the theme parks are Jimmy Neutron: Boy Genius and Shrek and Donkey's Fairy Tale Adventure, both at the Studios. Coming in 2004 will be the spectacular Return of the Mummy attraction. Both CityWalk and the Studios now serve Starbucks coffee. Gone from the Studios are Alfred Hitchcock: The Art of Moviemaking, Kongfrontation, and the FUNtastic World of Hanna-Barbera.

When to Visit

When it comes to crowds and weather, all of Orlando's attractions experience the same ups and downs of temperature and crowds. Our favorite time of year is January and the first two weeks of February, when Orlando's attractions are less crowded and discounts and specials are easy to come by. Crowded theme parks are not much of a factor at Universal Orlando, if you're staying in one of U/O's three hotels. See page 388 for details about "No Line, No Wait."

Weatherwise, a lot of the attractions at Islands of Adventure will get you wet. So it's worth considering that during the winter months in Central Florida, occasional cold snaps may make these attractions less than inviting. One thing about Islands of Adventure: It's particularly good during Florida's hot summer season. For more information about weather and crowds in Central Florida, see page 6.

During the course of the year, Universal Orlando features some special events and parties. If you visit on a New Year's Eve, Fourth of July, or during the busy summer months, you're likely to find a nightly fireworks show. If you enjoy parties, you might

Insider's Secret
Stay at a Universal hotel and don't worry about crowds. See page 388.

want to plan your vacation for the February–March Mardi Gras celebration, Halloween Horror Nights in October, or Rock the Universe in September. And of course, you'll find seasonal festivities around the Christmas Holidays.

Where to Stay

Your choices are to stay either inside Universal Orlando (at one of its three Loews Hotels: the Portofino Bay, the Hard Rock, or the new Royal Pacific) or outside in one of the many hotels or motels in the Orlando area. Of course, we're going to tell you to stay inside, where Universal Orlando makes it *very, very* inviting. The Loews Hotels are all first-class in every way: luxurious accommodations, great restaurants, unique ambience, wonderful service, and right next door to all the fun. (We'll tell you all you need to know about these great hotels later in this chapter.)

But there's something even better about staying in one of these hotels, a perk so special it made us feel like Michael Eisner at Walt Disney World. Guests of these hotels have merely to flash their resort ID cards at virtually any attraction in the Universal parks and ride without wait. It's called "No Line, No Wait." This privilege makes a stay in one of these hotels a real "no-brainer," especially during the summer months or the holiday seasons. "No Line, No Wait...*No Problem*." This feature and the convenience and luxury of the hotels makes a Universal Orlando holiday something so special, you'll have to experience it to believe it. We promise.

Trivia

Fun Fact

With "No Line, No Wait," staying at a Universal Hotel means that you won't have to stand in line even during the busiest seasons.

Finding the Right Admission Ticket

There are a variety of admission passes for Universal Orlando, from a 1-day, 1-park ticket to a pass that provides unlimited admission for an entire year to both Universal Studios and Islands of Adventure. At the Universal hotels, a full assortment of passes may be purchased at the concierge desk. Tickets can be purchased at all three Universal hotels and through Universal Orlando by calling (888) 322-5537, or on the Universal Orlando Web site (see appendix B). A small selection of passes is also offered at discount prices at many Florida AAA offices. You'll also find all these passes at the Destination Universal ticket desks at more than a hundred hotels in the greater Orlando area. Ask about special or discounted offerings.

Know, too, that price increases at all the Orlando attractions seem to happen several times a year. Therefore, expect the following prices, which include tax, to change slightly over time. Children two years of age and younger are free.

1-Day Universal Studios or Islands of Adventure Ticket $55.33 / $45.74 (for ages 3 to 9)

ℯ Provides admission to one theme park for one day only

2-Day Ticket with Third Day Free $103.26 / $89.41 (for ages 3 to 9)

ℯ Provides admission to both parks for two days, with unlimited park-to-park access. Third day expires seven days after first use of ticket. Second day does not expire.

ℯ Includes CityWalk Party Pass" (all-club admission, see page 447) for seven consecutive days from first use.

3-Day Ticket $119.23 / $103.25 (for ages 3 to 9)

ℯ Provides admission to both parks for three days, with unlimited park-to-park access. Unused days do not expire.

ℯ Includes CityWalk "Party Pass" (all-club admission) for seven consecutive days from first use

$ Universal Orlando 5-Day Bonus Pass $106.45 / $81.95 (for ages 3 to 9)

ℯ Available only online (see appendix B for Internet address)

ℯ Provides admission to both parks for five consecutive days, with unlimited park-to-park access.

ℯ Includes CityWalk "Party Pass" (all-club admission)

Universal Orlando 2-Park Annual Power Pass $117.10 for all ages

ℯ Provides admission to Universal Studios and Islands of Adventure for one year, with blackout dates around Christmas, Easter, and certain dates during the summer months

ℯ Parking ($8) not included

ℯ Does not get the discounts of the Preferred Annual Pass

2-Park Preferred Annual Pass $180.99 for all ages

@ Unlimited admission to both parks, valid year-round

@ Includes free parking

@ 30% savings at all three Universal Loews Hotels (based on avail-ability)

@ 15% savings in Universal Orlando theme park restaurants (ex-cludes alcohol)

@ 20% savings in merchandise shops and carts at theme parks

@ 10–15% savings at CityWalk clubs and select restaurants

Length-of-Stay Passes

For Loews Universal hotel guests only, these passes provide admission to both Islands of Adventure and Universal Studios and are tailor-made to fit the length of your Universal visit. These will save you some money, but passes expire when your visit ends. They are available only at the concierge desks of the Universal Loews Hotels. Prices below in-clude all applicable taxes.

2-night / 3-day pass: $113.91 adult, $97.93 ages 3 to 9

3-night / 4-day pass: $124.56 adult, $108.58 ages 3 to 9

4-night / 5-day pass: $135.21 adult, $119.23 ages 3 to 9

Money-Saving Tip

The length-of-stay pass for hotel guests will save money over other tickets as long as you use the pass every day. See a movie and save even more.

Orlando FlexTickets

Universal Orlando also offers the Orlando FlexTicket, which provides admission not only to the two Universal theme parks and CityWalk but also to SeaWorld Orlando and Wet 'n Wild. Good for fourteen consecutive days, this bargain pass costs $187.39 ($152.24 for ages 3 to 9). A 5-Park FlexTicket is also good for fourteen consecutive days and adds Busch Gardens Tampa Bay (with transportation from select Or-lando hotels). Cost is $223.60 ($187.39 for ages 3 to 9).

Forget Retail!
Get a Discount for Your Universal Vacation

If you take the time to look for them, you'll discover a surprising number of discounts. Universal Orlando's Web site frequently features a variety of special offers (see appendix B). The Universal Orlando 2-Park Preferred Annual Pass offers the best all-around assortment of discounts (see above). Make good use of them, and this pass can easily pay for itself.

Florida AAA (American Automobile Association) local offices offer tickets and annual passes at discount prices that are available to any AAA member. You can also get a slightly smaller discount right at the Universal box offices by showing your AAA card. Once inside the parks, your AAA card will get you 10 percent off for your entire party at most restaurants, as well as discounted merchandise at Universal Orlando theme park shops. Florida chapters of AAA feature exceptional deals for AAA members.

Universal Entertainment MasterCard works like a frequent-flyer club: You get points for using the card, and those points go toward benefits such as front-of-the-line passes, free movie screenings, special offers, and other theme park priveleges. To apply for this credit card, call (800) 293-9080.

Destination Universal has ticket booths at more than a hundred hotels around Orlando. During the year, they offer discounted admission tickets and passes to the Universal attractions.

Military discounts up to 10 percent off admission are available for active duty, reserve, and retired military personnel and are available at the ITT office on base.

Coupon offerings and ticket brokers can be found everywhere in and around Orlando. The Central Florida tourist market features some serious competition and some of these coupons offer limited savings. As for unofficial "ticket brokers," you'll find them everywhere from mini-marts to gas stations. A few offer good deals but others . . . well, let buyers beware. Before purchase, always compare their "deals" to our list prices.

Our Tips for Universal Orlando Admission

@ Unless you're spending only one day at Universal Orlando, avoid the one-day ticket.

@ At the current price, a Preferred Annual Pass features some impressive discounts and if you're planning to return within a year, you will save even more.

@ Check for special offers on the Universal Orlando Web site (see appendix B).

@ Check with your AAA club for Universal/Orlando discounts.

Looking for a Package Vacation?

There are a nearly infinite number of vacation package offerings for Universal Orlando. However, we'll cover only those that include a stay at Universal Orlando's on-site Loews hotels. Such packages typically include accommodations and admission to the Universal attractions and are available from a number of sources: local travel agents, AAA, and Universal Studios Vacations—Universal Orlando's own travel service.

Universal Studios Vacations offers a variety of basic packages that, when broken down, seem designed more for convenience because they don't appear to save money. For information about offerings or to make reservations, call Universal Studios Vacations at (800) 224-6035, or visit them online (see appendix B).

For discounted packages, we turned to AAA, which offers some of the same packages with discounts up to 25 percent. They seem to be attractive deals. For details and to make reservations, call your local AAA office.

Whatever packages you may be considering, we suggest that you compare their costs with what you can do by making the arrangements yourself. Use our resort rates, and call for the most current admission prices. Simply add them up to see which is the best deal.

The Loews First Card

This is a great deal for anyone planning a stay in a Loews Hotel and an even greater deal if you are a frequent Loews Hotel guest. Having a Loews First Card will get you a nice welcoming gift, delivered to your room, and if available, a room upgrade. There are several types of cards, depending on how many times you've stayed at Loews. The more often you stay, the more you get. It costs nothing to join and you can do it either online (www.Loewshotels.com) or by telephone (800-LOEWS12).

Making Your Hotel Reservations

Given the fabulous benefits of Universal's three on-site hotels, and given that together they have only about 1,400 rooms, you'll need to make your reservations as far in advance as you can. Universal Orlando reservationists can be reached toll-free at (888) 837-2273 or (800) 232-

7827. Later in this chapter, we'll tell you all about the Loews Hotels. Decide which resort suits you best and what kind of room you want, and then call with your dates. Reservations can also be made online (see appendix B).

Your First and Last Days at Universal

It's wise to make arrangements for the first and last days of your vacation. If you're flying to Florida, we urge you to make your ground transportation plans before you leave home. You won't want to waste precious vacation time waiting around the airport.

Getting to Universal Orlando

If you're driving in, Universal Orlando is just off I-4, about midway between Walt Disney World and downtown Orlando. The exit is clearly marked. Simply follow the road signs either to your Universal hotel or to the huge parking garage. Parking at Universal Orlando costs $8 per day ($10 for RVs or trailers). Parking for CityWalk after 6 P.M. is free. For $10, you can use "preferred parking," which will get you closer to the attractions, especially if you arrive later in the day. Valet parking for CityWalk, Islands of Adventure, and Universal Studios is $14 per day (plus gratuity).

If you're flying in to Orlando International, a Mears shuttle costs $24 per person, round trip. However, these shuttles usually make stops at other hotels and can take a surprisingly long time to get you to your destination. For rental car information, see page 42.

We prefer Florida Town Cars (800-525-7246), a service that gets rave reviews. Prices for round-trip town car transportation is $80 for up to five passengers. It's a nice way to go. (See appendix B for Web address for this and other town car services.)

> **Helpful Hint**
>
> For a stay at *both* Universal and Disney resorts, Florida Town Cars will get you to and from the airport and in between, from your Universal hotel to your Disney resort (or vice versa), all for only $130 to $140 (for up to five persons). Great company, great service, great price.

Mears runs round-trip shuttles from Universal Orlando to Disney for $13 per person. For details and schedules, call (407) 423-5566. At $70 round trip, a taxicab seems too expensive.

Arriving at Your Loews Hotel

If you're arriving early in the day, you probably will not get in to your room until after 3 P.M., especially during busy times of year. However, you'll be able to register, have your luggage put in storage, and begin your Universal Orlando vacation. If you're arriving later in the day, we suggest you forego purchasing theme park admission for that day and either visit CityWalk (no admission) or explore your hotel or the other Universal hotels.

Your Last Day at a Loews Hotels

If on your last day, you're departing after the 11 A.M. check-out time, you can have your luggage put in storage and enjoy your last few hours at Universal Orlando. You can even join the hotel's health club for the day and use the facilities to shower and change.

A late checkout of 1 P.M. can be granted to a limited number of rooms each day. Call the front desk early on the day of your departure to make arrangements.

The On-Site Hotels of Universal Orlando

We love all three Loews Hotels. They are luxurious and beautiful, and all provide the services seasoned travelers like ourselves have come to expect. Besides these things, you'll find lots of other important benefits to staying in one of these on-site hotels.

Guest Privileges for the On-Site Loews Hotels

@ "No Line, No Wait" access to almost all Universal Orlando attractions

@ Unequalled convenience to theme parks and CityWalk

@ Priority seating at select Universal Orlando restaurants, shows, and character dining at resorts

@ Concierge desk for information, admission passes, and restaurant reservations

@ Resort ID cards to charge merchandise, dining, and entertainment throughout Universal Orlando

@ Courtesy water taxi and bus transportation between resorts, theme parks, and CityWalk, every fifteen minutes

@ Special length-of-stay pass available to enjoy unlimited admission to theme parks and CityWalk

- Free next-day package delivery from theme park shops to hotel
- Full bell service
- Twenty-four-hour room service
- Valet parking, $12 per night; self-parking, $6 a day
- On-site car rental
- Valet laundry service
- Fitness centers, per person daily charge varies with hotel
- Privileges at the nearby Keene's Pointe Jack Nicklaus golf course
- Childrens activities centers, after 5 p.m.
- In-room babysitting with Kids Night Out (see page 37 for details)
- The "Did You Forget Something Closet," an offering of items you might have left at home

Loews Hotels' Kid-Friendly Features

Loews is a company that proclaims "Loews loves kids!" Of course, children stay for free in all Loews Hotels, and Loews features a variety of extras designed to meet the needs of their youngest guests. Couples staying at these resorts can get a special discount on an adjoining room for their children and separate room cards with pre-loaded spending limits that allow children to make their own purchases. Rollaway beds and cribs are complimentary.

The "Kid's Kloset" is another special feature for children. Simply pick up your phone to request games, books, car seats, strollers, nightlights, potty seats, baby bathtub and blankets, and even outlet protectors.

Perhaps the most interesting kid-friendly feature (found only at the Hard Rock and Portofino) is the two-room children's suite. These popular accommodations feature an adjoining room designed especially for kids. TV and Sony PlayStation, childhood themes, two single beds, a small table and chairs, and a separate closet with child-size hangers and even children's bathrobes make them especially memorable. The kids rooms can be accessed only through the main king bedroom and are perfect for a romantic family visit. With off-peak prices beginning around $470 per night, a children's suite is a viable alternative to having two rooms or sharing your bedroom with your children. *Parents* magazine cites Loews as the top U.S. hotel chain for family travel. It's easy to see why.

If you're traveling with kids, you'll also want to know about Campo Portofino, the Lil' Rock Club, and the Mariner's Club. These children's activity centers are for kids ages 4 to 14 (young children must be potty trained), and all three feature carefully supervised arts and crafts programs, interesting activities, and nightly movies. The centers all open at 5 P.M. Cost at Hard Rock and Royal Pacific is $10 per hour, per child, and $45 per child at Portofino Bay for the entire evening, dinner included. We suggest you call the resort before your arrival for more information and to make reservations (see appendix C for telephone numbers).

Loews "Generation G" Program

This program offers amenities and services designed for grandparents traveling with grandchildren. From connecting rooms to a keepsake photo album, this clever program offers quite a bit, including customized packages. Inquire at your Loews Hotel for details.

Loews Loves Pets, Too!

Much to our surprise, all three hotels feature a limited number of designated pet-friendly rooms. These special accommodations feature pet mats, toys, treats, a welcome amenity, and even a pet room-service menu. A nice touch. A maximum of two pets is allowed per room. Owners must present a current health certificate and keep pets leashed while on hotel property.

Loews Hotels Seasons

All three hotels feature an off-peak (value), a regular, and a peak season. Here's how they go:

> **Off-peak Season:** All of September; December 1 to several days before Christmas

> **Regular Season:** January 2 to a week before Easter; a few days after Easter to the end of August; and October and November

> **Peak Season:** Ten days around Easter; and a few days before Christmas to January 1

> Resort rates quoted in this book include up to two adults per room (no charge for children). Additional adults cost $25 each per night. Standard resort rooms can accommodate four persons. Cribs are available at no charge upon request.

Portofino Bay Hotel

While strolling this resort's harborside avenue of shops, we heard a window washer singing an Italian aria as he worked. It seemed typical

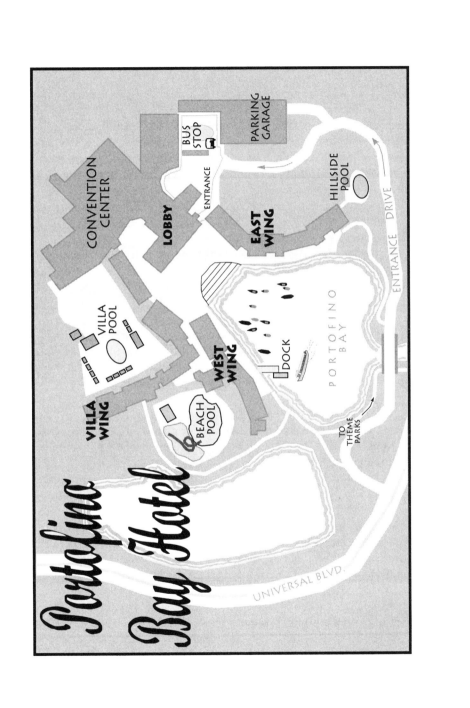

of this charming place, which seems more like a village in Italy than a hotel with Italian theming. Small vineyards, beautiful piazzas, and sparkling fountains give it a real feeling of enchantment.

We walked the narrow, cobbled streets of this quaint, seaside "town," to discover its pleasant plazas and its cafes and restaurants. Later, as the water taxi ferried us off to the theme parks, we looked back on the fishing boats that lay anchored in its small harbor. Gathered around the shore we saw the romantic and picturesque Mediterranean village that was our hotel. Already, we were anxious to return.

We love beautiful and luxurious hotels. For us, it's what travel is all about. The Portofino Bay is all this and more: exceptionally comfortable accommodations, lavish dining, a luxurious spa, and more than enough opportunity to lay back and relax. If the Universal Orlando theme parks have a pause button, this is it.

The Portofino Bay Hotel enjoys the essence of its namesake, a getaway for the world's rich and famous on the Ligurian Coast of northwestern Italy. The quiet elegance of Portofino's lobby is enhanced by polished Italian marble, classical music, and a sunlit fountain courtyard. Outside, the colorful style and decorative trompe l'oeil evoke the sun-drenched Riviera, bringing this captivating creation to life. If you're like us, you'll want to mix your theme park adventures with some of this European-style comfort. After a few days at Portofino, you'll know the meaning of "la dolce vita," the sweet life.

The Rooms at Portofino Bay

We've always expected a lot from a luxury hotel. If all it took to satisfy us were "all the comforts of home," we'd probably stay at home. Portofino did not disappoint.

Our standard room featured a sense of old-world charm and all the sensibilities of a new-world space. An antiqued armoire, an exceptionally comfortable king bed with fluffy comforter and duvet, and such upscale amenities as bathrobes, coffeemaker, a small table and chairs, well-stocked mini-butler, and umbrella made everything simply "elegantissimo." Our room enjoyed a soothing palette of Mediterranean tones: sand, gold, and emerald. Except for our garden view, little about it seemed "standard." Larger than any Disney resort room, Portofino rooms average a stunning 450 square feet.

Even our bathroom was exceptionally large and well appointed. Its double vanity featured a granite counter top and a large mirror trimmed with colorful Italian tile. Plush cotton towels, bathroom scale, small television, makeup mirror, and upscale toiletries all spoke of uncompromising quality. From evening turndown to morning newspaper, our Portofino nights were splendid and restful.

Room Rates as of 2003 for Portofino Bay Hotel (prices include taxes)

Accommodation	Off-Peak Season	Regular Season	Peak Season
Garden View	$289	$322	$345
Bay View	$311	$345	$378
Deluxe Pool View	$333	$367	$400
Kids Suite	$512	$556	$601

Here at Portofino, standard rooms such as ours offer garden or bay views. Rooms with pool views are larger deluxe rooms, featuring separate shower and tub, sound systems, and video cassette players. Portofino's 750 guest rooms are located in the resort's four wings: East, West, Villa, and Hospitality. Rooms feature either two queen beds or a single king.

Suites at the Portofino Bay Hotel

Suites at Portofino include the lavish Presidente and two Governator suites. These luxurious accommodations each include a bedroom with walk-in closet, a study, a comfortable entertainment area, and a whirlpool tub. Not for every traveler, prices for these suites begin at $1,672.

Another suite well worth considering for a family is the Kids Suite. This marvelous accommodation includes a large king bedroom with an adjoining themed and decorated kid's room. We tried one with our grandkids Ben and Guin and were delighted. They loved their bunk beds (not all kids suites feature these) and their very own space. And of course, we enjoyed having a space that was ours. A bit more expensive, yes, but it made our little holiday all the more special.

Dining at the Portofino Bay Hotel

Dining opportunities are numerous here, but it is worth mentioning that even by theme park standards, prices seem high. Still, you'll find a good variety of restaurants at Portofino Bay. Guests looking for an assortment of foods for each of the day's meals will find it all at Trattoria del Porto. Breakfast offerings include either a large buffet or a variety of à la carte items. Trattoria's lunch menu includes sandwiches, salads, soups, pastas, and wood-fired pizzas, and the dinner menu adds a variety of entrées, including seafood and cuts of beef.

Mama Della's Ristorante serves up a family-style dinner menu of Italian favorites along with plenty of Mama Della's own homespun Italian hospitality. With a stunning view of the harbor, Delfino Riviera ♥♥♥♥ is Portofino's fine-dining destination. It's one of Orlando's gourmet choices for upscale, authentic Northern Italian cuisine and, for us, the most romantic meal we've ever enjoyed. For more details about both Mama Della's and Delfino Riviera, see chapter 10.

One of our favorites at Portofino is Sal's Market Deli. You'll think you're in Italy when you step into this charming, neighborhood cafe. Sal's offerings include pastries, baked goods, wine, sandwiches, salads, and wonderful wood-fired pizzas. It's open from 11 A.M. to 11 P.M. and features a beautiful outside patio overlooking the harbor.

Splendido Pizzeria is poolside at the Beach Pool, and it's a great place to grab a pizza or a sandwich while catching some sun or on your way to or from the parks. And if you're sweet tooth begins to act up, treat it with a gelato or a sorbet at Gelateria. Next door is Cafe Espresso, the perfect place for a cappuccino or a cup of brew, and a tempting assortment of pastries. Mornings at Cafe Espresso feature a modest continental breakfast, including cold cereals.

And for food and beverage anytime, Portofino offers round-the-clock room service.

Lounges at Portofino Bay

Bar American is this resort's handsome lobby lounge. Stylish and comfortable, it features a full-service bar and a variety of cordials and Italian wines. On the piazza and overlooking the harbor is the Thirsty Fish, a casual and family-friendly bar that features live entertainment on Friday nights. Its outside seating area is right on the waterfront. Poolside at the Beach Pool is the full-service Splendido Pool Bar.

Live Entertainment at Portofino Bay

There's a surprising amount of entertainment here. Featured on Thursdays, Fridays, and Saturdays at Trattoria del Porto are character dinners, with a variety of entertainers. Mama Della's has a strolling musician and Delfino Riviera is made even more romantic by an Italian guitarist and vocalist. On weekends, you're likely to find singing Chef Luciano serenading guests at Sal's Market Deli. Even Splendido Pizzaria features a calypso steel band on Saturdays and Sundays.

Shopping at the Portofino Bay Hotel

As you might expect, there is an impressive assortment of shops at this hotel. If you're looking for that last-minute souvenir, you'll find it at Portofino's Universal Studios Store. For unique gifts from Italy and Portofino logo apparel, you'll want to visit Le Memorie di Portofino, adjacent to the lobby.

Harborside shopping includes the classy men's and women's apparel and accessories of Alta Moda. You'll find everything here from undergarments to hats. Nearby is L'Ancora, Portofino's place for gifts and remembrances, sundries, over-the-counter medications, and snacks and beverages. And for some really unique browsing, you'll want to visit Galleria Portofino, a veritable art gallery of Italian glass, paintings, sculptures, and jewelry. All in all, it's shopping that befits any small Italian village.

Recreation at Portofino Bay

This resort features three large pools, all with "zero entry," a feature that allows bathers to simply wade into the beach-like shore of the pool. Portofino's pools are located in charming garden areas and have an ample number of comfortable chaise lounges. At the more adult-oriented Villa Pool, you'll find private rental cabanas and at the Beach Pool, a Roman aqueduct water slide, white-sand beach, and a children's wading pool. The Hillside Pool is particularly quiet.

- Three large, heated pools
- Three whirlpool tubs
- Greenhouse Spa fitness center, $12 per day
- Rental cabanas with refrigerators, video, and ceiling fans
- Children's wading pool
- Video arcade
- Jogging and walking path
- Two bocce ball courts
- Teen hotline for resort activities for teens

The Greenhouse Spa & Salon at Portofino Bay Hotel

After a day in the theme parks, let your tired feet find their way to this heavenly place. The beautiful Greenhouse Spa is what great vacations are all about. You'll find a blissful assortment of massages, facials, hydrotherapy treatments, and even a full-service salon. Its quiet and luxurious atmosphere is permeated by the soothing aromas of citrus and herbs, and merely stepping inside the door will give your senses a taste of what delights await.

The Greenhouse Spa & Salon features a large and inviting menu of services, including a men's spa escape, an exotic coconut rub, and an aroma stone therapy massage. There's even a large, coed whirlpool tub.

Fun Fact

Gift certificates are available to the Greenhouse Spa (hint, hint).

The Greenhouse Spa also offers in-room massage by appointment. To see the entire menu of services, visit the spa's Web site at www.cbeauty.com/menu.asp. Greenhouse prices are comparable to other spas of this caliber, with most services costing around $90 an hour. For more information and to make reservations, call (407) 503-1244. We suggest you make your reservations several weeks in advance.

Our Impressions of the Portofino Bay Hotel

@ A beautiful and luxurious resort. First-class in every way. So much like Italy that it will simply transport you.

@ Rooms are some of the largest in the industry. Ours was a spacious, comfortable, and restful retreat from the hubbub of the theme parks.

@ With "No Line, No Wait," a stay here makes for the ultimate Universal Orlando vacation.

@ Portofino Bay has been recognized as one of the "World's Best Places to Stay" by Conde Nast Traveler.

@ Our only dread here at Portofino Bay: check-out time.

@ There is no concierge level service here at the Portofino Bay Hotel.

Our Recommendations for the Portofino Bay

@ If you want to be near the water-taxi dock, ask for a room in the West Wing.

@ Opt for harbor view room

Romance at Portofino Bay

@ Overall theming ♥♥♥♥

@ Luxurious rooms ♥♥♥♥

@ A romantic dinner at Delfino Riviera ♥♥♥♥

@ An after-dark stroll to CityWalk or the Hard Rock for dinner or a drink ♥♥

@ Breakfast in bed ♥♥♥

@ Stroll this resort's piazzas after dark ♥♥

@ A glass of wine from Sal's under the stars on the Harbor Piazza ♥♥♥

@ A Kids Suite ♥♥♥

@ A late-night hot tub ♥♥♥

The Hard Rock Hotel

This hotel has a story. It was once a huge mansion, owned by an internationally renowned rock star. The tale tells how with his career in decline, he decided that rather than part with his home, he'd turn it into a luxury hotel. It would be the perfect place for his friends to come and stay, and he'd call it the Hard Rock Hotel. A cute story, of course, and quite engaging.

We arrived at the Hard Rock Hotel in the evening, and from a distance, the California Mission–style "mansion" seemed grand, indeed. Its red-tiled roof, parapet gables, and Spanish belfries hearken back to Hollywood's golden era. The long, palm-lined drive passes under a large porte cochere to make a graceful turn around a beautiful fountain. Under its cascade of sparkling water is a spiral sculpture of bronze electric guitars. It speaks volumes about this hotel. Once inside, we found ourselves immersed in the classic rock music that this hotel so faithfully celebrates: the Beatles, the Stones, Led Zeppelin, and a generation of other superstars.

Hard Rock's reception area is an uncluttered expanse of marble floor. Throughout the lobby are displays of this hotel's vast collection of rock memorabilia: autographed guitars, sequined costumes worn by Elvis and Elton John, and the psychedelic posters of legendary music festivals. But there is more to this place than simply nostalgic music and unusual memorabilia. The mood here at Hard Rock is one of a perpetual party, but what might have become a contradiction in moods, comes off instead as an atmosphere that's both luxurious and lavish, as well as casual and fun. This hotel claims to be the first in a new generation of resorts aimed at a new generation of guests. We couldn't agree more.

After check-in, we explored the lobby's trendy and Art Deco sitting area. A stylish and contemporary California chic, it's comfortable and inviting. Out on the long balcony that overlooks the pool, we gazed down upon the beautiful palms and fountain courtyards that give Hard Rock's pool area its Southern California beach atmosphere. Everywhere outside, the hotel's powerful sound system drives the nonstop rhythms of rock 'n' roll. In the huge pool, we watched a throng of swimmers playing water basketball while other guests cheered them on from the nearby pool bar. Beyond Hard Rock's lively courtyard and

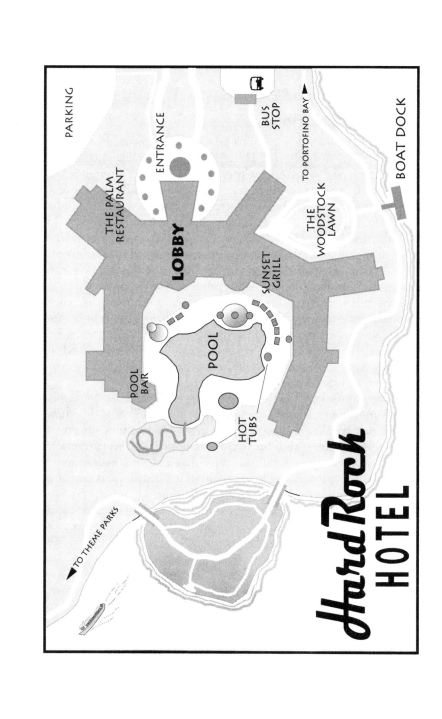

PARKING

ENTRANCE

THE PALM
RESTAURANT

LOBBY

BUS
STOP

TO PORTOFINO BAY

THE
WOODSTOCK
LAWN

BOAT DOCK

SUNSET
GRILL

POOL
BAR

POOL

HOT
TUBS

TO THEME PARKS

Hard Rock
HOTEL

Room Rates as of 2003 for The Hard Rock Hotel (prices include all taxes)

Accommodation	Off-Peak Season	Regular Season	Peak Season
Garden View	$233	$255	$278
Pool View	$255	$278	$300
Deluxe Room	$300	$322	$356
Hard Rock Club	$345	$367	$411
Kids Suite	$467	$512	$556

above the tops of its surrounding palms are the colorful lights of City-Walk and the brilliant search lamps over the theme parks. This, we knew, was going to be a vacation to remember.

Hard Rock Hotel Rooms

Although this resort is a place of nonstop music and partying, our room was a safe haven of luxury and peace. Like the atmosphere of this hotel, our spacious and well-appointed accommodations also enjoyed some smart and stylish contrasts. The monotone beige of walls, bedspreads, and drapes are elegantly contraposed by the simple black and white photos of rock superstars and by the gentle curves and warm wood tones of bedstead and dresser. As modern as these furnishings are, they also seem to evoke the stylish opulence of the 1920s. A plush carpet of teal and green brings these elements together, to create an overall effect that is chic, soothing, and even glamorous.

While there are no balconies here at the Hard Rock Hotel, guest rooms feature a comfortable, stuffed chair with "starburst" ottoman as well as a cozy table with seating, perfect for in-room dining. A stylish mini-butler is cleverly recessed into a mirrored niche and provides both a coffeemaker and a well-stocked selection of beverages and snacks.

Hard Rock baths include a small vanity, plush cotton towels, hair dryer, makeup mirror, telephone, bathroom scale, and specialty toiletries. Other room amenities include two-line speakerphones with data ports, an integrated entertainment center with on-demand movies, and CD player/radio. With 650 rooms, guests can choose a room with either two queen beds or a single king. Average standard room size is 365 square feet. A larger, deluxe room features the addition of a built-in desk and a window seat area.

Concierge Service and Suites at the Hard Rock

Concierge service here at the Hard Rock means a stay in the Hard Rock Club, on the hotel's private seventh floor. The stylish Club lounge features a comfortable sitting area, large-screen TV, a library of more than 600 music CDs, and a selection of rock 'n' roll books, all available for guest checkout. A complimentary continental breakfast is served each morning and beer and wine and hors d'oeuvres are featured from 5 P.M. to 7 P.M. A variety of complimentary beverages are available throughout the day and after 8 P.M., cookies, milk, and coffee are served.

And of course, the Hard Rock Club has its own private concierge desk, ready to make dinner reservations, obtain tickets to shows, or to help you plan any part of your vacation. Club guests also enjoy complimentary use of the hotel's fitness center and a 50 percent discount on poolside rental cabanas.

Rooms in the Hard Rock Club feature additional creature comforts such as bathrobes, umbrella, nightly turndown, large-screen TV and entertainment center, cordless phones, and a special amenity package. Our Hard Rock Club stay was one of the highlights of creating this edition of our book.

Also here on the exclusive Club level are a handful of suites, all of which enjoy Club privileges. The Graceland Suite is one of Orlando's most lavish accommodations, and features a large king bedroom, plush parlor with fireplace, and a stunning panorama of pool and theme parks. The Graceland's large bathroom includes both an oversize whirlpool tub and a fireplace. Prices begin at $1,200 per night. Also on this private floor are two Club Suites ♥♥♥ that feature a single king bed, comfortable parlor room, and the option to connect to a room with two queen beds. For just the Club Suite, prices begin at $395.

At other pool-view locations throughout the hotel are ten King Suites, each similar to the Club Suites, and each with the option of an adjoining room (but none including concierge Club service). We enjoyed one of these wonderful suites and found it spacious, luxurious, and romantic. Prices begin at $400 per night.

Dining at the Hard Rock Hotel

There are three restaurants here at the Hard Rock. The Sunset Grill serves an innovative California cuisine for each of the day's meals. The Palm is both a chophouse and a fine Italian restaurant, serving both lunch and dinner. For more about these restaurants and our take on their offerings, see chapter 10.

Guests enjoying the pool will also like the Hard Rock Beach Club, with its casual menu of burgers, salads, sandwiches, wraps, and poolside service. New at the Hard Rock is Emack & Bolios. This delightful cafe is on the ground floor adjacent to the Sunset Grill. It features Star-buck's coffee, a variety of baked sweets, and the gourmet delights of the Emack & Bolios ice cream company of Boston. Mornings here feature good coffee, pastries, cinnamon rolls, and bagels.

Lounges at the Hard Rock

The Velvet Bar is one of the most comfortable lounges we know of. Its name says it all. Inside, you'll find cozy sitting areas, plush sofas, and a full-service bar. Poolside, guests looking for a cold beer or a cocktail will find it all at the Hard Rock Beach Club.

Shops at Hard Rock

Adjacent to the lobby you'll find a large Hard Rock Store that features a large variety of Hard Rock Hotel logo merchandise as well as a small offerings of snacks, beverages, and sundry items such as film and sunscreen.

Recreation at Hard Rock

There's so much to do here, you might think you're at summer camp. Much of it revolves around this hotel's fabulous pool area, which features a 266-foot water slide and an underwater audio system.

- Large "zero entry" pool with water slide and a sand beach
- Two hot tubs (one more secluded)
- Water basketball and water polo
- Complimentary floats for pool
- Beach volleyball, shuffleboard, life-size chess, and ping pong
- Kids wading pool and interactive "pop jet" fountains
- Rental cabanas with stocked refrigerators, video, and ceiling fans
- Video game room
- The Workout Room fitness center, $8 per person, per day
- Jogging and walking path
- Pet walking area (pets need recreation, too!)

Our Impressions of the Hard Rock Hotel

- This is one of our favorite hotels anywhere. It's casual and fun, and the rooms are luxurious and comfortable. We love staying here.
- With "No Line, No Wait," a stay here makes for a great Universal Orlando vacation.

- Great recreational offerings around the pool. A virtual summer camp.
- Kids just seem to love this place. We can't blame them.
- We love having a CD player in our room.
- Considering the room rates here and the caliber of this hotel, Hard Rock is a deal.
- This is a place of non-stop rock music.

Our Recommendations for the Hard Rock Hotel

- Hard Rock Club level is well worth the extra money.
- A pool-view room on a higher floor.
- Try a King Suite. Nice! ♥♥♥
- Visit here off-season for real bargain luxury.
- Bring a few favorite CDs to play in your room.

Romance at the Hard Rock Hotel

- Overall "theming" ♥♥♥
- A Club Suite ♥♥♥♥
- A King Suite ♥♥♥
- An after-dark stroll to CityWalk or Portofino for dinner or a drink ♥♥
- Breakfast in bed ♥♥♥
- Late evening in the secluded hot tub ♥♥
- A nightcap at the Velvet Bar ♥♥
- Dinner on Sunset Grill's patio ♥♥♥

The Royal Pacific Resort

The lilting songs of the Far East and the melodious music of rushing water greeted us as we arrived at this enchanting resort. A covered footbridge took us across a small river, its terraced ravine dense with tropical foliage. Purple taro, bamboo thickets, variegated ginger, and frangipani are but a few of the many plants native to the lands this resort celebrates: Fiji, Tonga, Bali, Samoa, and Tuvalu.

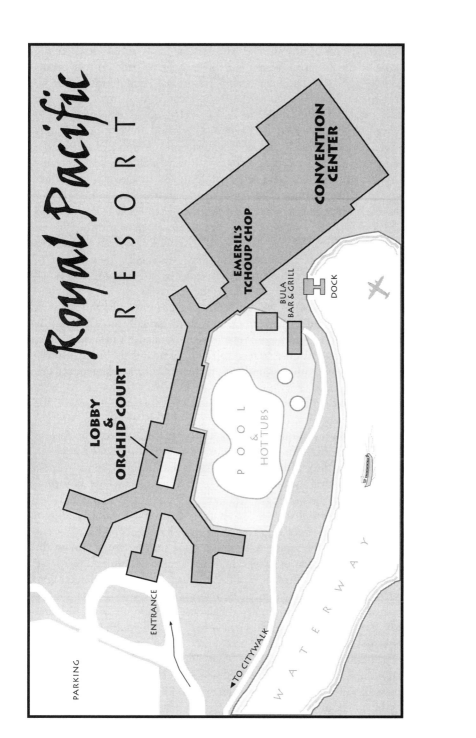

The islands of the South Pacific and the lands of Indonesia are the theme of this beautiful place. But this is a theme park, so that means there's a story, too. The Royal Pacific Resort was "built in the 1930s" to be the jewel in the crown of the Royal Pacific Company. Here in the exotic heart of tropical Polynesia, pampered guests enjoyed tranquil layovers as they explored the surrounding island archipelagos. Visitors arrived and departed by Royal Pacific steamer or onboard one of the company's seaplane clippers. "Today's" Royal Pacific Resort will transport you to this golden era of romantic travel, an age of worn leather luggage, big band music, and mysterious ports of call.

We'll admit that we were a bit surprised by this place. Promoted as Universal Orlando's moderately priced resort, it seems someone forgot to tell the architect. To us, the Royal Pacific Resort is from top to bottom, a deluxe hotel. Although its rooms are smaller than the Hard Rock's, they are very comfortable, even luxurious. In short, the Royal Pacific is a bargain.

The resort's central area surrounds its beautiful Orchid Court, a lush, open-air garden that can be seen from virtually anywhere in the lobby. In addition to dozens of exotic plants and sculptures, the Orchid Court also showcases the largest collection of orchids in Florida. In the large, stone fountain, a family of sculpted Balinese elephants frolic while resort guests enjoy quiet sitting areas.

The Orchid Court is a sunny and stunning centerpiece to the lobby area that surrounds it. Here we found the front desk and the concierge counter, numerous cozy sitting places, one of the resort's shops, and the beautiful Orchid Court Lounge. It's all richly themed in an eclectic melange of Indonesian cultures that include carved Balinese lanterns, batik wall-hangings, and painted murals. It's serene, beautiful, and classy.

We took a stroll around the resort to discover a veritable garden of flowering plants, towering palms, thickets of bamboo, and banana trees. On one side of the resort, we found a quiet putting green next to the beautiful luau garden, home to the Royal Pacific's Wantilan Luau feast.

On the other side of the resort is the Lagoon Pool. The largest pool in Orlando, it features zero entry, rental cabanas, and a "half sunken steamship" playground, the Royal Bali Sea. This unique water play area will keep children busy for hours, frolicking in its fountains and dueling with its water cannons.

There's a real lagoon at the Royal Pacific, too. And it's here you'll catch the shuttle boat to City Walk and the Universal theme parks. If you're like us, you'll want to just laze around here under the palms and daydream about the seaplane that lies at anchor in the lagoon. It's the perfect bit of theming for this resort.

The Rooms at the Royal Pacific Resort

The comfortable accommodations of the Royal Pacific enjoy a romantic Dutch colonial decor of dark wood furnishings with woven reed accents. Fabrics are tropical floral prints of rich rusts and subdued ochre. Each room features a hand-carved Balinese mahogany wall panel, vintage travel posters, and enough luxury to make your stay a special one.

Room amenities include a small table and chairs, a mini-butler, television, two-line phone with data port, hairdryer, coffeemaker (with coffee), and iron and ironing board. Guest rooms have either a single king bed or two queen beds. Some king rooms also have a sleeper sofa. If that is your wish, you must request it when you make your reservations. Average standard room size at the Royal Pacific is 335 square feet (Disney's moderate resort rooms are 314 square feet).

Each resort accommodation has a separate (but rather small) vanity area and lavatories that feature a standard shower/tub. Although there are no balconies at the Royal Pacific, there are a variety of pleasant views. Our view of the pool area and lagoon was memorable, especially after dark. Other views are of the resort's garden areas, Islands of Adventure theme park, or Orlando.

For the price of a room, you get a full-service hotel with luxurious rooms, numerous dining and entertainment options, and all of it just a stone's throw from the Universal theme parks. Toss in the "No Line, No Wait" perk of staying here, and the Royal Pacific makes for a great deal, one we highly recommend.

Concierge Service and Suites at the Royal Pacific Resort

The Royal Club Level is this resort's exclusive concierge area. Rooms on this private floor include a variety of suites and standard guest rooms. Extra amenities mean nightly turndown, cotton bathrobes, and access to the resort's modern health club. The comfortable Royal Club

Room Rates as of 2003 for the Royal Pacific Resort (prices include taxes)

Accommodation	Off-Peak	Regular	Peak
Standard	$200	$222	$244
Water View	$233	$255	$278
Club Level	$311	$333	$356
King Suite	$289	$311	$333

lounge provides a daily continental breakfast; beer, wine, and hors d'oeuvres in late afternoon; and desserts and beverages in the evening. Be it a rental car or restaurant reservations, the knowledgeable concierge staff will be there to help with your needs. We love staying in concierge and our stay was made truly special by a staff that is exceptionally friendly. We simply can't wait to return.

There are a variety of suites at the Royal Pacific, and they begin with the Stateroom (or King) Suite and its king bed. Although this suite is not on the club level, it does feature a comfortable adjoining parlor room with sleeper/sofa, sound system, television, and small desk. At $289 (off-peak), it's the perfect accommodation if you are traveling with one child or simply desire the extra space.

Other suites include the First Officers Suite and two extravagant Captains Suites. Each of these pricey, multi-room accommodations provides more than enough space for a small party as well as such amenities as a butler's pantry, powder room, study, and luxurious master bath with spa tub. Traveling in this style certainly has its appeal, but at around $1,500 per night, a Captains Suite is not for those of us who travel on a budget.

Dining at the Royal Pacific Resort

Food is certainly one of this resort's strong suits. Tchoup Chop, celebrity chef Emeril Lagasse's second Orlando restaurant, takes Asian food and "kicks it up a notch." It's one of Orlando's premier dining destinations. We strongly suggest you make plans to dine here. Islands Dining Room is this resort's "all-purpose" eatery, but don't let this description fool you. Islands features a varied and creative menu for each of the day's meals, with a specialty buffet on select evenings. It's one of our favorite Universal dining spots. For more details and our take on these restaurants, see chapter 10.

For a more casual meal, we suggest Jake's American Bar, where the small but mighty menu features everything from salads and sandwiches, to pasta and baby back ribs. And if you're looking for a continental breakfast, head to the lobby to the Orchid Court Lounge. In the morning, you'll find coffee and an assortment of pastries, bagels, and dry cereals. It's an economical and convenient place to start your day.

You'll find even more good eating poolside under the thatched umbrellas of the Bula Bar and Grill. While away your afternoon around the pool and begin it with lunch at Bula, savoring an inviting selection of salads, Asian snacks, and wraps. In addition to all these restaurants, Royal Pacific guests are but a few minutes away from City

Walk, where there are more dining opportunities than can fit into a single vacation.

Lounges at the Royal Pacific Resort

There's no shortage of interesting and comfortable places to have a drink at the Royal Pacific. Our favorite is Jake's American Bar and its 1930s aviator atmosphere. We like Jake's so much, we wouldn't dream of returning to the Royal Pacific without a visit to this great place. Other choices include the Orchid Court Lounge's decidedly Asian ambience and the Bula Bar's outdoor, island charm.

Live Entertainment at the Royal Pacific Resort

Did we mention there's live entertainment here, too? Drop by Jake's on a weekend evening to enjoy the dusky and romantic tones of jazz singer Sarah Hayes. And each night in the Islands Dining Room, you'll find something a little different. Whether it's Balinese dancers, strolling Polynesian musicians, or a bevy of Universal characters, something's almost always happening here.

At the Royal Pacific, you'll also find the evening Torch Lighting Ceremony. Based on an ancient Hawaiian tradition called "kukui hele po," this is something you won't want to miss. Check with the concierge desk in the lobby to find out when it's offered during your visit.

The Royal Pacific also features the marvelous Wantilan Luau. With a feast of South Seas and Asian foods and authentic and exotic entertainment, this popular dinner show is one you'll want to enjoy. When you reserve your room, be sure to ask when it is available during your visit and make reservations.

Shopping at the Royal Pacific Resort

There are two shops here, and both offer the usual variety of Universal and resort logo merchandise, as well as a selection of South Seas souvenirs. Toko Gifts is on the lobby level, while Treasures of Bali is poolside.

Recreation at the Royal Pacific Resort

- ℮ The Lagoon Pool features a pool area with steamship water playground
- ℮ Three hot tubs (two at pool, one in health club)
- ℮ Scheduled activities such as water aerobics, bocce ball, ping pong, beach volleyball

- Rental cabanas with TV
- Children's wading pool
- The Gymnasium Health Club with beautiful coed hot tub
- Putting green
- Video arcade

Our Impressions of the Royal Pacific Resort

- We love this enchanting and charming resort. We can hardly think of a better vacation than to stay here and visit the Universal Orlando theme parks.
- Great dining ♥♥ and a great lounge, Jake's
- Amazingly convenient to Universal theme parks

Our Recommendations for the Royal Pacific Resort

- Reserve an upper floor room.
- Club level is very good here; the staff is the friendliest we have known.
- The Stateroom (King) Suite

Romance at the Royal Pacific Resort

- Resort Theming ♥♥♥
- A Club Level room ♥♥
- The Wantilan Luau ♥♥♥
- An evening at Jake's American Bar
- Hot tub after dark (outside or in the health club) ♥♥
- Breakfast in bed or in-room dining ♥♥♥

CHAPTER 10

The Attractions of Universal Orlando

Universal Orlando proves that you don't have to be big to be BIG. There's a truly impressive amount of entertainment packed into its 240 acres: Universal Studios, Islands of Adventure, and CityWalk. And strangely, it doesn't feel crowded.

"Ride the Movies!" is the motto of Universal Studios, and it's not only a great movie theme park, but it's also a working studio. Right next door is Islands of Adventure (IOA). Really five different theme parks rolled into one, IOA is a place of over-the-top coasters, wild thrill rides, and even heartwarming children's attractions. There's something here for everyone.

Not exactly what we'd call a theme park, CityWalk is the focal point of after-dark excitement here at Universal. It features lively avenues of clubs, restaurants, unusual shopping, and a 20-screen Cineplex.

The Lay of the Land

However you arrive, you'll come first to CityWalk, the central "hub" of Universal Orlando. From here, you can go to either Universal Studios or IOA, the entrances to which are at opposite ends of CityWalk (see our map on page 384), or you can stay and explore CityWalk. Universal's compact size makes getting around a breeze. Nothing seems very far from anything else, and you'll find it easy to skip from one park to another whenever you wish, or leave the parks and enjoy lunch or dinner at CityWalk.

What You'll Find at Both Parks

Theme parks everywhere seem to have certain things in common. Here's what you can expect at both Universal Studios and IOA:

@ Both parks usually open at 9 A.M. Closing times vary from 6 P.M. to as late as 11 P.M., depending on the time of year. Expect later closings during holidays, on weekends, and during the busy summer months. To find the exact times during your visit, call (800) 232-7827. Dial 0 to speak with a person.

@ Each park features a full-color map of attractions, shops, restaurants, first aid, rest rooms, and so on. Whatever you're looking for, you'll find it in Universal Studios' Studio Guide or IOA's Adventure Guide. Each also has an insert that lists the times of shows and special events. Be sure you get them both first thing and look them over to get an idea of what you want to see and do.

@ Guest services are located at the entrance to either park, just outside the turnstiles. They will be happy to help with special dining needs, disability guides, and any problem or request you may have. Theme park guest services phone number is (407) 224-6350.

@ Ticket booths and automated ticket machines are located at the entrances to both parks (you can also purchase tickets from guest services). Also near the entrances: ATMs, telephones, stamp machines, and rest rooms.

@ Rental counters just inside the entrances to both parks rent strollers ($9 for singles, $15 for doubles), wheelchairs ($8), and electric convenience vehicles ($40 per day plus deposit).

@ Rental lockers ($6 a day) are located near the entrance to both parks.

@ A Family Services Center is located just inside the gate of both the Studios and Islands of Adventure. Each provides first-aid, a diaper-changing station, and a small room with rockers for nursing.

@ Tip Boards are located throughout both parks and will tell you how long you can expect to wait at the various park attractions, and what attractions might be closed.

@ Check your Studio Guide and Adventure Guide for "Character Meet and Greet" places where you can meet the Universal characters for fun and photos.

@ What we call "attraction-action" photos are featured at some rides in both parks. Your photo will be taken during the attraction, and you can see (and purchase) it as you exit. Prints cost $13 or more, depending on size and frame. These are a great opportunity for photos that are otherwise impossible to get.

@ Other souvenir picture opportunities range from roving photographers to artists who will sketch your caricatures. Check these out. They make good souvenirs. Most prices begin around $13.

@ "Kid Swaps" allow parents to ride certain attractions when their children are too small to accompany them. Here's how it works: Go to one of the many rides that features this and ask where you can find the "kid swap" entrance. Then, one of you takes your child there while the other enters the attraction in the normal fashion. After the ride, you then "swap the baby" and the other one rides. It's simple, once you get the hang of it.

@ Pet boarding is available at the Universal Kennels and costs $5 per day. You'll need to provide food and walk your pet several times during the day. A current health certificate is required. Ask a parking attendant where to go. The kennel closes one hour after the closing of CityWalk. For complete details, call (407) 224-9509.

@ Free, computerized storage lockers are available while you ride certain attractions that won't let you on with backpacks, camera bags, or whatever else you may be lugging around. Several rides even require you to empty your pockets.

@ Many shops at both parks sell film and even cameras, in case you've forgotten yours.

@ Certain attractions have minimum height requirements. We'll post these with each ride, where applicable. They are also shown on the guide maps for each park.

@ Vegetarian meals are available at restaurants throughout the parks. No advance notice is required.

@ Personally guided VIP tours are available at both parks. Choose from a variety of packages, with prices beginning around $130. Reservations must be made at least two to three weeks in advance. For more information and reservations, call (407) 363-8295.

@ Face painting, hair wraps, video game arcades, snack carts with ice cream, drinks, and snacks are available everywhere throughout both parks.

Universal Express Pass

Like its cousin across town, Disney's *FASTPASS*, the idea of the Universal Express pass is to allow you to avoid waiting in line by assigning an hour-long time period during which you can return and ride the attraction with little or minimal wait. It's worth mentioning that during the busiest times, this wait might be as long as fifteen minutes.

Universal accomplishes this with two notable differences from Disney. The first difference is that Universal Express includes nearly every attraction in both parks. (We'll mark those that are not participating later in this chapter.) The second difference is that guests can chose either of two one-hour time slots.

Here's how the Universal Express pass works: Scan your admission pass at one of the Universal Express Distribution Centers at various locations around either park (each location is for a specific attraction). You'll receive a pass that will allow you into a specific attraction during a one-hour time period. You can get another Express Pass only after you have either used it, after the one-hour time slot has expired, or at a time printed on the pass.

Our Tips for Both Universal Studios and IOA

℮ If you're planning a visit during a holiday or a busy season such as summer or school vacations, we *strongly* suggest you stay in one of Universal Orlando's three resorts and make use of "No Line, No Wait." You won't have to stand in line for attractions. It's the best and only way to beat the crowds. For details, see "Where to Stay" on page 388 for more details.

℮ Most people arrive between 10:00 A.M. and 11:30 A.M. Arrive earlier and make use of the few hours to see the most popular attractions.

℮ Head to the back of the park first, where there are fewer people. Most people work their way around from the entrance.

℮ Make full use of the Universal Express pass when the parks are busy. See page 418.

℮ Travel light. Avoid large knapsacks, purses, and bulky camera bags.

℮ To avoid crowded restaurants, eat earlier or later, and then take advantage of rides while most others are eating.

℮ A card from AAA (American Automobile Association) will get you a 10 percent discount on food and merchandise in select restaurants and shops throughout Universal Studios and IOA.

℮ Save your shopping for either your last day or late in the day, to avoid having to carry around bags full of souvenirs.

℮ On certain holidays and on certain dates, both theme parks sometimes feature special shows and nightime fireworks. To see what is happening during your visit or to answer other questions, call Universal Orlando's Event Hotline (407) 224-5500.

Universal Studios

This park really lives up to its motto of "Ride the Movies!" The attractions here feature many of the most popular films of all time. Some even take you "backstage" for an interesting look into how movies and special effects are created. Others make you feel as though you're in the movies. All in all, this is a great park with a real emphasis on entertainment for adults. Happily, it also seems to be a place that teens enjoy and it even features an entire area dedicated to younger children.

Our Tips for Universal Studios

@ Get a Studio Guide and times guide and look them over to get a good lay of the land. Keep them with you for reference.

@ Lines get longest at Men in Black. If you wish to ride it, go there first thing and ride it or get an Express Pass.

@ Because this is a working studio, you'll have the opportunity to join the audience for shows that might be taping. Tickets are first come, first served, and are available at the Studio Audience Center (near the front gate). To find out what might be in production during your visit, call (407) 224-6355, after 11 A.M.

@ Lost & Found is located at Studio Audience Center. Call (407) 224-6355.

@ Some of the attractions at the Studios are rated PG-13. This means "parental guidance suggested for children under 13 years of age."

@ Kodak Trick Photo Spots are featured at various places throughout the park. These utilize a "miniature matte" special effects technique still used in the movies. Simply place your camera in the designated spot and "take your mark."

Our Tips for Eating at Universal Studios

@ During the slower seasons of the year, when the park closes at 6 P.M., you'll find that many restaurants begin to close around 4 P.M., so don't wait too long to eat. During the busier times, when the park is open until late at night, almost all restaurants are open until well past the dinner hour.

@ Grab a continental breakfast just inside the park at Beverly Hills Boulangerie.

Universal Studios
SAN FRANCISCO / AMITY

WILD WEST STUNT SHOW

JAWS

MEN IN BLACK

WORLD EXPO

CURIOUS GEORGE

AMITY AVE.

THE LAGOON

BACK TO THE FUTURE

WOODY WOODPECKER'S KIDZONE

NUTHOUSE COASTER

EMBARCADERO

EXPOSITION AVENUE

ANIMAL PLANET LIVE

FIEVEL'S PLAYGROUND

EARTHQUAKE

SUNSET BLVD.

E.T. ADVENTURE

MAKE-UP SHOW

THE MUMMY COMING 2004

5TH AVENUE

7TH AVENUE

PRODUCTION CENTRAL

STAGE 54

8TH AVENUE

HOLLYWOOD BLVD.

TERMINATOR 2 ADVENTURE 3-D

HOLLYWOOD

NEW YORK

TWISTER

SHREK

RODEO DRIVE

NICKELODEON STUDIOS

JIMMY NUTRINO

57TH STREET

ENTRANCE

ISLANDS OF ADVENTURE ←

UNIVERSAL HOTELS →

@ Remember that CityWalk and the Universal hotels are right out-side the front gate and offer much better food, most of it for prices only slightly higher than in the theme parks.

@ At the Studios, only Lombard's Landing takes priority-seating arrangements for meals. Do this up to twenty-four hours ahead at the Studios guest services, with Lombard's maitre d', at the concierge desk of any Universal hotel, or by calling (407) 224-9255.

@ There are only two table-service restaurants here at the Studios, and they're both merely OK: Lombard's Landing (San Francisco) and Finnegan's Bar & Grill (New York).

@ Kosher meals (prepared and frozen) are available with forty-eight-hour notice at both Finnegan's Bar & Grill and Lombard's Landing.

Money-Saving Tip

You can get a 10 percent discount at restaurants throughout Universal Studios by showing your AAA membership card.

Universal Studios Live Entertainment

Each day, you'll find a variety of live entertainers at Universal. On a stage in front of Mel's Diner, catch 4 Girls Only, a talented 1950s vocal group. In New York, the Blues Brothers perform live daily. And throughout the park, you're likely to see the Studios' roving characters: Charlie Chaplin, Marilyn Monroe, and the Marx Brothers. These char-acters will be happy to pose with you for photos and these will be some of your favorites.

Production Central

The focus of this area of huge sound stages is how movies and televi-sion shows are created. Exhibits, demonstrations, movie clips, and even a ride are all featured here.

🌟 *Shrek and Donkey's Scary-Tale Adventure*

@ Sensory 3-D movie with special effects.

@ Lasts about twenty minutes, including pre-show.

This attraction hadn't opened before we completed this edition, but it is supposed to feature fifteen minutes of all-new Shrek animation with spectacular effects. We guess it will be a lot like It's Tough to Be a Bug at WDW.

WILL LIKELY BE OUTSTANDING; one not to miss. May be frightening to very young children.

💥 *Jimmy Neutron Nicktoon Blast*

℮ Bumpy "flight simulator," riders must be at least 40 inches tall

℮ Lasts about 5 minutes; continuous shows

This blends state-of-the-art computer graphics with the same "ride" platform as the old Hanna Barbera ride. Of course, the new movie features Jimmy Neutron and a gang of Nickelodeon characters.

LOTS OF FUN, especially good for families but we enjoyed it, too.

Nickelodeon Studios Gamelab

℮ Audience participation game show

℮ Lasts about 25 minutes

This attraction allows you to play games based on those on the Nickelodeon Network. Someone always gets slimed.

GOOD FAMILY FUN, fairly engaging.

Stage 54

℮ Walk-through exhibit

℮ No set time, usually no lines

This area displays props and sets from a recent Universal Studios film production. Video clips and a behind-the-scenes look into the making of the film are featured.

INTERESTING AND ENGAGING, especially if you're a film buff.

Hollywood

Besides some great attractions, this area features a wonderful Art Deco street of shops, eateries, a 1950s drive-in, and even a theater. There's a lot of fun here for movie (and TV) lovers, and most of it is aimed at teens and more mature audiences. One of our Hollywood favorites is Movietime Portraits, where you can get your photo taken dressed in any of an interesting selection of costumes, complete with real background set. It's a great souvenir idea! Prices begin around $26.50.

Universal Studios Restaurants

Restaurant	Location	Price	Fare	Service	Our Comments
Classic Monsters Cafe	Production Central	$	Salads, pizza, pasta, soup, rotisserie chicken	Counter service L/D	Noisy fun, OK food
Cafe La Bamba	Hollywood	$	Burgers, wraps, BBQ, rotisserie chicken	Counter service L/D	Pretty good food
Mel's Drive-In	Hollywood	$	Burgers, fries, shakes	Counter service L/D	Great atmosphere, decent food, good shakes
Schwab's Pharmacy	Hollywood	$	Turkey and other sandwiches, ice cream treats	Counter service L/D	Nostalgic atmosphere, OK fast food
Beverly Hills Boulangerie	Hollywood	$	Gourmet sandwiches, pastries	Counter service B/L	Continental breakfast and good sandwiches
International Food Bazaar	Hollywood	$	Pizza, fried chicken, tacos, burgers	Counter service L/D	Skip it!
Finnegan's Bar & Grill	New York	$$	Irish pub menu with full-service bar	Table service L/D	Authentic atmosphere, OK food
Louie's Italian Restaurant	New York	$	Italian cuisine with espresso bar	Counter service L/D	OK fast food

Universal Studios Restaurants *(continued)*

Restaurant	Location	Price	Fare	Service	Our Comments
Lombard's Landing*	San Francisco	$$	Fresh seafood, steak, pasta, sandwiches	Table service L/D	Quite good: reservations a must (See page 454.)
Richter's Burgers	San Francisco	$	Build your own burgers	Counter service L/D	Good topping bar
Chez Alcatraz	San Francisco	$	Clam chowder, sandwiches, beer	Counter service L/D	Some good choices
Midway Grill	Amity	$	Hoagies, Philly cheesesteaks, beer	Counter service L/D	OK fast food
BoardWalk Snacks	Amity	$	Seafood and chowder	Counter service L/D	Pretty good stuff
Animal Crackers	Woody's Kidzone	$	Hot dogs, chicken fingers, sandwiches	Counter service L/D	Kid stuff!

B/L/D: Breakfast/Lunch/Dinner (when parks are open late)
$ most entrées less than $10
$$ most entrées less than $25
*See chapter 10 for our reviews of these restaurants.

The Gory, Gruesome & Grotesque Horror Make-Up Show (PG-13)

@ Stage show and demonstration of special effects makeup

@ Lasts 25 minutes, continuous shows after 12 P.M.

Both entertaining and interesting, this humorous show demonstrates the ins and outs of special effects makeup. We enjoyed both the humor and the insights into moviemaking.
VERY GOOD, don't miss it.
WARNING: Some humor is not suitable for youngsters.

Terminator 2: 3-D Battle Across Time (PG-13)

@ 3-D film with live action

@ Lasts 20 minutes

This adventure is one of Orlando's best attractions and is nothing less than a sequel to the *Terminator* feature films. It includes original cast members (even you-know-who), first-rate action scenes, and over-the-top special effects. Maybe movies will be this great someday.
TERRIFIC ENTERTAINMENT, don't miss it, especially if you enjoyed the films.
WARNING: Loud and in-your-face. Too intense for very young children.

Lucy: A Tribute

@ Walk-through exhibit

@ No set length, rarely crowded

For our generation, there is but one great TV sitcom: *I Love Lucy*. All others that have followed are mere shadows of this television pioneer. This stroll-through display features film clips, artifacts, and stories about the life and comic genius of Lucille Ball. For older guests, some great nostalgia.
FOR LUCY LOVERS, an attraction not to be missed.

New York

This large "set" features several city blocks of New York City. It's so real that you'll want to stroll into some of the shop facades. There are plenty of other open doors though, including several attractions, an arcade, some shops, restaurants, a Starbucks, and even an Irish pub. Don't forget to get some pictures of your visit to the Big Apple.

Twister . . . Ride It Out (PG-13)

@ Stand-up special effects show

@ Lasts 15 minutes

We loved the movie and enjoyed this "show," which was heavy on effects but short on story. Still, the set and effects are very good and the pre-show features some good insights into how this feature film was created.

GOOD, but didn't move us as much as it did Twister's set.

WARNING: Definitely too loud and too intense for small children.

NEW The Mummy [opens 2004] (PG-13)

Universal is keeping pretty tight-lipped about this coming attraction, but it will be done by the same team that created Spiderman at Islands of Adventure. Part roller coaster, part who-knows-what, we expect this to be one of the most advanced theme park attractions in the world and a not-to-miss ride.

WARNING: Might be too intense for very young children.

The Blues Brothers

@ Musical street show

@ Lasts about 20 minutes; check the Studio Guide for times

From the Dan Ackroyd and John Belushi movie of the same name, this street party can be found on Delancy Street and features blues standards and the film's signature tune, "Soul Man."

OK, music is good and the Jake and Elwood look-alikes are entertaining.

San Francisco/Amity

These areas feature a San Francisco waterfront set and a street that's supposed to be from Amity Island, the fictitious location of the movie *Jaws*. It reminds us of the Massachusetts seaside town of Rockport (or at least how we remember it from our youths). Amity features shops, restaurants, several attractions, and even a midway. Universal's San

Francisco enjoys several popular attractions, a show, some shops to browse, and even a waterfront seafood eatery, Lombard's Landing.

Earthquake: The Big One

@ Special effects show and ride

@ Altogether, lasts about 25 minutes

This attraction includes a display of models, matte paintings, and artifacts from the feature film *Earthquake*. A short movie narrated by Charlton Heston and an audience-participation demonstration show how the film's award-winning special effects were created. For the finale, you'll experience an "earthquake" of 8.3 on the Richter Scale while riding Universal's subway. Fiery explosions, crashing walls, and a tidal wave make for great fun.

TERRIFIC, what great movie attractions are all about. Don't miss it.
WARNING: Probably too intense for young children.

Beetlejuice's Rock 'n' Roll Graveyard Revue (PG-13)

@ Stage show; check Studio Guide for scheduled times

@ Lasts 18 minutes

This open-air theater features a talented cast of ghouls that sing and dance through an updated show that features a neat set, great costumes, special effects, and pyrotechnics.
ENTERTAINING.

Jaws

@ Rocky boat ride through "shark-infested" waters

@ Lasts about 5 minutes

Hop aboard an Amity Island launch to be terrorized by a large and very hungry mechanical shark (actually a whole school of them). Special effects are memorable, the story line is good, and if your pilot is as good a performer as ours was, you'll enjoy this attraction a lot.
ONE OF UNIVERSAL'S BEST. Don't miss it.
WARNING: Too intense for young children.

The Wild Wild Wild West Stunt Show

@ Live show

@ Lasts 18 minutes

With more than one hundred stunts, thunderous gunfights, action-packed horseplay, and special effects, this show provides plenty of excitement and comedy.

GREAT FUN and an attraction not-to-miss.

World Expo

We guess the theme here has something to do with the future or perhaps the world. Whatever it is, this area is the home of two very neat attractions.

Men in Black Alien Attack

@ Interactive ride (cars move slowly), six seats, riders must be at least 42 inches tall

@ Lasts about 5 minutes

Based on the blockbuster movies, this ride takes you through a cityscape where you'll battle aliens, who literally infest the place. If they blast you, it sends your car into a tailspin. You rack up points, both individually and as a team. At the end, you're rated by star Will Smith. Will you be "bug bait"?

GREAT FUN FOR ALL AGES. Gayle's favorite ride at Universal Studios. Don't miss it!

TIP: Before riding, you must stow all bags in (free) lockers near the entrance.

Back to the Future . . . The Ride

@ Flight simulator, eight passengers; riders must be at least 40 inches tall

@ Lasts about 5 minutes

This attraction has it all: a great story, time-traveling DeLoreans, Christopher Lloyd as Doc Brown, and an over-the-top adventure skipping through time to catch the villainous Biff Tannen. When you hear Universal's claim "Ride the Movies!", this is what they're talking about.

STILL FUN, despite the no-longer-cutting-edge technology.

WARNING: Gets a bit rough.

Woody Woodpecker's Kidzone

Even though this area is mostly for kids, there are still attractions here you might wish to see. If you're coming with kids, you won't want to miss this great place. It features innovative play areas, kiddie shows, Barney, and a pint-sized roller coaster.

E. T. Adventure

@ Slow ride on "flying" bicycles

@ Lasts 5 minutes

Of course, these bikes don't really fly, but they do seem to soar around this large soundstage filled with impressive sets and special effects. Best appreciated by those who have seen the film. We guess that's about everyone.
FUN FOR ALL AGES, great sets and effects, a kids' favorite.

Animal Planet Live

@ Live animal show

@ Check Studio Guide for show times

This attraction is the result of a partnership between Universal and the Animal Planet television network. This show features animal demonstrations, live sketches, video clips, and visits from the stars of Animal Planet's most popular shows.
ENTERTAINING. For all ages.

Woody Woodpecker's Nuthouse Coaster

@ Gentle kiddie coaster; riders must be at least 36 inches tall

@ Lasts about 1 minute

@ No Universal Express here

This is a very mild coaster, perfect for young children.
FUN FOR KIDS, otherwise skip it.

Fievel's Playground and Curious George Goes to Town

@ Both attractions are hands-on playgrounds

@ Stay as long as you wish

@ Neither playground participates in Universal Express

Be sure to have your camera along for the many great photo opportunities in these areas. Kids can stay occupied for hours in either of these playgrounds. Be advised that children can get very wet playing here. LOTS OF FUN FOR KIDS, otherwise skip them.

Helpful Hint
Curious George Goes to Town is a water-filled playground. Bring a towel and bathing suit (or a change of clothes) for your young ones.

A Day in the Park With Barney

@ Musical show

@ Lasts 20 minutes, check Studio Guide for show times

Toddlers seem to love Barney, who sings and dances his way through this cute show. Afterward, he'll stay around long enough to greet your children and for you to snap a few photos. The theater empties into Barney's Backyard, a very nice playground, imaginatively conceived and colorfully executed. Your kids will love it. You don't even have to see the show to get into the play area. It has its own entrance.
FOR VERY YOUNG CHILDREN ONLY.

The Shops of Universal Studios
Nearly every attraction has an adjoining shop, and whether you're into looking for Terminator gifts or tornado apparel, you'll find all this and much more in the Studios' many shops. We promise, you won't have to go home without something that proclaims "I've been to Universal!"

Money-Saving Tip
Check out Second-Hand Rose for marked-down Universal merchandise.

Money-Saving Tip
You can get a 10 percent discount on merchandise at select Studio gift shops by showing your AAA card.

Universal Studios Best-of-the-Best List

Men in Black Alien Attack

The Gory, Gruesome, & Grotesque Horror Make-Up Show

Terminator 2: 3-D Battle Across Time

Jaws

Islands of Adventure

While Universal Studios draws its inspiration from the movies, IOA seems to aim simply at having great fun. IOA is made up of five themed "islands" that form a circle around a man-made lagoon named The Great Inland Sea. The five islands are Marvel Super Hero Island, Toon Lagoon, Jurassic Park, The Lost Continent, and Seuss Landing. Each enjoys unique attractions, shops, and restaurants. Theming throughout is very good.

Rides at IOA run the gamut from cutting-edge, high-tech 3-D to a gentle and heartwarming carousel. State-of-the-art coasters, whitewater raft rides—this place seems to have it all. Whatever your age, IOA has plenty in store for you.

The IOA Roller Coasters

Theme parks everywhere boast coasters that are the biggest and the baddest. So, how do IOA's coasters stack up? Well, we'll admit we're not coaster experts. So, we consulted someone who is: Arthur Levine of www.themeparks.about.com. His expertise is legend. All three coasters (Hulk and the two Dueling Dragons) are "truly world-class" he says, and regularly appear on enthusiasts' top-10 lists. He describes Hulk as "both exhilarating and terrifying" as it "groars" through rollovers, corkscrews, and fog-shrouded tunnels. G-forces have everything to do with great coasters, Arthur tells us, and the Dueling Dragons really pour it on. "These rides," he says, "are not for the timid." We couldn't agree more.

Our Tips for IOA

@ Be sure to pick up a map of IOA. It's called the Adventure Guide and is available at the front gate and in many shops. You'll need it to find your way around.

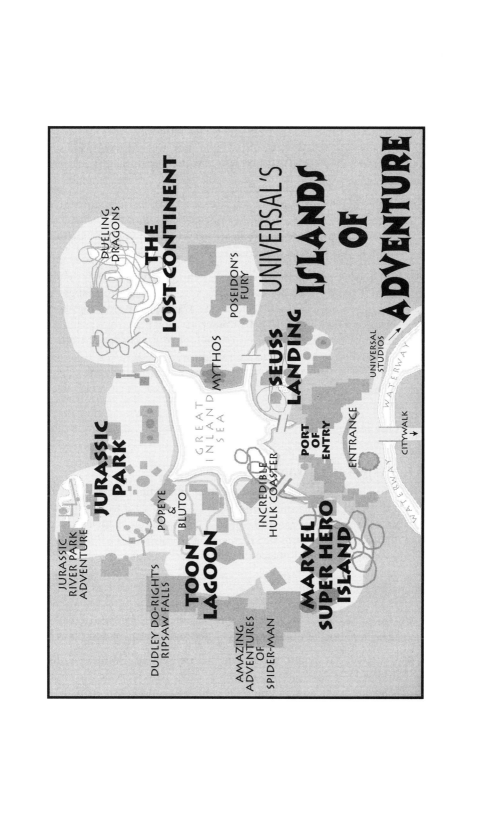

@ Make the best possible use of Universal Express. See page 418 for details and tips.

@ If you want to ride "Spider-Man," arrive early and ride it (or get an Express Pass, they may be unavailable later in the day). Afterward, make the best use of the first hours of the day to hit the coasters and thrill rides.

@ Unlike Universal Studios, there are no PG-13 warnings here. It's all about how tall you are (many rides feature minimum height requirements) and how brave you are. Mom and Dad, don't forget to exercise your parental discretion.

@ WARNING: Numerous attractions here (including some for children) feature water enough to get you anywhere from slightly spritzed to dripping wet. Ponchos are available at most shops and we recommend them. In the summer, you might arrive wearing T-shirts and bathing suits. At other times of year, a change of clothes might come in handy. Also, you might want to save these rides for later in the day, after it warms up. These rides are Dudley Do-Right's Ripsaw Falls, Popeye & Bluto's Bilge-Rat Barges, and Jurassic Park River Adventure.

@ Lost and Found at Islands of Adventure is located at the front gate at guest services. Call (407) 224-4245.

Our Tips for Eating at IOA

@ During the slower seasons of the year, when the park closes at 6 P.M., you'll find that many restaurants begin to close around 4 P.M., so don't wait until too late to eat. During the busier times, when the park is open until late night, virtually all restaurants are open until well past the dinner hour.

@ Grab a continental breakfast at Croissant Moon Bakery (Port of Entry).

@ Remember that CityWalk is right outside the front gate. It has a great selection of dining opportunities for both lunch and dinner.

@ Only two restaurants at IOA take priority seating: Confisco Grille and Mythos. You can make yours at either restaurant, at Universal Vacation Services (just inside the front gate), at the concierge desk of either the Hard Rock or Portofino Bay Hotels, or by calling (407) 224-9255.

@ $ Our favorite restaurant at IOA is Mythos, in the Lost Continent. The food is good, the prices reasonable, and the atmosphere imaginative and beautiful. Who could ask for more? For more on Mythos, see page 455.

Money-Saving Tip
You can get a 10% on food at restaurants throughout IOA by showing your AAA membership card.

Port of Entry
This is the entryway to IOA and you'll first notice this park's signature icon, inspired by one of the Seven Wonders of the Ancient World, the Lighthouse of Alexandria. The original, built by Ptolemy in 280 B.C., was nearly three times as tall.

Port of Entry is a striking melange of fantasy elements from old Venice, the Middle East, Africa, and a generous helping of unusual architecture from movies, literature, and imagination. It is marvelously created and deftly executed. Along its streets are shops, restaurants, and countless details of interest: a windmill, odd balconies and parapets, and a fantasy world of props and artifacts. It's some of the best theming we've ever seen. You'll surely wish to explore this place, but if it's still early in the day and you're just arriving, we suggest that you forge ahead and return later.

Island Skipper Tours

℗ Slow boat ride to the other side of the lake

℗ Lasts about 7 minutes

When it's operating, this boat will take you to the opposite shore of the Great Inland Sea, to a dock near Jurassic Park. If it's departing soon, it might even save a little time.

Marvel Super Hero Island
This is a brightly colored land of super heroes where everything seems just like the comics: two-dimensional, bold, bright, and bigger-than-life. The intense thrill rides here are some of the best in themedom. You can even meet your favorite super heroes in the afternoon. Check your Adventure Guide for times.

WARNING: This place is very loud.

Universal Islands of Adventure Restaurants

Restaurant	Location	Price	Fare	Service	Our Comments
Blondie's	Toon Lagoon	$	Variety of specialty sandwiches	Counter service L/D	Good sandwiches (and fun, too)
The Burger Digs	Jurassic Park	$	Burgers and chicken sandwich	Counter service L/D	A better burger
Cafe 4	Super Hero Island	$	Pizza, pasta, salads, and sandwiches	Counter service L/D	OK food
Captain America Diner	Super Hero Island	$	Burgers, chicken sandwich, shakes	Counter service L/D	The usual fast food
Circus McGurkus Cafe	Seuss Landing	$	Pizza, lasagna, fried chicken, spaghetti	Counter service	Kid food
Comic Strip Cafe	Toon Lagoon	$	Chinese, Mexican, Italian, & American	Counter service L/D	Just OK
Confisco Grill*	Port of Entry	$$	steaks, salads, burgers	Table service L/D	OK food, nice atmosphere. See page 451.
Croissant Moon Bakery	Port of Entry	$	Pastries, sandwiches, light breakfast	Counter service B/L	Pretty good food
Enchanted Oak Tavern	Lost Continent	$	Ribs, chicken, burgers, drumsticks	Counter service L/D	OK
Fire-Eater's Grill	Lost Continent	$	Gyros, chicken strips	Counter service L/D	Pretty good stuff

Universal Islands of Adventure Restaurants
(continued)

Restaurant	Location	Price	Fare	Service	Our Comments
Green Eggs & Ham Cafe	Seuss Landing	$	Egg sandwich, burgers, chicken	Counter service B/L/D	OK fast food
Pizza Predattoria	Jurassic Park	$	Individual pizzas, salads	Counter service L/D	Not our taste in pizza
Mythos*	Lost Continent	$$	Fine dining; good prices	Table service L/D	IOA's best food; see page 455
Wimpy's	Toon Lagoon	$	Burgers, dogs, chili, and fries	Counter service L/D	OK fast food

B/L/D: Breakfast/Lunch/Dinner (when parks are open late)
$ most entrées less than $10
$$ most entrées less than $25
*See chapter 10 for our reviews of these restaurants.

Incredible Hulk Coaster

@ Rapid-launch roller coaster; minimum height required 54 inches

@ Lasts 90 very long seconds

This state-of-the-art, catapulted coaster launches riders up and out of a nearly vertical 150-foot tube at G-forces similar to an F-16 fighter jet. And that's just the first few seconds. The thirty-two-seat cars then reach speeds of nearly 60 miles per hour as they whip around the lagoon, doing multiple corkscrew inversions. Get the picture? There's even a special line for the front row of the coaster (sorry, front-row seats don't participate in Universal Express).

OVER-THE-TOP FUN for coaster freaks.

Helpful Hint
As you exit this attraction, you can buy a picture of yourselves riding this coaster. It's a great souvenir.

The Amazing Adventures of Spider-Man

@ 3-D adventure ride, minimum height requirement of 40 inches

@ Lasts 5 minutes

This adventure is so high-tech that there isn't even anything to compare it to. We can tell you that it's a moving car and that the special effects include a simulated 400-foot freefall, real fire, and continuous in-your-face 3-D action scenes. In short, it's one great ride.

ABSOLUTELY GREAT FUN. Don't miss this attraction. WARNING: May be too intense for small children.

Helpful Hint
Arrive early and ride Spider-Man first thing, or get an Express pass. Ride it more than once to better enjoy all the effects.

Doctor Doom's Fearfall

@ Midway freefall; riders must be at least 52 inches tall

@ Lasts 30 seconds (seems much longer!)

Teenagers love this ride, which launches you up a 150-foot tower at nearly 50 miles per hour. That done, you then fall back to Earth only to be re-launched. There's a short story involved and the ride is over almost before you finish screaming.

GREAT FUN for the brave at heart.

Storm Force Accelatron

@ Spinning midway ride

@ Lasts about 2 minutes

This reminds us of another theme park ride we know of, one with spinning teacups. On this one, you'll be in colorful "orbs." There's a brief storyline and you can control the spin-speed yourselves.

MOSTLY FOR KIDS, but fun if you like to feel dizzy.

Toon Lagoon

Being in this colorful land is like being in a cartoon. It's a great place for families and great photo opportunities abound. Make good use of them. There are rides here, too, and they're wet ones.

Here with the kids? Be sure to bring them to the Toon Trolley Character Meet and Greet here in Toon Lagoon plaza. Don't forget your camera (and autograph book). Check the Adventure Guide for schedule.

Dudley Do-Right's Ripsaw Falls

@ Log-flume ride; minimum height required is 44 inches

@ Lasts 6 minutes

This log-flume ride travels through scenes featuring Dudley Do-Right, his gal Nell, and arch-villain Snideley Whiplash. There are several pleasant plunges along the way but none as breathtaking as the 60-foot finale. The wildest log flume we know of.

LOTS OF FUN, don't miss it.

TIP: You'll get wet on this ride.

WARNING: May be too intense for young children.

Popeye & Bluto's Bilge-Rat Barges

@ White-water raft ride; riders must be at least 42 inches tall

@ Lasts 5 minutes

This is the wildest, wettest, and most fun theme park raft ride we've ever been on. Avoid it on a cold day. Otherwise, prepare to get soaked. LOADS OF FUN. Perfect for a hot summer day.

Me Ship, The Olive

e Playground boat, kids will get wet

e No set time limit

This rubberized play area is particularly well executed. You might also want to know about the water cannons you can use to spray riders on the Popeye's raft ride below. Also, the top deck of The Olive provides an exceptional view of the park and a good photo opportunity.

Toon Amphitheater

Usually around holidays or for special events, you might find some sort of show here. Check the IOA showtimes guide or call (407) 224-5500 to see what might be happening here during your visit.

Jurassic Park

Okay, so some of this park *is* inspired by the movies, but it's done exceptionally well. Here amidst the exotic tropical foliage and the "electric fences," you'll get a real sensation of being in the imaginary Jurassic Park. There's a lot to do here in addition to looking around at all the great effects and props. The park includes some interesting exhibits, a restaurant and shop, a dinosaur encounter, a great playground, and several good rides.

Time-Saving Tip

You can catch the *Island Skipper* tour boat from here back to Port of Entry.

Jurassic Park Discovery Center

e Interactive displays and more

e No set time limit, but can get crowded

This area is really the heart and soul of Jurassic Park. Besides an interesting shop, the Center features numerous displays, photo opportunities, interactive exhibits, and even a few "mini-shows." It's interesting and well done.

INTERESTING, especially for kids. Drop in and take a look.

Triceratops Discovery Trail

@ Walking tour and encounter with robotic dinosaur

@ Lasts about 5 minutes

This attraction features a close-up (and hands-on, if you're lucky) encounter with an authentic, mechanical Triceratops. Seriously, it may be the most impressive animatronic creature we've ever seen and it feels real, too!

VERY INTERESTING, don't miss it.

WARNING: May be disturbing for very young children. Lines here can get very long.

Jurassic Park River Adventure

@ Raft flume-ride; minimum height of 42 inches

@ Lasts 5 minutes

Quite literally, this is one over-the-top attraction. It begins with a quiet river tour of Jurassic Park, but things quickly go haywire and you'll soon be worrying if you'll be lunch for one of the hungry 'raptors that pursue you. The ride ends with a thrilling 89-foot drop. Mood, story, and special effects are all first-rate.

A GREAT ATTRACTION, what you've come here to see. Don't miss it.

WARNING: May be too intense for small children.

Helpful Hint

Don't sit in the first few rows of the boat unless you want to get wet.

Insider Tip

Try to ride Jurassic Park River Adventure near or after dark!

Pteranadon Flyers

@ Mild, suspended coaster; riders must be 36 to 56 inches tall, or accompanied by someone this tall

@ Lasts about 2 minutes

@ Does not participate in Universal Express

This is a pretty neat ride, "flying" along a track above Jurassic Park. The problem is, guests over 56 inches tall must be accompanied by a child. An interesting twist.

FUN AND A GOOD VIEW, TOO. For kids or someone accompanied by one.

Helpful Hint

Lines at Pteranadon Flyers get very long. Try it first thing in the morning.

Jurassic Rock Climbing

This rock-climbing adventure is strictly supervised and allows little or big rock climbers to test their skills on an artificial cliff. Cost is $5.

Camp Jurassic

℮ Interactive playground, kids may get wet.

℮ Take as long as you like, usually not too crowded.

This is a splendidly conceived play area, complete with slides, nets, ropes, tunnels, and water-spitting dinos. Its jungle ambience, waterfalls, and smoldering volcano make for exotic hours of kid-fun. One of the best playgrounds we've ever seen.

FOR KIDS, but worth a look.

The Lost Continent

This entire area looks as though it's just emerged from centuries at the bottom of the sea. Theming is on a grand scale and we think it doesn't get much better than this. You'll want to spend some time just looking at the crumbling ruins of the Lost Continent. Afterward, be sure to visit its interesting shops and enjoy its variety of attractions. Our favorite Universal Orlando theme park restaurant is here: Mythos (see page 455 for details).

The Mystic Fountain

℮ Interactive architecture

℮ Lasts as long as you wish

This is one of the cleverest "attractions" we've ever seen and we don't want to give away any of its surprises. Check it out. Make a wish and see what happens. Then hang around to watch other guests unravel its mysteries.

LOADS OF FUN FOR EVERYONE. Don't miss it.

Poseidon's Fury

℮ Special effects show, must stand throughout

℮ Lasts 25 minutes, check show times guide for times

Part live action and mostly special effects, this show begins slowly and builds up to a really grand scale. Don't let anyone tell you the surprise ending and don't miss this attraction.

OUTSTANDING, great special effects. Don't miss this show.

WARNING: May be too intense for small children

The Eighth Voyage of Sinbad

℮ Stunt show

℮ Lasts 20 minutes; check show times guide for show times

Sinbad sets out on yet another voyage of adventure, this one with outlandish sets, colorful costumes, corny humor, terrific stunts, and great special effects. We found it entertaining and pretty funny, too.

A GOOD SHOW, worth the trip.

Insider's Secret

Get here early to catch a particularly entertaining pre-show.

Dueling Dragons

℮ Twin, intertwined roller coasters; minimum height requirement of 54 inches

℮ Lasts less than 2 minutes, seemed like an eternity

These are the world's only "dueling coasters" on which riders hang suspended beneath the track (known as "inverted coasters"). During this high-speed ride, the coasters come so close to each other that collisions appear unavoidable. Don't worry, they are. If you enjoy the taste of your own adrenalin, this one's for you.

WILD, WILD RIDE; for coaster freaks only, a world-class coaster experience.

Helpful Hint

Get here early in the day (or get an Express Pass) and ride both coasters: Fire and Ice. They are different experiences.

Insider's Secret

Dueling Dragons is much, much better if you're in the first row. It's worth waiting in the special lines for the front seats (sorry, they don't participate in Universal Express).

The Flying Unicorn

@ Relatively mild "family-style" roller coaster; riders must be at least 36 inches tall

@ Lasts about 1 minute

This is really a family-safe, kiddie coaster and its smooth, sloping curves pass through an enchanted forest. Definitely not thrilling, but pleasant.

MILD COASTER, especially fun for families.

Seuss Landing

This charming land is the world of Dr. Seuss brought to life: bright, colorful, and strangely eccentric. For our generation, who grew up on Seuss books rather than cartoons, it is especially engaging. Complete with gentle rides and wonderful music, and teeming with Seussian characters, this is a place young children will adore. And seeing your kids so happily involved will be a pleasure in itself.

Helpful Hint

Have your camera ready. Great photo ops are everywhere at Seuss Landing.

The Cat in The Hat

@ Slow ride with some bumps and spins, 6-passenger "sofas"

@ Lasts 2 minutes

This children's ride does a terrific job telling the story of Dr. Seuss's most popular book. Sets and effects are outstanding. This ride is a must-see for youngsters. Even we enjoyed it.

ONE OF UNIVERSAL'S BEST KID RIDES, not to be missed by youngsters and parents.

Caro-Seuss-el

@ Interactive merry-go-round

@ Lasts about 2 minutes

This carousel features the many odd creatures of Dr. Seuss and they'll wag their tales or blink their eyes when your youngsters pull on the reins or pull the levers. Have your camera ready for this attraction.

GREAT FOR YOUNG CHILDREN.

One Fish, Two Fish, Red Fish, Blue Fish

@ Spinning midway ride; riders get spritzed with water

@ Lasts 2 minutes

Reminiscent of an elephant ride we know, this one features flying fish. Riders can control up and down motion and even make futile efforts to avoid being squirted.

ANOTHER GREAT RIDE FOR YOUNGSTERS.

If I Ran The Zoo

@ Interactive play area

@ Stay as long as you wish, usually not too crowded

Score another success for the "Universal creator." This play area is imaginative, amusing, and even manages to tell a story. There are three different areas and nearly 20 interactive elements that are guaranteed to keep preschoolers busily engaged.

GREAT FUN FOR KIDS.

IOA Best-of-the-Best List

The Amazing Adventures of Spider-Man

Poseidon's Fury

Popeye & Bluto's Bilge-Rat Barges

Jurassic Park River Adventure

IOA's coasters (if you dare): Incredible Hulk and Dueling Dragons

A Meal at Mythos

Shops at IOA

You won't have any trouble returning home with merchandise that boasts of your visit to IOA. From T-shirts to mugs and from backpacks to stuffed animals, every island delivers shop after shop of character and logo goods. Some of it's actually quite nice.

What we like best about shopping here is that you'll also find an assortment of stuff you just might not expect: some exotic collectibles at Ocean Trader Market and a unique assortment of Christmas decorations at the Port of Entry Christmas Shoppe. Our other favorite browsing stops include The Lost Continent's Shop of Wonders and Metal Smith; Cats, Hats, & Things; and Jurassic Outfitters.

Money-Saving Tip

Get a 10% discount on merchandise at many IOA gift shops by showing your AAA card.

CityWalk

When it comes to nightlife, Orlando is indeed a lucky town. Between the theme parks and downtown Orlando, offerings are nearly limitless. CityWalk makes a big contribution. Here at the focus of Universal Orlando's nightlife is an assortment of clubs, restaurants, and shops. Reggae, jazz, Motown, and the laid-back tunes of Jimmy Buffet can all be found along the lively avenues of CityWalk. Food offerings include everything from Creole to Italian, Nuevo Latino to Caribbean, Starbucks Coffee, and, of course, pizza and lots of burgers.

Admission to CityWalk

There's no admission to CityWalk but most of its clubs charge a cover later in the evening for their live shows. While you can simply pay the cover charge, you can also purchase the CityWalk Party Pass (all-club access) for $9.53 (all prices include tax). It will admit you to any or all of CityWalk's clubs for one evening. Multi-day theme park passes and Orlando FlexTickets also include all-club admission to CityWalk.

For $12.78, you can add a movie ticket at Universal's twenty-screen Cineplex to the all-club admission. And for a total of $18.00, you can purchase either the Meal & Movie Deal or the Meal & Party Deal. With these tickets, you'll get a meal at a select CityWalk eatery and then either a movie at the Cineplex or unlimited access to City-Walk's clubs. Restaurants for both deals include Hard Rock Cafe, Jimmy Buffet's Margaritaville, Latin Quarter, Motown Cafe, NBA City, Pastamore Restaurant, and NASCAR Cafe. Even though menu selections are very limited, this deal can still save a few bucks.

Parking at CityWalk

After 6 P.M., parking for CityWalk is free. Parking before 6 P.M. is $8 ($10 for RVs or campers). Parking is free anytime for Preferred Annual Pass holders. There is a closer, preferred parking for an extra $3.

Our Tips for CityWalk

@ Be sure to pick up the CityWalk times and info guide, this area's map and schedule of entertainment and special events. It will tell you all about what's happening (and where) during your visit.

@ Most shops and restaurants at CityWalk are open by 11:30 A.M. It's a great place for lunch and convenient to the parks.

@ Want to dine at Emeril's Restaurant Orlando? You'll have to make your reservations at least several months in advance. We're not kidding. For reservations, call (407) 224-2424. For more information about Emeril's, see page 452.

CityWalk Information

For ticket and event information, CityWalk has its own guest services, open after 12 noon. Call (407) 224-2690.

The Universal Orlando Cineplex

This is not your neighborhood movie theater. It features awesome digital sound, comfortable stadium seating with high-back rocker seats, and five concession areas. Grab a pizza, some beer or wine, an espresso or cappuccino, or just a bucket of popcorn. Then sit back and enjoy any of Hollywood's most recent releases on one of the twenty wall-to-wall screens of this state-of-the-art movie house.

The Stages of CityWalk

There are several stages here and you're likely to find unusual entertainment happening at them: small musical groups and comedians that get passersby in on their antics. No set times but you won't have any trouble hearing when they begin.

The Clubs of CityWalk

One word of warning about the clubs of CityWalk: they are very, very loud, even ear-shattering. We wonder why this always seems to happen in today's clubs. Our latest theory: The sound engineers simply have blown out their eardrums. There's no other explanation.

CityJazz

This nightclub features jazz memorabilia and a performance stage surrounded by small tables. Jazz groups here are mostly from around Orlando, but name groups also perform here during busy holidays and the summer months. The music is good and the menu is mostly light fare, designed more to keep you munching than to provide a meal: burgers, steak sandwich, hot wings, onion rings, and other finger foods. Martinis in all their various incarnations are the specialty of the full-service bar. CityJazz charges a $5 cover.

Bob Marley—A Tribute to Freedom

This beautiful club is a replica of reggae superstar Bob Marley's home and garden in Kingston, Jamaica. It's definitely worth a look and while you're there enjoying the live reggae rhythms, you might want to sample some of the tasty Caribbean appetizers. There's even a small dance floor. After 8 P.M., this club charges a $5 cover, and guests must be at least 21 years old.

Hard Rock Live Orlando

This concert hall looks like the Roman Coliseum. Featured on weekends throughout the year are some of the biggest names in pop music. There's seating for 2,000, and both sound system and lighting are state-of-the-art. The hall even features an impressive amount of pop music memorabilia. You can find out about upcoming events by calling (407) 351-5483 or online at www.hardrocklive.com. Tickets can be purchased through Orlando Ticketmaster at (407) 839-3900 or the Hard Rock Web site.

Pat O'Brien's Orlando ♥♥

This club is an exact replica of Pat O'Brien's in New Orleans and if you've never been there, you'll be surprised by the beauty of this place. An open courtyard, red-brick walls, and a flaming fountain are just a few of its memorable features. If you visit only one club here at City-Walk, we cast our vote for this one. Be sure to drop in here for a taste of its small menu of Creole treats, some live piano, and the world-famous Hurricane drink. After 9 P.M., there's a $5 cover charge and guests must be at least 21 years old.

Jimmy Buffett's Margaritaville

This place is fun: three cool bars, a neat merchandise shop, and a lively restaurant. Theming is appropriately Caribbean and amusing. Everything seems related to the laid-back songs of Jimmy Buffett. In one of the bars, there's a huge volcano that erupts regularly, spewing gallons of margaritas into a giant blender. There are several stages that feature nightly live performances. Most of the entertainment is in the genre most appreciated by Buffet fans, known for some reason as "Parrot Heads." For our take on the food here at Jimmy Buffett's, see page 453. There's a $5 cover charge after 10 P.M.

Motown Cafe Orlando

What we like best about this club is the floorshow. Its five great entertainers sing, dance, and perform all the spins, walks, and gestures of the classic Motown sound. It's bright, flashy, and fun. This club also features a barbecue menu. For our opinion of the food, see page 455. There's a $5 cover charge after 9 P.M.

The Latin Quarter ♥♥

This is an attractive club and also one of CityWalk's best places to dine. With a retail store, live Latin rhythms, and a dance studio, you might consider spending an entire evening here. Have dinner, listen to some music, learn to salsa, and then do some dancing. Cover charge applies on certain nights. To read about our dining experiences here, see page 454.

The Groove

This club features a large (and crowded) dance floor, countless video monitors, special-effect lighting, and loud, loud music played by deejays. It's touted as one of Orlando's "hottest dance clubs." There's a $5 cover charge and patrons must be at least 21 years of age.

CityWalk Best-of-the-Best List

Best dining: Emeril's Orlando and the Latin Quarter

Most fun dining: Jimmy Buffett's Margaritaville

Most romantic dining: Latin Quarter ♥♥

Most romantic club: Pat O'Brien's ♥♥

The Shops of CityWalk

You'll find some interesting shopping here at CityWalk. Naturally, there's a Universal Studios Store, but you'll also find our favorite, the Endangered Species Store. Much of its nature-themed merchandise is original and beautiful. It's a great place for gift shopping. We also like the expensive apparel in Quiet Flight Surf Shop, and the colorful clothes of Fresh Produce. There's no shortage of novelty stores here either, and if you're looking for trendy gifts, lava lamps, oddball toys, or things that glow in the dark, you'll find it all here in vast quantities. These shops are a magnet for any kid with money, so be forewarned.

Other shops include Cigarz at CityWalk, a smoke shop and bar (cough, cough), and one fake jewelry store and one real jewelry store. It's more than a few hours of browsing and enough selection to assure that you'll see at least a few items that interest you.

Food at CityWalk

Whatever your taste and budget, you'll find something you want to eat here at CityWalk. Fast-food offerings include burgers, pizza by the slice, a sausage stand, Latin Quarter Express, and a deli; and table-service restaurants run the gamut from the pricey Emeril's to Jimmy Buffett's cheeseburger in paradise. See our reviews on the pages that follow.

Helpful Hint

For CityWalk dining reservations, call (407) 224-3663 or visit the CityWalk dinner reservation cart.

Dining at Universal Orlando

It's great to see theme parks "growing up" and offering some real dining. There are so many good places to eat here at Universal that we had a hard time fitting them in. Of course, we have our favorites and we'll tell you what they are.

Priority Seating Arrangements

These dining "reservations" mean that you'll be given a time and once you arrive, you'll get the next available table. This usually means a short wait. Universal dining (407) 224-9255 will make priority seating arrangements for select restaurants at the theme parks and for the following CityWalk eateries: Pastamore, Latin Quarter, Margaritaville, Bob Marley's, and Motown Cafe, phone (407) 224-3663. For priority seating at Emeril's call (407) 224-2424, and for The Palm, (407) 503-2383. For dining reservations at Universal's three hotels, call (407) 503-3643.

The Restaurants of Universal Orlando

Restaurants here at Universal Orlando run the gamut from unremarkable fast food to elegant and memorable fine dining. The restaurants following are those we thought deserving of mention. For the key to the symbols used here, see page 312.

Confisco Grille ★ $$

@ Port of Entry, IOA

@ Table service, lunch and dinner (when park is open later)

@ Beer, wine, and full bar

@ Priority seating recommended during busy times

This place is piled with props from all five islands, brought here by the "smugglers" who confiscated them. Hence, the name. Confisco is a bit dark though it makes for a nice break from the parks. The imaginative menu features a selection of burgers, sandwiches, salads, and pastas. After all the hype we'd heard about the food here, we were disappointed.

Delfino Riviera ★★★★ $$$$ ♥♥♥♥

@ Portofino Bay Hotel

@ Table service, dinner only

@ Priority seating a must

Passion permeates everything at Delfino Riviera: the serene ambience, the flawless and knowledgeable service, the authentic Ligurian cuisine of Chef Massimo Fedozzi, and, not the least of all, the charm and passion of Delfino's strolling guitarist and vocalist, Felix Cabrera. Our dining experience here was the most romantic of our lives.

With a beautiful view of the harbor at Universal Orlando's Portofino Bay Hotel, Delfino Riviera is a charming, quiet, and elegantly romantic dining destination.

Delfino's is about as upscale as Italian gets. Chef Fedozzi brings to Central Florida his hometown cuisine of Northern Italy's Portofino, and he executes it with creative passion and a well-deserved reverence for the ingredients of his land: Riviera olives, the finest virgin olive oils, and Italy's legendary wines. We think you'll certainly want to savor each of the three courses that comprise the classic Italian meal: the Antipasti, the Primi Piatti (usually a pasta dish), and the Secondi, the main course. We suggest that you do as we did and share your first two courses and then each order a main dish. We also urge you to ask your waiter to select a wine for each course.

Featuring seafood, chops, and poultry, the menu changes with what is best and freshest in the marketplace. Pricey yes, but if you are looking for an unforgettably romantic meal, Delfino's will not disappoint.

Emeril's Restaurant Orlando ★★★ $$ ♥♥

@ CityWalk

@ Table service, lunch and dinner

@ Full-service bar and exceptional wine list

@ Priority seating a must, call (407) 224-2424

When it comes to popularity, this restaurant is at the top of the food chain here at Universal. If you expect to eat here during your Central Florida visit, you'd best make reservations at least several months in advance (and for lunch, several days). We're not kidding.

Although TV personality and chef Emeril Lagasse is not at work in the kitchen here, the recipes reflect the essence of Emeril. The Creole-inspired menu includes a variety of imaginative creations. Emeril's banana cream pie with a cup of this restaurant's outstanding coffee is the perfect ending to any meal here.

Hard Rock Cafe ★ $ to $$

@ CityWalk

@ Lunch and dinner

❷ Beer and wine

❷ No priority seating

This themed restaurant is home to an impressive collection of rock music memorabilia. The menu features a good burger, a pig sandwich (barbecued pork), and a selection of entrées such as fajitas, pot roast, ribs, and a daily blue-plate special. Pretty good food but don't forget the loud, loud rock 'n' roll music.

Island Dining Room ★★★ $$$ ♥

❷ Royal Pacific Resort

❷ Breakfast, Lunch, Dinner (various live entertainment at dinner)

❷ Wine, beer, and full bar

❷ Priority seating suggested on weekend nights

This lovely, Asian-themed restaurant is one you'll wish to try, especially if you want to slip out of the theme parks and enjoy a quiet and wonderful lunch. Not an Asian restaurant, Islands features a variety of foods with something of a pan-Asian attitude. We found everything, from salads and sandwiches to dinner entrées, to be creatively conceived and well prepared. An additional bonus is that the prices are quite reasonable. It even features a special dining room for youngsters. We look forward to dining here again.

Jimmy Buffet's Margaritaville ★ $

❷ CityWalk

❷ Table service, lunch and dinner

❷ Full-service bar, specialty drinks, and modest wine list

❷ Priority seating suggested for busy seasons

Margaritaville features three bars and one restaurant. This says a lot about it. The well-known tunes of Jimmy Buffett are not only heard here almost nonstop, but are also the focus of the many sight gags and props that fill up this amusing place. From the "Live Bait Shop and Sushi Bar" to a large model of a Pan Am Clipper, Margaritaville evokes the laid-back whimsy and carefree style of this popular troubadour. The menu features a decent burger, a good chicken sandwich, and a variety of other dishes, all acceptable in quality and large in quantity. Not at all a dining experience, Margaritaville is, for us, a fun place to eat.

Latin Quarter ★★★ $$ ♥♥

@ CityWalk

@ Table service, dinner only

@ Full-service bar, good wine list

@ Priority seating

This attractive restaurant features a starlit sky and a Meso-American atmosphere of Mayan and Aztec ruins. The food here is surprisingly good. The menu is an imaginative and innovative mélange of the many cuisines of South and Central America known as "Nuevo Latino." Our *churrasco a la parilla* (grilled skirt steak served over garbanzo beans seasoned with ham and chorizo sausage) was outstanding, as was the roast pork marinated in sour orange juice and cilantro and served over black beans and boniato. We were in the mood for something exotic and Latin Quarter most certainly delivered. Just as we were finishing our meal, a small group of performers began playing some Latin music. Nice.

Lombard's Landing ★ $$

@ Universal Studios, San Francisco waterfront

@ Table service, lunch and dinner (when park is open later)

@ Wine and beer

@ Priority seating during busy seasons

This seafood restaurant is one of only two full-service restaurants at the Studios, and it's an acceptable choice for a meal during a day at the park. Attractive and comfortable, Lombard's Landing enjoys a pleasant view of the harbor and its outside patio is especially pleasant later in the day. The menu features a seafood Cobb salad, a variety of sandwiches, and such signature specialties as fried Ipswich clams, prime rib, five-cheese raviolis, and shrimp cioppini ratatouille.

Mama Della's Ristorante

@ Portofino Bay Hotel

@ Table service, dinner only

@ Good wine list with suggested wine pairings

@ Priority seating suggested

The mismatched chairs and eclectic assortment of tableware will make you feel like you're having dinner in Mama Della's dining room. She's even here, making the rounds, chastising diners for eating without wine or for not having dessert. Strolling musicians and a hug and kiss from Mama Della are all part of this Italian family-style restaurant

Mama's menu features calamari, bruschetta, lasagna, cacciatores, parmigianas, veal Marsala, and other Italian standards. Everything is quite good, servings are generous, and it's all freshly prepared. Dinners include a large salad from which you may help yourselves. The menu also includes some family-style entrées served on large platters. Save room for dessert.

TIP: Try one of Mama's wonderful Chiantis.

Motown Cafe ★★ $$

- ℮ CityWalk
- ℮ Table service, lunch and dinner
- ℮ Full-service bar and modest wine list
- ℮ Priority seating only during very busy times

The menu here features comfort foods from barbecue to fried catfish and it's all good. Ambience here is 1950s/1960s Motown with accompanying loud music and videos.

Mythos ★★★ $$ ♥

- ℮ IOA, The Lost Continent
- ℮ Table service, lunch and dinner (when park is open later)
- ℮ Very good wine list
- ℮ Priority seating suggested during busy periods

Perhaps the name of this restaurant has something to do with dispelling the myth of bad theme park food. Mythos features some of the best food we've eaten in a theme park. The openers of lobster and corn bisque and a butternut squash soup are very good. Other treats include the risotto of the day and cedar-planked salmon. The warm chocolate banana gooey cake alone is enough reason to visit Mythos. And at these prices, it's a place you'll want to try.

NASCAR Cafe Orlando ★ $

- CityWalk
- Table service, lunch and dinner
- Full-service bar
- No priority seating

This restaurant features a downstairs bar and video game area, and an upstairs dining room. Racing memorabilia (even full-size race cars) is everywhere throughout and for race fans, this atmosphere may seem very appealing. The food here is actually pretty good: a large burger, fried chicken, barbecued ribs, and char-grilled pork chops.

NBA City ★★ $$

- CityWalk
- Table service, lunch and dinner
- Full-service bar and modest wine list
- No priority seating

If you don't get the name, the basketball player sculpture that stands three stories tall out front ought to give you an idea of this restaurant's theme. Just inside the door, you'll find a basketball training zone and the dining room is located on the polished-wood floor of a real round-ball court. The big surprise here is the food. It is quite good. Menu offerings include an intriguing selection of pizzas, pastas, salads, and sandwiches as well as entrées like grilled salmon, stuffed chicken breast, and New York strip steak. This restaurant (operated by the Hard Rock Cafe) doesn't try to be fancy, just good. It succeeds.

Pastamore Ristorante & Market ★ $$

- CityWalk
- Table and counter service, dinner only
- Priority seating suggested during busy times

Owned and operated by Universal Orlando, this noisy restaurant features a menu of so-so Italian dishes. You'll find the usual assortment of pizza, spaghettis, piccatas, and parmigianas. Large, family-style servings

are an option. Simply, this is not our taste in Italian food. It may be
yours. The counter-service Pastamore Market serves espresso, cappuccino, ice cream, pizza by-the-slice, and a variety of entrées. It has both
indoor and sidewalk seating.

Sunset Grill   ★★ $$ Outside Patio ♥

- Hard Rock Hotel

- Table service, breakfast, lunch, and dinner

- Full-service bar and decent wine list

- No priority seating

This is the Hard Rock Hotel's "all-purpose" restaurant and serves each
of the day's meals, including a large à la carte menu for breakfast.
Lunches at Sunset Grill have an offering of sandwiches, salads, pizza,
burgers, and even a few entrées, such as steak and grilled chicken. Dinner adds to this a tasty mix of entrées that include grilled salmon, filet
mignon, and ribs, to mention only a few. Though nothing is memorable, the quality of food here is quite good and it is cerainly a good
choice for a meal.

Tchoup Chop   ★★★★ $$ ♥♥

- Royal Pacific Resort

- Lunch and dinner, reservations a must

- Good wine and sake list, full-service bar

Tchoup Chop is an embodiment of Feng Shui, the ancient Chinese science that seeks to create a balanced and harmonious environment with
its four basic elements: wood, fire, metal, and water. This is celebrity
chef Emeril Lagasse's newest Orlando eatery, and it harmoniously combines these elements into one very exciting dining experience.

The beautiful wood furnishings of Tchoup Chop are accentuated
by handsome metal accessories. In the middle of the dining area is a
serenely beautiful lily pond. The element of fire is most notable in the
open kitchen, where Chef Joel Morgan and his team work to create a
menu that is both imaginative and exotic.

There are two ways to dine here: at a table ordering from the menu
or at the food bar overlooking the kitchen. Tchoup Chop's menu features a fusion of the cuisines of the Pacific Rim. Banana leaf–steamed

fish, Kona-glazed duck breast, or braised Kobe beef short ribs, to give you just a glimpse of the many wonders. Appetizers, soups, and salads: all are uniquely delicious and beautifully presented on hand-crafted pottery.

On our first visit to Tchoup Chop, we chose the food bar. This prix fixe meal ($45 per person) was one of the most exciting dining experiences we've ever enjoyed. The food bar features three seatings per evening, each for eight lucky guests. We didn't have to order our food (although we did select some nifty mojitos from the bar). We just sat back, chatted with Chef Armando, and watched as he created each of our memorable courses. With a newly conceived menu each night, the food bar is a great way to put your toes in the water at Tchoup Chop.

We were so impressed, that we returned the next day to try a meal from the regular menu. No disappointments here at Tchoup Chop, simply delicious, beautiful, and exotic food in surroundings that are unique and beautiful. In short, a dining adventure we are most eager to repeat.

Trattoria del Porto ★★ Breakfast and Lunch $$/ Dinner $$$

 Portofino Bay Hotel

 Table service, breakfast, lunch, and dinner

 Good wine list

 Priority seating not needed

This attractive eatery is the only one at Portofino Bay to serve all three meals each day. Breakfast features a large à la carte menu or a generous buffet that includes eggs cooked to order. Lunches feature an assortment of salads, soups, and sandwiches, as well as a few pasta dishes and a pizza of the day. Dinners at Trattoria also offer pizzas and pastas and add a selection of entrées such as grilled salmon and steak. In addition to its à la carte menu, Trattoria del Porto also serves buffet dinners on Friday and Saturdays. From Thursday to Saturday, dinners feature characters from Universal Studios.

The Palm ★★★ Lunch $$/Dinner $$$

 Hard Rock Hotel

 Table service, lunch and dinner

Universal Orlando
Best-of-the-Best Restaurants

Best All-Around Dining:
Islands Dining Room at the Royal Pacific

For elegant and romantic dining:
Delfino Riviera ♥♥♥♥ at Portofino Bay Hotel

For a fun meal: Jimmy Buffett's Margaritaville, CityWalk

Best theme park food: Mythos, IOA

@ Full-service bar and very outstanding wine list

@ Priority seating for dinner a must

The Palm started in 1926 as an Italian restaurant and only more recently did it begin serving steaks. That was about 1930, we believe. If practice makes perfect, you'd expect that after seventy-five years, The Palm would have things right. And they do. The dark wood charm of this place would have you believe you'd landed in yet another chophouse, but there's more going on here than simply great cuts of meat. From a sublime linguini and clam sauce to veal Milanese, this place really has Italian right. Steaks, chops, giant lobsters, and a marvelous assortment of salads and side dishes together make this a great choice for any taste. The broiled crab cakes are the best we can remember having. Give some serious thought to leaving the theme parks for a lunch here at the Palm. In fact, give dinner some serious consideration, too.

Appendix A:
Our Favorites

Our Disney World Favorites

Our Favorite Fine Dining

Jiko: The Cooking Place (Animal Kingdom Lodge) ♥♥

California Grill (Contemporary) ♥♥

Victoria & Albert's (Grand Floridian) ♥♥♥♥

Cítricos (Grand Floridian) ♥♥♥

Wolfgang Puck Dining Room (Downtown Disney) ♥♥

Arthur's 27 (Wyndham Palace Resort) ♥♥♥

Shula's Steakhouse (The Dolphin) ♥♥

The Flying Fish (BoardWalk) ♥♥

Our Favorite Fast Food

Wolfgang Puck Express (Downtown Disney, two locations)

Tusker House (Disney's Animal Kingdom)

Our Other Disney World Favorites

Most Exotic Dining Experience: Jiko (Animal Kingdom Lodge)

Most Romantic Restaurant: Victoria & Albert's (Grand Floridian) ♥♥♥♥

Favorite Fun Dining Experience: 50's Prime Time Café (Disney-MGM)

Best Steak or Lobster: Shula's Steakhouse (Dolphin) ♥♥♥

Best Seafood: Narcoossee's (Grand Floridian)

Best Ice Cream Cone: Ghirardelli's (Downtown Disney Marketplace)

Best Gourmet Pizza: Wolfgang Puck Cafe (Downtown Disney West Side)

Best Buffet: Boma (Animal Kingdom Lodge)

Best Sushi: California Grill (Contemporary) and B's Bar at Wolfgang Puck Cafe (Downtown Disney)

Best Wine List: California Grill (Contemporary) ♥♥

Best Character Dinner: 1900 Park Fare (Grand Floridian)

All-Around Favorite Resort: Disney's Yacht and Beach Club Resorts ♥♥♥♥

Favorite Moderate Resort: Disney's Caribbean Beach Resort♥♥

Favorite Value Resort: Disney's All-Star Movies Resort

Favorite Home-Away-from-Home Accommodations: One-Bedroom Villa at Disney's BoardWalk♥♥♥

Most Romantic Resort: Disney's Grand Floridian Resort and Spa ♥♥♥♥

Most Romantic Room: Honeymoon Turret Suite (Grand Floridian) ♥♥♥♥

Most comfortable beds: The Swan (and in 2004, also the Dolphin)

Favorite Resort Lobby: Disney's Animal Kingdom Lodge

Favorite Pool: Stormalong Bay (Yacht & Beach Clubs Resort) ♥♥

Favorite Hot Tub: The Grotto (Swan and Dolphin) ♥♥♥

Favorite Thrill Ride: Rock 'n' Roller Coaster (Disney-MGM)

Favorite 3-D Attraction: It's Tough to Be A Bug!

Best Live Show: Cirque du Soleil (Downtown Disney) ♥♥

Favorite Recreation: Sammy Duvall's Watersports (Contemporary)

Our Universal Orlando Favorites

Our Favorite Fine Dining

Delfino Riviera (Portofino Bay) ♥♥♥♥

Tchoup Tchop (Royal Pacific Resort) ♥♥

Mythos (Islands of Adventure)

Islands Dining Room (Royal Pacific Resort)

The Palm (Hard Rock Hotel)

The Latin Quarter (CityWalk) ♥♥

Our Other Universal Orlando Favorites

Favorite Fun Dining Experience: Jimmy Buffett's Margaritaville

Most Exotic Dining Experience: The Latin Quarter ♥♥

Most Romantic Restaurant: Delfino Riviera (Portofino Bay) ♥♥♥♥

Best Steak: The Palm (and best crab cake!) (Hard Rock Hotel)

Best Hamburger: The Palm (Hard Rock Hotel)

Favorite All-Around Restaurant: Islands Dining Room (Royal Pacific Resort)

Best Coffee: Starbucks (CityWalk)

Favorite Dessert: Coconut Crème Brulee (Tchoup Chop)

All-Around Favorite Resort: Hard Rock Hotel ♥♥

Most Romantic Resort: Portofino Bay Hotel ♥♥♥♥

Favorite Resort Lobby: Royal Pacific Resort

Most Romantic Room: King Suite at Hard Rock Hotel♥♥

Favorite Pool: Hard Rock Hotel

Favorite Bar: Jake's American Bar at the Royal Pacific Resort

Our Favorite Universal Orlando Attractions (this is a tough one!)

The Amazing Adventures of Spider-Man (Islands of Adventure)

Terminator 2 3-D (Universal Studios)

Men in Black Alien Attack (Universal Studios)

Popeye & Bluto's Bilge-Rat Barges (Islands of Adventure)

Appendix B:
Online Links for
Walt Disney World and
Universal Orlando

Walt Disney World Resort

The Walt Disney World Resort Welcome Page	www.disneyworld.com
The Official Disney Home Page	www.disney.com
The Disney Cruise Line	www.disneycruise.com
Disney Fairytale Weddings and Honeymoons	www.disneyweddings.com
DisneyQuest	www.disneyquest.com
Cirque du Soleil	www.cirquedusoleil.com
House of Blues	www.hob.com
Sammy Duvall Watersports	www.duvallwatersports.com
Swan and Dolphin Resorts	www.swandolphin.com
Walt Disney Travel Company	www.disneytravel.com
Disney's Wide World of Sports	www.disneyworldsports.com

Universal Orlando

Universal Orlando	www.universalstudios.com/themeparks/
Universal Vacations and Tickets	www.usevacations.com
Universal Cineplex	www.enjoytheshow.com

Transportation

Airport Car Rentals	fcn.state.fl.us/goaa/ops/rac.htm
Florida Town Cars	www.florida towncar.com

Mears Transportation	www.mearstransportation .com/AirportTransfers/
Tiffany Town Cars	www.tiffanytowncar.com/

Unofficial Theme Park Sites

Themeparks.Com	www.themeparks.com
Deb's Unofficial WDW Information Guide	www.wdwig.com
MouseSaver Disney Discount Information	www.mousesaver.com
Our e-mail address:	perlmutter@msn.com

Appendix C: Phone Directory

Automotive Service

Disney Car Care Center: (407) 824-0976

Barber and Beauty Shops

Casa de Belleza, Coronado Springs: (407) 939-3965

Contemporary Hair Styling Salon: (407) 824-3411

Greenhouse Spa at Portofino Bay Hotel: (407) 503-1244

Ivy Trellis Barber and Beauty Shop, the Grand Floridian: (407) 824-3000, ext. 2581

Niki Bryan Hair Salon, the Dolphin: (407) 934-4250

Periwigs Hair Salon, the Yacht & Beach Clubs: (407) 934-3260

Child Care

KinderCare: (407) 827-5444

Disney children's activities centers: (407) WDW-DINE (939-3463)

Universal Orlando, hotel children's centers:

Camp Lil' Rock: (407) 503-2230

Campo Portofino: (407) 503-1200

Royal Pacific Mariner's Club (407) 503-3235

Dining

Disney Dining Experience: (407) 828-5792

Disney Dining Reservations: (407) WDW-DINE (939-3463)

Emeril's, CityWalk, reservations: (407) 224-2424

Arthur's 27, Wyndham Palace, reservations: (407) 827-3450

The Palm, Hard Rock Hotel, reservations: (407) 503-2383

Universal Orlando, dining reservations: (407) 224-9255

Victoria & Albert's "Chef's Table," reservations: (407) 939-7707

Florist

Walt Disney World Florist: (407) 827-3505

Foreign Language Services

Foreign Language Center (WDW Resort): (407) 824-7900

Health Clubs

Body by Jake, the Dolphin: (407) 934-4264

Wyndham Palace Resort & Spa: (407) 827-3200

Grand Floridian Spa and Health Club: (407) 824-2332

Greenhouse Spa Fitness Center, Portofino Bay: (407) 503-1244

Gymnasium at Royal Pacific Resort: (407) 503-3235

Hard Rock Hotel, Fitness Center: (407) 503-7625

La Vida Health Club, the Coronado: (407) 939-3030

Muscles and Bustles, the BoardWalk: (407) 939-2370

Olympiad Health Club, the Contemporary: (407) 824-3410

Saratoga Springs Spa and Fitness Center: (407) 827-4455

Ship Shape Health Club, the Yacht & Beach Clubs: (407) 934-3256

Sturdy Branches, the Villas at the Wilderness Lodge: (407) 938-4222

Swan Health Club: (407) 934-1360

Zahanati Fitness Center, the Animal Kingdom Lodge: (407) 938-3000

Information

Disney Tour Information: (407) WDW-TOUR (939-8687)

General WDW Information: (407) 824-4321

Hearing-Impaired Guest Information: (407) 827-5141

Universal Orlando, general information: (800) 232-7827

Universal Orlando Studio Audience Center: (407) 224-6355

Universal Orlando VIP Tours: (407) 363-8295

Kennels

Fort Wilderness Kennel and general kennel information:
(407) 824-2735

Universal Orlando, general information: (800) 322-5537

Lost and Found

Same day, TTI/Magic Kingdom: (407) 824-4521

Epcot: (407) 560-6105

MGM: (407) 560-4668

Animal Kingdom: (407) 938-2265

Central Lost and Found, TTC: (407) 824-4245

Universal Islands of Adventure: (407) 224-4037

Universal Studios: (407) 224-6355

Medical Facilities

CentraCare Walk-in Medical Care: (407) 239-6463

In-Room Medical Care and Emergency Dental Referral:
(407) 238-2000

Gooding's Pharmacy: (407) 827-1207

Recreation

Disney's Wide World of Sports, schedule information:
(407) 363-6600

All Disney Recreation: (407) WDW-PLAY (407-939-7529)

Richard Petty Driving Experience: (800) 237-3889

Resort Reservations

Best Western Lake Buena Vista Resort: (800) 348-3765

Courtyard by Marriott: (800) 223-9930

Disney Central Reservations Office (CRO): (407) W-DISNEY
(407-934-7639)

Disney Cruise Line: (800) 511-1333

DoubleTree Guest Suites: (800) 222-TREE (800-222-8733)

The Grosvenor: (800) 624-4109

The Hilton: (800) 782-4414

Hotel Royal Plaza: (800) 248-7890

Shades of Green: (888) 593-2242

Universal Orlando On-Site Hotels: (800) 232-7827
Wyndham Palace Resort and Spa: (800) WYNDHAM

Spas

Grand Floridian Spa: (407) 824-2332
Greenhouse Spa at the Portofino Bay Hotel: (407) 503-1244
Spa at Saratoga Springs: (407) 827-4455
Spa at Wyndham Palace: (800) 827-3200

Theaters and Clubs

AMC, Pleasure Island: (407) 298-4488
Cirque du Soleil (407) 939-7600
House of Blues, concert tickets: (407) 934-BLUE (2583)
Universal Cineplex, CityWalk: (407) 354-5998
Hard Rock Live: (407) 839-3900

Transportation

Florida Town Cars: (800) 525-7246, (407) 277-5466
Tiffany Town Cars: (888) 838-2161
Mears: (800) 759-5219, (407) 423-5566
Taxi Services at WDW: (407) 824-3360

Travel Services

AAA Disney Travel Center in Orlando: (407) 854-0770
Delta Travel, Delta Airlines Orlando: (800) 221-1212,
    (407) 849-6400
Universal Orlando Vacations: (800) 232-7827, (888) 837-2273

Weddings and Honeymoons

Disney Fairy Tale Weddings: (407) 828-3400

Index

The Perlmutters arrived at travel writing via a number of other careers. Both have educational backgrounds in writing, Gayle in English and Rick in journalism, and both have worked as registered nurses, Gayle in neonatal ICU and Rick in the operating room. Rick has also been a chef, pastry chef, and baker, and has taught gourmet cooking at a Florida community college (very helpful experience when it comes to restaurant reviews).

Walt Disney World for Couples is the product of the authors' love of travel and adventure, as well as their continuing quest for great Florida romantic getaways. Having lived for over 20 years aboard their sailboat, *Big Otter*, the Perlmutters have traveled extensively in the U.S. and abroad. Other interests include boating, diving, biking, cooking, and wines. The Perlmutters retreat regularly to their lakeside camp in Maine to enjoy hiking, exploring, and "life as it ought to be."

The authors have three grown children. Brian owns and operates a chimney sweep business, and Jennifer is a registered nurse. Both live in North Carolina. Tyra lives in California and does costume work in the movies. The Perlmutters particularly enjoy taking their three grandchildren, Guin, Ben, and Noah to Walt Disney World.